AMERICAN ZION

ALSO BY BENJAMIN E. PARK

American Nationalisms:
Imagining Union in the Age of Revolutions, 1783–1833

Kingdom of Nauvoo:
The Rise and Fall of a Religious Empire on the American Frontier

AMERICAN ZION

— A —

NEW HISTORY

OF

MORMONISM

BENJAMIN E. PARK

Liveright Publishing Corporation

A Division of W. W. Norton & Company
Independent Publishers Since 1923

For information about permission to reproduce selections from this book,
write to Permissions, Liveright Publishing Corporation, a division of
W. W. Norton & Company, Inc., 500 Fifth Avenue, New York, NY 10110

For information about special discounts for bulk purchases, please contact
W. W. Norton Special Sales at specialsales@wwnorton.com or 800-233-4830

Manufacturing by Lakeside Book Company
Book design by Brooke Koven
Production manager: Anna Oler

ISBN 978-1-63149-865-7

Liveright Publishing Corporation, 500 Fifth Avenue, New York, N.Y. 10110
www.wwnorton.com

W. W. Norton & Company Ltd., 15 Carlisle Street, London W1D 3BS

1 2 3 4 5 6 7 8 9 0

For Sara and Curtis
Who make the Zion ideal worthwhile

Are we not then traveling in the direction of American empire? Are not the mission of America and the mission of Mormondom identical in their greatest issues? . . . Fundamentally, we are on the track of America—extending the empire of the great republic of the United States. I grant that we expect Mormondom to form ultimately no insignificant part of them. And why should it not, if its empire-founding force brings forth the results?

—EDWARD TULLIDGE, 1866[1]

— CONTENTS —

A NOTE ON NAMES
AND NARRATIVES

T HE *MORMON* NICKNAME was originally born of derision. Critics of the movement led by Joseph Smith associated his followers
with the controversial scripture he had produced, the Book of Mormon, the textual symbol of their delusion. But the Latter-day Saints,
as they were wont to do, transformed the slight into a point of pride.
Though the church's official name changed several times over the
following two decades after its 1830 founding, the *Mormon* moniker
became a focal point for their cohesive identity. To be a true believer,
to gather all truths, to be a good friend—all of these, according to
Smith, were the ingredients to becoming "a pure Mormon." And so
the name became a badge of honor, a signal for the faithful, for nearly
two centuries. Indeed, during the height of the "Mormon moment"
in 2012, when the nation was infatuated with Republican presidential nominee Mitt Romney's faith, the Utah-based church plastered
Times Square with billboards that featured a diverse cast of saints
proudly declaring, "I'm a Mormon."[1]

That institutional preference came to an end in August 2018 with
Russell M. Nelson, president of the Church of Jesus Christ of Latter-
day Saints and Joseph Smith's sixteenth successor. Nelson, a retired
surgeon with a narrow face and unflinching gaze, firmly requested
that members and media alike cease using the *Mormon* label. While
any group should have a say in what they are called, such a mandate places the historian in a bind. Beyond the impracticality of

using the faith's full name in every instance, the suggested short-hand terms—"Church of Jesus Christ" or "restored gospel of Jesus Christ"—are difficult to differentiate from other Christian denominations. They also carry theological implications that do not belong in a nondevotional study.[2]

I have chosen to use *Mormon*, along with other shorthand terms like *saints*, in this book for a few reasons. First, and perhaps most important, it was the term that was most frequently used during the periods in question. It would be anachronistic to imply otherwise. Second, much of the history in this volume is claimed by different traditions, and not all of them belong to the institution based in Salt Lake City and led by Nelson. And finally, as I am more interested in the cultural experiences and expressions of the faith than in its truth claims, *Mormon* more aptly captures the book's human-centered frame. However, out of respect for the church's request, I have followed its proposed style guide when referring to the contemporary Latter-day Saint institution.

Similarly, I have at times mimicked the Latter-day Saint community's tradition of referring to those outside the faith as *gentiles*. This terminology is crucial to understanding how members of the church understood the world and those who inhabited it.

The politics of naming the Indigenous communities discussed in several chapters also deserve mention. For much of the church's history, many Mormons, like their American counterparts, envisioned a homogeneous group of "Indians." They even supplied a new title, "Lamanites," based on their belief that Native Americans were descendants of a particular Book of Mormon tribe. It was only the most recent label placed on peoples whose land and identities were robbed by Euro-American colonization. Wherever possible, I have therefore tried to refer to Indigenous persons by their nation. Whenever speaking of a general group of Natives, as Mormons often did, I have used the term *Indigenous* or *Native nations*. I have also capitalized *Black* and *White* when referring to racial identities to emphasize the social construction inherent in both categories.

It is nearly impossible not to take a stand on miraculous accounts when writing on a faith that adamantly believes in miracles. Did

Joseph Smith actually uncover ancient records written on golden plates? While answering questions like this is not necessarily outside the parameters of a historian's task, it can distract from telling a broader story of cultural evolution and historical change. This book therefore grants a degree of epistemic sympathy to its subjects while still making clear where the historical record counters otherwise sacred narratives.

I have faithfully preserved the creative spelling when quoting historic sources in order to capture the period's feel and have only edited when absolutely necessary for readers' comprehension.

AMERICAN ZION

PROLOGUE

Faith and History

Have you heard of the
All-American prophet?
He found a brand new book
About Jesus Christ!
We're following him to paradise;
We call ourselves Mormons!
And our new religion is . . .
All-American!

—*THE BOOK OF MORMON* MUSICAL[1]

I N JUNE 2009, the Church of Jesus Christ of Latter-day Saints completed a new library and archives. The massive five-story, 230,000-square-foot facility houses 270,000 books, pamphlets, and magazines, 240,000 collections of archival records, and tens of thousands of photographs and audiovisual recordings. Dozens of credentialed historians work in offices on the upper floors, and researchers frequent the desks and computers on the lower. The structure is evidence of a faith inescapably committed to preserving, minding, and detailing its past. Patrons who enter the reading room walk under a wood-paneled section of wall that features gilded wording from a revelation that Joseph Smith dictated on the day the church was organized: "Behold, There Shall Be A Record Kept Among You."

I was three months removed from graduating from Brigham Young University when the library opened. Having been raised in a committed Mormon family, with ancestry that could be traced as far back as the Mormon city of Nauvoo in mid-nineteenth-century Illinois, I had always been fascinated with my faith's history. My two years of service as a missionary in Washington, DC, invigorated a love for the nation's past, too. It was no surprise, then, when I chose to pursue a career in history, with a particular interest in the history of my spiritual forefathers. And when the new library opened, I eagerly perused its catalog, fingered through its many stacks, and submitted dozens of archival-collection requests to investigate in its reading room.

It quickly became apparent that the faithful stories I had been raised on did not entirely match the records I was now encountering nor the scholarship I was simultaneously digesting. Mormon history was far more complicated and divisive than I had come to—been led to—believe. Nor should this have been a surprise: my years at BYU were marked by student agitation, as I watched many fellow classmates protest the church's involvement in anti-LGBTQ legislation, appeal for more intellectual freedom, and oppose the university's selection of Republican vice president Dick Cheney as commencement speaker in 2008. It occurred to me that if Mormonism was characterized by a cacophony of divergent voices in the present day, it had likely been so for some time.

Today, as a professor of American religious history, I know that the history of Mormonism has in fact been contested from the very start. At the founding meeting for what was then the Church of Christ on April 6, 1830, Joseph Smith, the faith's "first elder," dictated the revelation that commanded the faith to keep "a record." But that order came with a specified purpose: such records would detail how Smith was "a seer & Translator & Prophet [and] an Apostle of Jesus Christ," and document how members of the church "give heed unto all his words & commandments." In other words, the new faith's historical record was primarily envisioned to reaffirm Smith's role as a prophetic leader and encourage followers to obey his dictates.[2]

Present at the meeting was John Whitmer, whose family hosted the gathering. Whitmer was soon assigned by Smith to "write & keep a regula[r] history," a charge he took seriously. He commenced writing a manuscript, "The Book of John Whitmer, Kept by Commandment." The title followed the pattern of scripture, including the Book of Mormon itself, and centered the faith's revelatory origin. Yet Whitmer was excommunicated from the church in 1838, taking his history and records with him. Mormonism's first historian was no longer able to attest to Smith's divine calling.[3]

Disputes over who should or can narrate the church's past have continued ever since. Smith's mother, Lucy Mack Smith, dictated a memoir in her later years that recounted her son's prophetic mission. Yet when Brigham Young, who claimed to be Smith's successor, came to feel that the work was a threat to his own authority, he ordered all copies burned. Young oversaw an "official" history of the church that included gathering, editing, and at times expanding accounts from the earliest decades. Those laboring on it even adjusted the language so that the story was told in Joseph Smith's own voice, although that voice was determined by contemporary leaders. The controlled and sanitized history that resulted fulfilled the original 1830 mandate.[4]

For the saints—the term by which the faithful wished to be known—history was a matter of life or death. Joseph Fielding Smith, born in Utah Territory in 1876, was raised hearing stories about how his grandfather, Hyrum Smith, the founding prophet's brother, was killed by an angry mob that was enabled, if not encouraged, by authorities in Illinois. Joseph Fielding's early teenage years were spent missing his father, Joseph F. Smith, who was on the run from federal officials intent on imprisoning the family's patriarch for polygamy. It was no surprise, then, that when Joseph Fielding Smith became the institution's assistant church historian in 1906—promoted to church historian in 1921—he remained invested in a polemical history of sanctified people fulfilling God's mission while persecuted by bloodthirsty enemies equally dedicated to Satan's cause. His textbook on the church, *Essentials in Church History*, became the faith's standard for generations. Smith was released as church historian only when he was ordained church president in 1970, a position that both his father and great-uncle had held before him.[5]

Joseph Fielding Smith's final years witnessed a new generation of historians within the faith who were less anxious to sacralize Mormonism's past and more eager to place it within its historical context. Participants in this movement, calling themselves proponents of the "New Mormon History," used tools from the secular academy to confront myths and stories that had long been taken for granted. One of the group's leaders, Leonard J. Arrington, was the first credentialed scholar to be appointed church historian, in 1972. He helped open the archives to all researchers and promoted a version of Mormon history that could, in his words, "stand on two legs—the leg of faith and the leg of reason."

Yet when Arrington's division produced a new one-volume history of the faith in 1976, *The Story of the Latter-day Saints*—it was meant to be a replacement for Smith's *Essentials in Church History*—some leaders feared that it did not grant enough space for divinity. Despite the book's immediate success in finding readers, church authorities decided not to issue a new printing for two decades. They also canceled a massive multivolume historical series that was scheduled for the church's sesquicentennial in 1980. By 1982, Arrington was unceremoniously released as church historian; within another decade, several of Arrington's fellow historians were excommunicated, and archival access was closely guarded once again.[6]

Not until the past two decades did the church again warm, ever so slightly, to critical research. Amid heightened public scrutiny, forward-thinking administrators persuasively argued that only by directly confronting problems from the past could they satisfy members in the present. The about-face was perfectly timed to meet rising national curiosity about the faith: Mitt Romney's run for the presidency, *The Book of Mormon*'s Broadway debut, television's fascination with modern-day polygamists all made 2012 the "Mormon moment." To match this new era, the church inaugurated another multivolume history, *Saints*, though it followed this one through to completion. While the new official history was still designed to build faith—to testify that Joseph Smith and his successors were "seer[s] & Translater[s] & Prophet[s]"—it did far more to reckon with more complicated topics than Joseph Fielding Smith's volume did. Leaders also allowed more access to archival sources and even published several collections previously considered off-limits. Simultaneously, a handful of universities across the nation started to host "Mormon studies" programs, funded by Latter-day Saint donors, that enshrine that tradition as a unique means of understanding and teaching American religious history.[7]

This is the first book since the so-called Mormon moment to tell the history of Mormonism. *American Zion* takes advantage of a plethora of new sources that have been available for only the past twenty years or so, including the personal records of church leaders and other consequential figures, to demonstrate how the Mormon tradition has been repeatedly transformed over two hundred years, often by internal and external battles over culture, not merely theology. It draws from a generation of new scholarship that has excavated lost voices and reconstructed forgotten alternative trajectories. While the book focuses in part on how the modern church came to be, it also emphasizes the contingent nature of its evolution, and highlights moments when the tradition might have taken a different route. Telling the story of how the people who longed to create Zion built one of the most powerful institutions in the nation reveals much about not only the history of Mormonism but also the culture out of which it arose.[8]

MORMONISM IS arguably America's most successful homegrown religion. It was born at a time of cultural transformation and religious disruption. The young American republic was only a few decades old and changing with each generation as existing political, industrial, and social systems gave way to novel experiments, and as large groups of people were migrating westward as part of an imperial and bloody expansion that seemed destined to encompass an entire continent. Amid these seismic shifts a series of spiritual revivals took place, each intending to restore communities to their divine roots. Many Americans were dissatisfied with the available religious options, and the marketplace had taught them that innovation would be rewarded. It was in that moment of crisis and opportunity that Joseph Smith, a farm boy with New England roots and limited education, who had recently settled in western New York with his family of seekers, offered his own contribution to America's already-crowded religious scene.

The faith was controversial from its very beginnings. Smith directly challenged Christianity's holy canon by publishing the Book of Mormon, a scriptural narrative of North America's ancient inhabitants he alleged to have translated from ancient gold plates. The text sacralized American soil by making it a Christian land long before European colonization. Yet American Christians rejected it as heretical. Nor did Smith's contemporaries appreciate his claim to dictate revelations in God's voice, his orchestration of his followers as a political body, or, in his final years, his introduction of polygamy as the divine form of family. For some Americans, though—starting with mere hundreds and then thousands—Smith's message was a divine light in a world of darkness. He answered the questions with which they had long struggled, including where their spirits came from and where they would go after death. Mormonism quenched their thirst for biblical roots through modern-day prophets and apostles, for familial certainty through temple sealing rituals, and for elusive knowledge through priesthood authority. Joseph Smith offered an anchor to people who felt themselves at sea.

Conflicts between those who embraced the Mormon message and the surrounding communities were numerous and, at times, deadly. Saints were forced to evacuate New York, Ohio, Missouri, and Illinois in succession. A majority of the faithful then followed Brigham Young to the Utah basin, while other schisms scattered across the Midwest. The federal government soon declared war on the Mormon practices of polygamy and theocracy, at one point dispatching the army to Utah to quell what the government believed to be an insurrection four years before the Civil War. The ensuing legal dispute would come to shape how American law still defines the limits of religious liberty today. Latter-day Saint leaders were eventually forced to forfeit both doctrinal pillars. Not all agreed with the decision: some saints chose to form their own dissenting and polygamous groups. A new movement, known as fundamentalists, continued to practice polygamy in America, much to the chagrin of Latter-day Saint and federal officials alike.

After it formally gave up polygamy, the Latter-day Saint church began a long and uneven march toward assimilation, a quest to gain acceptance from a nation that it had previously scorned. In doing so, it helped define, critique, and, in some cases, determine the place of religion in American life. The Mormons' trek from the margins to mainstream of US culture reveals the origins of cultural coalitions that still dominate modern society, including how Latter-day Saints became one of the most reliable conservative voting blocs in the nation.

Today the Latter-day Saint church is a global force. Its membership recently surpassed 17 million worldwide; nearly 7 million saints live within the United States alone. Though headquartered in Salt Lake City, Utah, the church boasts over thirty thousand congregations spread across nearly every country on the globe. Members of the church have an outsize influence on national politics, especially as part of America's religious right alliance. Mormon culture is often depicted—and sometimes skewered—in popular culture. Many believers of the faith have become celebrities, including singers, athletes, and businesspeople. In early 2023, the Securities and Exchange Commission announced an investigation into the church's investment practices, revealing a system that has succeeded in accumulating a massive portfolio as well as keeping its size private from the public. Even if not every American knows a Mormon, they still know Mormonism, and have a faint sense of its troubled—or troublesome—past.

What many Americans do not know, however, is the turbulent and, at times, radical transformations that the tradition has experienced in its two centuries of existence. Similarly surprising is how much of the modern faith has been shaped by cultural clashes that took place inside and outside the church. Mormonism, like most religions in American history, has been determined as much by the social sphere—by contemporary influences, internal battles, and political quarrels—as it has been by belief. *American Zion* narrates the long history of cultural wars waged over Mormonism's purpose and mission.

*　　*　　*

THIS IS not an exhaustive history of the Church of Jesus Christ of Latter-day Saints. Such a project would require many more pages, if not several volumes. Themes, events, and people covered in the chapters that follow can be, and often have been, given book-length treatments by other scholars. Mormonism is a deep well. Space constraints even necessitate excluding references to numerous significant works.[9]

Mormonism has been transnational since its earliest years. Preachers were sent north of the Canadian border before the church was formally organized, and missionaries were dispatched across the Atlantic Ocean before its first decade closed. Today more than 53,000 young men and women knock on doors across the globe every year to share copies of the Book of Mormon, which has been translated into 115 languages. There are more members of the faith who live outside the United States than inside, and nearly as many speak Spanish (35 percent) as English (45 percent) as their first language. But while any attempt to understand the Latter-day Saint church must understand its international dimension, I am particularly interested in the experience of Mormons within the United States, and how the faith has changed America itself.[10]

Joseph Smith's first revelations spoke of a "people" who were united through God's word. However, Mormon culture has never been fully homogeneous, despite an ecclesiastical emphasis on unity. The surrounding culture of religious competition and individual liberty—the same culture that enabled the Latter-day Saint church to exist in the first place—also ensured that members within the faith could fight over its true meaning. The tradition has, as a result, always been home to a wide spectrum of ideas and experiences. Some of these divisions resulted in denominational schism; scholars have traced more than four hundred different movements that have sprouted from Smith's original vision. The story this book tells reveals how competition with these rival sects, including the Reorganized movement that followed Joseph Smith's sons in the nineteenth century and the fundamentalists who perpetuated polygamy in the twentieth and twenty-first, influenced the Latter-day Saint church. But there has always been a marked degree of heterogeneity within the Salt Lake City–based institution, too. That includes dissenters who disagree with official doctrines and policies while still maintaining spiritual allegiance, as well as those who left the fold. America's religious marketplace has never been short on options.[11]

Many of Mormonism's internal disputes have related to issues of race and gender. Emma Smith was the first woman to push for changes within the faith her husband founded, and she inaugurated a legacy of feminist agitation over gender roles that has continued to this day. Similarly, the church's first congregation in Ohio, in 1831, was led by a man known only as "Black Pete," whose quick departure was indicative of the difficult place that non-White saints inhabited within the faith. Black believers continued to petition for belonging even after a racial policy was instituted in the 1850s that barred them from saving ordinances, a restriction that remained in place until 1978. Indigenous and Hispanic saints have likewise labored to join and exist within a community that long judged them according to the label *Lamanite*, a term that came from the Book of Mormon and reflected White-centered theologies. More recently, and as I witnessed as an undergraduate at BYU, LGBTQ saints have launched their own fight for acceptance. *American Zion* not only includes such marginalized voices but demonstrates how they helped form the modern church.

In June 1844, mere weeks before his death at the hands of an angry mob, Joseph Smith dictated a letter regarding the writing of history. Israel Daniel Rupp, a historian, had just published a volume documenting America's many denominations, including a passage on Mormonism that Smith had provided. The prophet was thrilled with their inclusion, as "every sect" deserved to "tell its own history." He then endorsed a vision of capturing a community's highs and lows. "Although all is not gold that shines," Smith confessed, they could take comfort that "by proving contraries, truth is made manifest." In other words, it is through the spirit of competition, the alchemy of refinement, that a people is formed. Smith's first month as prophet featured a revelation insisting that the historical "record" should entail divine destiny, but in his last month he conceded that the process was much more complicated.[12]

The modern Latter-day Saint community is a product of two centuries of proving contraries. Mormonism started as one family's quest to achieve domestic unity, and now exists as a global faith—surely one of the more remarkable threads in this nation's history. Though such a claim would have been laughed at in the nineteenth century, and for much of the twentieth, too, it is clear that the Mormon story *is* the American story. Now, finally, that history can be explained with authority and clarity and the necessary complexity. What follows is an account of not only religious but national transformation.

I

A Visionary Nation, 1775–1830

This prophet Smith, through his stone spectacles, wrote on the plates of Nephi, in his book of Mormon, every error and almost every truth discussed in New York for the last ten years. He decides all the great controversies;—infant baptism, ordination, the trinity, regeneration, repentance, justification, the fall of man, the atonement, transubstantiation, fasting, penance, church government, religious experience, the call to the ministry, the general resurrection, eternal punishment, who may baptize, and even the question of free masonry, republican government, and the rights of man.

—ALEXANDER CAMPBELL[1]

T HE HIGHLIGHT FOR Joseph Smith Jr. on April 6, 1830, was not when his new church, the Church of Christ, was officially organized near Fayette, New York. Nor was it when he was sustained by the forty or so attendees as the faith's "first elder." It was not even when he received a new revelation that declared, in God's own words, that he "shalt be called a seer & Translater & Prophet and Apostle of Jesus Christ." Such revelatory texts were common by this point.[2]

The highlight came when Smith saw his father's six-foot-two frame emerge from the water, a baptism that signified the aged seeker's religious commitment, an ordinance that made his family whole.

The younger Joseph embraced Joseph Sr. as soon as his father exited the water, still dripping. Joseph Jr. was two inches shorter than him and had a full head of brown hair, a large nose, and heavy eye-lashes. Neither man could keep his composure. "Oh, my God," the son exclaimed, "I have lived to see my own father baptized into the true Church of Christ!" Lucy Mack Smith, mother of the prophet and wife of the baptized, later recalled that Joseph Jr. buried his head in his father's chest and "wept like an infant." "His joy seemed to Be full," a fellow participant noted.[3]

The emotional scene was the culmination of decades of events within a single household. Just a few years before, the Smiths were a family divided by religion, beset by financial difficulties, and faced with an uncertain future. Now they shared a singular belief, were united in purpose, and claimed a network of supporters.

The Smith family experienced this shift just as America's young republic emerged as a dynamic marketplace for commerce, ideas, and religion. The newly formed United States offered both opportunity and instability. Citizens were afforded the chance to move, experiment, suc-ceed, and, just as often, fail within a nation that prioritized the individ-ual over the community. "This is the age of severance, of dissociation, of freedom," declared another of the era's prophets, Ralph Waldo Emerson. While enticing for some, this propulsive environment wrought chaos for many. The American people were "divided into an almost endless variety of religious factions," wrote one British visitor. The new Church of Christ was just one attempt to restore order and belonging, even as it took advantage of the period's liberality.[4]

The family of Joseph Sr. and Lucy Mack Smith felt the conse-quences of this new culture more than most. They had been tossed to and fro upon the waves of religious change, economic turmoil, and societal transformation. But out of those trials came a new prophet visited by God, ordained by angels, and empowered to translate an ancient record. "It is my duty to say to you that the need was never greater of new revelation than now," blasted Emerson to a shocked gathering of Harvard ministers-to-be in 1837. Though Emerson blanched at the type of revelation—and especially the revelatory authority—that eventually flowed from Joseph Smith Jr., he appreci-ated its audacity.[5]

Many who knew the Smiths before 1830 would have been startled at their becoming the founding family of a global faith. They had appeared destined for continued struggle and anonymity, or perhaps even ignominy. But the early American republic was full of surprises.

LUCY MACK SMITH was a frustrated religious seeker in 1802. Though raised in a family that encouraged spiritual devotion, the young wife and mother of two felt "a dark and lonely chasm between myself and Christ." She had lived a righteous life, married an upright man, and attended to her religious duties, but still felt something was missing. Now, as an illness brought her to the brink of death, she wondered if she was ready to meet her maker. Smith prayed that if God "would let me live, I would endeavor to get that religion that would enable me to serve him right." She heard a voice that quoted scripture and promised salvation. Though grateful to be physically cured, Smith was more excited about her spiritual assurance. She spent the rest of her life trying to fulfill that covenant.[6]

Early America was a society enflamed with religion and patriotism. Few families were more emblematic of that culture than those that begat the nation's preeminent prophet. Lucy Mack was born in

Photograph of a daguerreian button believed to show Lucy Mack Smith, circa 1840s or 1850s. Lucy Smith both influenced and documented the earliest years of the Mormon movement.

July 1775, only months after the fighting at Lexington and Concord. Her father, Solomon Mack, was a farmer and veteran of the Seven Years' War, and her mother, Lydia Gates, a schoolteacher. When independence was finally declared, Solomon, along with his sons Jason and Stephen, joined the patriotic cause.

The family soon set out on their own spiritual odyssey. Though Solomon initially stayed clear of organized worship, he later became a religious seeker who wrote an autobiography narrating his dramatic conversion. Prayers for deliverance from painful rheumatism resulted in "a bright light" and "a voice" that reminded him of "passages of scripture." The vision healed his ailments. He shared this deep and mystical devotion with the next generation. Mack's daughters Lovina and Lovisa claimed visionary experiences, and his son Jason formed his own religious community. Lucy's conversion experience therefore fit within a family pattern.[7]

The Macks' spiritual explorations occurred during a broader religious awakening. When Thomas Jefferson fought for religious liberty, he believed it would dissolve any "enthusiastic" and "evangelical" sects that could not withstand the light of reason. "There is not a young man now living in the United States," he predicted in 1822, "who will not die a Unitarian," a reference to the denomination known for rationalism and morals rather than miracles and dogma. America would be governed by modernity's enlightenment standards.[8]

Jefferson proved to be a poor prophet. Not only did rates of religious affiliation explode in the aftermath of political independence, but the most successful movements were those that discomforted the sage of Monticello. Evangelistic denominations like Baptists and Methodists surged as they embraced democratic ethos that empowered common men and women. Clerics and their followers created a Protestant quasi-establishment that dominated the landscape. Meanwhile, movements and ideas that were outside the mainstream found space for experimentation, even if not acceptance. Prominent deists like Thomas Paine argued that organized religion should be abolished altogether, while the less-aggressive Universalists posited that true republicanism meant forfeiting antiquated notions of damnation and hell.[9]

If Lucy Mack represented the evangelical mainstream, the family into which she married reflected the more experimental. Joseph Smith Sr.'s New England ancestry dated back to 1638 and Robert Smith, one of the first Anglo settlers of Topsfield, Massachusetts. They were puritans and then Congregationalists until Asael Smith, Joseph Sr.'s father, was drawn to the Universalist teachings of John Murray. Both Asael and Joseph helped found the Universalist Society in Tunbridge, Vermont, in 1797, the year after Joseph married Lucy. Joseph, however, remained aloof from organized religion for the next three decades, convinced that all the denominations were corrupt. It was a feeling shared in his family. After discovering that Lucy had coaxed Joseph into attending a Methodist meeting, Asael threw a copy of Paine's deistic book *Age of Reason* at him and "angrily bade him read that until he believe it." Lucy mourned the growing religious rift.[10]

Skepticism toward organized religion did not mean unbelief, however. Lucy later recalled her husband receiving a series of dreams throughout the following years, most of which reaffirmed a seeker's sense of spiritual yearning and ecclesiastical distrust. Lucy's own vivid dream, received after praying in a grove nearby their home, eased concern that she had married a man who would never settle: she envisioned two trees, one of which bent in the wind while the other resisted. The flexible tree represented her husband, who would eventually embrace true religion, while the other was Jesse, his brother who never would. Though it is impossible to gauge how much these remembered visions were shaped by the ensuing decades, it is clear that the Smith household adamantly believed in divine intervention outside official channels.[11]

The generations that immediately preceded Joseph Jr. were not just religious seekers but also economic opportunists anxious to take advantage of America's capitalist revolution. Solomon Mack, for example, attempted to escape the small farmstead through speculative endeavors. While he had little success, his son, Stephen, became a landholder successful enough to gift Lucy $1,000 for her wedding. Joseph Smith Sr., like his father Asael, also ventured into business. He and Lucy rented out their Tunbridge farm and became storekeepers in a nearby town. They soon collected ginseng to sell on the global market. The investment, however, proved disastrous. The merchant they hired to sell the product kept the proceeds, and the Smiths were forced to sell their farm and forfeit savings to cover their debts. They escaped "the embarrassment of debt," Lucy bitterly remembered, but not "the embarrassment of poverty." The new marketplace was as dangerous as it was enticing.[12]

It was in the wake of this crisis that Lucy gave birth to her fourth child and third son. They named him Joseph, after his father, in whom Lucy still held faith despite his failed financial gamble. "Nothing occurred during his early life," Lucy later summarized, "except those trivial circumstances which are common to that state of human existence." The most "common" feature of the future prophet's early years, however, was struggle.[13]

Whereas Asael Smith and Solomon Mack enjoyed the benefits of the new republic—religious freedom and economic experimentation—Joseph Sr. and Lucy experienced its downside. Spiritual wandering bred denominational vagrancy, and fiscal risks produced financial ruin. Over the next dozen years their family relocated seven times across New England, moving from one tenant situation to another. Just when they started to find their footing in Lebanon, New Hampshire, in 1813, a typhoid epidemic swept through the region and affected each of the seven Smith children. None of them died, but Joseph Jr., only seven years old, experienced an infection so severe that he would have lost his leg were it not for a nearby surgeon's experimental surgery. The young boy remained on crutches for some time and suffered physical and emotional consequences the rest of his life.[14]

The ensuing medical bills, coupled with a series of failed harvests made worse by a global "year without a summer" in 1816, devastated the Smiths financially. City officials "warned" them that the community would no longer help. The family chose to cut ties with New England altogether and flee to New York, following Joseph Sr.'s brothers, who had recently relocated to harvest large wheat fields that promised more lucrative rewards.[15]

*   *   *

THE UPSTATE New York village of Palmyra offered a fresh start, as it had for thousands of New Englanders who flooded the region. The Smiths ran a downtown store and contracted for a larger farm just south of the county line in Farmington, soon renamed Manchester, in 1819. While they began building a handsome frame home, they rented a small log cabin that was a tight squeeze for a family that included a father, mother, six boys between two and nineteen, and two girls aged fifteen and six. (Another daughter, Lucy, was born two years later.) Their measure of success was primarily due to the oldest son, Alvin, who was both industrious and savvy. He and the next oldest, Hyrum, compensated for their father, who remained spiritually earnest but increasingly adrift. Years of hard labor with little reward left Joseph Sr. disillusioned and, according to some, a drunkard. Though the patriarch's drinking habits were probably typical of the time, he later expressed shame for frequent intoxication. Regardless, the family proved quite capable during their first years in Palmyra.[16]

Financial stability was not the only obsession. Palmyra was amid what Lucy called "a great revival of religion," a series of spiritual upheavals known as the Second Great Awakening. Itinerant ministers preaching hellfire sermons were so pervasive in upstate New York that later historians referred to it as the "burned-over district." Rural and urban communities alike hosted camp meetings where thousands of attendees listened to energetic clergymen urging them to experience a "new birth," embrace God's grace, and reject the world's materialistic temptations.[17]

Many of these messages were conjoined with personal visions. The most prominent minister of the day, Charles Grandison Finney, told of how he fled into the woods to pray and "met the Lord Jesus Christ face to face," as plain as he "would see any other man." Another visionary, the Black preacher Jarena Lee, reported being "delivered" from a physical Satan through God's grace. Closer to Palmyra, Asa Wild claimed to have learned from Christ himself that all denominations were corrupt. Whereas visionary experiences had previously been seen as a threat to religious order, America's spiritual marketplace not only allowed but encouraged such episodes.[18]

With these expanded options came commensurate anxieties. How could a seeker know they had found the true religion? The young Joseph Smith Jr. inherited his father's curiosity as well as his restlessness. Lucy recalled that he "always seemed to reflect more deeply than common persons of his age." What his education lacked in breadth he made up for in depth. One neighbor described him as "proverbially good-natured," but "never known to laugh." This serious demeanor implied the solemnity with which he approached religion.[19]

Palmyra's religious awakening deeply affected the teenager. He attended revivals, listened to preachers, and explored the Bible. Yet the boy failed to find satisfying answers. The religious marketplace, he concluded, was saturated with possibilities but light on substance. He referred to this uncertainty as "a grief to my soul," as he could not help but feel despondent concerning "the contentions and divisions" that plagued "the minds of mankind." Whenever he attended worship services, he was impressed with their words but could "feel nothing" in his heart. He was both committed to finding truth and unmoored by the quest. The revivals only succeeded at stirring "division amongst the people," as "all good feelings" were "entirely lost in a strife of words and a contest about opinions." Chaos reigned.[20]

Like so many others at the time, the young Smith sought his own answer. The Bible, he later testified, informed him that if he "lacked wisdom," he could "ask God" (James 1:5). While still in his teens, he followed the example of his parents, the example of Charles Finney, the example of his many contemporaries, and secluded himself in a nearby grove to pray. In response, Smith claimed that God descended through "a pillar of light." The boy was told that while "the world lieth in sin at this time," his own sins were forgiven.[21]

Millions of believers today identify this moment as the "First Vision," the origins of a global faith. In the 1820s, however, it was just another manifestation of America's spiritual revolution, which opened the heavens for earnest seekers.

Joseph Smith eventually provided several accounts of his visionary experience. He revised the episode with additional details and increasing importance with each telling. His earliest descriptions matched other visionary narratives from the era, especially those within the Methodist tradition. But as Mormonism grew more distinct in doctrine and practice, so too was Smith's initial theophany reinterpreted by millions of believers to become the founding story for the evolving faith.[22]

The first person Smith told, a Methodist minister, immediately denounced the vision. Though many denominations, like the Methodists, had previously welcomed such religiosity, a growing majority were pushing for reforms and respectability, which resulted in a more staid climate. Smith may have hoped the vision would prove his place among the converted. The rejection, however, jarred the young seeker and made him reluctant to either share the story or join a church. It was the first time Smith learned that there were limits to religious exploration, and that the nation's spiritual forum did not require existing church structures to listen to new prophets. Ecclesiastically speaking, Smith was on his own.[23]

It is impossible to account holistically for the many influences that resulted in the young Joseph Smith's religious journey. Any individual component could be, and has been, emphasized as *the* crucial ingredient. When understood together, however, all of these factors combined to induce an anxiety that required individual conversion, an environment that enabled experimentation, and a family perfectly situated to take advantage of the age's opportunities. From his mother, Joseph inherited an expectation of divine manifestations; from his father, a commitment to unorthodox searching. And from his nation, the prophet-to-be was afforded the freedom to embrace both.

SIX YEARS LATER, as he appeared before a justice of the peace in Bainbridge, New York, in March 1826, Joseph Smith likely worried about his life's direction. The twenty-year-old was charged with being a "disorderly person" for claiming to use a seer stone while seeking buried treasure. Smith was arrested, imprisoned, and forced to listen to twelve witnesses who testified about his supposed seership abilities. The justice referred to the case as *People v. Joseph Smith the Glass Looker.* If found guilty, the young visionary could be sentenced to up to sixty days in jail.[24]

It was a traumatic turn of events for Smith in the wake of his spiritual experience. It also occurred during a family crisis. He later confessed that, following his First Vision, he "fell into transgressions and sinned in many things," but was vague with details; in another account, he merely referred to these moments as youthful "follies." Yet as much as Smith wished to distance himself from treasure-seeking activities and the period's folk-magic culture, in which citizens blended occult beliefs with traditional Christianity, they played a crucial role in his path to prophethood. They were also the primary prism through which many first viewed the gold plates project.[25]

The young Joseph inherited his fascination with magic culture from his father. Joseph Sr. searched for "Captain Kidd's buried treasure" before Joseph Jr. was even born and boasted in the 1830s that he knew "more about money digging" than most because he had "been in the business more than thirty years." He acquired a reputation in Palmyra for being "a firm believer in witchcraft and other supernatural things." Lucy later expressed embarrassment for these activities, assuring readers of her memoir that just because the family was "trying to win the faculty of Abrac[,] drawing magic circles[,] or sooth saying," it did not mean they were neglecting their financial and spiritual duties. For many Americans in the early nineteenth century, the notions of magic, industry, and religion converged into an enchanted world filled with wonder. Indeed, treasure-digging appeared ubiquitous. "There comes a time in every rightly constructed boy's life," Mark Twain wrote, "when he has a raging desire to go somewhere and dig for hidden treasure."[26]

Joseph Jr. discovered his first seer stone while digging a well with his neighbor Willard Chase in 1822. Willard's sister, Sally, then taught him how to use it. The group of seekers embraced the Smiths and actively searched for the region's treasures. One neighbor recalled Smith looking into his "peep stone" to see a cave where an ancient Indigenous king had buried his precious belongings; another recorded Smith's instruction to slit the throat of a black sheep to free treasure from its protective spell. The teenager soon developed a reputation for his skill. Among those impressed was Martin Harris, a successful Palmyra farmer. Once, while chatting with Smith, Harris dropped the small pin with which he was picking his teeth into a pile of straw. Smith, looking at his stone nestled in an "old white hat," immediately found the pin without glancing at the ground.[27]

Smith's religious and supernatural obsessions soon intersected. On the evening of September 21, 1823, following a family discussion concerning "the subject of the diversity of churches," Smith stayed up late in prayer. His pleas were answered with an angel dressed in white who informed Smith that he was to be a conduit for God's voice. Buried in a nearby hill—the same hill he had recently searched—were records "written upon gold plates, giving an account of the former inhabitants of this continent." The angel then recited a string of biblical verses referencing the coming millennium. After disappearing through "a conduit" that opened "right up into heaven," the angel returned two more times to repeat the same message. His last visit closed with the warning that Satan would try to tempt the young man who, due to his family's "indigent circumstances," might abscond with the plates "for the purpose of getting rich."[28]

Smith, exhausted from the visitations, proved worthless while laboring the next day. He was finally sent home, whereupon he was visited by the angel for a fourth time and told to relate everything to his father. Joseph Sr., inclined to believe the supernatural story, urged him to follow the angel's instructions and visit the designated hillside. Though he and his fellow seekers had failed to find treasure in the area just a few days earlier, Smith now claimed to uncover a box that contained the plates. He picked them up, set them to the side as he re-covered the opening, but discovered them missing when he turned around. "Why can I not obtain them!" Smith exclaimed. The angel informed him that it was because he had "saught the Plates to obtain riches," confirmation of the previous warning. However, if he reformed his ways, the angel promised Smith, he could access the records in a few years.[29]

Elements of this story fit both the magical and Christian contexts that shaped Smith's family. The promise of hidden gold records left by ancient communities confirmed suspicions of buried treasure. But the biblical references and appeal to a divine reward, rather than monetary gain, implied a spiritual priority. The angel directed him to become not rich but holy. The distinction between these simultaneous, and sometimes conflicting, impulses took several more years to untangle.[30]

The plates sprouted another fascination. Though Joseph did not yet have access to the records, he soon regaled his family with stories concerning its contents. "He would describe the ancient inhabitants of this continent," Lucy recalled, including "their dress, mode of traveling, and the animals upon which they rode," as well as their cities, buildings, warfare strategies, and religious worship. At least part of Joseph's divine mission included excavating the continent's history. Many Americans were fascinated with the nation's Indigenous ancestors. As early as 1660, British colonist Thomas Thorowgood's *Jews in America* hypothesized that Native nations possessed Israelite heritage. More recently, politician Elias Boudinot's *A Star in the West* (1816) and Congregationalist minister Ethan Smith's *View of the Hebrews* (1823) both posited that Indians descended from the Lost Tribes of Israel. But rather than offering more speculation, this new record promised direct evidence.[31]

Smith demanded that his parents not speak of the plates to anyone because jealous neighbors "will want to kill us for the sake of the gold." Yet word trickled out. Smith himself likely told several in his treasure-seeking circle, who immediately connected the buried records to their activities. The seekers' accounts of learning of the plates included details like toads that "assumed the appearance of a man," a "beast" that "arose and expanded as large as a dog," and even guardian gnomes, all frequent features of magic tales. They felt a sense of ownership over the mystical material, and their reflections revealed how the records were first understood. The seekers felt betrayed when they were later not given immediate access to the plates.[32]

Joseph's story of the plates united the Smiths, albeit momentarily. It was confirmation that theirs was a special family with a divine mission. Joseph's oldest brother, Alvin, was designated by the angel to accompany Joseph to the hill the next year. Lucy fondly remembered a feeling of "sweetest union" and "tranquility" during that period.[33]

The moment of peace, however, did not last long. Alvin died a few months later after a physician administered a lethal dose of calomel, or mercurous chloride. Alvin was not only the Smiths' favorite son, he had acted as the family's financial head and his demise brought ruin. They were already behind in mortgage payments and now lacked Alvin's manual labor as well as his fiscal management, both of which had been crucial. By 1825, they were at risk of losing their property once again.

Faced with such a crisis, the Smiths turned to what they knew best. Rumors of Joseph Jr.'s seership abilities had traveled over a hundred miles southeast to Bainbridge, New York. Josiah Stowell, a wealthy farmer, was convinced that Smith held "certain keys by which he could discern things invisible to the natural eye," namely a "silver mine" left behind by Spanish conquistadors in the nearby Pennsylvania town of Harmony. Both Joseph Jr. and Sr. readily agreed to be hired after Stowell offered a handsome salary and promised to put them in touch with another businessman, Joseph Knight, who could purchase their wheat. They signed a contract on November 11, 1825, along with four other diggers, to evenly split any uncovered "Gold or Silver." One of the witnesses to the contract was Isaac Hale, a distinguished farmer and hunter who came to rue the day he met the Smiths.[34]

The search was a bust. After weeks of digging, Joseph Jr. admitted that he could not see the proper location, and the company disbanded. The Smiths then lost title to their land, though the new owner allowed them to remain in the home as renters. Decades of labor went up in smoke. Lucy "felt the inconvenience of poverty" more than ever before. Given that rumors of the gold plates shaped the family reputation, young Joseph must have felt some blame.[35]

Losing the farm was not the end of their struggles. Several months after the silver mine search, Stowell's nephews sued Smith as a "disorderly person," instigating the 1826 Bainbridge case. They believed Smith, a fraud, had swindled their impressionable uncle. The relevant New York statute condemned anyone convicted of "pretending . . . to discover where lost goods may be found." Stowell insisted that he "had the most implicit faith in [Smith's] skill." Smith begrudgingly conceded that he possessed a "certain stone" through which he had successfully searched for "hidden treasures in the bowels of the earth," though he appeared embarrassed by the whole ordeal.[36]

The official outcome of the trial, one of Smith's most formidable early experiences, has been lost. However, a guilty verdict seems probable, given that Smith's and Stowell's testimonies verified the accusation. One early account alleged that Smith was found guilty but "allowed to escape" due to "his youth," while another reported he was discharged. Either result may have been possible, but it is also likely that the justice made an informal agreement with Smith to stay the trial in return for the young man's promise to reform.[37]

The Bainbridge episode was a turning point for the wandering seeker. Until 1826, Smith was focused on supernatural quests to discover lost treasure, an occupation deeply rooted in family and culture but increasingly at odds with a new skeptical generation anxious to rid themselves of their folkloric origins. Smith was now forced to reorient his priorities and reassess his abilities according to standards of respectability. His understanding of the yet-to-be-uncovered plates shifted accordingly.

EMMA HALE was torn between her inclinations toward love and family in January 1827. The tall twenty-two-year-old with dark hair and an olive complexion was born the seventh of eight children in Harmony, Pennsylvania, to Isaac and Elizabeth Hale. She grew up horseback riding, canoeing, and cooking. She also possessed a special affinity for religion. Hale was baptized Congregationalist but joined the Methodists after being swept up in the awakening revivals. One neighbor reported that she was "fine looking, smart, a good singer, and she often got the power"—that is, she manifested a spiritual rebirth. Her piety even drew her otherwise stubborn father into the faith. But now she was standing in the home of a family friend, Joseph Knight, as Joseph Smith begged her to marry him against her father's wishes. Her decision that moment determined the rest of her life.[38]

Smith first met Hale the previous November when he traveled to Harmony on the treasure quest. Isaac Hale served as a witness to the diggers' agreement and provided housing. While the search proved fruitless, Joseph fell in love with Emma and frequently visited her as he worked for Stowell and Knight the next year. At one point he even convinced another treasure seeker, Samuel Lawrence, to fund a silver mine search in Pennsylvania just so he could have an excuse to visit. Yet the two faced opposition from Emma's family, who disapproved of Smith's vocation. Emma, too, likely had reservations about Joseph's questionable activities, given her pious background. Joseph Smith had to reform his ways to win over the Hales.[39]

It was around this time that Palmyra hosted another series of revivals. While Smith's earlier visionary experience had commenced his spiritual journey, this new reawakening, coupled with his growing reservations toward magic and increasing desire to court Emma and her family, determined the young man's course. Smith once again tried his hand with the Methodists, Emma's faith, after "catching a spark" at one of their camp meetings. But other members of the Smith family were pulled elsewhere. Lucy formally joined the Presbyterians and took with her several of her children, including the oldest surviving son, Hyrum. Meanwhile, Joseph Sr. remained steadfastly opposed to organized churches. The Smiths were once again a household divided.[40]

Joseph Jr. sought solace through forming a new family. He approached his parents and, after noting that he had "been very lonely since Alvin died," expressed his desire to marry Emma. The Smiths approved but the Hales did not. Finally, after a year of courtship, Joseph rendezvoused with Emma at the Stowells' house on January 18, 1827, and urged her to take his hand. While she had "no intention of marrying when I left home" that day, she still preferred "to marry him to any other man I knew," and therefore consented. They moved to Palmyra and Emma did not write her parents until the following summer, when she requested that they forward her belongings.[41]

Smith's decision to marry Emma, and his continued hope to impress her family, transformed the young seeker. He swore to Isaac that he had "given up what he called 'glass-looking'" and would now seek more reputable employment. Smith continued to cultivate some of his seership powers, but they were now framed in an explicitly religious quest. "'*Peeping*' was all d—d nonsense," he explained to Emma's brother Alva, but the "gift in seeing with a stone" was "from God."[42]

Emma was soon committed to the gold plates story. Originally, Joseph's brother Alvin, who had shared the family's mystic beliefs, had been identified as the person to assist in retrieving the plates. After Alvin's death, that duty shifted to fellow seeker Samuel Lawrence, an indication that Smith still understood the records as related to treasure quests. But in 1827 Joseph Jr. explained that Emma was the newly designated partner. The plates were now conceived as a religious pursuit to be obtained with his more pious wife. Smith reported in mid-1827 that an angel had delivered "the severest chastisement that I have ever had in my life," signifying it was time to finally acquire the records.[43]

The long-awaited day finally came on September 22, 1827, four years after Smith first spoke of the plates. Joseph Knight, who had learned about the records and had become one of Smith's first converts, traveled to Palmyra in anticipation. Smith's former treasure-seeking associates, convinced they were due a share of the loot, scoured the hill. To surprise them both, the prophet left shortly after midnight that morning, accompanied by Emma, who was wearing her bonnet and riding dress. They utilized Emma's riding skills and took Knight's horse and wagon. Lucy prayed all night. Joseph and Emma returned with the plates after breakfast, just as Knight worried about his missing property. "Do not be uneasy," Joseph told them, "all is right." He instructed that nobody else could see the plates, which remained in a decayed "old birch log" outside, but insisted that they were "ten times Better then I expected."[44]

After years of failed treasure searches, Smith had finally uncovered precious material from the earth. He was struck by the stones that had been buried with the plates, an encased set of two sacred rocks fashioned like eyeglasses yet known as "interpreters" that were meant to help him translate the plates' content. "They are Marvelus," Smith informed Knight, for he "can see any thing." His previous quests and abilities now paled in comparison. His former colleagues, however, felt cheated. They hired a famous seeker to find where Smith hid the plates. The family moved the records from the log to beneath their hearth, and from the hearth to a barrel of flax seed in a nearby cooper's shop, always just one step ahead of their foes.[45]

The situation became untenable. Joseph and Emma decided that their only hope for peace was to relocate back to Harmony. To cover expenses, they turned to Martin Harris and his wife, Lucy, who had previously supported Smith's seeking abilities. Though Lucy demanded to see the plates for herself, Martin claimed a vision had convinced him of the plates' veracity. The issue eventually drove a wedge between the two, and Lucy forced Martin to sleep in a separate room before eventually divorcing him. Undaunted, Martin offered the Smiths $50, and the prophet loaded the plates into a ten-by-twelve-inch box, nailed it shut, hid it in a strong cask, filled the cask with beans, and set off for Pennsylvania.[46]

THE SMITHS arrived in Harmony to a cool reception from Emma's father. Isaac Hale still hoped he could reform his son-in-law, and Emma hoped she could keep both sides happy. Things did not start well when Joseph refused to show Hale the plates, who in turn refused to permit anything he was not "allowed to see" on his property. They therefore hid the box in which they kept the plates in the woods. Once the newlyweds moved into a small home that had been recently vacated by Emma's brother, the plates were left on a table while wrapped in a linen cloth. Emma, though tempted, never uncovered them, though she traced their exterior with her fingers. "They seemed to be pliable like thick paper," she recalled, "and would rustle with a metallic sound when the edges were moved by the thumb."[47]

Smith struggled for months with how to translate the record. At first he "drew of[f] the Caricters" hoping to break some type of linguistic code. He described the text as "reformed Egyptian," and his tracings exhibited a series of hieroglyphic-type figures. Once Joseph started dictating text, Emma, who served as his first scribe, was shocked at what she heard. Her husband "could neither write nor dictate a coherent and well worded letter," yet here he was "dictating a book" with characters, plot, and doctrine. At one point after sharing a passage that detailed walls surrounding Jerusalem, Joseph asked if such a thing were plausible. When Emma confirmed it was,

Characters copied by either Christian or John Whitmer, circa 1829–31. Though it is not known when this document was created, the characters are alleged to have been copied from Smith's plates.

he shouted, "Oh! I was afraid I had been deceived." Emma always referred to this work as a bedrock of her faith.[48]

Things escalated after Martin Harris arrived in early 1828 to serve as a full-time scribe. To validate Smith's abilities, Joseph sent Harris to New York City with a copy of the plates' characters to consult linguistic scholars. Accounts of the trip, especially Harris's visit with noted linguist and scholar Charles Anthon, vary substantially. Anthon, a specialist in Latin and Greek, claimed that he immediately saw the characters as a fraud and Harris as a mark. He believed the text was filled with sophomoric writings designed to fool the ignorant. Harris, conversely, came away from the interaction convinced of the plates' veracity. He asserted that Anthon had initially declared Smith's translation "correct" before ripping up his certificate of authenticity after hearing of their supernatural origins. Smith saw the episode as the fulfillment of biblical prophecy.[49]

Translation soon picked up speed. While Smith initially hung a sheet to separate himself as he pored over the plates, the prophet soon reverted to using his seer stone. Smith never provided firsthand accounts of the process—perhaps out of fear of association with magic culture—but observers stated that he would place the stone in his hat and that "Brite Roman Letters" would appear. Harris once tested Smith by switching his stone with a look-alike. "Martin! What is the

Joseph Smith's seer stone and pouch, photographed by Welden C. Andersen and Richard E. Turley Jr. This stone is assumed to be the one used by Joseph Smith while producing the Book of Mormon text. It is also assumed that Emma constructed the pouch in which it was stored.

matter!" Smith exclaimed. "All is as dark as Egypt." The two succeeded in producing over a hundred pages between April and June 1828.[50]

Tragedy struck that summer. Harris, still hoping to fix his marriage, begged Smith to allow him to take the manuscript home. Smith begrudgingly agreed. Days later, on June 15, Emma gave birth to their first child. The baby did not survive, and Emma nearly died as well. Once somewhat recovered, Emma urged Joseph to find the manuscript. Joseph, however, discovered that Harris had lost it, negating all their progress. Lucy remembered Joseph's pained exclamation that "all is lost." When Smith next looked in his stone he saw a divine rebuke: "Although a man may have many Revelations & have power to do many Mighty works," those who disobey "the councils of God" are destined to "incur the vengence of a Just God." Smith lost his translation "privileges" until he sufficiently repented. In the meantime, the angel revoked the plates.[51]

The revelation marked a new stage for the evolving prophet, as well as a new genre for sacred texts. He was now dictating commandments in the voice of God. By February 1829, Smith was receiving a string of divine commands, immediately written down, that directed both him and his small circle of believers.

The translation's pause was followed by a quick denouement in spring 1829. Oliver Cowdery, a sober, slim, and earnest schoolteacher, had arrived in Palmyra the previous autumn and boarded with the Smiths. He quickly became engrossed with rumors concerning the plates, which Joseph had eventually reacquired from the angel. At first reluctant to provide details, Joseph Sr. and Lucy eventually told him the story, and Cowdery became "so entirely absorbed" that he was ineffective at everything else. He set off for Harmony at the start of April. Once there, Cowdery and Smith worked feverishly at the translation. "These were days never to be forgotten," Cowdery jubilantly reminisced a few years later, "to sit under the sound of a voice dictated by the inspiration of heaven." Now fully invested in the project, Cowdery even received permission to attempt his own translation. Though his attempt failed—Smith dictated a revelation that explained that he did not do enough to "study [the scripture] out in your mind" prior to dictation—Cowdery remained astounded at Smith's prophethood.[52]

Hostility from the Hales remained an obstacle. Cowdery wrote David Whitmer, a friend whose family had heard whispers about the plates, to ask for assistance. The Whitmers, a German family with pietist roots located in Fayette, New York, about thirty miles southeast of Palmyra, immediately offered to house the translation project. Cowdery and Joseph Smith arrived on June 1, with Emma trailing a few days behind. The number of Smith's followers quickly grew as the entire Whitmer family and many of their neighbors embraced the miraculous story. Buoyed by the friendly surroundings, Smith finished the entire manuscript by the end of June, having dictated nearly three hundred thousand words in less than twelve weeks.[53]

Smith arranged for several of his closest followers to share his burden of supernatural experiences. Cowdery, Harris, and David Whitmer reported that, while praying with Smith on June 28, they saw an angel, viewed the gold plates, and heard a voice proclaim the records' divinity. A few days later, eight more witnesses—Joseph

Jr.'s father and brothers Hyrum and Samuel, as well as four Whitmer siblings (Christian, Jacob, Peter, and John) and one Whitmer in-law (Hiram Page)—were allowed to both see and "heft" the plates. "Father, mother, you do not know how happy I am," Joseph Jr. declared as he collapsed in his parents' house; "I am not any longer to be entirely alone in the world." The testimonies from these three and eight witnesses were designated to appear inside the book as additional evidence. (Not all were convinced: Mark Twain would later quip, "I could not feel more satisfied and at rest if the entire Whitmer family had testified.")[54]

Only publication remained. Smith secured copyright on July 11. An announcement for the book appeared in a Palmyra newspaper by the end of the month. The title, "The Book of Mormon," came from a title page found on "the very last leaf, on the left hand side of the collection or book of plates." Martin Harris agreed to mortgage his farm to convince a local printer to take on the project. Learning from previous mistakes, Smith directed Oliver Cowdery to make a duplicate manuscript for the printer. Hyrum Smith, designated to oversee the publication, took only the necessary pages for each day, hiding them under his coat as he walked from home to publisher. John Gilbert, who helped with typesetting, recalled that the manuscript was "closely written and legible" but lacked any punctuation. The publication of America's newest religious text was underway.[55]

The twenty months between September 1827 and June 1829 were a transformative period for Smith. After years of wandering through various conversion experiences and supernatural activities, Smith now escalated through several significant prophetic steps at a rapid pace. He had finally produced tangible results from his seership, had dictated hundreds of pages of scripture, and was now declaring revelatory edicts in the voice of God. Early America had no shortage of prophets, of people searching for fresh revelation, or even of new scripture. But the Palmyra seeker's project pushed in new directions, both a culmination of and diversion from broader cultural pursuits.[56]

* * *

WHILE STORIES of buried records fit, albeit awkwardly, in early America's magic culture, the text that Joseph Smith produced is unique. The Book of Mormon was America's most substantial contribution to the world's scriptural canon. A multilayered story with numerous narrators, mixed genres, and elements that both drew from and challenged cultural currents, it was destined to elicit strong responses. Critics called it "the greatest piece of superstition that has ever come within the sphere of our knowledge" even before its publication. But the book was immediately embraced by Smith's followers as profound scripture. Today, it inspires millions of believers and fascinates scores of religious scholars.[57]

The book begins with a tale of dissent. Lehi, the story's founding patriarch, escapes corrupt Jerusalem with his family around 600 BC to settle their own godly civilization on a new continent with his family. Once in the Americas, Nephi, a righteous and self-confident third son who becomes Lehi's successor, leads his followers to separate from their more rebellious siblings. Now identified as "Nephites," as opposed to the disaffected "Lamanites" (named after Nephi's older brother), they are taught to "observe to keep the judgments, and the statutes, and the commandments of the Lord in all things." The people are so righteous that they learn Jesus Christ's name and mission centuries before his birth, and Christ himself ministers to them following his resurrection.[58]

The Book of Mormon was not the first text to posit an Israelite heritage for America's Indigenous inhabitants. Nor was it the first to present their continent as a "chosen" land. But by presenting the Native nations as not only godly but proto-Christian, the book both sacralized and Christianized the ground upon which the young United States was built.[59]

Even as the Nephite saga echoes some cultural myths concerning Native peoples, it directly challenges others. Most Americans of the era subscribed to the theory of the "vanishing Indian," an assumption that the continent's original inhabitants would give way to Anglo-American dominance. Contemporaries estimated that there were fewer than five thousand Iroquois remaining in New York by 1830, a vastly diminished number after centuries of violence, dispossession, disease, and forced migration. Yet the Book of Mormon promises a redemptive—and even vindictive—future for the Lamanite descendants. (The Nephites are wiped out at the end of the book due to their turn to wickedness.) During Christ's visit to the Americas, he predicts that the "remnant of the house of Jacob" was given this land as its irrevocable "inheritance," even after the arrival of White "gentiles." These Indigenous nations, though surrounded by colonists, would still triumph "as a young lion among the beasts of the forest." Indeed, the entire book was directed "to the Lamanites" as its primary audience.[60]

The text laid a foundation for early Mormonism's complicated racial views. When the righteous Nephites separate from the wicked Lamanites, the former are described as "white" and "exceedingly fair and delightsome," while the latter are given "a skin of blackness." The Lamanites are described with racist stereotypes: scantily clothed, idolatrous, and fundamentally uncivilized. Yet they do not always fulfill the role of villains, and at times are even more righteous than the Nephites. One of the book's most powerful prophets, Samuel the Lamanite, is reminiscent of the Pequot activist William Apess, a Methodist minister famous for calling White America to repentance. Further, given the constantly changing racial complexions, the book demonstrates that race is malleable, a rejection of the growing American conception that racial identities were forever fixed. While many Christians were now positing that the different races were forever separated by biological barriers, Joseph Smith's text introduced the idea of racial fluidity. Though far from systematic or cohesive, the Book of Mormon's theology of race reflected the church's ensuing struggle to develop a consistent approach to non-White bodies.[61]

The text promises that God "denieth none that come unto him, black and white, bond and free, male and female." Yet with very few exceptions, women mostly go unnamed and unnoticed. Righteous and wicked men take center stage, with their wives, mothers, and daughters living in the literary shadows. Mormonism's entrenched and consistent patriarchal culture was rooted in its founding scripture.[62]

In many ways, the Nephite record reaffirms a culture of personal liberty. Salvation is an isolated affair accomplished through faith and private works. Adam's choice in the Garden of Eden is recast as a fortunate development that granted individual agency, and the text consistently emphasizes that a nation's chosen status can change with each generation. But the new scripture's communal message, hierarchical structure, and narrative of priestly authority also portends critiques of American society. The Nephite civilization's fall came after they were "divided into classes," no longer looked after their poor, and prioritized worldly wealth over divine commandments.[63]

Much of the Book of Mormon's narrative demonstrates a deep uneasiness toward democracy. Nephi's followers desire that he rule as "their king," a position he reluctantly accepts because it was "according to the commandments of the Lord." (Or not so reluctantly: Nephi has a penchant for, as narrator, highlighting simultaneously his own importance and his humility.) The only problem with monarchies is a pragmatic one: the impossibility of choosing "just men" for rulers. Even when a system of judges is established in lieu of a hereditary monarchy, the new law is based on God's commandments rather than majority vote. "Now it is better that a man should be judged of God than of man," Mosiah, the last of the prophet-kings, cautions, "for the judgments of God are always just, but the judgments of man are not always just."[64]

The work's most direct cultural challenge is its critique of America's Bible-centrism. The young nation had splintered into competing denominations, but nearly all of them shared the belief in a closed scriptural canon. The Book of Mormon, however, while incorporating long passages from the Bible, also undercut its supremacy. In a passage foreseeing the modern world, God denounces those who declare, "A Bible! A Bible! We have got a Bible, and there cannot be any more Bible." Such were the assertions of "fools," for it was God's will to speak to civilizations across time and space. It is not that the Bible could be replaced, but that it was only one part of a larger scriptural tapestry. "I command all men, both in the east and in the west," God declares, "that they shall write the words which I speak unto them." Rather than supplanting the Bible, as many of Joseph Smith's critics accused him of doing, the Book of Mormon reaffirmed the importance of scripture for the modern day even as it tore the canon open.[65]

Smith's book emphasizes the importance of prophetic leaders who worked in tandem with divine law. Nephi is the first in a string of prophet-leaders placed in charge of both God's people and God's record, passing down the sacred tablets from one generation to another. Their primary opponents, conversely, are wicked men, often termed "anti-Christs," who challenge church authority and teachings. Several closely resembled Protestantism's enemies during the 1820s. One, Shem, attempts to turn the Nephites away from truth by lying about Christ's reality, a swipe against groups like Unitarians that failed to prioritize Christ's divinity. Another, Nehor, establishes a fraudulent church in an attempt to earn riches, a common narrative in anti-Catholic literature. Perhaps the most charismatic anti-Christ is Korihor, who mimics Deistic arguments against an interventionist God and organized religion. The only thing to save humanity from social chaos and spiritual anarchy was a divinely appointed prophet.[66]

The last of these authorities, a father-son tandem named Mormon and Moroni, compile and edit the extensive records into the gold plates. Moroni, after his father perishes and leaves him the sole remaining righteous Nephite, buries the plates around 400 AD. It was Moroni, according to Smith, that visited in upstate New York, which happened to be the same place the records had been deposited. (Mormons referred to the mound as Hill Cumorah, a place named in the Book of Mormon.) Smith was now the latest of divinely appointed prophets placed in charge of sacred records. His translation fulfilled Moroni's prophecy that their records would speak "out of the dust."[67]

Smith's neighbors immediately cried foul. One newspaper claimed the book was "Salem Witch-craft-ism" and "the very summit" of "blasphemy and imposition." The most rigorous of the book's early critics, Disciples of Christ minister Alexander Campbell, declared that he "would as soon compare a bat to the American eagle, a mouse to a mammoth," than to equate the Book of Mormon to the Bible. Later attacks explained the book's production by claiming it was plagiarized from other works, though evidence never surfaced. Whatever its origins, the Book of Mormon was seen as a blasphemous subversion of religious liberty whose only converts were deluded fanatics.[68]

Smith's followers paid no regard to these critics. To them, the book dispensed divine truths and represented God's voice. Lucy Mack Smith excitedly wrote her family about receiving "the fullness of the Gospel," profusely quoting its content. Soon the book itself drew converts. Months after its publication, Parley Pratt, an itinerant minister as zealous as he was devout, became engrossed with the text. "I read all day," he recalled, so much so that he "had no desire for food" and "preferred reading to sleep." Pratt became the faith's foremost missionary for the next three decades. To both Lucy Smith and Parley Pratt, the Book of Mormon signified a modern House of Israel and laid the foundation for a unique Mormon theology.[69]

This enthusiasm did not result in immediate sales, however. Jesse Knight recalled once seeing Martin Harris, who had mortgaged his farm to pay for the book's printing, carrying a pile of copies under each arm. "The Books will not sell," he complained, "for no Body wants them." Harris eventually lost his property.[70]

Even if not a commercial success, the Book of Mormon launched a new religion. Joseph Smith's followers were thereafter known as "Mormons" to reflect the scripture's centrality. Their distinctive scripture forever marked them as a people apart. The text signified a fundamental belief in an open scriptural canon and continued prophecy. Though the movement later evolved in theology and practice beyond that found in the text, the Book of Mormon would always be its symbolic keystone.

JOSEPH SMITH and dozens of followers gathered in Fayette, New York, to officially organize the new church on April 6, 1830. They opened the meeting with "solemn prayer" and those in attendance accepted Smith and Oliver Cowdery "as their teachers in the things of the Kingdom of God." The two men ordained each other as first and second elders. Once concluded, many walked to a nearby creek to be baptized into the Church of Christ.[71]

The ecclesiastical path to this meeting was an intricate one. While several Americans took advantage of the young republic's religious liberty to establish new denominations, it was not predetermined that Smith would take that route. Many religious innovators, like Charles Grandison Finney and Jarena Lee, both prominent ministers with disruptive teachings, chose to operate within existing movements. Others took a moderate course by forming a schism within religious traditions. (The Methodists, Baptists, and Presbyterians already boasted numerous fissures by 1830.) Those that formed fundamentally new churches, like the Shakers, faced severe backlash and alienation. Yet even before Smith had completed translating the Nephite record he received a revelation that God "will establish my church" that was "like unto the church which was taught by my disciples in the days of old." Smith's solution to the problem of competing denominations was not to create something new, but to restore something old. Mormonism tapped into a broader primitivist impulse to uncover core ancient truths buried under the morass of modern corruption.[72]

The question of authority was at the heart of Smith's denomination. Who could act in the name of God, especially in a world already filled with earnest ministers? On the one hand, the new faith incorporated the period's democratizing impulse to obliterate any connection between ordination and elite education. The Book of Mormon referred to "priests and teachers" who "labored with their own hands" and did not place themselves "above [their] hearers." But the movement did not merely rely on personal intuition, either. The priesthood, or the authority to both preside over and officiate ordinances, was determined not by a body of believers but by divine authorization. The mere opinion of man could not be trusted.[73]

Smith's lineage of authority went directly to an ancient source: he claimed ordination to priesthood leadership through a series of angelic visitations. The first, in April 1829, featured John the Baptist appearing in Harmony to lay his hands on Smith's and Cowdery's heads, authorizing them to baptize. Later, the two were visited by Christ's original apostles, Peter, James, and John, who similarly ordained them to a "high priesthood." Smith began ordaining other men to the position of "elder" that fall, necessary steps toward forming his own church.[74]

The new church also required rules. To satisfy legal and cultural expectations, Smith and Cowdery prepared an official governing document, presented at their founding meeting. Titled "Articles and Covenants of the Church of Christ," the manifesto listed offices, ordinances, and procedures, though it downplayed doctrinal differences with other Christian sects. Members were to be baptized by full immersion, and the church was led by men ordained to the various positions of "Elders, Priests, Teachers, and Deacons." After partaking of communion, which Mormons call the sacrament, congregants listened as Smith dictated a revelation for the day. "Behold there Shall a Record be kept among you," it declared, establishing Mormonism's tradition of meticulous documentation. Members of the church would forever after mark April 6 as a sacred date.[75]

Smith's prophetic confidence escalated in the months following this founding moment. He had been dictating revelations in the voice of God for two years, but now the texts proliferated. The seer issued at least six more revelations that month, with over a hundred more over the following three years. His followers immediately embraced these texts as scripture. "The scribe seats himself at a desk or table, with pen, ink and paper," explained one witness, and as Smith was "moved upon by the Holy Ghost," he dictated "sentence after sentence," slowly and distinctly. The texts were seen as binding and distinct from their orator. When Smith asked John Whitmer to be the faith's first historian, Whitmer was reluctant. If God "desires it," Whitmer responded, "I desire that he would manifest it through Joseph the Seer." Smith, through the same mouth that issued the first request, then proclaimed, "Behold it is expedient that my servent John should write & keep a [regular] history." Whitmer now accepted. These revelations were collected into their own compilation, more additions to an ever-expanding scripture canon.[76]

The archive of sacred texts continued to grow as Smith embarked on another audacious project. At some point in June 1830 he dictated a revelation that expanded the story of Moses, narrating the biblical prophet's visit with God and vision of the cosmos. This theophany, not contained in the Bible, allegedly took place during Moses's life and provided a new foundation for modern religion. "Look & I will shew thee the workmanship of mine hands," God declared to the patriarch, "but not all for my works are without end & also my wo[r]lds." Moses learns of Christ's divinity, the earth's creation, and his own prophetic mission. The text made a direct connection between ancient and modern prophets. After generations would corrupt the biblical record, God would "raise up another like unto thee," another revelator to restore God's truth. Smith's calling was bound up in a cosmic matrix of grandiose visions and revelations that stretched the eternities. The brash text commenced an expansion and revision of the Bible that reflected Smith's imperious sense of his own sacred mission as a modern-day Moses.[77]

More and more believers followed Smith's increasingly daring teachings. The young Church of Christ had devoted clusters surrounding the Smiths in Palmyra, the Whitmers in Fayette, and the Knights and Stowells in Colesville, New York. Preachers, starting with Smith's own brothers, spread through the region with copies of the Book of Mormon. The church soon claimed over a hundred converts, each conversion based on individual experiences whose stories often spread like wildfire. Joseph's younger brother, Samuel, for example, met Methodist minister John P. Greene, whose wife, Rhoda, embraced the message. She then converted her husband as well as her own extended family. That cohort eventually included her seeker brother, who exhibited a devotion as fiery red as his hair. His name was Brigham Young.[78]

AMONG THOSE baptized at a large Colesville gathering in late June was Emma Smith. The prophet's wife had spent much of the past year alone in Harmony as her husband managed the Book of Mormon's printing, the church's organizing, and the gospel's spreading. Her cows were now the family's primary source of income, and she continued to sell milk, butter, and cheese to the local market. Complaints from her family concerning Joseph's career path continued, and Emma might have even had questions herself. Joseph had added a two-story saltbox structure to the west side of their humble home. Emma likely appreciated the additional space, but the new six rooms meant their domestic sphere doubled as church headquarters. She had missed the official founding in April, probably due to pressing matters in Harmony, but perhaps also from internal turmoil.[79]

Yet she pressed on. After an April 16, 1830, revelation commanded that the faithful be rebaptized under the "new and everlasting covenant," Emma decided to formally enter the new church. Joseph watched from the water's edge as she was baptized by Cowdery and covenanted herself to the movement.[80]

The fledgling church's early victories brought costs. A mob who viewed Mormonism's claims as heretical hurled taunts during Emma's baptism and then destroyed the saints' dam to prevent further services. They also heckled Joseph and his followers wherever they went, a constant chorus of opposition that believers felt accompanied God's chosen. When intimidation failed, Knight's neighbors turned to the law, and Smith was brought to court on two succeeding charges of disorderly conduct. The accusations were likely related to the old treasure-seeking case, but Smith saw it as persecution. Both sets of judges ruled in Smith's favor. The second court authorities allowed Smith to escape out the back door because a mob had gathered in the front. These two early trials demonstrated not only the belief of Mormonism's critics that the faith was outside the boundaries of acceptable religion but also the broad berth that America's religious freedom allowed. They were merely the first of Smith's many legal obstacles.[81]

It is impossible to know how Emma reacted to these developments. Watching her husband be arrested on her baptismal day dampened an otherwise sacred experience. The crisis delayed her confirmation as a new member. Now she was forced to flee with him back to Harmony, where her angry family awaited. Her own home was now filled with Joseph's growing number of followers and scribes, making it clear that she would forever have to share her husband with a wider community. Emma was soon in the early stages of pregnancy with twins, a prospect that provided hope while also raising unpleasant memories of their first child's death. It would have been impossible not to have second thoughts about her life's direction.[82]

In response to these concerns, Joseph dictated a revelation directed

Woodcut of Joseph Smith and devil. The earliest public image of Joseph Smith, this appeared in an anti-Mormon tract that framed how most of Smith's contemporaries viewed the upstart prophet: as an unlearned dupe under the influence of Satan.

to his wife in July. It was the first with a woman recipient. Emma was called an "elect lady" with a clear, but circumscribed, role. Publicly, she would be "ordained" to "expound scriptures, and to exhort the church," as well as compile a hymnal; privately, she would be "a comfort unto my Servant Joseph thy husband in his afflictions with consoleing words in the spirit of meekness." The revelation addressed issues with which Emma had either secretly struggled or openly complained. She was told not to "murmur" about "the things which thou hast not seen," likely the gold plates, as well as to "not fear" over the family's finances because "the Church" would support them. If she followed this counsel, "a crown of righteousness thou shalt receive."[83]

The text reflected both immediate and broader anxieties. Joseph hoped it would provide Emma comfort during their current difficulties. But the revelation also demonstrated much about women's roles in the new movement. While ministerial work remained a man's domain during this era, the burned-over district saw a rise in women orators and preachers, especially among upstart groups like Freewill Baptists and Universalists. Joseph's revelatory promise to Emma that she would be "ordained" to "expound" and "exhort" fit this broader trend; Methodist women were also appointed as "exhorters." But this ordination did not imply priesthood ordination. None of the women converts were welcomed into the growing number of ecclesiastical offices, nor were they given authority to officiate ordinances. Emma's instructions spent as much time on domestic issues as they did on public duties. As with most antebellum religions, women filled the pews but lacked access to the pulpit.[84]

If the revelation calmed Emma's concerns, it failed to do the same for her family. The Hales and their neighbors were alarmed with the church's growth, especially as their Edenic Harmony was invaded by its members. Smith finally dictated a revelation commanding that they relocate closer to the Fayette cluster as soon as the summer harvest was complete. So in September, after Emma tended her orchards one last time, the Smiths left their furniture, locked the doors to their first home, and abandoned Harmony forever. As they departed, an emotional Isaac Hale told Joseph that he would "much rather have followed [Emma] to her grave." Emma never saw her parents again.[85]

The Smiths were not the only saints on the move. "The judgements of the Lord are already abroad in the earth," Joseph wrote in August, "and the cold hand of death, will soon pass through your neighborhood." It was not enough for God's elect to embrace his truth; they must also relocate to his chosen headquarters. A September revelation confirmed that the faithful should be "gethered in unto one place," though the specifics were yet to come. In a republic where personal mobility was synonymous with freedom, saints were expected to forfeit that liberty to avoid what their prophet warned were ensuing calamities.[86]

Smith faced the most direct early challenge to his leadership when he arrived in Fayette. Oliver Cowdery, the second-in-command of the young church, questioned the prophet's authority. The "second elder" had misgivings about the faith's evolution from its initial, simple doctrines. He was especially upset that the "Articles and Covenants" contained a baptismal requirement that was not directly found in the Book of Mormon. "I command you in the name of God to erase those words," Cowdery ordered in a letter. Further, another of the faith's first believers, Hiram Page, had dictated enough revelations from his own seer stone that they filled a "role of papers." Many, including Cowdery, accepted Page's revelations. At stake was whether Mormonism was a democratic faith of equals, bound together through shared scripture and revelation, or a more centralized movement with Smith as its primary seer. Questions concerning equality and authority were especially rife during this antebellum era when citizens tested the boundaries of democracy.[87]

The answer soon became clear. "No one shall be appointed to Receive commandments & Revelations in this Church excepting my Servent Joseph," Smith's new revelation declared, "& thou shalt be obedient unto the things which I shall give him." Smith's authority was not to be questioned. Mormonism was a hierarchical structure, a check against democratic ethos, as "all things must be done in order." The Church of Christ went through several ecclesiastical evolutions over the following two centuries, but prophetic supremacy was a constant throughline.[88]

If the revelation checked Cowdery's authority in the church, it also provided a new assignment that forever shaped the church's direction. Cowdery was called to "go unto the Lamanites," assumed to be America's Indigenous peoples, "& cause my Church to be established among them." This was a fulfillment of Book of Mormon prophecy. The site for this mass Native conversion would be a "glorious New-Jerusalem" where "the Temple of God shall be built." Cowdery was assisted by several men, including Parley Pratt, on this quest. The four earnest elders departed for Missouri in October. Their mission resembled that of many evangelist groups from the era who assigned messengers to convert Indigenous tribes recently relocated to the West, yet they were armed with a scripture and a mission that made them unique. The Mormon gospel was going national.[89]

The Smiths' situation in Fayette worsened due to hostility that accompanied their missionary success. Neighbors worried that this new heretical faith would disrupt their traditional society. Another opportunity soon appeared. Saints received news in December that Pratt had succeeded in converting nearly an entire primitivist congregation of over a hundred people in Ohio. The frontier community appeared more accommodating to their expansion, especially after their leaders, Sidney Rigdon and Edward Partridge, traveled to meet Smith in New York. Recognizing it was time to leave the faith's birthplace, Smith dictated a revelation just before the end of 1830 that the entire church should "go to the Ohio." Another revelation soon promised that, once in Ohio, the faithful would receive "my law, and there you shall be endowed with power from on high." While some worried that Smith "invented" the revelation in order to "deceive the people," most followed the prophet's urging.[90]

Emma Smith, who had already relocated three times in her three years of marriage, was once again on the move. Twenty-six, pregnant, and having exerted so much energy helping her husband that she spent much of December bedridden, she crowded into a sleigh with Joseph and any belongings they could fit. She and many others "bade adieu to all we had held dear on this earth" as they followed their earnest prophet to an unknown future.[91]

SHORTLY BEFORE hearkening to her son's revelatory call to move to Ohio, Lucy Smith penned eager and poignant letters to her siblings. She hoped her brother and sister, both of whom had spent years seeking salvation, would join the steady stream of Mormon converts. "There have been three hundred [just] added to the church," she boasted, with more joining "almost daily." All the religious strivings her family had experienced—the deathbed prayers, dramatic conversions, biblical searching—had culminated in her own son's prophetic calling. Theirs was a modern House of Israel directed by a presiding patriarch yet still caressed by a determined matriarch.[92]

Though Lucy never heard from her siblings, she had more luck with her husband's family. Joseph Sr. and youngest son Don Carlos visited the aged Asael and the other Smiths who lived nearby. Just as Lucy's dream from decades before had predicted, brother Jesse Smith, the tree that refused to bend, rejected the gospel. He threatened that if they "say another word about the Book of Mormon," he would "hew you down with my broad axe." But much to Jesse's chagrin, the rest of the family believed "that cursed Mormon book, every word of it." The family of seekers had finally found what they sought. Joseph Jr., previously a wandering and wayward boy, now recognized as a prophet, exulted that he had "brought salvation to my fathers house." Before becoming an international phenomenon, Mormonism was a family affair.[93]

About a year before Smith formally organized the church, his family received a visitor. Solomon Chamberlin, a Methodist seeker who had just published a pamphlet narrating his own visionary experiences, heard rumors about Smith and desired firsthand knowledge. The erstwhile pilgrim made the voyage to Palmyra, knocked on the rumored prophet's door, and, when admitted, asked if there was anyone who believed in visions. "Yes," Hyrum responded, "we are a visionary house." It was a true enough statement, especially for the Smiths, but the label could have been given to the entire country. America in the 1820s was a visionary nation, filled with innovative believers, each proclaiming their own doctrines, detailing their own visitations, some even peddling their own scripture. Joseph Smith was just one of many that sought to capitalize on the moment even as he laid the foundation for an even more audacious future.[94]

2

The Voice of the People,
1831–46

No line can be drawn between the church and other governments, of the spi[r]itual and temporal affairs of the church.
Revelations must govern. The voice of God, shall be the voice
of the people.

—BRIGHAM YOUNG, 1844[1]

M ANY HAVE CLAIMED that America is a chosen land, but
very few could identify the exact coordinates for God's headquarters. Yet Joseph Smith did precisely that on June 20, 1831, in a
sparsely settled Missouri village. "Thus saith the Lord your God,"
he bellowed in his revelatory cadence, "the place which is now called
Independence is the centre place" for the "City of Zion." A divine
temple, the restoration of the biblical sanctuary that connected earth
and heaven, was to be built on "a lot which is not far from the court-
house." The juxtaposition between these two structures, one present
and the other prophesied, was emblematic: the house of man's law
would be overshadowed by that of God's.[2]

The dozen or so men who accompanied Smith that day, including
close associates Oliver Cowdery and Sidney Rigdon, squinted to see
any promise in the land around them. Independence, Missouri, could
not be categorized as a bustling hub. Mostly composed of brush, scattered trees, and open prairies, the community featured fewer than
two dozen homes, most of them log cabins, as well as a handful of

hotels, stores, and "alias grogshops." It was the literal edge of Anglo-American colonization, only twelve miles from Missouri's western boundary and the eastern terminus for the Santa Fe Trail. President Andrew Jackson's Indian Removal Act, signed the previous year, had designated all Indigenous people to be removed to land just a day's march away. (Independence settlers expelled the last of the Osage peoples in 1824.) Proximity to Indian Territory was what attracted Mormons in the first place: the first LDS missionaries, including Cowdery, had been called to bring the gospel to the Native inhabitants they believed to be "Lamanites." Yet they had yet to count a single conversion from the nearby Delaware Indians despite meeting with their aged leader, Kikthawenund.[3]

Smith, undaunted, pressed forward to consecrate the land. Twelve men symbolically laid a hewn shrub oak on top of a small cornerstone. Rigdon, a stern and bearded scriptorian who had quickly become the fledgling movement's primary orator, delivered a sermon and everyone covenanted to follow Smith's revelations. They then consecrated the designated plot for a divine temple, Smith laying the small cornerstone himself, over which they planted a sapling that featured a carved *T*. Smith's revelation commanded the saints to purchase every parcel of land between the temple and the state's western boundary. Recognizing the scandal such plans would prompt, they scrawled "Not to be printed at present" atop the divine command.[4]

Twelve hundred Mormon men, women, and children flooded the area within two years, much to the consternation of their "gentile" neighbors. But then, in a stunning reversal, every single one of these saints was evicted from the county over a span of months, many to never set foot in Zion again.

The county in which Zion was to be built was named Jackson, after the current president Andrew Jackson, whose personality and politics dominated what came to be known as the Jacksonian era. It was seen, in retrospect and at the time, as a moment of democratic governance, what French philosopher Alexis de Tocqueville termed the "tyranny of the majority." The concept of majority rule, even at the expense of minority rights, was sacralized as the central pillar of American society, especially on the frontier. This priority resulted in the ascension of the common man but also the subjugation of the marginalized. To a degree, Mormonism drew from this populist message. When asked if he was "ashamed" of claiming prophethood despite being "no more than any plough-boy of our land," Smith responded that the gift of prophecy "has returned back again, as in former times, to illiterate fishermen." But the faith was also meant to check this democratic impulse. Only the voice of God could settle disputes between the voices of humanity.[5]

The number of those who believed in the Mormon message grew from the hundreds to the tens of thousands by the 1840s. That growth invited internal divisions as well as external opposition. The movement established large communities in Missouri, Ohio, and Illinois, but members were also forcibly removed from all three, expulsions that marked the boundaries for American acceptability. At stake was how much religious freedom and cultural diversity a democracy could incorporate. In the end, many Mormons concluded that Zion could not be established within the United States' borders, while others, including some of the most prominent leaders, surmised that Zion was a failed mission altogether.

Those questions were far in the distance in 1831, however. That summer, Joseph Smith, Sidney Rigdon, and Oliver Cowdery, surrounded by followers, brush, and prairies, envisioned a profound future of divine glory that could take root only in American soil.

EVEN WHILE Joseph Smith envisioned Zion in Missouri, most saints were headquartered in Ohio. Many of the new converts came from close-knit congregations that worshipped with Sidney Rigdon, a primitivist pastor known for his eloquent oratory and religious excess. Rigdon's obsession with the Bible began at an early age. When basic Bible school failed to quench his spiritual thirst, he defied his father by secretly gathering hickory bark to burn in the fireplace so that he could study long past bedtime. He bounced around several denominations across the Ohio region, most recently splitting with prominent Disciples of Christ minister Alexander Campbell over Rigdon's belief that following God's law "required a community of goods"—that is, a community willing to share all its belongings. A hub of dynamic believers followed Rigdon's path.[6]

That group proved receptive when one of Rigdon's fellow itinerant ministers, Parley Pratt, arrived in the region with copies of the freshly printed Book of Mormon. After Pratt spoke to Rigdon's congregation near Kirtland, a town twenty miles northeast of Cleveland, Rigdon arose and declared that he had been a forerunner to God's true movement. Smith likened Rigdon to John the Baptist, one sent "to prepare the way." Mormonism suddenly claimed over two hundred people, nearly a third of Kirtland's adult population, almost overnight. A nearby newspaper bemoaned how so many "of good repute and intellect" had joined such an obvious fraud.[7]

The devoted believers who made up this new Mormon community were as disparate as they were impassioned. One critic described their services as scenes of "the wildest enthusiasm," in which the devoted barked like dogs, reenacted Book of Mormon scenes, and grasped written revelations from the sky. Even more scandalous was the fact that prominent members included a formerly enslaved man known only as "Black Pete" as well as a "prophetess" named Laura Hubble. These displays of religious exuberance, interracial worship, and women's authority threatened the frontier region's already tenuous claims to cohesion. Even Pratt confessed that these activities "were new and strange."[8]

New denominations experimented with novel forms of religious expression across the newly "United" States. But this anxiety for innovation was especially acute in its western regions. Ohio became the first and most successful attempt at American expansion, as White New Englanders flooded the area for new economic possibilities. With this migration came a concomitant fear of societal degradation. Churches therefore played an outsize role in colonization. Presbyterians, Methodists, and Baptists temporarily, albeit begrudgingly, put aside rivalries to prevent cultural backsliding. They formed interdenominational institutions like the American Bible Society (1816), supported joint evangelistic initiatives like the American Home Missionary Society (1826), and energized sweeping revivals, all in an attempt to keep the American experiment within mainstream Christianity's control. The result was a powerful, if informal, system of religious governance that privileged acceptable faiths while punishing those outside their boundaries.[9]

The Mormons were a direct threat to this quasi-establishment. The earliest, and most fervent, attacks on the movement identified it as alien to true religion. Critics cast Joseph Smith as both an "American Mahomet" and "another Jemima Wilkinson," references to religious leaders who challenged racial or gendered norms. The zealotry exhibited by Mormonism's Ohio converts was therefore an obstacle to the church's cultural acceptance, not to mention a challenge to Joseph Smith's own authority. Days after he arrived in Kirtland in early 1831, Smith dictated a string of revelations that further established "the law of the church" and commenced a formal organizing structure that has shaped the church ever since. "None else shall be appointed" to prophesy and teach "except it be through" Joseph Smith, one revelation proclaimed. The prophet then introduced a multilayered "higher priesthood" associated with the Old Testament patriarch Melchizedek that governed an increasingly vast and layered ecclesiastical hierarchy.[10]

These developments upset those who expected something more democratic. David Whitmer, one of Joseph Smith's first converts from New York and one of the Book of Mormon's Three Witnesses, later marked this turn from a more egalitarian "authority" to a stricter "priesthood" as a moment of declension. Both Black Pete and Laura Hubble disappeared from the community, casualties of the faith's narrower boundaries. Rigdon, conversely, was exuberant that he had finally found a church that matched his biblical vision. Smith appointed him a counselor in the First Presidency, a new three-man ecclesiastical body that governed the entire faith. As was repeatedly the case, Mormonism's evolution was a fulfillment for some and disappointment for others, as its allowance for personal revelation yet appeals to hierarchical authority made the movement ripe for schism.[11]

AMONG THOSE who followed Rigdon into Mormonism were Elizabeth Ann and Newel Whitney. Elizabeth, a self-determined woman who had left her parents' Connecticut home at eighteen to settle in

Ohio, described herself as "always religious." She had bounced around several denominations, including after her marriage to Newel. When Parley Pratt and the other Mormon missionaries arrived in Kirtland, the two believed they had finally found a faith that exercised biblical authority and exhibited spiritual gifts. Elizabeth became known for her ability to sing in tongues, Newel became the center for church business, and their home was Joseph and Emma Smith's first Ohio residence. It was while living with the Whitneys that Emma gave birth to twins on April 30, 1831. Neither child survived. However, when another recent convert, Julia Murdock, died after giving birth to twins John and Julia the next day, the Smiths adopted the infants. After years of tragedy, the prophet's family finally had progeny.[12]

The Whitney home was also where Joseph Smith dictated a revelation that promised a new financial system. "Thou shalt cons[e]crate all thy properties that which thou hast unto me," it instructed, "with a covena[n]t and Deed which cannot be broken." This fulfilled the wishes of Rigdon, the Whitneys, and others who desired to restore the "primitive" church: Mormonism required believers to "consecrate" all their belongings to the faith, only to receive "as much as shall be sufficient for him self and family" in return. God's chosen people, like apostles of old, were to hold "all things in common."[13]

Mormons were not alone in experimenting with communal living. The young republic's capitalistic empire created plenty of dissenters. The Shakers famously formed cooperative communities in which all possessions were shared. Nor did Utopianism appeal to only the religious. Followers of the French socialist Charles Fourier proposed a series of associative schemes during the antebellum era, most notably Welsh reformer Robert Owen's New Harmony in Indiana. "My desire now is to introduce into these States," Owen declared to a rapt audience in Washington, "a new social system" that would transform "the world." The cultural obsession became so immense that Ralph Waldo Emerson complained that every "reading man" had "a draft of a new community in his waistcoat pocket."[14]

Mormon communalism, soon called the Law of Consecration, drew from these broader currents even as it shaped its own. The initiative would not have been possible were it not for families like the Whitneys who sacrificed substantial wealth that had been built through the system they now decried. Newel was later called as a bishop, a new ecclesiastical position that presided over the spiritual and temporal well-being of local congregants. These parishes would later be named "wards," patterned after geographic divisions within cities. (Small congregations were organized as "branches.") Elizabeth fondly recalled organizing multiday "feasts for the poor" where they fed "the lame, the halt, the deaf, the blind, the aged and infirm" within their community. Mormons, from the beginning, watched over their own. To coordinate the church's economic activities, Smith organized the "United Firm," though leaders kept the organization secret and discussed it only with code names.[15]

Mormonism's consecration experiment, despite its ideals, fell apart almost immediately. Some took advantage of communal benefits. One convert, Herman Bassett, walked up to another, Levi Hancock, swiped Hancock's watch out of his pocket, and walked off "as though it was his." When confronted, Bassett retorted that "he thought it was all in the family." Broader economic woes and individual skepticism played larger roles. By the winter of 1833–34, most Kirtland saints were deemed indigent by city officials and threatened with expulsion. Smith dissolved the United Firm, with Whitney absorbing much of the loss. Undeterred, he and Elizabeth remained fully committed. And while the Law of Consecration subsided as a defined practice, its anti-capitalist principles remained, as did the role of bishops.[16]

Smith dictated over sixty revelations during their first three years in Ohio, a quantity and quality that would not be matched for the rest of his prophetic career. Some were mundane and provided practical instructions, while others introduced sweeping doctrines that challenged Protestant orthodoxy. One, titled the "Word of Wisdom," was dictated at the explicit request of Emma Smith. Emma had tired of cleaning tobacco stains after church gatherings and urged them to follow the example of wider reform movements. Temperance societies littered the American countryside during the era, including one that was founded in Kirtland mere weeks before the Mormons arrived. Many were led by women who used the cause to seize otherwise limited political opportunities. As a result of Emma's pleading,

Joseph's revelation warned not only about tobacco but "hot drinks," wine, and other foods that disrupted a healthy lifestyle. Though spottily enforced for decades after its reception, the "Word of Wisdom" later became a key marker of Mormon identity.[17]

Few revelations compared in scope and audacity with one Smith received on a cold February day in 1832. While Smith and Rigdon worked on their translation of the Bible, the two were struck by a passage that implied multiple heavens. This prompted a shared vision of a three-tiered afterlife. Entranced, Smith and Rigdon alternately asked, "What do I see?" Once provided a description, the inquisitor responded, "I see the same." A crowded room of observers watched in silence as the two leaders regaled each other with descriptions of God and a multilayered system of eternal reward. Other than the "sons of perdition" who followed Satan into outer darkness, everyone inherited one of three degrees of glory: the "Celestial Kingdom" for the most righteous, the "Terrestrial" for those who fell short of their covenants, and the "Telestial" for sinners who refused to heed the gospel message. The theophany lasted several hours, and due to its enormity became known as "the Vision."[18]

The Vision was Joseph Smith's most audacious theological break with mainstream Christianity. Universalists, with whom some of Smith's family had previously affiliated, similarly promised that every human soul would receive some degree of salvation. And some iconoclastic theologians, like Emanuel Swedenborg, had posited a tri-layered heaven. But the Mormon cosmos was a blend of universal salvation, Christ-centric redemption, and a heavenly hierarchy centered around Smith's ever-growing conception of priesthood authority. Smith believed "the sublimity of the ideas" contained in the Vision were so powerful "that every honest man is constrained to exclaim: 'It came from God.'"[19]

The revelation proved divisive. Critics accused Smith of blasphemy, citing this as evidence that Mormonism was even more heretical than initially conceived. Even converts were hesitant to accept such a radical departure from traditional doctrines. Brigham Young, who finally joined the church in spring 1832 after a year of investigation, confessed that he "could not understand" the new teachings. He remained committed, however, though still living away from church headquarters. An entire branch of believers in New York, conversely, chose to leave the faith rather than accept its radical cosmology. The gulf between Mormonism and acceptable religion widened.[20]

The combination of Smith's heresies and his instructions that all believers would eventually move to Missouri courted a violent reaction. A mob of members, former members, and their families gathered late on March 24, 1832, to put an end to the prophet's cause. They painted themselves black, drugged the dog who stood watch, and broke into the house where the Smiths were staying. They pulled Joseph from the trundle bed where he slept with a sick infant. Once dragged outside, Smith saw Rigdon inert on a nearby road, presumably dead. (Rigdon was in fact unconscious from his head being thumped on the frozen ground.) The mob initially hoped to pour nitric acid into the two Mormon leaders' mouths, and a doctor was assigned to castrate the prophet, but they instead decided to just tar and feather them. Hours later, when Smith limped his way back to the home, Emma fainted at his ghastly sight. She spent the remaining hours before dawn using lard to peel tar off her husband's body.[21]

Smith escaped the episode with skin sores, a bald spot, and a chipped tooth. Rigdon, meanwhile, likely suffered permanent brain damage. His increasing unreliability saw him decline in prominence within the movement. Most heartbreaking, Smith's sick child, Joseph Murdock Smith, died a few days later, probably from exposure. The trauma from this early episode of persecution framed how the saints understood their relation to the wider world.[22]

An upswing in violence did not deter Mormonism's growth, nor their migration to Missouri. British writer Nancy Towle, then touring the region, was shocked to meet "so many men of skill" who were "duped" by Smith and dedicated to relocating to Zion. "We are now going to that Land," they gleefully shouted as they departed, "which is to be our dwelling-place, forever more!" Persecution seemed only to breed more devotion.[23]

Emma Smith, meanwhile, regrouped as Joseph left town mere weeks after the mobbing. She had now buried four children, and therefore clung to her one remaining daughter, the adopted Julia

Murdock Smith. While Emma, soon pregnant again, hoped she could find solace by staying with her good friend Elizabeth Whitney, a family dispute resulted in the prophet's wife being whisked around three other homes over the next few months. Her first five years with Joseph brought equal parts tumult and tragedy.[24]

THOUGH ONLY eight years old, the young Emily Dow Partridge was struck by the differences between Ohio and Missouri. Her parents, Edward and Lydia, successful merchants, were among Mormonism's first Kirtland converts; Edward was called as the faith's first bishop, months before Newel Whitney. He accompanied Joseph Smith on the prophet's first trip to Zion in summer 1831 and was then assigned to preside over the Missouri settlement. When Emily and the family joined him the next year, they rented a single room from a local state senator named Lilburn Boggs until they could build their own home on a corner near the proposed temple block. The apostle Parley Pratt recalled that it was not unusual for "ten families" to squeeze into one log cabin, which was often "open and unfurnished, while the frozen ground served as the floor." Establishing Zion was the hope that made all these sacrifices worthwhile. It was both "days of rejoicing and also days of mourning," wrote another Mormon migrant, Phoebe Lott.[25]

Joseph Smith taught that Zion was not some mere ephemeral idea but a physical reality. He supplied blueprints in the form of two detailed plats in 1833. The town was divided into ten-acre blocks, which in turn were broken into twenty rectangular lots "laid off alternately in the squares." No details escaped the prophet's meticulous vision. He provided instructions for the width of streets, size of homes, location of farms, and even total population—an astounding twenty thousand people, which would have made it the eleventh-largest metropolis in the nation. Nor would that be Zion's limit: once that entire plot is filled, Smith pronounced, "lay off another in the same way, and so fill up the world in these last days." The Mormon Zion would grow until it encompassed the entire earth.[26]

That his detailed plats did not fit with an already-settled Independence did not deter the prophet. Nor did the fact that his vision for a

Revised Plat of the City of Zion, circa August 1833. The second of two plats Joseph Smith envisioned for the establishment of Zion in Missouri, this City of God was designed to house twenty thousand believers. Saints were evicted from the county before they could begin acting on the plans.

sacred urban center did not mesh with mainstream religious thinking. Many ministers decried what they saw as urban corruption, arguing that the faithful should flee the materialism that dominated big cities. The Second Great Awakening's wilderness revivals embodied a call to return to nature. And yet Joseph Smith desired a sprawling metropolis that could take advantage of modernity's virtues even as it revolved around divine rule. Zion's center squares, areas typically reserved for civic or commercial activities, were instead set aside for twenty-four temples in which saints could perform sacred work. God, not money or politics, would be the hinge upon which society pivoted.[27]

The people who already inhabited Independence were not convinced. Oliver Cowdery described the old-timers as a mix of "Universalists, Atheists, Deists, Presbyterians, Methodists, Baptists, & professed Christians"; the only thing they held in common was their "uniting and foaming" against the saints. They feared being overrun by a deluded sect seeking unlimited dominion. These critics accused Mormons of blaspheming God and agitating nearby Indigenous groups. Given that many of Missouri's inhabitants were southerners, and most Mormon converts came from the Northeast, cultural clashes were inevitable. One Mormon editorial in their newly established newspaper was misread as inviting Black migration. The editor quickly clarified that he did not seek to disrupt Missouri's slaveholding society, but the divide became unbridgeable.[28]

Mob violence was a common way to handle such clashes on the American frontier. In an era when government oversight, and even local police, was mostly invisible, communities turned to vigilance committees to protect both legal and extralegal boundaries. In 1835, after newspapers reported 109 riots over just four months, one editor concluded that American politics were based more in "mobocracy" than in "democracy." A young Abraham Lincoln bemoaned how mobs, especially in Missouri, were permitted to "burn churches, ravage and rob provision stores, throw printing presses into rivers, shoot editors, and hang and burn obnoxious persons at pleasure and with impunity." In such circumstances, he warned, "this government cannot last."[29]

Independence residents, after they decided vigilante justice was the only way to solve their Mormon problem, started with intimidation. Emily Partridge recalled ruffians setting aflame her family's hay storage, which "made a tremendous blaze." More radical actions followed. Hundreds of residents signed a manifesto that as "the arm of the civil law does not afford us a guarantee" against dangers posed by the "pretended" religion, they must "rid our society" of the saints, "peaceably if we can, forcibly if we must." Mormonism, far from being an acceptable denomination worthy of religious rights, was a heretical fraud that threatened social stability. A mob comprising "lawyers, magistrates, county officers[, and] religious ministers" then marched into the Mormon settlement and "treated" Emily Partridge's father "to a clean suit of 'tar and feathers.'" They also destroyed the saints' printing press. The Mormons were told that they had until the end of the year to leave.[30]

At first, Joseph Smith instructed the saints to stay firm. But after more violence that November, they were forced to surrender, and a mob overseen by just-elected Lieutenant Governor Lilburn Boggs pillaged their goods and burned their homes. "Men, women and children, goods, wagons, boxes, chests, provisions," reported Emily Partridge, were strewn along the Missouri River during a hasty winter exodus. Hundreds of Mormons moved "in every direction; some in tents, and some in the open air, around their fires, while the rain descended in torrents." The image of fraught desertion stuck with the young girl her entire life.[31]

Smith demanded justice. He dictated a revelation that urged saints to appeal for redress from government officials, demonstrating faith in the Constitution's provisions for religious liberty. "For this purpose have I established the constitution of this Land," the revelation implored, "by the hands of wise men whom I raised up unto this very purpose." Many Americans believed the Constitution was divinely inspired, but the Mormons nearly canonized it. The saints wrote a letter to President Andrew Jackson pleading for him to help "wholly native born citizens being deprived of those sacred rights . . . guaranteed to every religious sect." Government officials responded that such complaints were handled at the state level. But while Missouri governor Daniel Dunklin admitted that the Mormons were wronged, his hands were tied because "the public has no other interest in it." In other words, in a majoritarian culture, the majority's voice ruled.[32]

Denied a chance at official redress, the saints hoped to follow the American tradition by reclaiming their rights through force. A new revelation declared that "the redem[p]tion of Zion must needs come by power," and commanded the saints to raise an army of five hundred men. While they were only able to muster just over two hundred, the modern-day Army of Israel, known as Zion's Camp, began their march for Zion in May 1834. Among their ranks were nearly a dozen women, including Aidah Clements, who marched with her husband, Albert. The couple were recent converts from New York who were baptized after personally hearing the Mormon message from Sidney Rigdon. Now they were part of God's army. Aidah likely assisted the camp's other women by performing domestic chores while also participating in the daily prayers and religious services.[33]

The crusade fizzled. Smith hoped a showing of strength would force the state to intervene, but no truce seemed imminent as they neared Jackson County's borders. A major thunderstorm followed by a cholera outbreak dissolved any chance for action. Smith eventually disbanded the camp by the end of June, but not before thirteen Mormon soldiers died from the disease. Instead of marching to their land in Independence, the saints returned to Ohio. Emily Partridge and her family stayed in Missouri, though in nearby Clay County, which temporarily welcomed the beleaguered saints. Yet fears of "another Mormon invasion" once again required resolution. Missouri authorities therefore created a new county in the northern part of the state, named Caldwell, that was reserved for Mormon settlement. The solution echoed what was posited for Indigenous peoples during the same decade: forced removal and geographic segregation.[34]

Mormons never recovered from losing Zion. Smith's vision that Jackson County was God's chosen gathering place never abated. His followers have ever since dreamt of their triumphant and prophesied return. Nor did Mormons ever forgive the Missourians for evicting them from their property, or the government for failing to intervene. Their many grievances, piled high, shaped how the saints understood their relationship to American society.[35]

ELIZA R. SNOW was a tall, thin, and strikingly brilliant poet. A journalist later described her as a "delicate woman with raven hair and piercing black eyes" who possessed an intellect that "would scare the muses out of their senses." Snow, who had just completed her third decade, watched Mormonism's developments with a close eye. Part of a large and energetic family settled near one of the church's Ohio hubs—"we never knew what it was to be idle," she recalled—Snow had joined Rigdon's primitivist church in 1828 but hesitated to follow him into Mormonism three years later, even when her mother and a sister did. Finally, after hearing reports about their "frequent manifestations of the power of God," she was baptized in April 1835 and moved to Kirtland that December. Her poetic talent found an immediate home, and her work soon appeared in Emma Smith's new hymnal:

> We'll praise [God] for a prophet's voice,
> His people's steps to guide:
> In this, we do and will rejoice,
> Tho' all the world deride.

Joseph Smith designated Snow as "Zion's Poetess."[36]

Snow was far from alone in finding a sense of purpose in the Mormon gospel. Across the American nation, hundreds and then thousands of converts embraced the message that was shared by the faith's army of missionaries. Many claimed that the gospel's organization fulfilled their belief that biblical Christianity—with its prophets, patriarchs, and apostles—would once again be restored, a final answer for a culture drowning in questions. They found convincing the Mormon elders' appeal to both rationality, in the form of biblical interpretation, as well as their supernatural claims, typically in the form of promises that sincere investigators would receive spiritual confirmation. One of the faith's early converts, Esaias Edwards, noted that "a close examination of the scriptures" had led him to conclude that only the Mormons "believed and practiced [biblical principles] in full." Many others agreed and chose to follow the modern-day prophet to Ohio.[37]

The new converts who gathered in Kirtland found it to be a bustling city. Snow was awed by a new structure in the town's center then nearing completion: a three-story stucco temple they believed to be the gem of northeastern Ohio. The building echoed other New England churches and drew from Gothic, Greek, and Federal architectural styles. It featured an earth-red roof, two large olive-green doors, and an imposing tower capped with a weather vane. The walls sparkled with glass and porcelain and had the look of polished blue granite. Inside, both the first and second floors comprised large assembly halls bookended by tiered pulpits. A pulley system raised and lowered curtains from the ceiling to separate the large rooms into smaller meeting quarters. The third floor was a more conventional arrangement of small offices and classrooms.

The entire structure cost around $40,000, an astronomical price for a cash-strapped faith. Lucy Smith, the prophet's mother, recalled that they endured "great fatigue and privation" during construction, and that the extended Smith family "parted every bed in the house for the [builders'] accommodation." Emma, who had finally given birth to a healthy boy, Joseph Smith III, and was now pregnant with

House of the Lord, Kirtland, circa 1900. Saints sacrificed most of their money to construct this "House of the Lord," which they soon had to abandon.

yet another, often slept on the floor with her husband. She hoped life would stabilize soon.[38]

The new temple with its intricate layout housed an evolving ecclesiastical system. Joseph Smith had returned from the failed Zion's Camp with a renewed energy to transform his church into something that could withstand persecution's many torrents. He introduced a series of hierarchical positions between 1833 and 1836 that matched, according to him, the "order of heaven in ancient councils." He ordained his own father as "presiding patriarch," a status that redeemed his domestic legacy while also reaffirming the significance of sacred lineages. Smith Sr. pronounced "patriarchal blessings" upon members, designating lineal connections to the House of Israel and predicting future rewards. The prophet also introduced layers of councils to oversee the expanding church, each based on biblical precedent: High Councils of twelve priesthood holders to preside within church headquarters, as well as a Quorum of the Twelve Apostles and a Council of Seventy to oversee missionary work without. Even the name of the church was changed: they were now known as the Church of Latter-day Saints, reflecting a renewed millenarian zeal.[39]

This leadership structure was the fulfillment of the primitivist strain that had been embedded within Mormonism since its beginning. Smith informed all those ordained to these new positions that they could trace their authority back to ministrations from resurrected biblical figures like John the Baptist and Peter, James, and John. Some within the fold were skeptical. David Whitmer later claimed that he did not hear about any angelic ordinations until Kirtland. But many embraced the new hierarchy and saw the organization as fulfilling biblical prophecies and providing necessary stability. That included Brigham Young, who had finally migrated from New York to join the saints. Young's first wife, Miriam, had died of consumption, and he now married another convert, Mary Ann Angell, shortly after arriving in Kirtland. He proved his dedication by marching in Zion's Camp and was rewarded by being one of the first called, along with Parley Pratt, to the new Quorum of the Twelve. It was the first of many ecclesiastical positions Young would eventually hold in the faith. The fiery redhead's ecclesiastical ascension had begun.[40]

It was during this period of excitement that Smith found another connection to antiquity. Due to Napoleon's recent excavation of Egyptian antiquities, early Americans were swept up in "Egypto-mania," a cultural obsession that allowed opportunists to tour the nation with ancient artifacts. One of these entrepreneurs, Michael Chandler, arrived in Kirtland in the hot summer of 1835 hoping to sell damaged mummies and papyri after a long circuit. Smith immediately pronounced that they contained "the inspired writings of Abraham." Though later scholars have classified these fragments as traditional funeral texts, Chandler, anxious to unload the material, pronounced Smith a competent translator. The prophet purchased the scrolls and two mummies for a hefty $2,400; the latter he put on display in the unfinished temple, while the former he translated into yet another scriptural text. Where critics saw a pretentious fraud misunderstanding foreign languages, believers celebrated a visionary equipped to find meaning in mundane objects.[41]

Mormon women took advantage of this spiritual outpouring. They gathered to pray, read scriptures, and strengthen one another's faith. After receiving a patriarchal blessing that promised her "the gift of singing inspirationally," Elizabeth Whitney stood and sang in unknown tongues, a form of spiritual gift known as glossolalia. Parley Pratt interpreted the song to be about ancient and modern prophets uniting in the power of priesthood. Joseph Smith Jr. assured Whitney that she "would never lose this gift if she used it wisely." She took him at his word and continued to sing for decades. Many women also helped prepare for the temple's completion by weaving clothes for the workers, sewing veils for the interior, and crafting curtains to separate the great halls. Impressed, Smith "pronounced a blessing upon the Sisters for the liberality in giving their servises so cheerfully."[42]

The culmination of these developments came when the temple was dedicated on March 27, 1836. Over a thousand saints crowded inside at nine in the morning, with the overflow moving to an adjacent schoolhouse. Sidney Rigdon delivered a two-and-a-half-hour sermon and Smith read a dedicatory prayer that Oliver Cowdery helped prepare. Dozens of leaders sat in their designated spots among the tiered pulpits, each of whom received an affirming vote. The order, unity, and energy thrilled Smith. One participant noted that it became a day "of our pentecost," as "Angels of God came into the room, cloven tongues rested upon some of the servants of the Lord like unto fire, & they spake with tongues and prophesied." Eliza Snow, who was rarely short of words, failed to find the right ones to capture that moment. "No mortal language can describe the heavenly manifestations of that memorable day," she testified.[43]

The period of Pentecost continued a week later when Smith and Cowdery alleged that, while privately praying near the pulpits, "the vail was taken from their minds" for yet another theophany. They were visited by a string of heavenly messengers, including Jesus, Moses, Elias, and Elijah, who accepted the temple and bestowed further authority. The visitation was the last entry recorded in Joseph Smith's diary that had been meticulously kept by a scribe for over a year. The journal cuts off mid-page, and the rest of the volume is blank. (Smith would not start another journal for nearly two years.) It was as if the temple's completion was the end of the story, a climax that could not be topped. At least for the moment, Smith felt content with what he had created.[44]

By the time Mary Fielding arrived in Kirtland in spring 1837, all the unity that Joseph Smith had carefully cultivated was crumbling. Fielding, born in England in 1801, migrated to Toronto in 1834, and was baptized by Parley Pratt in 1836. She had dark brown hair, a writer's sensibility, and a zealous commitment to her new faith. But now she witnessed her church facing a deep schism. Inside the same temple that had housed the pentecostal dedication a year earlier, Pratt, the faith's most prominent missionary, now accused the prophet of "commit[ting] great sins." Fielding was shocked. "I know not what the Lord will have to do with his church," she wrote to her sister. Tensions escalated until a fight broke out in the temple two months later and several church leaders were charged with assault.[45]

The tumult within the faith was mirrored by the nation at large. Andrew Jackson had run on a platform of transforming America through the destruction of long-held traditions and institutions. This included the National Bank, a program that funded and regulated the booming marketplace. Jackson insisted it benefited only elites. He signed the bank's death warrant by vetoing its federal funding in 1833, and its charter officially expired in 1836. The end of federal currency, however, meant that people had to pay in specie: gold, silver, or copper minted into coins. These coins were always in short supply, especially in the frontier. Small banks appeared to step into the void by printing their own notes. These local notes, in turn, proved vulnerable and unreliable. The entire system was poised for collapse.[46]

Mormons contributed to this financial panic with their own doomed scheme. The Kirtland region had experienced an economic boom since 1830, with the population growing 150 percent and housing prices skyrocketing 500 percent. The cost of food in the city doubled between 1836 and 1837. Further, the temple's construction costs plunged the church into debt. Smith took an impulsive and ill-begotten trip to search for treasure in Salem, Massachusetts, but soon came to a more fashionable solution: the saints would create their own bank. They raised $4,000 in investments and announced the creation of the Kirtland Safety Society Banking Company on November 2, 1836, with Sidney Rigdon as the president and Joseph Smith as cashier. The society immediately appealed for a legislative charter.[47]

Ohio politicians, concerned about the proliferation of these small banks, feared collapse. They denied all new charter requests in the 1836–37 session, including Kirtland's. Undeterred, the saints switched course and restructured into a joint-stock company called the Kirtland Safety Society *Anti*-Banking Corporation. Private joint-stock companies, which did not require a charter, were common but unregulated and therefore unstable. Within its first week, the society issued $10,000 in notes and seemed to succeed in stimulating the local market. Among the beneficiaries was Smith himself, who sold a house to Parley Pratt for $2,000 despite having bought it for $100.[48]

The fall came quickly due to internal mismanagement and external circumstances. A nearby agitator purchased a substantial amount in society notes with the immediate intent to demand redemption in specie. Soon there were rumors that a mob intended to "destroy our bank & take our property." Leaders found a temporary remedy by purchasing controlling interest in a chartered bank in Michigan, the Bank of Monroe, and appointed Oliver Cowdery president. But a national crisis wiped out any silver lining. The disappearance of federal currency and Jackson's executive order that land sales be paid in specie led to a run on banks, which were, in turn, unable to back up investments. Inflation, plummeting land values, and devalued currency followed. New York institutions failed in March, leaving little chance for rural banks—not to mention rural *anti*-banks.[49]

Kirtland was hit especially hard. Smith continued to urge patience, and even encouraged more investment in early April, but the society ceased issuing notes a week later. The prophet went into hiding due to the public outcry. "I wish it could be possible for you to be at home," Emma wrote him after several weeks on the run. Joseph eventually returned, but he and Rigdon withdrew from the Safety Society in early July. He had invested more than anyone else and therefore lost the most, around $6,000. He also now faced a series of lawsuits. Things were so bleak that the church mortgaged the temple to a New York firm. Smith dealt with financial and legal ramifications for the rest of his life.[50]

Fiscal challenges bred spiritual discontent. Despite being assured that these banking problems were "common to our whole country," members expected more from prophetic leaders. Pratt was especially irate. His year had already been tumultuous: after years of infertility, his wife, Thankful, gave birth to a son in March, but died shortly after childbirth. Parley then married a recent convert, Mary Frost, in May. And like many in Kirtland, Pratt was now in financial ruin, a crisis made more acute with a new bride and child. He blamed Smith for the home he could no longer afford. The "whole scene of Speculation," he bitterly wrote the prophet, "is of the Devel." Pratt accused Smith and Rigdon of "leading this people astray." Several church leaders, including other members of the Quorum of the Twelve, publicly denounced Smith for exercising "tyranny" and "oppression," even "a principle of popery." Those who no longer believed in Smith's prophethood formed their own faction.[51]

Not all lost faith in the Smiths. Amid this chaos Jerusha Smith, the wife of Joseph's brother Hyrum, died shortly after birthing her sixth child. Hyrum then married Mary Fielding, the recent convert who had arrived in Kirtland a few months earlier, in December. Mary was suddenly the stepmother to a large family with several young children; she was also the wife to a man who had just been added to the First Presidency, the most powerful council in the church. It was a chaotic time to enter the faith's First Family. Much to her satisfaction, Parley Pratt soon reconciled himself to the church and made amends with the prophet.[52]

Tensions within the community grew. Martin Harris, who had served as scribe for the Book of Mormon and funded its publication, was among those cut off in September. A slew of other prominent leaders were excommunicated in December. The Quorum of the Twelve lost nearly half of its members. Lucy Smith complained that critics had "contaminated the minds of many of the brethren against Joseph, in order to destroy his influence." By January 1838, Joseph no longer saw a future in the city he helped build. A hurried revelation instructed him to flee for Missouri, which he did in the middle of the night, leaving behind the temple he so loved. A mob set the church's printing press on fire and destroyed the printing office's contents only days after his escape. Mary, perhaps fearful of her new life, gathered her stepchildren and, alongside Emma and her three children, followed their husbands west.[53]

THE SMITHS arrived in Far West, Missouri, in March 1838. The town was the capital of Caldwell, the county set aside for Mormon settlement, and had swelled to several thousand residents as many relocated from Kirtland. Emily Partridge, who had remained in Missouri ever since the Independence crisis, was thrilled to once again be surrounded by saints. Eliza Snow arrived in the spring with her family and settled in nearby Daviess County, a secondary gathering place. When Smith visited the rural settlement, he declared it the place where Adam and Eve had gone after being evicted from the Garden of Eden. He named it Adam-Ondi-Ahman, which Smith said was drawn from Adam's pure language. (*Ahman* was allegedly

Adamic for "God.") The prophet declared that these new Missouri settlements would be "a pure and consecrated land" and home for another temple. Reflecting the faith's fresh start, a revelation changed the church's name once again, this time for good: the Church of Jesus Christ of Latter Day Saints.⁵⁴

Yet Oliver Cowdery was ready to break away. While financial matters played a role—he had been left penniless by the banking fiasco—he posed a more explosive accusation: Smith hid a "dirty, nasty affair" with Fanny Alger, a young woman hired to assist Emma with the Smith children. Many Mormons, including Alger's family, later claimed that she was actually Smith's first plural wife. Rumors of polygamy were already circling the church by 1837. It was not rare for new religious movements to be the center of such speculation. Beyond a desire to echo biblical patriarchs, however, there was little theological scaffolding to justify Mormon plural unions. At least not yet. A lack of contemporary evidence makes it impossible to fully explicate Smith's relationship with Alger. It is hard, however, to dismiss Cowdery's assertion that it was an affair.⁵⁵

Cowdery and Smith publicly feuded at a church conference in November 1837, after which Cowdery was dropped from his hierarchical position. The dispute resulted in an excommunication trial in April 1838. Cowdery claimed the church was threatening "my Constitutional privileges and inherent rights" in its attempt to "control me in my temporal interests" and beliefs. He and David Whitmer, another early founder, chose to "withdraw" their memberships rather than be formally cut off. All three Book of Mormon witnesses were now out of the church. Sidney Rigdon delivered a bombastic address weeks later that likened dissenters to salt that had lost its savor, which "is henceforth good for nothing but to be cast out." Nearly a hundred saints signed a petition ordering Cowdery and Whitmer to leave the community over which they had previously presided.⁵⁶

Having inwardly cleansed the church, leaders turned their attention outward to their neighbors. Rigdon once again ignited a flame, this time in a Fourth of July sermon declaring that though the saints had "suffered [constant] abuse without cause," from that time forward "we will suffer it no more." Violent threats would no longer be tolerated. "That mob that comes on us," Rigdon bellowed, "it shall be between us and them a war of extermination"; the saints were willing to "follow them till the last drop of their blood is spilled." Smith praised the address as a valiant "decleration of independence from all mobs and persecutions." Saints backed up their words with action by organizing their own vigilante group known as the Society of the Daughters of Zion, commonly called the Danites. Having learned from their previous Missouri experience that "all power belongs Originally and legitimately to the people," their militia was ready for war.[57]

Missourians were happy to oblige. A drunken mob sparked a brawl when Mormons voted in Daviess County that August. Lucy Smith rightly noted that Missourians "were determined to prevent them from exercising the priviledge of franchise." Rumors of more vigilante violence, casualties, and desecrated corpses began to swirl. The Danites and Missourians exchanged fire at the Battle of Crooked River that resulted in four deaths, including senior apostle David Patten. In retaliation, apostle Parley Pratt fired and injured a Missouri militiaman. Exaggerated reports soon reached Lilburn Boggs, a previous antagonist now elected governor. Boggs was fed up with the faith, which he believed had been given sufficient time to either reform or relocate. He signed an executive order that enlisted 2,500 state militiamen to quell the rebellion. "The Mormons must be treated as enemies," he dictated, "and must be exterminated or driven from the state." Though Rigdon was the first to use the "extermination" rhetoric, Boggs had the resources to carry through.[58]

The grisliest episode was yet to come. Days after Boggs's order, but likely without knowledge of it, a Missouri militia approached a small settlement where thirty Mormon families huddled near the mill of friendly non-Mormon Jacob Hawn. When they saw 240 armed men advancing near sundown on October 30, the women and children ran into the woods while the men and older boys gathered in the blacksmith shop. The militia then fired thousands of bullets into the poorly defended building for up to an hour, killing seventeen. Two of the deceased were young boys shot at point-blank range. "Nits make lice," one of the men allegedly quipped after firing a bullet into a ten-year-old's head.[59]

Joseph and Hyrum Smith turned themselves in to authorities shortly afterward. They were charged with treason in connection with supporting a Mormon-led militia at Crooked River. Parley Pratt, charged with attempted murder, was also imprisoned. A dozen leaders were then held in jails for a long, cold winter as thousands of followers were forcibly evicted from their homes. Some women claimed to have been raped. Eliza Snow may have been among those molested, though details are sparse. She bemoaned how the Missourians had "pollute[d] the holy sanctuary of female virtue" and "barbarously trample[d] upon the most sacred gems of domestic felicity!" Hundreds of Mormon families later submitted petitions to the federal government that meticulously detailed their travails. Emily Partridge's father, for instance, claimed he lost nine hundred acres, five houses, and one barn. Other losses could never be recouped: Aidah and Albert Clements, the family who had accompanied Zion's Camp in 1834, lost their infant son, Paul.[60]

Mary Fielding Smith gave birth to her first child on November 13, two weeks after her husband was arrested, and barely survived the impoverished conditions. She named the infant Joseph Fielding Smith. Hyrum was able to see young Joseph when they visited the frigid jail in December, but the guards quickly forced the mother and son to depart. Mary was irate that Hyrum "was taken from me by an armed force," especially "at a time when I needed, in a particular manner, the kindest care and attention." She and Emma huddled together as they migrated out of the state along with their mother-in-law Lucy, who witnessed misery "enough to make the heart ache." Some of Joseph Smith's most sacred documents were attached to the inside of Emma's dress. Snow estimated that eight thousand Mormons spent that blisteringly cold winter in the wilderness, worried that God had forsaken them. "Description fails; Tho' language is too mean," Snow penned a year later, "to paint the horrors of that dreadful scene."[61]

Led by Brigham Young, the saints pooled their resources and migrated across the state, over the frozen Mississippi, and to a temporary refuge in Quincy, Illinois. Young, Snow, the Smiths, and the rest of the saints, as well as their descendants, never forgot what had happened to them in Missouri under the supposed banner of American democracy.[62]

THE SAINTS' wilderness wandering, albeit traumatic, was temporary. Missouri officials lacked either the interest or the will to pursue legal charges against Mormon leaders. Satisfied a civil war was averted, they allowed Smith and his fellow prisoners to escape in April 1839 once all their followers had vacated the state. The church, anxious to start fresh, purchased nearly a thousand acres of Illinois land on a scenic peninsula that jutted into the Mississippi River. The area had previously been called Quashquema by Indigenous tribes but had recently passed through the hands of White speculators, who named it Commerce in hopes that it would be a trading outpost. But the location was now transformed into a refuge for God's elect. Mormons drained the swampy areas and built homes on both the flats near the river and the bluff above. Smith rechristened the new city, which soon boasted thousands of saints, Nauvoo, a Hebrew word for "beautiful situation."[63]

Smith, believing that the American experiment could still be redeemed, set off for Washington, DC, to petition federal leaders. "If their was any virtue in the government," his mother, Lucy, reasoned, they would grant redress. Yet the prophet faced stiff resistance from everyone he encountered, including President Martin Van Buren. "What can I do," Van Buren, famous for his political calculations, retorted; "if I do anything, I shall come in contact with the whole state of Missouri." Discussions with legislators similarly went nowhere. Many hid behind the doctrine of states' rights, while others admitted basic politicking. Smith and his followers never forgave Van Buren and his ilk for informing them that, while their cause was just, nothing could be done for them.[64]

Mormons found much more luck with Illinois politicians. The state, already known for its democratic ideals, inclusion of disparate groups, and the scheming of ambitious young congressmen like Stephen Douglas and Abraham Lincoln, was ripe for Mormon courtship. Illinois, like the rest of the nation, was emerging from financial recession, leaving politicians anxious for immigrants. A population boom netted the state three new congressional seats and a prominent role in the growing republic. Because Illinois was evenly split between Democrats and Whigs, both parties eagerly counted the saints among potential voting blocs.[65]

The saints were desperate to take advantage of this favorable climate. Aided by new arrival John C. Bennett, a talented yet egotistical climber who introduced Smith to powerful Illinois politicians, they secured extensive powers through a very generous city charter. (Mormons were so enthralled with the legislation that they called it their "Magna Charta.") They established their own militia, the Nauvoo Legion, with Smith as its head, which soon boasted more active soldiers than the state's own reserves. Politicians like Douglas frequented the town to court their support. Other than the Shawnee leader Tenskwatawa's Prophetstown in neighboring Indiana, Nauvoo was the most successful religious city-state since puritan New England in the seventeenth century.[66]

Thousands of Mormon immigrants, those who had survived the travails of Ohio and Missouri as well as those who had joined since, flooded the region. A growing number arrived from Britain, where the Latter-day Saint message was spreading like wildfire. England's Industrial Revolution had left thousands of beleaguered residents impoverished and seeking purpose and a new life; missionaries from an upstart American religion provided them both. Brigham Young, now president of the Quorum of the Twelve, managed this missionary effort, which stabilized the faith through the infusion of thousands of new believers and the expansion of the faith's footprint. Smith therefore elevated the Quorum's authority to preside over not only the mission field but also church headquarters in 1841. The First Presidency was the only remaining council that outranked the Twelve. Young's power now exceeded that of High Councils as well as stakes, the ecclesiastical grouping of local ward congregations. Though not yet achieving his future status as the "Lion of the Lord," the imposing Young relished his growing reputation.[67]

Emma Smith enjoyed extended influence in the new city, too. As the faith's first lady, she helped organize and participate in women's gatherings where they facilitated relief for the poor and support for construction projects. Their efforts culminated in the creation of the Female Relief Society, a powerful body that consolidated reform activities. Benevolent societies had cropped up throughout the nation during this era as women capitalized on the expectation that they could help redeem society's flagging morality. Protectors of hearth and home, these mothers, sisters, and daughters were empowered to save families through voluntary institutions outside government channels.[68]

But Emma Smith desired more. Though the society's idea originated with Sarah Granger Kimball, a dedicated convert from New York, the prophet's wife quickly became its driving force. She did not want the society to operate like the "other Societies in the world." Eliza Snow argued that "as daughters of Zion, we should set an example." Joseph promised that they would become a "kingdom of priests," a phrase that indicated an evolution in the Mormon conception of "priesthood," and one that participants like Snow carefully noted. The society soon carved out space for women to play a large role in civic discourse and reform. Emma was chosen as president, and she then appointed Elizabeth Whitney as a counselor. Eliza Snow served as secretary. "The spirit of the Lord like a purifying stream," Snow reported, "refreshed every heart."[69]

Nauvoo proved to be a home for a multitude of sorts. That included Elijah Able, a Black convert who was born, possibly enslaved, in Maryland around 1810. Able joined Mormonism in 1832, was ordained an elder in Kirtland, and served missions to Canada and Cincinnati. In Nauvoo, he worked as a carpenter and undertaker and even owned land. He was joined in 1843 by Jane Manning, another Black saint who walked from New England to Nauvoo with a group of other African American converts denied steamboat passage because of their skin. When she told her story to Joseph Smith, the prophet wept at the tale and offered to house her. Not all Black residents of Nauvoo were similarly satisfied with their own situations, however. Several White converts from the South took advantage of Illinois's porous laws and brought their enslaved men, women, and children.[70]

Mormonism's racial policy remained inchoate. Members like Able and Manning were not denied full fellowship, but only because most saints believed their faith would help them transcend their Blackness. "Thou shalt be made equal to thy brethren," Able's patriarch blessing promised, because "thy soul [will] be white in eternity." Manning's blessing identified her as a descendant of "the lineage of Cainaan the Son of Ham," though promised that she could be redeemed from her racial "mark." Smith's Book of Abraham, completed in 1842, spoke of Ham's descendants being "cursed" from "the priesthood"—an anti-Black idea common during the era—but leaders had yet to codify it into a coherent policy. Smith approved of Able's priesthood ordinations and offered some form of temple ritual to Manning. For the moment, Black members found an interracial home for worship.[71]

Many saints reveled in novel religious doctrines and practices, many of which continue to shape Mormonism today. While circling the deathbed of the aged patriarch Joseph Smith Sr., who never recovered from illnesses acquired in Missouri, Joseph Jr. declared in September 1840 that his deceased brother, Alvin, would meet them in the Celestial Kingdom. This was made possible by a novel ordinance. Saints had the opportunity to be baptized on behalf of ancestors and other deceased who, if they accepted the ordinance, would receive full exaltation. To house this new rite, as well as others not yet specified, Joseph Jr. envisioned a new temple, to be built on the bluff, that was much larger than and distinct from what they left behind in Kirtland. Its exterior was packed with symbols carved into stone that reflected earth's place in the eternities, all governed by priesthood authority.[72]

Smith did not wait for the temple's completion to inaugurate some of its ordinances. In May 1842 he introduced a small circle of men into what he called an "endowment," a ritual based on "the principles and order of the priesthood." Many of the elements were drawn from Masonry, into which he was recently inducted. The men were washed and anointed, and they participated in a ceremony that reenacted sacred scenes like the Garden of Eden while also receiving key words and signs necessary for exaltation. This was the type of formalized worship most American Protestants had eschewed as too Catholic, yet Smith exulted in how they bound believers to God. He promised that all members would be able to participate once the temple was completed.[73]

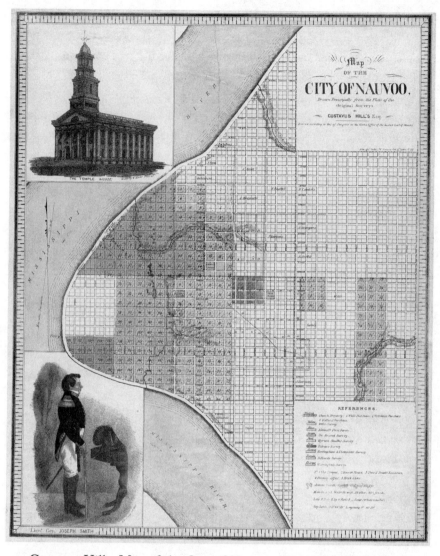

Gustavus Hills, Map of the City of Nauvoo. This map features early architectural plans for the Nauvoo Temple as well as Sudcliffe Maudsley's portrait of Joseph Smith in his Nauvoo Legion uniform.

It was around this time that Smith inaugurated another secretive biblical practice that would play an outsize role in the faith's image ever since.

* * *

BY THE 1840s, Elizabeth Whitney had dedicated over a decade of her life to Mormonism. She had survived two forced evictions and the collapse of her family's finances. But her biggest challenge came in the summer of 1842 when Joseph Smith asked to be wed to her seventeen-year-old daughter, Sarah. The union was part of Smith's expanding theology regarding families and eternity and forced Elizabeth to reluctantly lay "aside all our traditions and former notions in regard to marriage." To accomplish "the works of Abraham," Smith taught, required entering into unions consecrated by priesthood power. Sarah's father, Newel, officiated the ceremony. Smith, in his mid-thirties, took the teenage girl by the hand and the two were promised "honor and immortality and eternal life."[74]

Two days later, on June 29, Smith wed Eliza Snow as another plural wife. These marriages, called "sealings," were to transcend death. They reflected Smith's new and expansive temple doctrine. All involved were sworn to absolute secrecy. "This is a day of much interest to my feelings," Snow coyly wrote in her diary. Neither Elizabeth nor Sarah ever recorded their thoughts.[75]

The Whitneys and Snow may have been more open to the proposal because the antebellum period was an era of sexual experimentation. Religious and secular groups alike transgressed traditional boundaries of monogamy in their attempts to find a new, consecrated form of familial unions. On one end, Shakers abolished marriage and sexual relations altogether, believing that celibacy was the route to sanctification; on the other, John Humphrey Noyes's utopian society sacralized free love through "complex marriage." Some opined that women's access to divorce was a necessity, while others clamored for a return to patriarchal priorities. A common thread across these efforts was a belief that traditional family structures had failed. Few proposals were as radical, or as long-lasting, however, as Mormon polygamy.[76]

Emma Smith was unaware of the full details concerning Smith's new unions in 1842. As stalwart defenders of traditional morality, both she and Hyrum Smith promised to banish all those found practicing polygamy. When Nauvoo's mayor, John C. Bennett, was caught in multiple relationships, Joseph was forced to evict his close associate from the city. (Smith then became mayor and Bennett became the saints' most prominent foe.) Both Emma and Hyrum eventually accepted polygamy in spring 1843, however. Hyrum became the practice's most zealous defender because he could now be sealed to both his deceased wife, Jerusha, and his current spouse, Mary Fielding. Emma's support proved more transient. She agreed for Joseph to be sealed to Emily Partridge, now nineteen, and her sister, Eliza, twenty-one, who had lived with the Smiths since their father died in 1840. Unbeknownst to Emma, however, Joseph had already wed the two a few months before. Emma was livid when she found out. It was "a strange way of getting married," Emily later summarized.[77]

The prophet spent much of 1842 and 1843 expanding his sealing web, feverishly keeping it secret, and trying and failing to avoid his wife's wrath. At Hyrum's request, Joseph dictated another revelation, perhaps his most consequential, on July 12, 1843, that detailed "the order of the priesthood." It posited the doctrine of polygamy as the center of an eternal patriarchal structure and declared that faithful men and their wives would become "Gods" who populated innumerable worlds with their "seed." Emma was commanded to submit

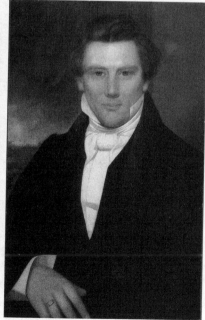

David Rogers, portraits of Joseph and Emma Smith, 1842.

lest she "be destroyed." Undeterred, Emma threatened Joseph with divorce. Reconciliation came months later when Joseph agreed to no more plural unions. By then, he had been married to over thirty wives, some of them teenagers, most of them without Emma's consent or knowledge. The number of men and women who participated in the practice now neared one hundred. Yet Smith's July 1843 revelation would outlive them all as part of the church's scriptural canon.[78]

Those who practiced polygamy in Nauvoo did so under strict secrecy. Very few plural wives lived under the same roof, and all involved denied their relationships in public. "O, how shall I compose a thought / Where nothing is compos'd," Snow penned; "How form ideas, as I ought / On subjects not disclosed?" Though reproduction was one reason for the unions, conditions made conjugal visits difficult, and as a result few children were born to polygamous couples. None of Joseph Smith's wives became pregnant, though several of

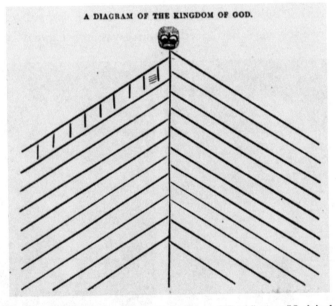

A DIAGRAM OF THE KINGDOM OF GOD.

Orson Hyde, "A Diagram of the Kingdom of God," 1847. Hyde's depiction of an eternal hierarchy centered on the priesthood captures the dynastic nature of Mormon theology. Each patriarch would preside over a new branch of God's kingdom, with every individual sealed together through both polygamous and adoption rituals.

them, including Emily Partridge, later insisted that their marriages were consummated. It is impossible to know whether teenage brides, like Sarah Whitney or Helen Mar Kimball, the fourteen-year-old daughter of apostle Heber Kimball, had sex with their prophet husband. Nor is it possible to know how much of a say they had in the first place. Given the power disparity, however, it is unlikely they exercised much agency.[79]

Mormon conceptions of family, heaven, and exaltation were now interwoven in what they called "celestial marriage." Joseph Smith's teachings became only more iconoclastic. "You have got to learn how to make yourselves God, king and priest," he declared to a General Conference in April 1844, just as their God had previously evolved from being a human himself to becoming a divine monarch. Eliza Snow found redemption in this doctrine, arguing that if celestial beings were akin to earthly ones, then it was unreasonable that "in the heav'ns parents are single." Mormon doctrine dictated that "I've a mother there," meaning a Heavenly Mother who co-presided with her husband over the cosmos. The eternities were filled with deific beings. "Gods, angels, men," wrote Parley Pratt, "are one great family, all of the same species, all related to each other, all bound together by kindred ties." Mormonism's radical theology was in full bloom.[80]

JOSEPH SMITH's doctrines grew alongside his political prowess. For their first few years in Nauvoo, the saints skillfully manipulated the electoral system to ensure civic leaders prioritized their interests in return for votes. We "care not a fig for Whig or Democrat," Smith trumpeted, but "we shall go for our *friends*." The process proved effective, as the saints became a powerful voting bloc. Their neighbors, conversely, saw corruption. Critics denounced the "clannish principle of voting in mass, at the dictation of one man," which was "repugnant to the principles of our Republican form of Government." While it was common for interest groups to vote together, to have it managed by ecclesiastical leaders destroyed any sense of disestablishment. Critics detested so much power being centralized in one man, as Smith played the role of prophet, mayor, chief judge, and political broker. A New York editor admitted he would not be surprised if Smith was also their "chief cook."[81]

Most alarming to Nauvoo's enemies was the city's ability to shield Smith from justice. When Missouri officials embarked on a series of attempts to extradite him back to the state, Mormons utilized legal maneuvers to keep the prophet out of harm's way, each more daring than the last. Politicians and judges were, at least for a time, willing to work with Nauvoo leaders, much to the disappointment of Smith's opponents. Illinois's growing anti-Mormon body concluded that the church operated above the law. Finally, after a state election in August 1843 when the saints flipped their votes at the last moment to support someone who offered a backroom deal, the chance for compromise was closed. Thomas Ford, Illinois's governor, observed that both parties became "determined upon driving the Mormons out of the state."[82]

Mormon leaders scrambled to find solutions. They appealed for Washington to designate Nauvoo as federal territory outside state control. The petition fell on deaf ears in an era of weak federal oversight. Hoping to ride the popular support for manifest destiny, Nauvoo officials proposed that Smith be deputized over an army of one hundred thousand troops to march to Oregon Territory, both securing an outpost for the saints and reaffirming America's control over the region. They petitioned presidential hopefuls to ask how, if elected, they would help the church. When John C. Calhoun, the South's most powerful senator, responded that those issues were managed at the state level, Smith rejected such a "fragile" understanding of the Constitution. "The States rights doctrine," the prophet believed, is "what feeds mobs." Given his experience, it was a fair point.[83]

Eventually, Smith declared himself a candidate for the White House. His proposed platform was an awkward conglomeration of popular, though incongruent, principles including restoring the national bank, cutting Congress members' salaries, annexing Texas, and instituting the gradual abolition of slavery. Hundreds of Mormon men, including Brigham Young, swarmed the nation campaigning for their prophet to become president.[84]

Smith's boldest proposal came in March 1844 when he organized a clandestine council to govern the entire world. Though the official title was a convoluted phrase that began with "The Kingdom of God and his Laws," it was colloquially known as the Council of Fifty due to the number of participants. Their goals were to "establish a Theocracy" so that God's word could finally rule humanity's world. They even drafted a new constitution: "We, the people of the Kingdom of God," it began, before blending theocratic governance with democratic language. The Mormons were not the only Americans to critique the Constitution as too secular, or even the first to submit a replacement. Abolitionists and woman-suffrage activists, for example, proposed solving the nation's ills through an infusion of divine correction. Yet the Mormon Council of Fifty was perhaps the most radical experiment to critique America's political tradition, even as it drew from its spirit of innovation. To reflect Smith's exalted station in this new world order, he was sustained as "Prophet, Priest & King."[85]

Skeptics had seen enough. A group of Mormon dissenters organized that spring and established their own newspaper, the *Nauvoo Expositor*. Its sole issue appeared on June 7, 1844, and detailed Smith's polygamous activities and political ambitions. The prophet immediately denounced the newspaper and ordered its destruction, insisting that he "would rather die to morrow" than see their slander "go on." Hyrum urged the Nauvoo Legion to "mash the press all to pieces and pie the type." Once the press was destroyed, the dissenters fled the city and called on the state to help. Governor Ford issued warrants for Joseph and Hyrum's arrest. The Smiths surrendered after two weeks of negotiations and were taken to the county seat in nearby Carthage. Fearing further incrimination, Joseph ordered that the Council of Fifty's minutes be destroyed.[86]

Mormonism's devoted critics were not satisfied with Smith's being held in state custody while charged with treason. They organized a Committee of Safety, the name a reference to American revolutionaries who protected their rights through extralegal action. Like the Mormons, they, too, had little faith in existing systems of justice. American democracy had proved too fragile to maintain order. So instead of trusting the legal process, they blackened their faces, loaded their guns, and marched to Carthage.[87]

Their actions were as swift as they were vengeful. The mob of 250 men arrived at suppertime on June 27, 1844, and overwhelmed the jail's outmatched guards. Joseph, Hyrum, and apostles John Taylor and Willard Richards tried to fend them off at the door to their upstairs room, to no avail. Hyrum was the first to fall, after a bullet entered near his nose and exited the back of his head. Taylor was hit a number of times, though without any mortal wounds. Joseph, faced with the violent end he always knew was possible, raced for the window but was struck several times before falling two stories to the ground outside. "Joseph and Hyrum are dead," Richards wrote after the mob had left; "the job was done in an instant." The simple words belied the catastrophic shock inflicted upon an expansive religious community.[88]

DECADES OF sorrow could not prepare Lucy Mack Smith to see her two sons' corpses. Before walking into the room where the bodies were displayed, she "braced every nerve, roused every energy of my soul, and called upon God to strengthen me." It was not enough. Surrounded by sobbing family members, Lucy cried out, "My God, my God, why hast thou forsaken this family!" She dreamt of her family bringing redemption to the world. Instead, the world filled them with bullets. Emma, "in a state of insensibility," collapsed and was carried out. Mary Fielding pleaded for Hyrum to speak. She lifted her five-year-old son, Joseph F., to see his father's mangled body, an image he kept with him his entire life. Joseph Smith III, the prophet's oldest son, laid his cheek against his father's. Eliza Snow captured the agonizing spirit when she wrote, "The blackest deed that men or devils know / Since Calvry's scene, has laid the brothers low."[89]

Mourning eventually evolved into a period of transition. Mormons had never chosen a prophet before. Joseph Smith's leadership came prepackaged with their initial conversion. But now they faced an unexpected, though always inevitable, choice: Who would replace him? Smith had never been clear or consistent in a succession plan. The apostle Wilford Woodruff described the city of saints as "sheep without a shepherd." The Quorum of the Twelve, most of whom were away on missions, returned to Nauvoo in August 1844 to find that Sidney Rigdon had claimed the throne. He had, after all, been as instrumental as anyone, save Smith, in building the faith, and was the last remaining member of the First Presidency. The previous fourteen years seemed to point to this moment. Yet Rigdon's erratic behavior resulted in a fallen stature, and Brigham Young's rise as president of the Quorum of the Twelve placed the ambitious apostle much closer to the now-deceased prophet. That he had presided over the missions that had courted thousands of converts also bolstered Young's reputation.[90]

The two primary challengers squared off before five thousand saints on a blustery August 8, 1844. Rigdon spoke in the morning, reciting his long history of leadership. Young, conversely, focused his afternoon remarks on the Twelve holding the necessary "keys" to govern Smith's expanding religious empire, especially the new temple rituals. When Young called for a vote, the vast majority supported the Quorum of the Twelve as their new guardians. Among those present who supported Young was Aidah Clements, the mother who had marched in Zion's Camp and lost a son in the Missouri War. Her husband Albert, however, chose Rigdon, who had initially brought him into the faith. Rigdon left the city after being excommunicated a month later, taking followers like Albert Clements with him. Mormon schisms divided not only allegiances but families.[91]

Young moved quickly to consolidate power. He released leaders who did not support the Twelve's succession. "If you don't know whose right it is to give revelations," he bellowed, "I will tell you[:] It is I." Few principles were as central to his tenure as a desire to never be undercut with dissent. Another was to expand and codify polygamy. Young and other senior apostles were sealed to dozens of women over the next year, which included inheriting many of the martyred prophet's own wives. Among those sealed to Young were Eliza Snow and Emily Partridge, while Sarah Whitney was sealed to

Heber Kimball, another apostle and Young's closest colleague. Much to Emma Smith's horror, the aspect of her husband's religious mission with which she had the most trouble was now becoming a defining feature. Her relationship with Young quickly deteriorated.[92]

Another Smith woman soon occupied Young's attention. Lucy Smith, Mormonism's founding mother, spent much of the next six months narrating her memoir to two eager scribes. Day after day, week after week, she dictated the faith's origin stories and placed her family at the heart of God's work. The work finished with a stinging indictment, as Lucy emphasized that despite her being a proud patriot and descendant of Revolutionary War veterans, in her eyes the country had become "so corrupt that there are none to defend and maintain the sacredness of the law." The memoir, which became one of Mormonism's most important texts, rebuked America's failure to ensure religious liberty.[93]

Revisiting her family's centrality to the church's past made Lucy worry about their role in the present. Her only surviving son, William, while an apostle, often battled with Young. Was the Smith family to be sidelined in the faith they founded? Lucy gathered family and friends together in June 1845 and revealed a series of dreams that contained an ominous warning. Men with "blacker hearts" had failed to recognize that William held familial claim to "the Presidency of the Church." (Joseph Smith had, at times, hinted at lineal succession.) The vision also reaffirmed her position as "mother" of the movement. Immediately recognizing the threat, Young and the other apostles gathered at Mother Smith's home to ease her "hurt feelings." Yet tensions with William continued to fester, and the last remaining Smith son was excommunicated in October.[94]

The greater threat to the Twelve's supremacy came from outside Nauvoo. James J. Strang had been a member of the faith for less than a year, yet he claimed to have a letter from Smith, allegedly written days before his death, appointing him as his successor. Strang also boasted about having been led to ancient buried records that he translated as scripture, along with there being witnesses who attested to their divine veracity. This prophetic mimicry of Mormonism's founder convinced several prominent members, including several of the Smith family and old-time believers like David Whitmer and Martin Harris. Lucy may have seen in Strang's tale an echo of her son's. Especially as allegiance to Young meant accepting a polygamous order and likely westward expulsion, the Strangite narrative compelled thousands of converts.[95]

Young never forgave the Smiths' role in enabling a string of challengers. His animosity launched a rivalry between the LDS tradition and their founding family that would last for over a century. Further, Young's belief that Emma's opposition to polygamy was responsible for her husband's death led him to curtail the limited advances Mormon women had achieved in Nauvoo. He denounced the Relief Society and counseled wives to fully submit to their husbands. "When I want Sisters" to organize, he trumpeted, "I will summon them to my aide." Until then, "let them stay at home." Young's patriarchal Mormonism was shaped in response to the Smith women.[96]

THE SAINTS continued to face external hostility on top of their internal schisms. State politicians, no longer courting Mormon support after it had proved to be too unpopular, stripped Nauvoo of its chartered rights. Roaming mobs molested saints in outlying settlements, prompting Young to order an armed response. The entire region seemed ripe for war by September 1845. "A determined spirit exists among the Anti-Mormons," wrote Thomas Sharp, the anti-Mormons' ringleader, to either evict the saints or "die in the attempt." Governor Ford assembled a convention of county and state leaders to find a solution. They all concluded that "the Mormon must and *should* leave the state," preferably before the next spring. Ford confessed that such an order exceeded his constitutional powers, yet he encouraged the saints to migrate.[97]

Brigham Young and the saints agreed. They had decided that America's promises of rights and liberties held no value. Leaders explored alliances with Indigenous tribes in the West, viewing them as fellow sufferers of American oppression. (These Native nations, however, rejected Young's paternalistic overtures.) The Quorum of the Twelve considered a move to the West, outside the country's oppressive borders. "The continued abuses, persecutions, murders, and robberies practiced upon us . . . in a (Christian) republic, and land of liberty," proclaimed John Taylor, left them to conclude that only in "our exit from the United States" can "we enjoy" freedom. They commenced organizing one of the largest and most successful mass migrations in American history. Fourteen thousand saints left Illinois over the next year.[98]

The last thing left for the saints before fleeing Nauvoo, however, was the temple's completion. The towering structure at the heart of Joseph Smith's religious vision, and the center of the Twelve's succession claims, was finally dedicated in December 1845. Young presided over sacred rituals for five thousand members, who were endowed and sealed to their families. Many were sealed into new polygamous unions and connected to prominent leaders through a new ordinance called an "adoption," which forged hierarchical families more reflective of monarchical dynasties than democratic couplings. By the time he closed the temple doors, Young claimed nearly forty women as plural wives, and over two hundred men and seven hundred women had entered the practice.[99]

While most saints followed Young across the Mississippi River in February 1846, many stayed for a few more months. Among those who remained were Mary Fielding Smith and her children. Her delay was in part due to depleted financial resources but also perhaps due to Mary's connection with Emma and Lucy Smith, who had chosen not to leave. Mary seemed torn over which direction to go. Finally, in September, she cast her lot with the Twelve and made her way west. Her daughter, Martha Ann, recalled how they left behind their home filled with furniture and their orchards filled with rosy peaches and ripe apples. Like most saints-turned-pioneers, they took only the bare necessities for the trek. A battle soon erupted as another mob evicted the last Mormon holdouts. Seven-year-old Joseph F. Smith forever remembered cannon fire being the last thing he heard in the city of his childhood, a sound he permanently associated with the lie of America's religious liberty.[100]

3

Of Empires and Wars,
1846–69

Thrones, Kingdoms, Dominions, and all Institutions
Of human erection, are bound to decay;
But the heavens introduce, in this last dispensation,
Their own order of things, that will not pass away.

Lo! here in the midst of the snow-cover'd mountains
We call to all nations—all people forsooth;
Come, come to our Standard, the Deseret Standard,
The Standard of Freedom, Salvation, and Truth.

—ELIZA R. SNOW, 1849[1]

As his wagon crested the last of the Rocky Mountains on July 22, 1847, Green Flake likely felt exhausted. His entire life had centered on hard labor. The broad-shouldered and good-natured man with a round face and short hair was born enslaved on January 6, 1828, in rural North Carolina, but relocated to Mississippi in the early 1840s. When his enslaver, James Madison Flake, embraced the Mormon message on April 7, 1844, the enslaved man followed suit. "Ordained two elders[,] brother James M. Flake & Washing[ton] N. Cook," recorded missionary John Brown; "I also baptized two black men, Allen & Green," he added, nearly as an afterthought. It is impossible to know whether Flake's baptism was consensual or coerced. Regardless, he found himself in Mormonism's vanguard after James sent him to accompany Brigham Young's advance pioneer party in 1847. Flake entered the destination two days before the prophet. By the time Young viewed the Salt Lake Valley and declared it "the place," Flake was already planting crops.[2]

Flake worked hard to grow food and build a cabin for his enslaver, who arrived the next year. Settling Mormonism's new home required plenty of effort. The land between the large Salt Lake and the majestic mountains was filled with tall grass and sand. But the work brought sacred rewards. Flake and many others were rebaptized on August 8 to demonstrate their devotion to a spiritual, as well as physical, cause.[3]

Brigham Young and the saints who followed him exulted in their promised land. They were finally separated from the country that had failed them and granted the opportunity to build Zion from scratch. Yet the United States acquired the territory at the end of the US-Mexico War less than a year later, inaugurating another phase of conflict between the LDS church and the nation in which it was born but could never escape. Nor was the land uninhabited: the Ute, Shoshone, Paiute, Goshute, Navajo, and other Indigenous nations laid claim to the very space the saints believed was theirs. Mormon appeals to theocratic rule were never as unchallenged as their rhetoric implied.

America's, and Mormonism's, story of westward expansion is a tale of conflicting sovereignties. White citizens believed it their fate to colonize and conquer all land between the oceans. "Already the advance guard of the irresistible army of Anglo-Saxon emigration has begun," boasted John O'Sullivan in 1845, just after America annexed Texas, and right before acquiring the Northwest through diplomacy and the Southwest through blood. O'Sullivan even coined a new term for the push: manifest destiny. Pioneers were "armed with the plough and the rifle, and marking its trail with schools and colleges, courts and representative halls, mills and meetinghouses." Facing west, the country's future knew no boundaries; facing east, Indigenous peoples suffered violence and dispossession.[4]

Mormons both fled from and worked within America's colonizing impulse. Governing America's ever-expanding territory challenged both legislators and settlers. By the 1850s, the territories in the West claimed more American land than did the existing states, evidence of expansion hurtling beyond control. Disputes over how to govern western territories eventually resulted in civil war. Before that, however, the government declared war on the Mormons.[5]

The saints appeared as a distinct threat due to their twin allegiances to theocracy and polygamy. Both principles were deemed incongruous with American democracy. Not that the Mormons minded: they viewed America as a rotting carcass of moral decay and political failure. All Young and his followers wanted was to be left alone. With long-flowing hair and not yet possessing his distinctive beard—Big Elk, a leader of the Omaha, called him the "Big Red Headed chief"—there were few more divisive figures of the period than Young. "His followers deem him an angel of light," observed one visitor, while "his foes a goblin damned." Everything about Young, just like the religion he led, appeared polemical.[6]

Common saints struggled to make sense of these shifting borders. Phebe Pendleton, who arrived in Utah in 1852, was thrilled to once again be around Young, who had baptized her in Kirtland. But she was also despondent about having left her adult children behind in Ohio. She urged them to escape the coming storm when "the union [is] dissolved and peace taken from the earth." Only their Rocky Mountain refuge could provide peace. Her maternal letters offer a poignant prism through which to view the period.[7]

By 1870, the church had established over a hundred settlements that spanned hundreds of miles, ranging from the northern Rockies to southwestern California. Green Flake, after gaining his freedom in the 1850s, first lived near Salt Lake City before relocating to southeastern Idaho. He witnessed much of the turmoil of the following decades—war, expansion, reformation, political clashes—all springing from the land he tilled.[8]

Territorial Utah's first years were both the apex of Mormonism's empire building and the start of its imperial decline. In 1847, the church had achieved cultural isolation and exercised unchecked political sovereignty; by 1869, they could claim neither.

*   *   *

THE ROAD from Nauvoo to Salt Lake was long and hard. After poring over travel guides, especially one produced by explorer John C. Frémont, Brigham Young fixed on "the neighborhood of Lake Tampanagos" due to it being "a most delightful district" with "no settlement near there." He hoped that an advance company could make the entire trek in 1846. It would be followed by a mass migration of nearly 16,000 saints, few of whom had substantial frontier experience, along a trail that was hardly a thoroughfare.[9]

Young's optimism proved naïve. The exodus from Illinois in February 1846 was rushed and haphazard, with two hundred wagons scattered across Iowa along a slow-moving westward train. (Some saints, like Phebe Pendleton, opted to remain in the East until a permanent settlement was established.) Their early departure meant they faced muddy daytime trails and freezing nighttime temperatures. The eighteen-year-old Emmeline Woodward, whose small frame contained an indomitable spirit, traveled with Newel and Elizabeth Whitney after joining their family as a plural wife. (Her first husband abandoned her before the trek.) Her diaries detailed the "very muddy and bad roads" that impeded progress for their "houseless village." Another young plural wife, Eliza Partridge Lyman, believed the only thing that prevented her from freezing was there not being enough "room in the wagon for the frost to get in." Eliza Snow, plural wife to Young, called these first months on the trail "a growling, grumbling, devilish, sickly time." Snow's sister-wife, Emily Partridge Young, birthed a child in "a tent surrounded by mud," one of many born on the trail.[10]

The saints marched into Mexican territory just as America claimed it for its own. Federal officials had finally annexed Texas the previous year after a decade-long dalliance. They now eyed taking even more. American pioneers who lacked the Mormons' religious zeal but matched their enterprising spirit flooded western territories. James Polk vaulted to the White House in 1844 in part due to his advocacy for expansion. Despite loud critics who feared further colonization would extend slavery, and a smaller number who denounced encroachment on Native lands, manifest destiny continued apace. Riding this popular wave, Polk manufactured a crisis on the Texas-Mexico border to coax America's southern neighbor into a war.[11]

Polk immediately sent emissaries to meet with Brigham Young along the Iowa trail. He wanted to both enlist soldiers and keep the Mormons from siding with Mexico. His concerns were justified: most saints, including Young, had denounced America's current government and were open to supporting Mexico or even warring Indigenous nations. Yet Young was also a pragmatist. He knew the country's expanding borders might encompass their next settlement, and it was his emissaries who had first broached the idea of a Mormon regiment with Polk. Young also knew that the pioneers desperately needed federal salaries. A compromise was brokered by Thomas Kane, an aristocratic philanthropist who, though not a Mormon, sympathized with their plight and continued as the church's gentile liaison for the next few decades. The saints raised a militia of five hundred men, named the Mormon Battalion, the first and only religion-based militia regiment in American history. Young promised Polk that they were open to settling in America again so long as they could establish "a territorial government of our own."[12]

The combination of a slow start and the loss of enlistees forced Young to reconsider initial plans. Instead of making it to the Great Basin that first year, the pioneers camped on federal territory along the Missouri River on land otherwise reserved for the Omaha. Saints proceeded to build a hasty village, named Winter Quarters, with eight hundred cabins that housed upwards of 3,500 people. Zina Huntington, one of Young's plural wives, called it a "City of log huts." She and several of her sister-wives lived in what Eliza Snow called "the 2d Mansion of Press. B. Young," a crude cabin specifically built for the prophet's large "female family." These devoted women developed a strong sisterhood. Meanwhile, thousands of others spent the winter scattered across the prairies. One woman, Abigail Abbott, wrote of the "dark prospect" of surviving the winter along the plains without her husband. Hundreds died due to disease, weather, and malnutrition.[13]

The "Lion of the Lord" consolidated priesthood authority as he prepared for the trek's second stage. He dictated his first and only canonized revelation on January 14, 1847, titled the "Word and Will of the Lord." It organized the camp into companies of hundreds, fifties, and tens, with captains over each, all forming a strict hierarchy

Photograph of Zina Diantha Huntington Young, Bathsheba Smith, Emily Dow Partridge, and Eliza R. Snow, 1867. These women converted to Mormonism during the 1830s and remained influential leaders for the rest of the century. Young, Partridge, and Snow were all first sealed to Joseph Smith but then later became plural wives to Brigham Young.

with Young at the top. The revelation provided practical guidance, gave moral commands, and even encouraged singing and dancing. The mixture of sacred dictation, mundane instruction, and merriment were a hallmark of Young's tenure. "I feel all the time like Moses," he remarked two months later.[14]

Young embarked on the 1,031-mile trip from Winter Quarters to the Great Basin in April 1847. He led an advance pioneer company of 150 people, including five women, three enslaved men, and several children. The trek's best chronicler was Wilford Woodruff, an earnest forty-year-old apostle with piercing eyes and large sideburns. Woodruff had begun his diary in 1835 shortly after his conversion and he kept daily records for the ensuing sixty years. The resulting thirty volumes totaling more than six thousand pages became one of nineteenth-century Mormonism's most crucial records. "We are now about to start on the pioneer Journey to go to the mountains of Israel," he wrote on April 3, "to find a location as a resting place for the saints." Woodruff's account captured the camp's strict order: everyone awoke by horns at five in the morning and, after breakfast and prayers, departed by seven. Besides lunch, they traveled until early evening, when they formed a protective wagon circle.[15]

The company finally arrived in the Salt Lake Valley in late July 1847. Based on advice from famed trapper Jim Bridger, they decided on this valley as opposed to one farther south near Utah Lake, and one to the north, because the former was a hub for Timpanogos and the latter for Western Shoshone. Woodruff was immediately taken by the scenery. The valley was "surrounded with a perfect chain of everlasting hills & mountains coverd with etrnal snow," and featured "peaks like pyramids towering towards Heaven," the "grandest & most sublime scenery Probably that could be obtained on the globe." Young officially deemed it the "resting place" for the saints on July 24. What Woodruff called "an important day" is still celebrated as Pioneer Day, an official state holiday.[16]

The saints immediately went to work. The valley, bordering a lake and surrounded by mountains, proved an especially healthy location for settlement. Mormons plotted a two-square-mile plat with 10-acre squares, each divided into 1.25-acre lots. A center square was reserved for the temple. They built an adobe-brick fort, established irrigation routes, and planted potatoes, buckwheat, turnips, and corn. A lack of timber meant that the saints turned to mud for their homes. No bother. "The children of Israel built of sun-dried bricks," mused apostle George A. Smith, and "we have done the same."[17]

The growing city welcomed a constant stream of immigrants. A second pioneer camp arrived in September 1847 with 1,500 people, more than half of them women, traveling with six hundred wagons and 5,000 head of livestock. Larger companies arrived over the next few years. The care needed to oversee such a project was substantial. One camp in 1848 included over 2,000 people as well as 2,012 oxen, 983 cows, 904 chickens, 654 sheep, 334 cattle, 237 pigs, 134 dogs,

131 horses, 54 cats, 44 mules, 11 doves, 10 geese, 5 beehives, 5 ducks, 3 goats, and, not to be overlooked, 1 squirrel. "I imagined myself on a large farm," quipped Caroline Crosby, who voyaged with this traveling zoo.[18]

Among those who made the trek in 1848 was Mary Fielding Smith, Hyrum's widow, and her children Joseph F. and Martha Ann. When the man who led her company, Cornelius Lott, urged her to stay behind in Winter Quarters, she pressed on, and eventually beat Lott to the valley. Young Joseph F., aged nine at the time, later claimed that her faith was so firm that she blessed their ox when it refused to budge. Though the story may be apocryphal, it captured what he believed to be his mother's zeal and determination.[19]

In an era defined by White encroachment upon Indigenous lands, Brigham Young officiated over what may have been the largest colonization scheme. He knew it. Woodruff recorded Young's boast that he had "accomplished more this season than can be found on record concerning any set of men since the days of Adam." Fifty acres of land just east of the temple block were reserved for Young's expanding familial kingdom. "Hail ye mighty men of Israel, / Who the hiding place have found," Eliza Snow praised in a poem that September; "The eternal God has blest you, / You have stood on holy ground."[20]

One step remained to confirm Young's status. Several apostles bristled at the gruff manner with which he lashed out at a number of his colleagues, including Parley Pratt, for questioning him. When apostle Orson Pratt, Parley's brother, argued that Young's position was akin to Speaker of the House, Young retorted, "Shit on Congress." Colonizing required a strong, singular hand. Finally, in December 1847, while visiting Winter Quarters, Young formally reorganized the First Presidency with himself as president. He would govern above the Quorum of the Twelve just as Joseph Smith had. The move was sustained at a church conference a few weeks later. "This is the best day I have seen in my life," the new prophet confessed. They celebrated by singing, dancing, and drinking "delightful Strawberry Wine." Young was officially a modern Moses, though one who lived to enter the promised land.[21]

*　　*　　*

THE SAINTS were excited to celebrate Pioneer Day, July 24, 1849, two years after arriving in the valley. They had survived meager crop returns and built an inchoate yet bustling town with several thousand residents. Eliza Snow designed a sixty-four-foot-long flag, which they flew with pride. Hundreds of youths marched in a parade with boys carrying a banner that praised Young as "the Lion of the Lord," and girls held one that said, "Hail to the Chief." The salvaged Nauvoo Temple bell filled the air. Young then read the Declaration of Independence to loud applause.[22]

That they read the Declaration on a day that commemorated their *exit* from America, and hailed a prophet, not the president, as their sovereign leader, marked the community's breach with the nation. The end of the US-Mexico War brought the Mormons under federal oversight due to Mexico ceding the territory to America. But Young still hoped to implement a theocratic rule he believed necessary for order despite Washington's governance. Only the priesthood offered "a perfect system of code laws." The reconvened Council of Fifty served as a temporary presiding body, and Salt Lake City was divided into nineteen ecclesiastical wards. Apostle John Taylor declared that the Kingdom of God was "both Church and state," designed "to rule both temporally and spiritually."[23]

Young realized such circumstances could not last. The federal government would not let a Mormon theocracy run unchecked. After advice from Thomas Kane, LDS leaders placed their trust in state sovereignty. They petitioned to form the "State of Deseret" in 1849 with sprawling borders that encompassed present-day Utah and Nevada as well as substantial portions of Colorado, Arizona, and Southern California. It would have been the largest state in the nation. Their new Mormon-only legislature repealed common law, therefore dismissing legal precedents not unique to Mormon society, and granted the church corporate status. This enabled LDS leaders to oversee the judicial system, solemnize polygamy, and hold massive amounts of both land and wealth. Young, hoping the government

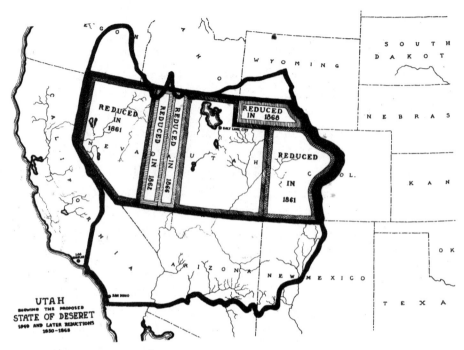

"State of Deseret." Changing boundaries of Utah Territory from the proposal for Deseret State in 1849 to Utah Territory's eventual boundaries after 1868.

would simply approve their proposal, instructed legislators to commence "act[ing] like a state."[24]

Deseret was not the only proposed state at the time. Thousands of migrants made their way to the Pacific coast after the discovery of gold in 1849. Both California and Oregon petitioned for statehood around the same time as the Mormons. How to govern these massive territories proved a difficult question for federal politicians. Northern reformers hoped to keep the land free from slavery; southern Democrats envisioned bolstering the slave power. Distrust of the Mormons was the only principle they shared.[25]

A solution came through a series of contested legislative actions that came to be known as the Compromise of 1850. The government rejected Deseret statehood and instead created the Territory of Utah, named after the Ute tribes who had lived in the region for generations. Though not as large as Young had proposed, the territory still encompassed much of the region between the Rocky Mountains and California. Perhaps most surprising, however, was Kane's success in lobbying federal officials to appoint Young as territorial governor.[26]

The delicate dance over territorial sovereignty proved treacherous. When the appointed territorial judges arrived in August 1851, they were aghast to hear what they deemed to be Mormon attempts to "alienate the affections of the people from the Government of the United States." The saints were equally upset when one of the judges implied Mormon women were no better than prostitutes. The clash continued for weeks until the appointees fled to Washington to spread salacious details concerning Young and his followers. Yet the saints succeeded in courting public sympathy and political alliances to stave off the threat, in part because they evaded the question of polygamy. Eliza Snow ridiculed the "runaway" officials with a poem sung by an approving crowd at the next Fourth of July's festivities: The men "have gone!—they went—but when they left us, / They only of themselves bereft us."[27]

Snow similarly scoffed at news concerning women's reform movements back east. "Let those fair champions of 'female rights,'" she penned in early 1852, come to Zion where men "cloth'd with the everlasting Priesthood" presided over a "perfect form of government." The suffragists who gathered at Seneca Falls in 1848, while well intentioned, were on the wrong path. Regulating society without priesthood authority was like "ships at sea" navigating without helms, oars, or steam engines. Only in Zion could women find fulfillment.[28]

Phebe Pendleton believed Snow's promise and made the fateful decision to travel to Utah in 1852. Much of her previous life had been full of "afflictions, privations, and hardships." She had survived three husbands, at least one of whom was abusive, and was now leaving her grown children behind. She was therefore anxious to live among believers once again. The patriarchal blessing she received decades before from Joseph Smith Sr. promised that her family would gather together in Zion, so she remained hopeful her nonbelieving children would eventually follow her to Deseret. "If you neglect this opportunity," she warned, "you will be left to regret it when it will be too late." She failed to mention to them her marriage to polygamist Jeremiah Woodbury, however.[29]

Even if Phebe Pendleton Woodbury's children never gathered, many others from across Europe and America did. Four thousand English saints arrived in 1854 alone. The church established the Perpetual Emigrating Fund to help up to thirty thousand converts who lacked resources over the next three decades. Not all travel experiments were successful, however. A handcart operation was created in 1856 to enable poorer migrants to cross the plains without oxen or horses. While several companies made the trek without problems, two were hampered by a late start and mismanagement, and were caught in harsh winter conditions. Saints in Salt Lake City heard the news at a large general meeting. "The sisters stripped off their Peticoats stockings and every thing they could spare," one observer recalled, and rescue wagons were dispatched. The companies lost 210 of their 980 members. Though Young insisted that his "skirts are clear of their blood," a lack of oversight and limited supplies enabled the tragedy.[30]

Leaders learned their lessons and implemented safer, and more efficient, policies that enabled continued emigration for decades. Utah's population boomed as the church's settlements expanded. Nearly forty thousand Mormons resided in Utah within a decade of its founding. At least for the time being, they had succeeded in securing their own rule.[31]

THE FAMED leader of the Timpanogos band of the Shoshone, Wakara, had already seen plenty in his life when he hosted the Mormon prophet in 1850. He presided over an expansive horse-raiding and slave-trading network that stretched from the Great Plains to California. Brigham Young reported, with a hint of jealousy, that Wakara acted "as proud and important as any potentate that ever flourished the ensigns of royalty." The Ute leader viewed his new Mormon neighbors as potential trading partners and drove hundreds of horses into Salt Lake City to sell. But when Mormons encroached on Timpanogos territory near Utah Lake in 1850, bloody battles ensued. After months of skirmishes, Young, calling himself "the Big Mormon Chief," traveled to Wakara's own home to reconcile.[32]

Wakara, a wise strategist, recognized the need for compromise. He welcomed Young and Shoshone, Timpanogos, and Paiute leaders at his tent. Wakara insisted that Young view him as "a friend" and not "throw me away." Young, in turn, pledged to "smoke the pipe of peace" and "make an everlasting covenant" of goodwill. While the Mormons had "come here to settle," God had provided "plenty of land" for both Native and Mormon. The meeting was so harmonious and spiritual that Young burst into tongues. One hundred and twenty-seven members from the various tribes were then baptized. Wakara and several other leaders, including Tut-se-gav-its and Taú-gu (Southern Paiute), Kanosh (Pahvant), Sagwitch (Shoshone), and Arapeen and Sowiette (Timpanogos), were eventually ordained elders. The Indigenous saints likely saw their conversion as a political alliance, but White saints viewed it as a fulfillment of prophecy.[33]

Mormons drew from their scripture as well as their surroundings in how they dealt with Utah's Numic peoples, as a number of Native tribes had lived and thrived in the region for centuries. Few were anxious to transform in order to meet Mormon expectations. The Book of Mormon testified that the "Lamanite" descendants, which saints interpreted as Native Americans, held a chosen place in God's kingdom. Yet most Americans, especially on the frontier, believed that colonization required evicting Indigenous inhabitants. Young, who held the title of Utah's Indian superintendent, proposed strategies that reflected both impulses. On one hand, his "uniform policy" was that "it is better and cheaper to feed and clothe the Indians, than to fight them." But Young also petitioned the government to remove all Native tribes to distant reservations. A constant priority was to build enough alliances with the Indigenous groups that they would support the saints in future conflicts with the government. Pulling from Book of Mormon prophecies, Young predicted the "Lamanites" would serve as "the Lord's battle axe." Phebe Woodbury believed the "numerous tribes" would form "an all protecting wall around us."[34]

These conflicting principles led to inconsistent results. Young insisted that he could manage the tenuous balance—"I know the difference between good Indians and bad Indians," he claimed—but the pioneers' expansionist tendencies courted conflict. "The Amer-

Defiant Attitude of Brigham Young and yᵉ Indians towards yᵉ Uncle Sam.

"Defiant Attitude of Brigham Young and ye Indians towards ye Uncle Sam." Americans feared an alliance between the Mormons and Native Americans against the federal government.

ican character is Go a head Davy Crockett like," the Lion roared. The saints listened. Both at Young's direction and through their own accord, Mormons scattered across the Mountain West to build over a hundred colonies during the 1850s alone, creating a thousand-mile corridor from southeastern Idaho to San Bernardino, California. Some of these settlements were focused on a singular commodity, like the Iron Mission in Southern Utah, while others were variegated. What they held in common was lusting after Native lands.[35]

Tensions boiled to the surface in 1853 when Wakara led a series of attacks against White settlers due to land, livestock, and slave-trade disputes. Fighting lasted until May 1854, when Young and Wakara once again compromised. White Mormons concluded that they had to do more to mollify Indigenous neighbors. Young announced a new Southern Indian Mission in October to convert and "civilize" the tribes. The program called 160 elders by 1855.[36]

The initiative provided opportunities for Mormon women. Eighteen women in Salt Lake City organized an informal "Soci[e]ty of females of the purpose of making clothing for Indian women and Children." Young, who had denounced Nauvoo's Female Relief Society, was impressed by their initiative and called for it to be standardized. There were soon twenty-four societies throughout the territory. When they produced more goods than could be supplied to Indigenous communities, the societies were tasked with helping the poor within their own wards. Wilford Woodruff recorded once returning to his home to find fifty women engaged in the "laudable undertaking" of "sewing, knitting, sewing carpet rags, making Quilts, &c."[37]

Deseret's limited success in befriending Native tribes concerned eastern Americans. Military officials and skeptical politicians worried about a grand conspiracy to overthrow federal control. One newspaper speculated that the saints were teaching Indians not merely "agriculture" and "the mechanical arts" but "military tactics." It was yet another reason to distrust the Mormons.[38]

Wakara died in January 1855, months after he had once again compromised for peace. He expressed from his deathbed a continued friendship with the Mormons and a "great anxiety for peace with the whites." After an elaborate burial ceremony, the great chief was buried with a letter from Young in his hands. Many hoped that ideals for cooperation would outlive the famous chief.[39]

THE MORMON KINGDOM, established in the middle of a desert, was a religious oasis. "We'll find the place which God for us prepared / Far away, in the West," sang a popular pioneer hymn. "Where none shall come to hurt or make afraid; There the Saints will be blessed."[40]

Of all those who took up this promise, perhaps nobody possessed a background as surprising as Qwack Walker Lewis, a middle-aged Black man who carried with him the abolitionist legacies of his upbringing. Raised in Massachusetts as the last of eleven children born to an enslaved mother, his given name reflected his Ghanaian ancestry. He was also named after his mother's brother, Quok Walker, whose freedom suit helped establish statewide emancipation in the 1780s. Lewis worked with David Walker (no relation) to form America's first all-Black abolitionist organization, the Massachusetts General Colored Association (MGCA). Walker later penned one of the period's most successful abolitionist tracts, *Appeal to the Colored Citizens of the World*; Lewis, for his part, aided those fleeing slavery through the Underground Railroad.[41]

Lewis accepted the Mormon faith while living in Lowell, Massachusetts, in the early 1840s. He was baptized by one apostle, Parley Pratt, and ordained to the priesthood by another, William Smith. When the Lowell branch's presiding elders resigned, Lewis became its default leader. Brigham Young bragged in early 1847 that Lewis was "one of the best elders" the church had to offer. It was also around this time that Lewis's son, Enoch, married Mary Webster, a White member of the church.[42]

Not everyone was happy with the union. William Appleby, the newly appointed eastern states mission president, was aghast that the congregation had welcomed an interracial family. He hoped it was a mistake. "I wish to know if this is the order of God," he wrote Young, whether it was right "to ordain Negroes to the Priesthood and allow amalgamation?"[43]

Young was outraged. He declared that were it not for gentiles who could prosecute the murderers, the Lewises "would all have to be killed," because "when they mingle seed it is death to all." The news was particularly ill-timed because Young had recently dealt with the troublesome case of William McCary, a convert in Winter Quarters described as "a half blooded Indian," "Coolurd man," and "a half breed Indian negro." McCary had married a White woman, Lucy Stanton, and soon formed his own break-off sect. While originally assured that his racial background did not bar him from fellowship, the Twelve exiled the "Indian prophet" after he courted White women into unauthorized plural unions. Now the Lewises confirmed Young's deepest fears. In a church that merged priesthood authority and familial relations, ordaining Black men to the priesthood opened the door to miscegenation.[44]

Oblivious to these discussions, Lewis personally informed Wilford Woodruff of his intent to gather to Utah in 1850. The move involved leaving his network of activists, his abolitionist heritage, and even his immediate family. Not knowing what was before him, he prepared a final will and testament, passed all his belongings to his family, and set out for Zion in the spring of 1851, alone.[45]

Lewis's time among the Mormons was short. The people were as alien as the environment, and the culture as oppressive as the weather. Having left one of the largest hubs of free African Americans, Lewis now found himself in a territory with only around two dozen free Blacks; more odiously, having previously surrounded himself with antislavery activists, he now lived among enslavers. Several of Utah's most prominent men brought their chattel practice from the South, including Charles C. Rich, an apostle from Kentucky, who enslaved around a half dozen men and women; Abraham Smoot, a Salt Lake City bishop, enslaved a woman named Lucy. There were around fifty enslaved persons in the territory by 1851.[46]

The final nail came when the territorial legislature met during the frigid first months of 1852. Apostle George A. Smith introduced a bill to legalize slavery in Utah Territory. Brigham Young, despite previously expressing moderate antislavery sentiments, backed the legislation and delivered a series of sermons that offered the most explicit anti-Black theology yet uttered in the Mormon tradition. Young declared himself "a firm believer in slavery," though the legislation he supported differentiated Utah's practice from that existing in the South. Those of African descent were "naturally designed" for service, as "the seed of Canaan"—the very genealogical marker placed on Lewis in his patriarchal blessing—were irrevocably cursed.[47]

Young's position did not go unchallenged. Apostle Orson Pratt made a valiant abolitionist stand that included an impassioned plea for Black suffrage. Pratt, known for his philosophical mind and stubborn spirit, proclaimed that it was inhumane and hypocritical to allow slavery within their religious refuge. His efforts went unheeded, however. The all-Mormon gathering ratified the prophet's recommendation, as well as legislation that outlawed interracial sex.

Legalized slavery was only the first step. Black residents would also be second-class citizens in the church. Young proclaimed, for the first time in public, that those with African ancestry could not be ordained to the priesthood. The same inherited curse that bound them to slavery also relegated them to spiritual subordination. "If there never was a prophet or apostle of Jesus Christ [who] spoke it before," he trumpeted, "I tell you [now], this people that are commonly called Negroes" could never "bear rule in the priesthood." It was this sermon, delivered on February 5 before a political body, that entrenched Mormonism's anti-Black theology.[48]

It is unlikely that Lewis heard a rationale for these changes from church leaders. If any of the apostles met with Lewis during his Utah sojourn, none chose to record it. Perhaps they could not bring themselves to face the Mormon elder who no longer had a place in their kingdom—not Parley Pratt, who had baptized him; not Wilford Woodruff, who had urged him to gather; and certainly not Brigham Young, who only five years earlier had praised him. Lewis, who had dedicated decades to celebrating his African ancestry and fighting for racial equality, discovered his church had formally cursed both.

Repulsed, Lewis fled Zion and returned to the East. Not that Young minded. The prophet boasted later that year that the legislature's actions had "nearly freed the territory of the colored population." His sermons and the church's policies had the desired effect of defining their empire's racial boundaries. The saints had found the place that God had prepared, but it was not open for all.[49]

Lewis was back near Boston by October 1852, the land of abolitionist agitation, the region where he had worked with David Walker to foment revolution for the cause of emancipation. A local newspaper announced the reopening of his barber shop. Lewis hoped to focus on cutting the hair of little children.[50]

MORMON POLYGAMY was Utah's worst-kept secret. Many plural families lived openly well before leaders ever announced it. What many had merely dismissed as outlandish rumors was now clear to all. "I have heard some things since you went away which you nor I never thought of," wrote one recent convert, Ellen Bishop, to her sister, Lucretia, who had just migrated to Utah. Rocked by details that "make one stagger," Ellen admitted that the news of plural marriage threatened her faith. She pleaded for Lucretia to never marry "an already married man" without "*deep* considerations."[51]

Young officially announced what everyone already knew in August 1852. He chose Orson Pratt to deliver the discourse. Polygamy, Pratt declared, was God's marital system and had been practiced since before the earth's beginnings. It restored order, meaning, and sacredness to humanity, and would raise a chosen generation sired by righteous patriarchs. Young optimistically, if naïvely, hoped that the announcement would "sail and ride triumphantly above all the prejudices and priestcraft of [the] day." Observers outside the faith knew otherwise.[52] A global missionary force was called to spread the message. Over a hundred men were sent to remote locations, including Calcutta, South Africa, and the Caribbean. Hosea Stout, assigned to Hong Kong, expressed his excitement to "publickly declare the true and greatest principle of our holy religion." While their success at changing public opinion was limited, their efforts bound the missionaries to the church. Nearly all became polygamists upon their return.[53]

Among those who served missions during this time was Joseph F. Smith. His mother, Mary Fielding, passed away from pneumonia in 1852, leaving him an orphan. He received support from First Presidency counselor Heber Kimball, who had married Mary as a plural wife, but the young son of Hyrum bucked all forms of authority. He was expelled from school two years later for assaulting a teacher. Leaders decided his energy could be better spent spreading the gospel. Smith was dispatched to Hawaii in 1855 at the age of fifteen, where he was tutored by Parley Pratt.[54]

Women were not among the missionary crop. One of Young's wives, Augusta Cobb, petitioned her husband to "send us on a mission," anywhere, "for we are so heartily tired and sick of our dear *Companions*, that we can hardly live." Yet other women found ways to share their voice through publication. Belinda Pratt, one of Parley's plural wives, penned America's first polygamous defense authored by a woman. She argued that polygamy was the only way to save women from a life of ruin and men from lasciviousness.[55]

Was American pluralism inclusive enough to allow plural marriage? Orson Pratt argued that the government could not prohibit a practice "conscientiously and sincerely believe[d] to be essential to their salvation." If the United States was based on biblical truths, then surely it would allow biblical marriage. He posited that all modern ills—especially prostitution and spousal abuse—were the results of monogamy. In response, politicians and journalists denounced the barbaric practice as uncivilized. One popular anti-polygamy book represented many when it claimed that "Mormon women are degraded and subjected by the system to a state of mental and physical slavery more abject and perfect than attaches to the inmates of a Turkish harem." Religious liberty could not cover such depravity.[56]

The daily reality of polygamy varied. Eliza Snow lived with a dozen sister-wives in a long cabin called Log Row. By the mid-1850s they moved into a set of homes constructed within the Young compound just east of Temple Square: the Beehive House, named for its beehive sculpture, was an adobe structure that doubled as the executive mansion; the Lion House, which featured a lion statue over its entrance, was Gothic Revival with twenty small bedrooms. Between the two massive homes were smaller buildings that served as territorial and church headquarters. The compound was surrounded by nine-foot stone walls with a gate featuring a sweeping arch topped by a sixteen-foot eagle. Young's familial kingdom, what Wilford Woodruff called the "tribe of Brigham," eventually numbered fifty-six wives and nearly sixty children.[57]

Life was not easy for even the most privileged families. Emily Par-

Image of the Brigham Young family compound by Edward Martin, 1861. Young's family was split between the Lion House (left) and Beehive House (right). Between the two houses were Young's territorial and church offices. In the far back-right corner is the Young family schoolhouse. A large gate surrounded the compound.

tridge, who was a young plural wife to Joseph Smith before joining Young's tribe, eventually bore Young seven children. The loneliness inherent in sharing Young with so many other women was torturous. After her oldest child died, she mourned not having a doting spouse. "As I am not essential to your comfort or convenience," she pleaded to her prophet-husband, "I desire you will give me to some other good man who has less cares." While she soon changed her mind, six of her sister-wives eventually sued for separation. Indeed, Utah's divorce laws were more liberal than most states', and Young oversaw the dissolution of over 1,600 marriages before 1866. As one historian posited, "Divorce was perhaps the safety valve that made polygamy work."[58]

Other polygamous unions were disrupted through more traditional circumstances, like death. Emmeline Woodward lost her second husband before the age of twenty-two when Newel Whitney died in 1850. She taught school to provide food for herself and two young daughters. Finally, at her own insistence, Emmeline became the fourth plural wife of Daniel Wells, a prominent religious and civic leader, in 1852. "I feel my lonely situation sensibly," she wrote Wells, which left her hoping to be "united with a being, noble as thyself." Though she gave birth to three more children, the marriage proved distant. These experiences taught her that despite her community's patriarchal structure, or perhaps because of it, she could not rely on men for support. "I am determined to train my girls to habits of independence so that they never need to trust blindly," she explained. Emmeline Wells's tenacity later became a hallmark of Mormonism's unique brand of feminism, one primarily aimed to carve out space for agency within, rather than against, an overwhelmingly patriarchal system.[59]

Non-elite plural families were much more intimate. Most polygamous men had only two wives and squeezed all dependents under a small roof. Frontier living was rough and providing for multiple families was rougher still. Poverty was common, especially in outlying settlements. Many women who became plural wives hailed from struggling economic backgrounds or arrived in Utah young and without parents. Around half of Utah's population was part of a polygamous family by the end of the 1850s. The percentage of men

Charles R. Savage, photograph of unidentified Mormon family, 1888. Most polygamists lived with fewer resources and in smaller homes than the Young family.

and women who married plurally was similar to those who served missions or paid tithing. The practice caused the Mormon population to explode: by 1870, 60 percent of Utahns were younger than twenty.[60]

Elizabeth MacDonald and her husband, Alexander, did not expect to become polygamists when they immigrated from Scotland in 1854. Yet she soon allowed four women the "privilege" of being sealed to her husband. They formed "one family household" that was held together through three things: "plenty of work" to stay busy, an earnest promise to "keep our own business and cares within our family circle," and a commitment to "family prayer" every night, where they "received strength from the proper source to remember our covenants and obligations to each other." Yet MacDonald still experienced plenty of "trials" despite these principles.[61]

No matter the sacrifice, leaders soon feared the community was losing its zeal. Young instructed in March 1856 that it was time for leaders to "put away their velvet lips and smooth things," and instead "preach sermons like pitch forks tines downward [so] that the people might wake up." Apostles scorched the region with fiery rhetoric. "It is a time of cleansing and pruning here in the valley," wrote one congregant, Harriet Doremus; those unwilling to fully commit were cut off, "root and branch." This push for redoubled commitment came to be known as the Reformation, and it convinced many to be rebaptized and renew their covenants. Local leaders were given a list of questions to ask each member concerning their faith and practice through a home-visiting program that reaffirmed ward authority.[62]

At times Young's rhetoric turned violent. He warned that there were some sins that exceeded Christ's atonement and could be redeemed only through "the life & blood of the individual." Though the sincerity of his words could be questioned—"I frequently say 'cut their infernal throats,'" Young once confessed, but "I don't mean any such thing"—his statements on "blood atonement" both instigated and justified vigilante attacks, castrations, and perhaps even a few deaths. For a population that viewed his sayings as scripture, the promptings created a combustible and dangerous environment.[63]

The Reformation's correlation of polygamy with faithfulness resulted in other tragic consequences. "Nearly all are trying to get wives," Woodruff reported, somewhat aghast, "until there is hardly a girl 14 years old in Utah but what is married or just going to be." With a shortage of marriage-age women, wives became younger. Young approved one man to marry a thirteen-year-old so long as he "preserve her intact until she is fully developed into Womanhood." One local community's median age for wives dropped to sixteen by 1860.[64]

The Mormons' practice of polygamy, coupled with their theocratic governance, fed already-tense national debates over popular sovereignty. LDS leaders hoped to capitalize on the Democratic Party's emphasis on local autonomy, a principle reaffirmed in the 1854 Kansas-Nebraska Act. Young wrote to Senator Stephen Douglas, who had previously befriended the saints in Illinois and was now popular sovereignty's primary defender, that their "strictly constitutional domestic regulations" should be protected. The Mormons posed a problem for the Democrats. As Utah's delegate John Bernhisel astutely noted, if the Democrats argued that the government should do more to reform Utah, their opponents could point out that such a principle "would apply everywhere," especially with southern slavery.[65]

The upstart Republican Party, which coalesced around stringent opposition to the slave power, also focused on what its members called the Mormon problem. Their founding platform in 1856 dictated that it was "the right and the imperative duty of Congress to prohibit in the territories" what they deemed the "twin relics of barbarism": slavery and polygamy. Abraham Lincoln skewered Douglas over the issue in their famous 1857 debates. If "the sacred right of Squatter Sovereignty [was] secured to every people," he asked, why not support the Mormons? Douglas's hedge was that the Mormons did not deserve the right because they were "alien enemies and outlaws, unfit to exercise the right of self-government." Woodruff called Douglas's remarks "contemptible," and Mormons never forgave him the slight.[66]

Utah appeared safe so long as the parties were gridlocked. But the combination of local and national tensions proved an incendiary blend.

"THE SPIRIT of the times" were filled with "the great excitement and predjudice," Phebe Woodbury bemoaned to her children in 1858. Though she insisted that Utah remained the safest place in a doomed world, she admitted the last year had been tumultuous. A swirl of rumors and accusations had brought them to the brink of war and, at least on one occasion, to bloodshed.[67]

Democratic president James Buchanan faced pressure to solve the Mormon problem as soon as he moved into the White House in early 1857. Journalists speculated that the saints had allied with Indians for a full-scale rebellion, and demanded action. Woodruff felt like "all hell is boiling over." More interested in settling territorial issues than any president before him, Buchanan was aware of the complexities at play. But his concern was piqued when he received the Utah legislature's memorial threatening that they "will not tamely submit to being abused by Government officials." He took this as a "declaration of war" and felt it necessary to reassert federal dominance. Buchanan's anxiety was especially acute given the crisis that had taken place in Kansas, where pro- and antislavery activists fought over the state's— and the nation's—future. He ordered 2,500 troops in May to march to Utah to support the latest group of federal appointees, including a new territorial governor to replace Young.[68]

News of a coming army set Utah Territory aflame. Woodruff worried that the "United States had turned mob," and the church decried the "tyrannical Administration" for "totally disregarding" their freedoms. Brigham Young was furious. He was determined "not to let any troops enter this territory," as the saints would "make every preparation to give the U.S. a Sound drubbing." Feelings were already on edge when they received word their beloved apostle Parley Pratt had been killed in Arkansas. The murderer was a man named Hector McLean, who was furious that Pratt had been sealed to his former wife, Eleanor. The death of Mormonism's most famous missionary added weight to the crisis. Violent conflict seemed inevitable.[69]

Young's animosity remained after meeting with army representatives in September. He declared martial law in the territory, forbade saints to sell grain to emigrants, and instructed everyone to prepare for battle. "We are invaded by a hostile force" intent on "our overthrow and destruction," he declared, and it was their duty "not to tamely submit to be driven and slain." Attendees at one raucous meeting in Salt Lake City unanimously pledged to defend their families and burn their properties rather than turn them over to troops. Local militias, organized at the ward level, trained every morning and evening. Young met with Indigenous leaders in early September and urged them to join forces with the saints, perhaps even encouraging them to plunder gentile migrant trains. Phebe Woodbury noted that she would "sooner seek for asylum among the savages" than in America's "Christian nation."[70]

The fiery message quickly spread throughout the territory, where it reignited embers left from the previous year's Reformation. Tasked with providing instructions to the Southern Utah settlements was apostle George A. Smith, a towering man at six feet and over 250 pounds. Because of his ability to remove his wig, glasses, and false teeth, Southern Paiutes named him Non-choko-wicher, or "he who takes himself apart." But this trip in August 1857 took a solemn tone. His heated sermons blazed a trail as he spread rumors of the army's intent. Ominously, Smith relayed Young's message that no gentiles were to be trusted, as well as the threat to no longer restrain Indians from attacking California-bound emigrants. A series of scuffles between Utah saints and transient gentiles soon followed.[71]

The full weight of these escalating conflicts was felt by innocent bystanders who had not contributed to any of them. A migrant train that had largely originated in Arkansas, with a few from Missouri and other states, slowly crossed Utah. Like other trains passing through that September, they grew frustrated when Mormons refused to sell them goods. Mormons, in turn, distrusted their intent, and likely coveted what appeared to be rich supplies. After tepid skirmishes resulted from hostile accusations, the Mormon community that had been on edge for months snapped. Local leaders ordered an attack while the train traveled across a scenic valley known as Mountain Meadows. They hoped it would appear to be an Indian raid. When the plot failed, and the migrants circled their wagons, Mormons planned more nefarious actions. They concluded that in order to prevent an army marching from the east or west, none of the witnesses who had learned of White Mormon involvement could survive.

The episode that ensued on September 11 was as bloody as it was heinous. Under direction from his local superiors, John D. Lee and other Mormon elders led the entire train out from their encampment into a single-file line, unarmed, under the guise of peace. Lee claimed it was to protect them from vengeful Indians. Instead, once they reached a designated mark and a signal was given, Mormons slaughtered more than one hundred men, women, and children, only sparing the youngest, who were deemed unable to tell tales.[72]

Rumors about the massacre spread quickly. When Lee reported to Young and apostle Wilford Woodruff later that month, Woodruff recorded Lee saying that the migrants had "belonged to the mob in Missouri & Illinois," that there "was not a drop of innocent blood in their Camp," and that it was the Indians who had done the killing anyhow. Massacre leaders and perpetrators continued for years to lie to Young that Indians were solely responsible for the massacre, and Young chose to believe them despite contrary evidence. Further, the impending crisis with federal troops meant Mormon leaders had no interest in any investigation. Even though he did not directly order the massacre, Young's enflamed rhetoric and policy of encouraging Indian raids at the very least created the circumstances for the atrocity and cover for the treacherous plot.[73]

Young was right to be concerned. When US Major James Carleton viewed the Mountain Meadows site two years later and witnessed its remains, he wished the Mormons could be wiped out. "All fine spun nonsense about their rights as citizens, and all knotty questions about Constitutional Rights," he concluded, "should be solved with the sword."[74]

Both federal and Mormon officials spent the rest of 1857 and the first few months of 1858 hoping to avoid such a conflict. A Mormon counterinsurgency, coupled with Buchanan's late decision to send the troops, resulted in the army not making it to Salt Lake City before the end of the year. "Our orders from the commanding officers," wrote one Mormon agent, "was to harass the Army, keep them awake and not let them sleep day or night, stampede their stock, burn every patch of grass that would burn, but not fire a gun only in self defense." Women supported the efforts by knitting wagons' worth of quilts and blankets for their own soldiers that were then transported into the mountains.[75]

Their efforts worked: over the next few months, they burned over fifty army-wagon loads of supplies, drove off hundreds of cattle, and forced the troops to stay still. Phebe Woodbury believed the troops' inability to press forward was God's will. She boasted that the only thing that kept the army alive was kindhearted Mormons who brought them supplies. The frigid winter also allowed tempers on both sides to cool.[76]

Young had already decided he would rather evacuate, and even burn, Salt Lake City than wage a doomed war. Saints who lived there and in other northern settlements were told in April that "we should vacate our homes" and move south. "The whole territory has been upon wheels," Phebe Woodbury reported, as "our City has ben deserted and prepared for a burnt offering." She was one of thirty thousand saints who made the journey to Provo. Another was Emmeline Wells, who had a close view of the events as her husband, Daniel, served as lieutenant general of Utah's militia and as one of Young's counselors

in the First Presidency. She complained of Provo's "dismal dark looking houses and dirty streets," though her family's privilege ensured
better living. The coordinated show of resolve impressed federal officials when they finally arrived to find only a ghost town.[77]

The brief détente enabled Thomas Kane, America's unofficial delegate to the Mormons, to arrive and once again broker a compromise. Buchanan felt pressure from Congress to quell the conflict.
He granted a pardon to any Mormon willing to pledge allegiance to
federal rule and accept a new territorial governor, which the saints
did. The president believed it would have been "mere madness" for
the Mormons, with their "limited resources," to "successfully resist
the force of this great and powerful nation." But his attention was
now drawn elsewhere. Young, conversely, mocked the government's
inability to follow through on its threats. "They float over it as having
obtained a victory," he mused, but "we consider them badly whipped."
Both sides declared victory. "The Lord has beh[e]ld our sacrifice,"
Woodbury summarized, "and our city has been spared." Impressed
with Daniel Wells's leadership during the crisis, Salt Lake City later
voted him mayor. Emmeline was increasingly part of Deseret royalty.[78]

The Utah War was a turning point for the Mormons. Young never
again served as the territory's civic leader, and the question of federal sovereignty seemed resolved. Within a few years, the Buchanan
administration further curtailed Utah's footprint by carving out substantial portions for the Nevada and Colorado Territories. Deseret
was reduced in both size and autonomy. The Mormons had to learn
how to operate within America's constricting borders.

MORMONS ADMITTED relief when America's war powers shifted
from Utah to the South. Shortly after the Civil War commenced in
1861, Young quipped that he "prayed for the success of both North
& South" in their attempt to kill each other. Sardonically, he privately mused that once the war was completed, "the brethren will
have many wives to take care of." Young was more diplomatic when
he had to be, of course. When the telegraph finally arrived in Utah
that October, the prophet's first message placated President Abra-

ham Lincoln: Utah "has not seceded," Young assured, "but is firm for the Constitution and laws of our once happy country." That he specified their loyalty was to the Constitution, rather than the Union, was a clever way to soothe fears without pledging full allegiance.[79]

Young was not alone in his reluctance to cheer on Lincoln's troops. Phebe Woodbury's letters during these years balanced a sincere concern for her children with a confident reminder that she had warned them such a fate was coming. She begged them to join her in Utah as "the only place of safety." American blood was being shed because the nation killed Joseph Smith and oppressed his followers. "Do not flatter yourself that war will soon be ended," she scolded, as "it is only the beginning of sorrow." Young refused to raise troops to support the Union, though he did agree to protect the telegraph line and mail routes. Utah's saints were, in general, happy to merely be observers. Yet the Civil War brought changes that would soon directly impact Utah's peculiar religion.[80]

Few people received as close a view of America's transformation as George Q. Cannon. The thirty-five-year-old had a distinctive look—round frame, high forehead, and well-manicured beard—but was better known for his mastery of words. Cannon was born in Liverpool in 1827 and migrated with his family to Nauvoo in 1842. The teenager became close to John Taylor, an uncle-in-law, after both parents died. Though part of one of the first pioneer companies, he spent very little time in Utah due to successive mission calls: first to California to evangelize gold diggers, then to the "Sandwich Islands" where he helped translate the Book of Mormon, and then once again to San Francisco, where he ran a pro-polygamy newspaper. Brigham Young was so impressed that Cannon's next assignment was to preside over the church's eastern states mission. Finally, in 1860, Cannon became an apostle, filling the slot that had been vacated by Parley Pratt's death. His first assignment was to oversee their European branches. Few Mormon men experienced such a meteoric rise as Cannon prior to 1860, and none could claim as large an influence in the decades after.[81]

Cannon's rise in reputation was such that, when Utah legislators petitioned for statehood in 1862, they chose the young apostle as a presumptive senator. The "unexpected news literally took my breath away," Cannon confessed in his diary, forcing him to cling "to the desk for support." He boarded a ship from Liverpool to New York City and then a train to Washington. Though not technically an elected official—his appointment was mostly symbolic, as Mormons hoped Congress would ratify their petition—Cannon spent the next congressional session lobbying politicians. The lofty, and unrealistic, goal was to finally achieve statehood; the more pressing agenda, however, was to stave off anti-polygamy legislation.[82]

Now shed of southern Democrats, northern Republicans in 1862 implemented policies for robust federal oversight that they had trumpeted since 1854. They argued that three things, beyond the abolition of slavery, were necessary to spread liberty across all federal territory: a homestead act, a railroad, and the destruction of polygamy. Leading the charge was Vermont representative Justin Morrill, a tall and slender entrepreneur who had been targeting polygamy for years. Riding this new Republican wave of robust federalism, he recycled his previously defeated anti-bigamy bill for a vote, and it appeared destined to pass.[83]

Cannon, the apostle-delegate, pushed forward regardless. He suffered through "oppressively sultry" heat as he met a series of representatives, senators, and newspapermen. He even met with Lincoln, whom he described as "awkwardly built" with a frame that was "heightened by his want of flesh." The president, while "quite humorous," did not offer much support. Nor did most of the other powerful figures with whom Cannon held "agreeable" chats. Massachusetts senator Charles Sumner, for instance, insisted he could not support Utah's "theo-republican" structure. When Cannon felt he had convinced another senator that Utah's proposed constitution was sound, the cornered politician could only respond that "as far as the text went it was, but and but and but"—he could not explain why, but his answer was still no. Dozens of private meetings and meals resulted in similar outcomes. After one especially rancorous meeting, Cannon described Senator Garrett Davis as "the most contemptible, ill-natured little wasp."[84]

Cannon's mission would have failed at any point during the era, but it was especially doomed during this historic congressional session. The same summer that he was in the nation's capital, May to July 1862, was a period in which American federalism was fundamentally transformed. Lincoln and the Republicans fulfilled their promises to secure enough federal power to add order to colonial expansion, exert territorial control, and regulate societal morality. On May 20, Lincoln signed the Homestead Act, which lowered the barriers for White settlers. A month later, another bill forever outlawed slavery in any federal territory. On July 1, Lincoln approved an act to fund the Pacific Railroad. And finally, a week later, on July 8, the president signed the Morrill Anti-Bigamy Act, which criminalized polygamy in all territories. These acts set the stage for that September when, in the culmination of the Republican Party's quest for an activist government, Lincoln announced his intent to sign the Emancipation Proclamation. These bills strengthened congressional power once and for all, only five years after the Supreme Court's 1857 Dred Scott ruling had seemingly neutered it by declaring Congress's limited authority.[85]

The specifics of the Morrill bill appeared to make its threat substantial: those convicted of bigamy could be jailed up to five years and fined $500; the church's territorial incorporation was annulled; and no religious organization could own more than $50,000 in real estate, a measure clearly aimed at the Mormons. Brigham Young fumed. It was heresy "to dictate the Almighty in his revelations," he bellowed. Young was also upset when the government established a new military fort in the foothills overlooking Salt Lake City, which they named after Senator Stephen Douglas, who had been the faith's friend before becoming a foe by preaching that it was "the duty of Congress to apply the knife and cut out th[e] loathsome, disgusting ulcer" of Mormonism.[86]

Yet the legislation proved feckless. As long as probate courts were controlled by elected officials, no Mormon would be indicted for practicing what they deemed to be a higher law. In blatant disregard for the new bill, Young married the twenty-four-year-old Amelia Folsom. Folsom, thirty-seven years Young's junior, was the prophet's first plural wife in seven years. Federal judges expectedly threw a fit and pressed to prosecute Young. But Lincoln, realizing energy was better spent elsewhere, removed the animated officials rather than confront the Lion. Deseret headquarters made it clear to Lincoln that if he "let [Young] alone, [Young] would let them alone."[87]

George Cannon felt deflated after watching his efforts in Washington fail. He took comfort in surmising that the church would outlast the country, as it appeared North and South were forever intertwined in war. America seemed "determined to re-enact" bloody scenes from the Book of Mormon. Satisfied that he, at least, was enlisted in a worthy cause, Cannon set sail to Europe to save souls.[88]

THE WAR'S violence soon reached the West. If the government was not yet determined to confront the Mormons, it was equipped to suppress those rumored to have conspired with them: Indigenous nations. Lincoln's administration used the Civil War as justification to eradicate Native peoples who were deemed troublesome to the Union's cause due to a perceived lack of allegiance. The same congressional session that passed the Republican Party's sweeping reforms also granted Lincoln the power to terminate treaties with rebellious tribes. Reservations became the most common solution. In late summer 1862, troops waged war against the Santee Sioux in Dakota Territory, resulting in hundreds of casualties and forced relocation. The army then turned its attention to those in the Mountain West.[89]

The Shoshone, who had labored to remain on good terms with the Mormons, bore the brunt of the violence. Colonel Patrick Edward Connor led a group of California Volunteers to northern Utah after reports that the Shoshone were raiding nearby settlers, migrants, and miners. The Shoshone, however, were merely trying to survive on depleted rations. The soldiers eventually massacred around 250 men, women, and children at Bear River, just north of the Utah-Idaho border, in January 1863. It was one of the bloodiest episodes of imperialism during the era. For his efforts, Connor was promoted to major general. He proceeded to attack more Native nations across the West.[90]

The massacre was a turning point for the region's Indigenous pol-

Photograph of Daniel D. McArthur baptizing Shivwits Indians in a stream near St. George, Utah, 1875. Nearly two hundred members of the Shivwits (sometimes *Shebit*) tribe, part of the Southern Paiute, were baptized by Mormon elders on March 20, 1875, one of several mass baptisms of Native communities during the territorial period. Mormons saw these conversions as evidence of their gospel's reach, while at least part of the Indigenous calculus was forming alliances needed for survival during an era of colonialism.

itics. Chief Sagwitch and many of the Shoshone survivors, having lost their foothold, were baptized into the LDS church. But while the saints welcomed their conversions, they also embraced America's imperial spirit. Mormons only tepidly approved of the Bear River Massacre in early 1863 but enthusiastically supported the congressional act of 1864 that forced the Timpanogos to forfeit their lands and move to the Uintah Reservation. Utah's White settlers participated in the series of violent clashes known as the Black Hawk War, to subjugate Ute, Paiute, Navajo, and Apache tribes for the next decade, though the extent of violence and land loss varied with each tribe. While they initially sympathized with the "Lamanite" descendants, Mormons had now fully appropriated the American quest for suppression and removal. Embracing colonization opened land for more White settlement, facilitated conversion, and reduced conflict. Mormons were agents of White colonization.[91]

JUST TWO months after the Civil War's conclusion, a large number of saints gathered in Wellsville, a small town about seventy-five miles north of Salt Lake City, in early May 1865. Hundreds came to hear from their prophet in the midst of a nation reeling from the devastation of battle. The prophet, however, was ready to wage another civil war, this one religious.

Young's anger was particularly piqued during the sermon. He had discovered a copy of Lucy Mack Smith's memoir at a local church leader's home the night before, a text he had denounced when it was first released in 1853 for alleged factual errors. Why was anyone still reading this "tissue of falsehoods," he demanded, when he had counseled otherwise? Young required that all members submit their copies to church leaders for destruction. The venom of his denunciation exceeded previous instances and reflected recent developments: Young's Mormonism was under threat from that of the faith's founding family.[92]

The schismatic movement led by James Strang that challenged Young in the 1840s quickly collapsed in the 1850s. Strang led hundreds of his followers to settle on Beaver Island, in Lake Michigan, in 1848, but many soon dissented due to his quixotic teachings and actions. While he initially denounced polygamy, Strang secretly preached the practice after 1849 and eventually married five women. (One of them, the nineteen-year-old Elvira Field, accompanied him on his speaking tours dressed as a man named "Charlie Douglas.") Strang was even crowned "king" of the new world order in 1850. But like his predecessor, he ended up assassinated, due to internal division and external opposition, in 1856.[93]

Strangism's remnants joined other saints who rejected Brigham

Young and formally called for a reorganization of pure Mormonism. They eventually convinced Joseph Smith III, Joseph and Emma's oldest son, to succeed his father's prophetic position. With his mother's support, the twenty-seven-year-old formally joined the "New Organization" in 1860. They denounced Utah Mormonism, especially its practice of polygamy, as a corruption, and denied that Joseph Smith had ever condoned the practice. Deemed more "pragmatic" than his father, and far more moderate than Young, Joseph III gathered hundreds of believers across the Midwest. It was a Mormonism stripped of its more radical teachings and therefore less of a threat to society. They sent missionaries to Utah in 1863 to preach to those who were sick of Young's theocratic and polygamous practices.[94]

LDS leaders were outraged. Young dismissed the missionaries as "apostates" and blamed the entire ordeal on Emma. "More hell was never wrapped up in any human being than [her]," he groused. George Cannon blasted the "New Organization" missionaries he encountered in England as wolves in sheep's clothing. The movement was a "crew of false, traitorous and malignant apostates." The feud was personal for Joseph F. Smith, Hyrum Smith's son who, after successful missions to Hawaii and Britain, was gaining leadership responsibility. Joseph F. believed his cousin, Joseph Smith III, was lying about their fathers. He canvassed Utah settlements and encouraged women who had been sealed to the founding prophet to produce affidavits and notarized statements asserting the veracity of their plural marriages. Eliza Snow signed hers as "Eliza R. Snow Smith." As if to counter the New Organization's Smith-centric claims, Young called Joseph F. as an apostle in 1866. The entire Smith family was rent asunder, with two Joseph Smiths competing over the legacy of a third.[95]

In a nation known for denominational schisms, the chasm between these two movements only grew over the years. More waves of New Organization missionaries came through Utah, including Joseph Smith III and several of his brothers. By 1870 they claimed several hundred converts in Brigham Young's own territory, and thousands across the nation. The latest Smith prophet eventually moved their headquarters to Independence, Missouri, where the first

Smith prophet had designated Zion. They added *Reorganized* to their name to distance themselves from their heretical cousins.[96]

Not all was a triumph. David Hyrum Smith, Joseph and Emma's last son, who was born five months after his father's death, was a poet, singer, painter, and devoted RLDS minister. But the charismatic missionary suffered a breakdown in 1870 while preaching the gospel. Some suspected he could not reconcile the conflicting stories concerning his family. He spent his final three decades in an asylum. Theological competition, ecclesiastical schism, incompatible histories—it was enough to drive one mad.[97]

THE RAILROAD was supposed to be America's greatest modernizer. The transportation revolution would better connect America's vast empire, moving goods and people into a new world. Indeed, Henry David Thoreau worried it brought too much change, too quickly. "We do not ride on the railroad," he mused in *Walden*, but "it rides upon us." Most eschewed Thoreau's pessimism: the railroad was a symbol of the future and would rapidly spread civilization. Its only victims were those who refused to assimilate—outcasts like the Mormons. "The first shovelful of dirt" turned over for the railroad in Utah, prophesied one journalist, "will be the commencement of the grave of [Brigham Young's] religion and authority." The railroad would bring the religious, ideological, political, and economic threats required to spell Mormonism's death.[98]

Brigham Young rejected such theories. He had supported a transcontinental line as early as 1852 and purchased $5,000 in Union Pacific stock once it became available in 1862, an acquisition large enough for a ceremonial spot on its board of directors. As the railroad's construction approached, Young publicly urged those constructing it to "hasten the work! We want to hear the iron horse puffing through this valley." George Cannon proclaimed that while many expected that the "flood of so-called 'civilization'" would imminently obliterate "every vestige of us," he expected it to do wonders for the faith.[99]

Beneath their expressions of certainty was an anxiety that

increased gentile migration and commerce could weaken Mormon cohesion. Young organized a small group of priesthood leaders, called the School of the Prophets, to orchestrate a united response. They tried, and largely failed, to resurrect a communal economic order. At the very least, they hoped to minimize reliance on non-Mormon merchants. Cannon instructed members that they should prioritize business "with our own brethren." They incorporated a sprawling conglomerate, Zion's Co-operative Mercantile Institution (ZCMI). In the religion sphere, leaders either created new or buttressed existing institutions for Sunday school instruction, youth participation, and ward services. Cannon became editor of the church's newspaper, the *Deseret News*, and transformed it into a daily organ that could withstand competition. All this to build a wall against the anticipated cultural invasion.[100]

The most formidable institution that gained new life during these years was the Relief Society. Though the local Indian Relief Societies had dissolved a decade before, Young hoped that reviving them would provide another tool for remaining self-sufficient. He instructed bishops to let the "many talented woman" organize societies at the ward level. "The sisters will be the mainspring of the movement," he promised. Women cultivated their own silk, sewed their own clothes, and designed their own hats. Eliza Snow recognized an opportunity when she saw one. "The time had come for the Sisters to act in a wider sphere than they had previously done," she proclaimed. Mormon women were nothing if not determined to fill a role when offered.[101]

Like Emma Smith before, Snow took advantage of the circumstances to create a program much larger than initially envisioned. She believed she was fulfilling prophecy dating back to Nauvoo. Carrying the original minute book she had carefully maintained in the intervening decades, Snow traveled the territory to teach women a detailed blueprint. "These Societies were after the pattern of Heavenly things," she claimed. Unlike Emma, however, Snow took pains to avoid threatening male authority. The local Relief Society presidents "should be subject to the Bishop," she warned, and never overstep priesthood boundaries. Their primary objective was to *"relieve the Brethren"* of requested obligations. Snow was always skilled at, as she once put it, "conform[ing] to circumstances."[102]

Young's desire for women to help control the region's economic marketplace granted them a degree of influence that had previously been denied. Sarah Kimball, in whose Nauvoo home the Relief Society was first conceived, became president of the Fifteenth Ward Society in 1867. She immediately went to work raising funds for a Relief Society Hall that housed a cooperative store on the first floor and a gathering place on the second, just like Nauvoo's Red Brick Store. There would eventually be over 140 similar structures throughout the territory. Kimball declared that traditional gender spheres did not supply space "sufficiently extensive" for women to exercise their "God-given powers and faculties." Emmeline Wells served as the assistant secretary in the Thirteenth Ward Relief Society. Her

Fifteenth Ward Relief Society Hall. This was one of many Relief Society halls constructed after the society's renewal in 1867. Most were patterned after Nauvoo's Red Brick Store, with a store on the first floor and meeting space on the second. The mixed purposes matched the society's aims during the era.

efforts proved impressive enough that she was later assigned to assist Snow in overseeing broader operations. These were just the first steps in her leadership climb.[103]

Backed by these multiplying societies, Young was finally ready to welcome the railroad and all it brought. While several non-Mormon businessmen hoped that the transcontinental hub would be built in Corinne, a mostly vacant community physically distant from Mormon settlements, saints maneuvered to keep it closer to their control. Young purchased over a hundred acres of land, which included several developed buildings, in Ogden, a city only forty miles north of Salt Lake. He then offered to donate it all, along with Mormon labor and a privately funded connection to Salt Lake City, if the government made Ogden the railroad's nerve center. Congress agreed, much to the chagrin of Corinne's backers. Mormonism was to be the victor, not the victim, of the galloping iron horse. The Central Pacific and Union Pacific lines finally met at Promontory, Utah, at a grand celebration on May 10, 1869, once and for all connecting America's continental union.[104]

Young did not attend the festivities at Promontory Summit, but he participated in a groundbreaking for the Utah Central Railroad in Ogden a week later. The company, presided over by Young, immediately set to work constructing a rail link to Salt Lake City, which was completed by January 1870. Young drove the final spike with a ceremonial mallet that featured the faith's slogan, "Holiness to the Lord." The mixing of sacred and secular marked the quixotic place that Utah now held in America's expanding empire.[105]

FEW PEOPLE looked forward to the coming railroad as much as Phebe Woodbury. She hoped it would finally connect her to the children she had not seen in decades, and she begged them to "come and see me when the pacific rail road is completed." Woodbury warned that they would hardly recognize her: while her hair had not grayed, her face was now "rincled" and she had only one remaining tooth. But she assured them that she was as "young in spirit as ever," as the gospel provided all the energy she otherwise lacked.[106]

That her children never visited did not deter Woodbury. The last letter she wrote, only six months before her death in 1868, regarded a historic meeting that took place in October 1867. "We have had the greatest conference here that was ever known," she reported, as members traveled "over two hundred miles to attend it and see our new tabernacle." The Salt Lake Tabernacle, which took three years to build, featured a domed roof that stretched 250 feet and sat seven thousand people. It was regarded as an engineering marvel: there were no interior pillars that obstructed audience views. Woodbury called it "one of the great wonders of the world." The structure, especially its famed organ, immediately became a prominent symbol for the community.[107]

It was not just the building that gave Woodbury pride. She was more grateful to hear "from the mouths of prophets and wise men the words of eternal life and salvation." Her sixteen years in Deseret were certainly filled with anxiety, especially as the boundaries and priorities of the United States shifted in fundamental ways. She still feared as late as 1867 that "Uncle Sam" would send "several thousand more troops" to "wipe out the Mormons." But her faith remained undaunted, and her trust in Brigham Young was absolute. The dispute between America and the religion it had birthed seemed only to be growing. Woodbury, along with tens of thousands of others, knew on which side they stood. Though she did not live to see it, her coreligionists were ready for the next war to come.[108]

4

The Boundaries of Citizenship, 1870–90

We are not only members of the Church of Jesus Christ of Latter-day Saints, but we are citizens of the republic. The Lord in His revelations to us impresses us with this fact, and it is our duty to uphold the government and to do all in our power to be loyal to it and to observe its laws, except of course when any of its laws conflict with the laws of God. In the latter event our duty to our God is paramount, and rather than violate the law of God we become martyrs under the law of the land.

—GEORGE Q. CANNON, 1887[1]

MORMON WOMEN ENTERED the year 1870 ready for battle. Ever since the 1862 Morrill Anti-Bigamy Act proved ineffectual at stopping polygamy, congressmen had tried to pass bills that would abolish what they saw as a barbarous practice once and for all. The most recent attempt was spearheaded by Illinois Republican Shelby Cullom and would bar polygamists from being "admitted to citizenship of the United States," voting in any election, or holding public office. Utah's antagonists hoped the Mormon question might finally be settled and that thousands of Mormon women could be "saved."[2]

Utah's women did not see the government as their savior. At a meeting held in the Salt Lake City Fifteenth Ward's Relief Society Hall, Eliza R. Snow declared that "the Ladies of Utah had too long remained silent while they were being so falsely represented to the world." It was time to make their voices heard. Snow, now in her sixties, had become the faith's most prominent spokeswoman. One journalist described her as possessing "a quiet, refined manner" as well as "a very precise and deliberate mode of speech." Sarah Kimball, another longtime Relief Society leader, urged sisters to remember how their ancestors "suffered and bled for the principals of civil and religious liberty." These saintly women would be "unworthy of the names we bear" if they bowed to tyranny. All they desired was to practice their religious freedom. The women planned a "mass indignation meeting" to take place the following week.[3]

The resulting gathering was a public spectacle. Some six thousand Mormon women filled Salt Lake City's "old" tabernacle, an adobe structure next door to its domed replacement. Reporters were the only men allowed in the building. The women proclaimed their sincere belief in polygamy as a salvific practice, denounced the proposed Cullom bill, and, perhaps most radically, called for woman suffrage. "Our enemies pretend that in Utah, woman is held in a state of vassalage," Snow said. "What nonsense!" Recalling her grandfather's Revolutionary War service, she denounced congressmen who "tear the Constitution to shreds" and were "sapping the foundation of American freedom." At least fifty-eight similar meetings, with some 25,000 participants, were held throughout Utah over the next two months.[4]

Whether they knew it or not, Snow and her sister saints were participating in a nationwide debate over the parameters and privileges of citizenship. The Civil War reaffirmed the Union's perpetuity, and westward expansion had largely settled its geographic borders, but crucial questions concerning how to govern its inhabitants remained. A congressional investigation to determine the precise meaning of *citizen* in 1866 concluded that while the word was found ten times in the Constitution, "no definition of it is given anywhere." Debates over the ensuing twenty-five years tried to solve that problem.[5]

The result was more restrictive for some than for others. The federal government further constrained the rights and lands of Indigenous persons, reversed legal advances attained by African Americans, forbade Chinese immigration, and did not extend suffrage to women. The grand promises that seemed to be associated with America's Civil

War victory gave way to a backlash that prioritized White supremacy and hierarchical authority over equality.

America's quest to settle these questions was the project of Reconstruction. The two dominant political parties, Democrats and Republicans, battled over how to govern America's sprawling and evolving empire. They accused each other of corruption and disloyalty, and changing circumstances often bred unexpected results and realignments. Mormons were just one of many groups attempting to navigate tempestuous political waters.[6]

George Q. Cannon both watched and participated in these debates. Derisively described as "stout of flesh, low of stature, rubicund of countenance, and ready of tongue," Cannon became Mormonism's most prominent ambassador after being elected territorial delegate in 1872. He was a close advisor to Brigham Young and, after Young's death in 1877, the second-in-command to Young's successor, John Taylor. Besides the prophets, no man received as much love from the saints or hatred from their opponents. Young told Cannon that "next to himself [Young], I was the most hated of any of the authorities." One observer named him the "Mormon Richelieu," a reference to the Catholic cardinal who exercised consolidated power in seventeenth-century France.[7]

Snow, Cannon, and thousands of saints hoped to find space within the American polity that would grant them full rights as citizens. Instead, they witnessed the nation's political, social, and legal boundaries being drawn to exclude them. Even their dominance over the Utah Territory evaporated. In 1870, 98 percent of Utah's 86,750 residents identified as Mormon; two decades later, that figure dropped to 56 percent of 210,779. Their isolationist empire evaporated as the transcontinental railroad brought "gentiles" by the thousands.

Among all the points of conflict, it was polygamy, which Mormons deemed a central religious principle, and theocracy, which Mormons deemed necessary for order, that drew the most ire. The contest over whether America's imperial power could extinguish the practices, or whether the saints could ever give them up, became the most dramatic episode in America's debates over religious liberty.

* * *

THE CARRION CROW IN THE EAGLE'S NEST.

"The Carrion Crow in the Eagle's Nest." After two decades in Utah, Mormons were increasingly seen as a deadly threat akin to a carrion crow lurking in an eagle's nest.

HUNDREDS OF Salt Lake City residents filed through City Hall to vote on February 14, 1870, among them Seraph Young. The twenty-three-year-old grandniece of Brigham Young came early before her job teaching primary school at the University of Deseret. She walked by gawking journalists as well as a brass band that celebrated the occasion. Her vote, one of around twenty-five by women that day, was the first cast because of a woman-suffrage law in American history.[8]

When the Fifteenth Amendment was ratified in 1870, it granted all male citizens, regardless of race, the right to vote. Many woman suffragists who had labored with abolitionists, however, felt betrayed that it failed to extend that same right to women. They continued a push for woman suffrage that dated back decades to the inaugural women's rights convention held in Seneca Falls, New York. Western territories were especially eager to offer new voting experiments, as some politicians envisioned it, to attract new settlers, and Wyoming was first to pass a bill granting woman suffrage in December 1869. Others wondered if the experiment could be used to solve a more pressing problem. Politicians had assumed that Mormon women, if they were given the opportunity, would overthrow their patriarchs. A handful of agitators proposed to give it a try. "Perhaps [Utah woman suffrage] would result in casting out polygamy and Mormonism in general," the *New York Times* opined.[9]

Mormon women were happy to embark on the test. At the January 1870 indignation meeting where they denounced the Cullom bill, they also called for "the right of the Franchise." George Q. Cannon heartily supported the measure, arguing there was "no place where the experiment can be so safely tried as in this Territory." The Utah legislature listened and voted unanimously to grant all White women suffrage in early February. Wyoming had passed such a bill three months earlier, but Utah's municipal elections came first, so Mormon women were the first to vote. "Utah is a land of marvels," observed one newspaper. "She gives us, first, polygamy, which seems to be an outrage against 'woman's rights,' and then offers the nation a 'Female Suffrage Bill.'" The juxtaposition was jarring. "Was there ever a greater anomaly known in the history of society?"[10]

Suffragists did not quite know how to react. Two leaders, Susan B. Anthony and Elizabeth Cady Stanton, visited Utah in the summer of 1871. Though they had been invited by a group of dissenters to speak in the anti-Mormon Liberal Institute, they accepted a request to address the saints in the tabernacle. Stanton admitted being impressed, even if she still denounced polygamy. "I would rather be a woman among Mormons with the ballot in my hands," she proclaimed, "than among Gentiles without the ballot." The two suffragists would maintain a strong, if often complicated, relationship with Mormon women, whom they simultaneously praised and pitied.[11]

Few struck as contradictory a chord as Eliza R. Snow, who led the sprawling Relief Society program. While an advocate for suffrage, Snow retained a trenchant belief that true freedom could be achieved only through patriarchal order. She distrusted those "who are strenuously and unflinchingly advocating 'woman's rights'" based on worldly ideas, and abhorred the "war of sexes which the woman's rights movement would inevitably inaugurate." Snow believed that women's subservience was the result of Eve's disobedience, a sin against patriarchal rule. Women deserved the vote, yes, but only to reaffirm religious unity. She insisted that male authority, not to mention polygamy, was paramount.[12]

Some Mormon women were more open to reformers, however. Emmeline Wells, whose marriage to prominent leader Daniel Wells had elevated her into elite society, was animated by Stanton and Anthony's lectures. "Woman" should strive "to attain to an equality with man and to train herself," she argued, "to fill any position and place of trust and honor as to appropriately and with as much dignity as her brother." Wells also drew ideas from agitators like Margaret Fuller in defending self-dependency. A woman should not become subservient to her husband, but rather maintain "rights and privileges peculiarly her own." Such a message seemed especially important given that her plural marriage featured a husband who was often emotionally and physically distant.[13]

Wells soon discovered a new vehicle for experimentation and advocacy. Louisa Lula Greene received support from her great-uncle, Brigham Young, to start a newspaper for Mormon women in

1872, the *Woman's Exponent*, dedicated to both agitating for rights and defending the church. Wells spent any spare hour at the newspaper's offices, activities she acknowledged appeared "out-of place" for a woman but necessary for the higher cause. She pseudonymously wrote forty-three editorials arguing for women to play a larger public role and for husbands to involve their wives in financial decisions. Wells took pride in her work and was thrilled when her husband bragged to Cannon "of my being a journalist."[14]

Other Mormon women lacked Wells's optimism. Fanny Stenhouse, an English convert who migrated to Utah with her husband in the late 1850s, found liberty outside the faith. She was horrified when confronted with polygamy and struggled for over a decade

Emmeline B. Wells, 1879. This photograph was taken two years after Wells, appropriately posed as if writing, became editor of *Woman's Exponent* and one of the most prominent voices in the faith.

to change her feelings and welcome a second wife. However, her husband's courtship of a third wife prompted investigation into its origins. Stenhouse concluded that Joseph Smith's revelation on polygamy was nothing more than a "strained effort" to "justify, under the sanction of a commandment, the leadings of his own passions." Such an abhorrent principle could not be "of God," as "from beginning to end, it is man, and weak man only." She and her husband left the church, and her 1872 exposé, *A Lady's Life among the Mormons*, which included Smith's revelation as an appendix, became one of the most popular anti-Mormon tracts of the era. For Stenhouse, a woman could achieve equality only once freed from the patriarchy.[15]

The tensions between the activisms of Snow, who prioritized patriarchal authority, Wells, who was open to external reforms, and Stenhouse, who rejected Mormonism entirely, were never fully reconciled. Indeed, these competing impulses remained at the heart of Mormonism's unique varieties of feminism ever since. Stenhouse's spotlight ebbed by the end of the decade, but Wells's influence and reputation grew, especially after she took charge of the *Exponent* in 1877. She remained its sole editor and publisher for thirty-seven years. Her masthead proclaimed, "The Rights of the Women of Zion, and the Rights of the Women of All Nations." In that role, she corresponded with suffragists throughout the nation even as she offered unapologetic defenses for polygamy.[16]

The conflict over Mormonism's domestic rights was only beginning.

AMONG THOSE who doubted Mormons sincerely believed in equal rights, none were as vociferous as the journalists of the recently established *Salt Lake Tribune*. They argued that extending suffrage only empowered "the female dupes of the priesthood." The *Tribune* had been founded by a cadre of dissenters who followed businessman William Godbe in denouncing Brigham Young as tyrannical. Mormons had made the "fatal error," they argued, of believing "that God Almighty intended the priesthood to do our thinking." They called for more liberality in thought and commerce. Fanny Stenhouse and her husband, Thomas, were among those who joined what became known as the Godbeites. While Young excommunicated those within the movement, their success at attracting a national audience demonstrated his weakening grip over the region. The *Tribune's* creation in 1870 inaugurated a long-lasting hub for local opposition.[17]

This animosity was matched by a renewed national focus on the "Mormon question." Republican Ulysses Grant's presidential election in 1868 commenced Reconstruction governance, which increased federal power in order to ensure African American rights in the South and White dominance in the West. With polygamy paired with slavery in the party's pre–Civil War platform, plural marriage stood out after the war as the remaining "twin relic." Enforcing the 1862 Morrill Anti-Polygamy Act would require weakening local control and strengthening federal oversight. President Grant sent Vice President Schuyler Colfax to Utah in 1869 to gather information. Colfax declared that "no assumed revelation justifies any one trampling on the law." The brief era of benign neglect was over.[18]

Saints immediately felt federal pressure. William Nebeker, a tall man with a full beard who had recently returned from presiding over the Swiss mission, confessed that "the feeling that government contemplates molesting" was "increasing in the minds of the faithful saints." All they could do was "ask the Lord to give us the integrity and strength to cleave to the truth under any and all circumstances." Nebeker condemned the "Godbeite" dissenters for aiding federal animosity in a vain attempt to achieve "the praise of the world."[19]

But local heretics were not as dangerous as national politicians. The church's *Deseret News* denounced new proposed legislation, like the Cullom bill, as gross violations of their liberties. "The slavery from which the blacks of the South have been emancipated," the paper bellowed, "would be delightful compared with the crushing bondage which this Bill would bring." Grant's choice for the territory's chief justice, James McKean, proved especially zealous. He charged Young with "lascivious cohabitation" in October 1871, forcing the prophet to spend the rest of the year in hiding. Young surrendered only when promised mere house arrest as punishment. Cannon denounced McKean as the "most unrelenting, persevering and active enemy" the faith had ever faced. Many others would follow.[20]

After his experience as a criminal defendant, Young concluded that a more robust political defense would be required. The formation of an anti-Mormon party, the Liberal Party, prompted the saints to create their own: the People's Party, a name that preceded the nation-wide populist swell two decades later. Their platform prioritized the church's interests. George Cannon was chosen as their first candidate for territorial delegate in 1872. With the church's endorsement, the apostle, who was soon added to the church's First Presidency, received 20,969 votes to his opponent's 1,942.

Cannon spent the next decade splitting his time between Utah and Washington and gaining national prominence. The polyga-mous yet refined and articulate delegate fascinated journalists. The *Washington Post* described him as "a benevolent-looking gentleman," though suspected that his "earthly tabernacle gives but little outward token of the blackness of the soul within." When asked how many wives he had, Cannon merely responded, "enough to keep me from meddling with the wives and daughters of other men," a reference to Washington's salacious reputation. His wit and congeniality won him admiration even among his rivals.[21]

The dynamic political scene required Cannon to adapt quickly. Grant visited Congress in February 1873 to officially make clear his wish for Republicans to pursue a united front against the polygamists. Therefore, when the GOP challenged Cannon's qualification to serve in public office, the delegate decided to align with the Democrats. He courted southern congressmen, presented himself as an "unostenta-tious but cultivated Virginia farmer," and supported Democratic oppo-sition to Reconstruction policies. Young even sent Cannon $3,000 to bribe anyone teetering on the fence. Cannon recorded the more scan-dalous instructions in his diary in Hawaiian, a language he had learned as a missionary decades earlier. These efforts, along with general Dem-ocratic resistance to federal power, brought immediate, if tepid, results: Democratic support allowed him to retain his seat, and the surprising coalition avoided any major anti-polygamy legislation that year.[22]

This new political alliance could not slow the growing cultural obsession with polygamy. Indeed, nefarious Mormon characters dup-ing converts and seeking additional wives became a popular genre

Thomas Nast, "Violators of the Laws of the Land." When Utah elected apostle George Q. Cannon as territorial delegate, critics saw him as a pawn for the church. This cartoon depicts Mormons approaching Congress with their "cannon."

within American and British literature. Arthur Conan Doyle's first Sherlock Holmes novel, *A Study in Scarlet*, included evil Mormon patriarchs determined to marry young brides and stop the escape of disenchanted members. These stereotypes—typically featuring references to polygamy, blood atonement, Danites, and secretive temple rituals—

became a staple of Mormon depictions in print and on stage for another half century, the origins of a long cultural fascination with Mormons through print, theater, and eventually television and cinema.[23]

Eventually the national outcry resulted in direct action. Ann Eliza Young, who had married Brigham in 1869 when she was twenty-four and he sixty-seven, divorced the prophet in 1873. (She credited Fanny Stenhouse for instigating her "awakening.") Ann Eliza then went on a preaching circuit across America and called on politicians to take a stand. Cannon feared any collaboration between her and Congress: "When a drunkard and a whore unite," he wrote, "the product should be filthy." Vermont senator Luke Poland proposed a bill in early 1874 to strengthen anti-polygamy enforcement: civil and criminal cases would be tried in federal district courts, the territorial marshal would be replaced by a federal marshal, and polygamists would no longer be eligible for jury service. Cannon claimed the bill would destroy "all local government." On the day the House passed the Poland Act, Cannon's mind filled with violent scenes reminiscent of Carthage Jail. "Our enemies are jubilant," he mourned. Grant signed the bill later that month.[24]

The Poland Act inaugurated a new era of anti-polygamy prosecution. Armed with strengthened judicial tools, Judge McKean found Brigham Young guilty in a divorce suit brought by Ann Eliza Young. The prophet was imprisoned for one night. A prosecutor also charged Cannon with both cohabitation and polygamy in October 1874. Both cases were eventually dismissed or overturned, and McKean proved so aggressive that he was replaced as territorial judge. But problems were clearly mounting.[25]

The saints remained convinced that polygamy was a protected religious practice. Leaders concluded that it was time to prove their constitutional rights. On October 21, 1874, the same month as his arrest, Cannon invited George Reynolds to walk with him along Temple Square. Reynolds, known for his studiousness and devotion, was a thirty-two-year-old clerk to the First Presidency. Young and Cannon wished Reynolds, less famous than his superiors, to serve as a test case. Cannon arranged with the US attorney, William Carey, to charge Reynolds with polygamy. The hope was that the case would eventually be heard by the Supreme Court.

Young and Cannon almost immediately feared they had been duped. They now shifted course and instructed Reynolds to deny any polygamous involvement. His first wife was told to stay hidden and, if found, deny. However, prosecutors surprised those in court when they found and supplied Reynolds's second wife, Amelia, to testify. "The ghost of Joe Smith would scarcely have produced a more profound sensation," one observer noted when the very pregnant second wife entered the room, as Reynolds sunk in his seat "with a look of hopeless terror." The first trial resulted in an acquittal, but a second jury convicted him after a half hour's deliberation.[26]

Both sides remained convinced that they were the true patriots, that their opponents were wrong, and that their position would be vindicated.

BRIGHAM YOUNG spent the twilight of his career shuttling between church headquarters in Salt Lake City and his winter residence in St. George, a growing settlement near the territory's southwestern corner. The aged prophet, who turned seventy in 1871, faced a series of medical ailments, including bouts of rheumatism. An enlarged prostate in 1874 required assistance in draining his bladder. He learned how to administer his own catheter, which he sometimes lubricated with consecrated oil. Even the most profane activities could be sacralized. While critics continued to harpoon him as the nation's most mischievous villain—the *New York Tribune* described him as "a portly, frank, good-natured, rather thick-set man," who seemed "to enjoy life, and in no particular hurry to get to heaven"—he earned fervent devotion from the saints, who heralded him as their modern-day Moses.[27]

Young's enormous family experienced substantial changes during these years. The prophet reported a $100,000 salary and $2,000,000 in assets in the 1870 census, but that wealth was unevenly split among his wives. Many, including Eliza Snow, moved out of the Beehive and Lion houses and into their own smaller residences. The large-scale communes were riven by rivalries and ill will. Yet Snow insisted that polygamous life brought happiness. She assured one gentile visitor that "the women here felt like queens."[28]

Brigham Young, circa 1870.

America's 1873 economic panic proved especially painful in Utah. Hoping to turn the crisis into an opportunity, Young rekindled his dream for all saints to practice the Law of Consecration, Joseph Smith's audacious vision for communal living. Starting with the St. George community, Young traveled across the territory urging saints to establish United Orders. Snow and the Relief Society echoed the message. "Sisters we have much to do with Cooparetion," she urged. "It is the Ordar of Enock, and those that cannot abide it will loose their exaltation." Edward Bunker, a dedicated bishop near St. George, pushed his congregants to donate all their wealth. For him, that included "the labor of myself, two teams, and two boys," as well as "a nice crop of grain growing, said by the appraisers to be the best in the field." It was a chance to prove one's willingness to sacrifice. More than 150 United Orders were established across the region.[29]

Not all were as enthused as Bunker. Nebeker, for instance, confessed to having "a few fears on the subject." A successful farmer and investor with a growing portfolio, he recognized it would be a challenge to his finances. But he remained resolute. "If the pill is bitter but must be swallowed," he explained, "I would like to know how to pucker or square my mouth and verve up my stomach, and if necessary, shut my eyes and hold my nose." The saints' reluctance embittered the prophet. Young seethed at their lack of enthusiasm. "They almost say by their conduct that they do not want the Lord to reveal any thing unto them," he griped. Most local orders dissolved within a year. That Young never consecrated his own property signaled its impending demise. Bunker was so disgusted with his congregation that he took a group of its most dedicated to settle a new town across the Nevada border, named Bunkerville. They instituted their own strict form of consecration. But capitalism's appeal proved too robust, and Bunkerville's experiment perished a decade later.[30]

Polygamy already demanded enough sacrifice. Worried that a younger generation of men and women were reluctant to embrace the practice, leaders reaffirmed its centrality to the faith. Plural marriage was far from a "superfluity" or a "non-essential to the salvation of exaltation of mankind," taught apostle Joseph F. Smith, but the linchpin. Smith's first wife, Levira Smith, disagreed: she divorced him in 1867, a year after he was sealed to a second wife, Julina Lambson. That did not faze Smith, however, as he married Sarah Richards in 1868 and Edna Lambson in 1871.[31]

Cannon surpassed all others in his insistence on the practice. He instructed leaders to instill in their congregants polygamy's significance. He chastised one monogamous bishop for not setting a good example. "He seems to have entertained the idea" that one wife was enough to be considered "celestial marriage," Cannon recorded. But "the Lord requires practical obedience to the revelation." Indeed, Young had insisted that Cannon expand his own family even while the delegate was assuring congressmen that polygamy was winding down. "If this is heard by our enemies," Cannon recorded in his diary in Hawaiian, "they will resist me in Congress." By the 1880s, most Cannons lived south of Salt Lake City in a farming compound that featured its own schoolhouse for over forty children.[32]

Emmeline Wells, conversely, struggled with regrets and despair. She constantly fretted over the lack of attention and her loneliness. "My nervous system is impaired with the trials I have undergone in silence and alone," she mused. "What can I do to gain favor in his sight?" Her diaries featured long passages about a romance-less union. She compensated by dedicating herself to church and suffragist duties. And she continued to publicly defend the practice. Polygamy "gives women the highest opportunities for self-development," she wrote, "making them more truly cultivated in the actual realities of life, more independent in thought and mind, noble and unselfish." She may well have been trying to convince herself.[33]

Some families proved more combustible. An extreme example was William and Maria Jarman, who converted to Mormonism in Exeter, England, in 1866, prior to migrating to Zion. Maria hoped the faith would reform her drunkard husband, who had already been excommunicated by two prior churches. But upon arriving in America, she discovered that William had impregnated her young dressmaking apprentice, Emily, who traveled with them. Maria realized that he had "only embraced Mormonism" for specific benefits when he proposed that Emily join the family as a plural wife.

William proved to be no better at polygamy than he was at monogamy. He continued drinking, stole goods from his employers, and abused both wives. Maria appealed for, and was granted, a divorce in 1869. Emily did the same five years later. William's life continued to spiral. He was excommunicated after being tried for larceny, was reinstated after appealing, but then resigned and left Utah altogether, hoping to make a career on the anti-Mormon lecture circuit. He became the church's most prominent critic in England, filling pamphlets and auditoriums with salacious details. One of his most alarming accusations was that the church had killed his son, Albert, in retribution for his activism. This claim was countered when Albert arrived in England as a missionary and confronted his father himself.[34]

Most who entered plural marriage, however, found ways to cope. The institution was a sacred one that provided order and meaning. For some women in elite families, polygamy even offered chances that were rare in America at the time. Snow announced in 1873 that the Relief Society would sponsor several women to travel east and be trained in medicine. This was part of a wider effort in the church to send their best and brightest to America's top universities in order to prove their cultural competency and bring various expertise back to Utah, so long as the students refused to forfeit doctrinal fundamentals. Martha Hughes, who soon married George Cannon's brother Angus, studied at both the University of

Michigan and the Philadelphia Medical College. Romania Bunnell, plural wife first to Parley Pratt Jr. and then, after divorce, to Charles Penrose, studied at medical colleges in New York City and Philadelphia; she became the first Mormon woman to receive a doctorate in medicine. Both relied on the support of their extended families, including sister-wives. The Relief Society then helped establish Deseret Hospital, one of several medical institutions built by American women at a time when health was a focus for moral reform. Susa Young Gates, Brigham's daughter, captured the irony when she noted that polygamy enlarged "my sphere of usefulness," largely due to shared housework.[35]

Young dedicated his final years to reorganizing the church's hierarchy. He formalized the succession process within the Quorum of the Twelve in a way that demoted Orson Pratt and Orson Hyde, two apostles with whom he had clashed, in favor of leaders who had proved to be reliable allies. He standardized stake and ward structures, dividing the former into more manageable units and granting bishops more control over the latter. Relief Societies were firmly embedded within each stake. Later, building on the grassroots work of Aurelia Spencer Rogers, a new organization called Primary was established to develop programs for children, and similar organizations were created for young men and women. The church's network became more sophisticated and all-encompassing.[36]

Eliza Snow's fingerprints were found in all these initiatives. Finally, in 1880, she was appointed the Relief Society's general president, the first to hold the title since Emma Smith. She named fellow Nauvoo veterans Zina Diantha Huntington Young and Elizabeth Ann Whitney as her counselors. Their new positions came after decades of dedicated labor. When Snow and Young visited one remote community, they were hailed as presidents of "all the feminine portion of the human race."[37]

SNOW RELISHED these organizations, but her most cherished rewards came from participating in temple rituals. Brigham Young had dedicated Salt Lake City's central square for a temple when the saints arrived decades earlier—he envisioned the "almightiest big Temple that ever was, instead of a nasty little one"—but the construction took far longer than expected. The tabernacle served the function of a gathering place, but did not house the rites associated with the more sacred structure. Saints performed ordinances in smaller buildings until completing a two-story adobe Endowment House in 1855 that they called a "Temple Pro Tempore." An annex with a stone baptismal font was added the next year. Snow helped initiate thousands of women into these secret rites over the following decades. Susa Young Gates referred to "Aunt Eliza" as "the high priestess in the temporary House of the Lord." But she and everyone else looked forward to another majestic temple that matched what they had left behind in Nauvoo.[38]

The Mormons soon returned to being a temple people. The first temple to be completed in Utah was not in Salt Lake City—its grandiose design met numerous delays—but in St. George. Saints broke ground in 1871 and spent years hauling rock from quarries eighty miles away. Locals worked every tenth day on the project. Cannon first saw the nearly completed structure in fall 1876 and was astonished at its beauty. The white walls "stood out in bold relief" against the "red hills which surround the little valley." Even more important was the interior, where rooms were designed for sacred rituals. Cannon was overcome with emotion as he witnessed the "elegant" decoration. "I felt as though I trod on holy ground," he confessed.[39]

Young and members of the Quorum of the Twelve began using portions of the unfinished temple on January 1, 1877. "We are this day blessed with a privilege that but few since the days of Adam have Ever Enjoyed," exulted Wilford Woodruff, who delivered a dedicatory prayer. Young, whose health was so poor that he was carried to the pulpit while on a chair, expressed that he was "not half satisfied," nor would he be "untill the devils is whip[p]ed and driven from off the face of the Earth." To express this point, Young struck the pulpit with his cane with such force that he left a dent in the polished wood. The prophet spent the following months "laboring" to "get up a perfect form of Endowments," writing down and standardizing temple rituals.[40]

St. George Temple under construction, 1876. This was the first Latter-day Saint temple completed in Utah. The ordinances performed and refined here in 1877 provided the foundation for Mormon temple work ever since.

The resulting ordinances formed the basic structure for Latter-day Saint temple worship ever since. Much of it was drawn from the rituals Joseph Smith introduced in Nauvoo. But Young was meticulous in formalizing elements like words in the script, decorations in each room, and clothes worn by attendees. Young and Woodruff, who was placed in charge of the temple, also expanded the temple liturgy: members were now encouraged to be not only baptized for their ancestors but also endowed and sealed. The ability to perform these ordinances for the dead conjoined generations across time but also necessitated repeated and frequent temple attendance. Months later, Woodruff claimed a vision of many "eminent men," including America's founders, who pleaded for their temple work. Besides proving a stark juxtaposition of Mormons completing ordinances on behalf of deceased federal officials while simultaneously despising those who were currently alive, the episode commenced a tradition of gathering genealogical information and performing temple rituals for everyone, not just one's ancestors.[41]

Participants were thrilled to perform these ordinances. Cannon recorded the "blessed privilege" when he was endowed and sealed on behalf of his father. "There was a holy influence plainly felt," he insisted. By the end of the year, saints performed 30,000 proxy baptisms and 13,000 endowments for their deceased ancestors. These rituals provided everlasting linkages that tethered families together for all eternity. Such promises seemed grand given the tempestuous circumstances of their contemporary world. Temple work became the heart of the Mormon experience. They now redoubled efforts on the Salt Lake City Temple, and Young dedicated land for two new temples in the towns of Manti, in central Utah, and Logan, at the northern edge.[42]

Some elements practiced in St. George became a perpetual core of the temple experience, but others proved more controversial. Young's most contested teaching was that the Garden of Eden's Adam was God, a divine being who, after creating the world, had then taken human form in order to inaugurate the human race. This complicated cosmology, never widely embraced, was temporarily codified in a lecture delivered at the temple's veil, yet abandoned years later. Rumors of a temple oath that pledged vengeance against the United States were constantly featured in exposés as evidence that Mormons should never be admitted as full citizens. Plural unions were also solemnized in these temples, which meant that their records and activities were crucial to the anti-polygamy crusade.[43]

Young's sermon at the St. George Temple's dedication in April 1877 was one of his last. He lived only four more months before his appendix burst in August. Cannon spent nearly every waking minute by the dying prophet's side and witnessed his last breaths on August 29. "To describe my feelings upon the death of this man of God, whom I loved so much," Cannon noted in his journal, "is impossible." Nearly three thousand saints packed into the tabernacle for Young's funeral, upwards of two thousand more crowded outside, and more than double that watched the procession. The congregation sang one of Eliza Snow's most popular hymns, "O My Father," an elegy to divine parentage. The choice was apt: Young was the father of Mormon colonization, the patriarch for polygamy, the lion for Mormon impetuosity, the lightning rod for both devotion and scorn. He died having married fifty-six wives and siring nearly sixty children, but also claiming spiritual adoration from over one hundred thousand adopted saints across the globe. His burial in the Young family estate marked the end of one of the most consequential and polarizing American lives in the nineteenth century.[44]

The controversy over Young's image did not end with his death. Not everyone was as bereft with grief. "He is not so much mourned as one would imagine," noted Emmeline Wells, never as enamored with Young as were her Relief Society sisters. Cannon was devastated to learn that some apostles felt that Young was at times too overbearing, even tyrannical. They did not "approve" of his leadership style, Cannon recorded, which featured "so strong and stiff a hand" that "they dare[d] not exhibit their feelings to him." Lingering feelings of distrust made it impossible for the Quorum of the Twelve to sustain the next prophet for another three years.[45]

Joseph Ferdinand Keppler, "In Memoriam Brigham Young," 1877. National journalists continued to poke fun at Young's living arrangements after his death, while still noting his significance.

The man who succeeded Young was John Taylor, the English-born apostle with a long face and a tuft of gray beard below his chin. His position as senior member of the Quorum of the Twelve—in which he had served for four decades—ensured his position, but Taylor also held much in common with his immediate predecessor. Like Young, he had boasted a close relationship with Joseph Smith, and was even with the founding prophet at Carthage Jail. That he witnessed Smith's death at the hands of an angry mob, and received bullet wounds himself, ensured in him deep distrust of their foes. The battle to preserve Mormon truths was a matter of life and death. The new prophet was adamant that the church would never retreat. When Taylor finally received enough apostolic support to reconstruct the First Presidency in October 1880, he chose as his counselors his nephew Cannon, who shared Taylor's approach and vision, and Joseph F. Smith, who restored the Smith family to the faith's highest echelon.[46]

Young died before the culmination of the battle between his church's commitment to polygamy and the federal government's commitment to wiping it out. But Taylor, Cannon, and Smith, as well as those who followed them, carried on the fight into the 1880s. None could expect that everything would change within a decade.

EVEN IF Emmeline Wells was not distraught over Brigham Young's death, she soon felt betrayed by her fellow suffragists. Several reformers, headlined by prominent women like Harriet Beecher Stowe and Julia Ward Howe, organized an Anti-Polygamy Society that held large protests throughout the nation in 1878. George Cannon mused that placing women at the head of the opposition was Satan's "latest and shrewdest move." Among their petitions to Congress was for the federal government to revoke suffrage for Utah's women. "We never thought woman could rise up against woman," Wells fumed. She left for Washington in January 1879 to fend off the coming storm.[47]

The national press was amazed to witness an educated and eloquent woman defend polygamy. Aided by Susan Anthony and Elizabeth Stanton, Wells gained an audience with President Rutherford

Hayes as well as Congress. Stanton argued that if Cannon were allowed to serve as a delegate "without compromising that body," then Mormon women should also gain a "platform without making us responsible for their religious faith." Wells felt satisfied she had "said just what I had time to say," and that politicians were "strongly impressed." Even Cannon, often skeptical of women's activism, wrote John Taylor that Wells had accomplished good work.[48]

Much to Wells's chagrin, however, the work proved fruitless. The ground shifted only days before she arrived in the nation's capital. The George Reynolds case, which had been on the Supreme Court's docket since 1876, had already cast a long shadow. Cannon learned in early 1878 that "our enemies evidently are pushing this case" to settle the Mormon question once and for all. Arguments finally took place later that year. The Mormons employed George Washington Biddle, a prominent Philadelphia attorney, for their defense. Biddle argued that Mormons were merely practicing sincerely held beliefs and drew from the notorious 1857 Dred Scott decision to demonstrate how Congress lacked authority to interfere with territorial matters. Federal attorneys, in response, attacked polygamy on humanitarian grounds and argued that allowing unlawful acts in the name of religion enabled even more nefarious crimes like ritual murder.[49]

The Supreme Court's verdict, issued January 10, 1879, was one of the weightiest in the institution's history. The justices concluded that religious belief could not trump the law. Allowing Mormons to practice polygamy would "make the professed doctrines of religious belief superior to the law of the land"; in such a circumstance, "government could exist only in name." Definitively repudiating the doctrine of *Scott v. Stamford*, the court held that the federal government was both empowered and obliged to regulate the public good at all levels. And finally, because marriage was deemed a crucial ingredient for civic virtue, it was in the nation's interest to abolish polygamy. Citizens were granted freedom for religious belief but not for religious action. Though complicated over the years, this "belief-action distinction," as it came to be known, has guided First Amendment interpretation ever since.[50]

The saints were crestfallen. Cannon denounced the ruling as

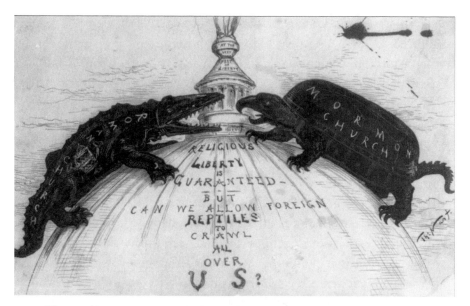

Thomas Nast, "Religious Liberty Is Guaranteed but Can We Allow Foreign Reptiles to Crawl All Over Us?" Mormons were grouped with other "unwanted" groups, like Catholics, as un-American threats.

"superficial, careless, and immature" and as proving America's promises hollow. John Taylor remained resolute in his defiance. He trumpeted that the government lacked "any right to interfere with my religious views, and in doing it they are violating their most sacred obligations." Emmeline Wells flooded the *Woman's Exponent* with poignant appeals to higher laws and cries of clemency. Wilford Woodruff spoke for many when he recorded in his diary a determination to never forfeit divine law. "I would rath[er] go to prison and to Death," he threatened. It was not an idle promise: shortly after returning from Washington, Wells learned that her husband Daniel had been arrested and imprisoned for refusing to cooperate in a polygamy trial. She proudly recorded that his bravery "will be handed down to posterity."[31]

Cannon worked swiftly to limit fallout. He met with congressmen and held a series of meetings with President Rutherford Hayes. The consensus was that if the Mormons wanted leniency, including pardons, the only course was to forfeit polygamy. If "the leading men among the Mormons would give a pledge that this practice would cease," Hayes assured, "then clemency would be extended." Yet Cannon and Taylor refused to give an inch. "My blood sometimes boils at the treatment we receive," Cannon fumed. Mormons, Cannon believed, were more often treated "like a conquered people than as citizens." He lost faith that any compromise was possible, especially after he and Taylor were arrested and convicted over a dispute concerning the sprawling Brigham Young estate. The faith's two most prominent leaders spent three weeks in jail that August 1879. "The air of liberty is sweet," Cannon reported once free. But that sweetness dissipated when Secretary of State William Evarts issued a proclamation to several European nations that October urging them to bar Mormon immigrants as "potential violators" of the Constitution.[52]

The *Reynolds* decision was a defining moment in the larger story of American federalism. It pushed the Mormon question from that of persuasion to coercion. No longer would politicians hope that Mormons would reform themselves, especially now that the Supreme

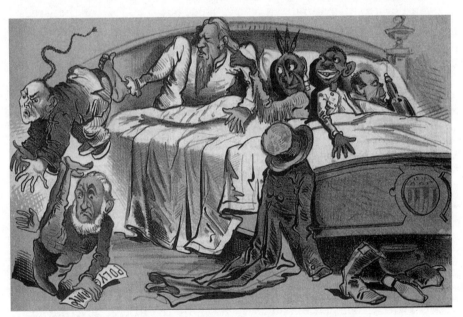

"Uncle Sam's Troublesome Bed Fellows." Many Americans grouped the Mormons with Asian Americans, African Americans, Native Americans, and Irish Americans as foreign bodies who did not fit into the nation's culture. The federal government capitalized on these fears by passing legislation to curtail the rights of all these groups during the 1880s.

Court had granted Congress authorization to legislate public goods. Even as Democrats and Republicans battled for partisan supremacy, the government increasingly evolved into an imperial power that was both willing and able to enforce moral values and restrict citizenship boundaries, both with Mormons and with other groups. Congress soon passed the Chinese Exclusion Act of 1882 as well as the Dawes Severalty Act of 1887, both of which expanded federal authority to regulate who was embraced within the national body. These debates over the rights of citizenship—the right to immigrate, the right to own land, the right to marry plurally—encapsulated America's modern, and increasingly constricting, definitions of liberty.[53]

Cannon felt the shifting tide. Politicians were "very noisy of late" and moved to revoke Cannon's delegate seat. Though he had won the 1880 election handily, defeating his non-Mormon challenger, Allen Campbell, by a vote of 18,567 to 1,357, Campbell petitioned to void the results. He claimed a host of reasons, including that Cannon had never been naturalized as a citizen, but the heart of the issue was whether a polygamist could hold office. Territorial governor Eli Murray, a Republican, supported the protest and certified Campbell as the winner. Cannon initially succeeded in retaining support in Washington, especially once Democrats were in power, but times were changing. After spending a sleepless night in December 1881, he wrote one of his wives that "prospects look more discouraging" than ever before.[54]

Cannon's political career ended in early 1882. George Edmunds, a Republican senator from Vermont, whom Cannon denounced as "one of the most, if not the most, dangerous man in the government," proposed the next anti-polygamy legislation. Acknowledging the difficulty of proving polygamous marriages, the Edmunds bill targeted "unlawful cohabitation," a much easier standard, as a crime with a sentence of up to two years in prison and a $300 fine. A board of five commissioners, chosen by the federal government, would oversee elections. This board could implement a test oath that required all potential voters and officeholders to declare that they were not in violation of the law. (This oath, which disenfranchised 12,000 saints, was soon ruled unconstitutional, but other versions were later resurrected.) It was the most substantial escalation in anti-polygamy laws yet encountered. "All hell seems to be boiling over," Cannon mourned.[55]

Among those who supported the new bill were "Reorganization" missionaries, representing the midwestern Mormon denomination, who denounced polygamy. They sent delegates to Washington to cheer on its passage. The Speaker of the House read a letter from Joseph Smith III, son of the man who originated Mormon polygamy, that praised Congress for defending "the honor and dignity of the nation," including "all true Mormons who abide in the original faith of the church." Cannon fumed. "The apostates flock like vultures to the feast," he wrote. The Edmunds bill was signed by the president on March 22, 1882.[56]

Because this new legislation barred polygamists from public office, Cannon's seat was finally vacated. "Maintain your principles," John Taylor telegraphed, in cipher; "make no compromise with apostates or corrupt men." Cannon had spent a decade in Washington witnessing the federal government evolve into an imperial power, often with his own community the target for the transition. After his final speech on the House floor, Cannon boarded a train to Utah, where he was met with large brass bands and crowds of people who cheered him as if he were a military veteran. Cannon, moved with emotion, reveled in the attention. He shook as many hands as he could. Such public spectacles, however, soon disappeared.[57]

BELIEVERS AND missionaries alike gathered for Sunday worship in rural Lewis County, Tennessee, on August 10, 1884. They were meeting at the home of recent converts James and Malinda Conder because their chapel had been burned to the ground three months earlier. The national outcry over polygamy, coupled with a slew of recent baptisms in the region, had resulted in growing animosity throughout the community. Critics were especially angry when two young women joined the faith and moved to Utah, which seemed to confirm suspicions that Mormons were brainwashing converts and gathering polygamous brides. A mob led by David Hinson, a Protestant minister living in a neighboring county, decided to settle the crisis with bullets.

The mob arrived at the Conders' home, located near Cane Creek, while most congregants were mingling outside. Two of the Conders' sons, Martin and Riley, raced inside for guns. The mob followed to search for the missionaries. Hinson struck Martin in the head while wrestling away the young man's shotgun, which he then used to shoot a Mormon elder, John Gibbs. A second missionary, William Berry, was then shot while saving a third, Henry Thompson. Martin reengaged Hinson before being shot himself. As the mob attempted to flee, Riley, the other Conder son, descended the stairs and shot Hinson. Gunmen fired back, killing Riley and seriously wounding his mother, Malinda. In total, five individuals died: the Conder siblings, two missionaries (Gibbs and Berry), and Hinson. A local newspaper proclaimed that "public opinion" justified the killings.[58]

Tasked with securing the missionaries' bodies, which hostile locals threatened to keep, was B. H. Roberts, the twenty-seven-year-old acting president of the southern states mission. Roberts had emigrated from England to Utah at age nine, and eventually outgrew a rebellious streak to become a bright student and productive missionary. But he now faced the daunting assignment of entering hostile territory filled with southerners anxious to avenge Hinson's death. Roberts disguised himself in an "old suit of clothing, a hat[,] and rough cowhide boots," and covered his face with "soot and grease." Once Roberts succeeded, the elders' corpses were returned to their families in Utah. Cane Creek Mormons, conversely, were forced to either move west or relocate to nearby counties. Cannon praised the Conder boys for "their kindness and their bravery," and denounced the "depth of wickedness" displayed by the killers. Saints throughout Utah Territory raised money for the "Tennessee Martyr's Fund."[59]

The Cane Creek Massacre was a violent manifestation of the national conflict over Mormonism. While Cannon attempted to assure journalists that most Mormon men ceased taking polygamous wives after the Edmunds bill, privately he and Taylor doubled down on the practice. Taylor dictated a revelation in October 1882 that all priesthood leaders had to practice polygamy. At least one stake presi-

B. H. Roberts in disguise, circa 1884. Once he returned to Utah after his heroic quest to retrieve the Mormon bodies, Roberts donned his disguise once again for a photograph.

dent resigned when he refused to be sealed to an additional wife. The First Presidency and apostles did not trust men who were unwilling to sacrifice reputation for God's law. Yet leaders also took precautions for safeguarding people and property. They considered reclassifying temples from "places of worship," which might be seized if the government enforced the 1862 Morrill Act, to "educational establishments," on which they would pay taxes but hopefully retain control. Taylor also ordered men to explore Mexico for potential settlement options.[60]

Leaders prepared for the inevitable deluge of court cases. Woodruff instructed his wives that if they were ever called to testify, "dont *Perjure* yourselves," but "tell nothing but the truth and as *little* of *that* as you can." The first woman placed in that impossible position was

Lydia Clawson, the second wife of Rudger Clawson. When Rudger was tried in October 1884, Cannon encouraged Lydia to hide. The jury failed to come to a verdict without her testimony. However, deputies soon located Lydia and she was charged with contempt of court. At Rudger's urging, Lydia told the truth, which resulted in her husband being found guilty. Rudger remained unrepentant at sentencing. "I very much regret that the laws of my country should come in conflict with the laws of God," he told the court; "but whenever they do, I shall invariably choose the latter." He was sentenced to four years in jail and fined $800.[61]

Thousands of other Mormons persisted, as well. Polygamy remained a central part of belief and practice. The very month that Clawson was convicted, Cannon recorded in his diary his decision, again coded in Hawaiian, to marry yet another plural wife. Caroline Partridge Young, daughter of Brigham Young and Emily Partridge, had recently left her husband and now wished to be sealed to Cannon. They were married on November 3 by Woodruff. "The two of us are very happy," he wrote, once again in Hawaiian, after their first night together. But the new relationship blossomed in a period of surveillance: Cannon feared deputy marshals were following him and that an indictment was imminent. They planted saints in the sheriff's office so that they "might have timely warning and get out of reach." Leaders began taking alternate routes to meetings during the day and switching homes at night. Every gathering seemed perilous.[62]

Circumstances quickly became dire. Cannon suggested organizing an extralegal police force to always accompany church authorities. Taylor dictated a revelation that it was a time for "setting our houses in order in all matters" in case they went into hiding. He escalated efforts to find "a city of refuge" in Mexico, especially when several Mormons in Arizona were arrested. When Woodruff's wife refused a subpoena issued for her husband's arrest, the deputy marshal threw it at her and demanded the apostle's surrender. A man "acting strangely" was seen pacing outside their house for weeks. Woodruff was therefore sent on "a short mission" to St. George to avoid detection. Once there, he asked Cannon and Taylor if "it not be wisdom to have some public arms in the Temple for its defense." Cannon slept in a series of different residences, including a barn's upper floor. Once they were informed the marshals had a "fixed intention to arrest the First Presidency," the three men—Taylor, Cannon, and Joseph F. Smith—went into hiding.[63]

Taylor delivered what would be his final public address on February 1, 1885. He declared to the gathered saints that this was only the most recent instance of the wicked oppressing the faithful. Those considered "grey-headed folks" had already endured the expulsion from Missouri, the martyrdom in Illinois, the quasi-war in Utah. God's chosen had survived them all, and they would survive again. His devotion to following divine laws was absolute. Taylor was ready to "die for the truth," as he could not "disobey my God." When relating this point, the prophet struck the podium so hard that it echoed throughout the room. All attendees responded with a loud "Amen!" A few days later, at a secret meeting held by the reconvened Council of Fifty, Cannon anointed Taylor king of God's empire, an echo of one of Joseph Smith's last actions in 1844.[64]

And then the president of a church that claimed over a hundred thousand followers disappeared. Forced to choose between following federal laws or God's commandments, Taylor became a fugitive. Mormonism would now be governed from underground.

JOHN WHITAKER was a starry-eyed twenty-two-year-old excited to start his dream job in early 1886. Raised on a farm in Centerville, just north of Salt Lake City, and recently graduated from the University of Utah, Whitaker was hired to help apostle Franklin Richards in the Church Historian's Office. Though technically devoted to preserving the faith's historical record, the two-story adobe structure across the street from Temple Square had become the church's informal headquarters. While Richards had been married nearly a dozen times, most of his wives had passed away and he was now living with only one wife, making him immune from prosecution. He therefore became the only public apostle and the funnel through which all official and unofficial activities took place. The young Whitaker was now his right-hand man.[65]

Whitaker, who sported perfectly combed hair and an impressive mustache, quickly learned how to maintain secrets. He kept a detailed, yet clandestine, record of code names as well as "the whereabouts of the brethren in hiding." This included over twenty-seven homes in which John Taylor slept over the next two years. A similar list was kept for Cannon. Joseph F. Smith, who had married two more women, Alice Kimball and Mary Schwartz, in recent years, was sent to Hawaii. Sometimes a polygamist leader showed up in the middle of the night seeking refuge. In those cases, there was a precise knock on a designated window to confirm safe passage. Hideaways were constructed in the closets in Gardo House, which neighbored Temple Square, an ornate mansion that was built for Brigham Young and now served as the Taylor family residence. Once when a deputy marshal stormed the home and searched its rooms, he came within inches of local leader Charles Penrose—code name "Doctor Williams"—who was hidden "in a specially built closet on the top floor." Whitaker predicted that "a great EPOCH, STORY, OR DRAMA" would someday be written about this period.[66]

George Cannon continued politicking despite the circumstances. He took pride in a disguise that allowed him to travel to his office without detection. Other disguises were less successful. Once, despite wearing "a blue drilling jumper and pants," coloring his beard black, and donning a "flapping Panama hat," he was still identified by colleagues. "They would know my face anywhere," he was told, "thanks to my prominent nose and eyes." Yet Cannon pressed on. He surprised General Conference attendees in October 1885 when he snuck into an evening session after everyone was already seated. "My entrance created a great sensation," he noted in his diary before slipping back into hiding that night. The former delegate also corresponded with Democratic officials, including Democratic president Grover Cleveland, drawing on party privilege. Cannon promised that only a small percentage of saints practiced polygamy, but that nearly all voted Democratic. If party officials found a way to save the Mormons, they would be repaid with loyal voters. The consistent message from Washington, however, was that they would not negotiate until polygamy was gone.[67]

Cannon was in no mood for compromise. Rather than "bending

"Wanted" poster for John Taylor and George Q. Cannon while church leaders were on the underground.

our necks too much to our enemies," he insisted they not "tamely submit to the tyranny practiced upon us." He scoffed whenever anyone, especially members, suggested giving up, or even slowing, plural marriage. "Lord, deliver us from such people who have no more faith than this," he grumbled. True saints were willing to withstand the crisis without complaint. The unfaithful could join "the apostate organization which has the unworthy son of the Prophet Joseph Smith as its leader." When Caroline, his newest wife, became pregnant, Cannon was exuberant. He began a new editorial series for *Deseret News* under the name "No Retreat."[68]

Emmeline Wells's husband, Daniel, who had escaped to England, agreed. Responding to Cleveland's admonition to "be like us," Wells smoldered: "We would rather live behind your prison doors and look at the light of the blessed sun through your iron grated windows, than abate a single hair's breadth, nor one jot or tittle, of our most holy faith in God's most perfect and holy law." Meanwhile, his wife struggled to earn a living on her own back in Utah.[69]

Cannon soon had a chance to prove his mettle. He was finally captured on his way to Mexico in February 1886. Yet when Taylor recorded a revelation that the church should forfeit the $45,000 bail rather than allow Cannon to face trial, the apostle returned to hiding. The episode animated thousands of saints who looked to Cannon as a martyr. "Few men are more thoroughly entrenched in the affections of the Latter day Saints than Bro. George Q. Cannon," wrote the farmer William Nebeker, "and therefore any hardship put on to him is likely to be a great source of trial to our people." Saints must stick to their principles, even if "God should see fit to allow the wicked to annihilate us." Many Mormons were willing to die for the cause.[70]

It was easier for Cannon, who wielded substantial means, to withstand the underground life. Scores of Mormon men with fewer resources were soon on the run as arrest warrants multiplied. More than fifteen hundred criminal cases were processed in Utah during the 1880s, over 95 percent of which were related to polygamy. It was an episode of prosecution rarely rivaled in American history. "The City of the [Latter-day] Saints," mused Martha Hughes Cannon, had become more like "the city of Desolation now-a-days." As many as fifty families fled to Mexico, though political disputes caused continued relocations. Soon families were sent to find another refuge, in Canada. Local wards, especially the Relief Societies, organized food and resources for families of men either in prison or in hiding. Cannon's wives flung themselves across the country, with several taking new names and living in other states. One local leader, who was underground for over a year, wrote his wife expressing a desire for just one more "walk in any City" with her and their children. In the meantime, "all must sacrifice." As one local leader put it, "Terror reigns in the City among the Saints."[71]

Among those who experienced the underground's difficulties was B. H. Roberts. After his daring acts in the South, Roberts became a prominent writer and orator. He also became a polygamist, having married Sarah Louisa Smith in 1878 and Celia Dibble in 1884. While working in the newspaper office he was arrested by two deputy marshals for cohabitation. The church enabled his escape the next day, and Roberts was then called on a mission to England for the next two years, leaving his wives and children to fend for themselves. Once again he donned a disguise in order to avoid detection while traveling on a train. Roberts finally returned to Utah in 1888, surrendered himself to authorities, and was sentenced to four months in jail. Yet his family remained a target. His second wife, Celia, joined a group of other polygamous wives fleeing the law in neighboring Colorado.[72]

Eventually over a thousand Mormons were indicted for unlawful cohabitation. Most served sentences of around six months and found brotherhood with their fellow inmates. Moroni Brown loved the half dozen Mormon men with whom he spent six months in jail. They held worship services, read the Book of Mormon, and wrote letters. The cadre mourned, however, when the warden forced them to shave their beards. Other prisoners kept autograph books and recorded the feelings and names of their fellow sufferers. "When you pas the prison gate / Hustle home never wate," penned one man. "Be true to those you love so dear / God is with you—never feer." Other poems were not as poignant:

> Straight and narrow is the way
> And few there be who find it
> You are on that road to day
> Press forward now I'v rhymed it

Suffering did not always engender poetic brilliance. But these martyrs were certain that it was more "honorable" to own up to their beliefs than to deny their religion by making their wives "a widow and her children Basterds."[73]

As was often the case, Mormon women performed needed diplomacy. Emmeline Wells returned to Washington in early 1886. She once again met with congressmen and gained a meeting with Rose Cleveland, President Grover Cleveland's sister and the White House's host. Wells delivered a memorial signed by thousands of Relief Society sisters pleading for clemency. But Wells was distraught that she was now stonewalled by suffragists she had previously considered friends. "Is there not work enough for women to do among their sisters in the world," she bemoaned, "without reaching away over to Utah[?]" She came home without any progress.[74]

These tense conditions made even the most basic activities difficult. While working in the Historian's Office, Whitaker fell in love with John Taylor's daughter, Ida, an educated woman in her midtwenties with wavy dark hair and a soft smile. But because Ida's father was constantly on the run, Whitaker never had a chance to ask his permission to propose. Eventually Taylor heard rumors of Whitaker's intent and concluded the young man was too cowardly to make a direct request. "There should be nothing clandestine, nor undercover" when it came to marriage, the prophet chastised. That Taylor wrote such a rebuke while underground due to his own marriages went unsaid. Whitaker eventually received Taylor's approval and married Ida in September 1886, though the president-in-hiding could not attend.[75]

Not all marital crises were as easy to solve. Whitaker noted that "it became so that one hardly knew who were and who were not married," because "the principle of polygamy had such a hold on many unsuspecting desirables." John Q. Cannon, son of George and counselor in the presiding bishopric, had married Elizabeth Ann (Annie) Wells, daughter of Emmeline. But this union, which conjoined two of Mormonism's most elite families, unraveled in scandal. John was caught having an affair with Annie's sister, Louie, in September 1886. Though Annie had encouraged her husband to marry Louie as a polygamous wife, the sealing never happened. Instead, Louie, still single, became pregnant. John was publicly excommunicated, and he and Louie became targets for marshals. The *Salt Lake Tribune* argued that polygamy, which enabled "promiscuous" fathers, made infidelity inevitable. At his father's urging, John divorced Annie so he could marry Louie, yet the pregnant Louie fled Utah's media and legal spotlight and stayed with another sister in San Francisco. The drama turned tragic when both Louie and her infant died the following spring. John then remarried Annie, who birthed nine more children.[76]

The episode devastated Emmeline Wells. "I shall never be myself again, never," she wrote. The bereaved mother blamed Cannon for prioritizing his son's reputation over her daughter's health and safety. Wells also learned of an attempt by Eliza Snow to have her removed as *Woman's Exponent* editor. "Whether [Snow] is a real friend or only one who does for her own sake," Wells mused, "I cannot determine."[77]

But Wells's star continued to rise as Snow's fell. The aged Snow's public appearances decreased in 1887 as her health deteriorated. Zion's "Poetess" had dedicated over half a century to defending her faith, exploring its doctrines, and empowering her sister-saints. "There is no Women on the face of the earth that are more respected and hon[ored] th[a]n the Latterday Saint Women," she declared in 1884, just as she had declared since 1835. She lived long enough to see the completion of the St. George and Logan temples, and knew Manti's was nigh. The temple ordinances over which she presided were at the heart of her religion. "Women who have received their Indowments," she taught, were part of a salvific mission.[78]

Snow joined the world of the dead on December 5, 1887. She requested that her funeral not be a dirge, and so the Assembly Hall was draped in white and feather roses and attendees wore bright colors. Wells wrote that Snow was buried in "her wedding dress" and looked "like a beautiful bride." Local Relief Society presidents marched in a procession overseen by priesthood leaders, a fitting tribute to Snow's lifelong fascination with woman's authority, albeit within a patriarchal framing.[79]

Snow was not the only prominent loss during 1887. John Taylor, increasingly frail, spent his final months being whisked between homes, never appearing in public. He dictated a string of revelations prophesying that polygamy would never disappear from the earth. When President Cleveland opened correspondence through back channels to avert further escalation, Taylor's answer, through Cannon, was clear: "No surrender of principle." He supported one last statehood push in 1887, a political compromise supported by Cleveland that would have returned control of prosecutions to the local level. Taylor sent delegates—and bribes—to Washington, who canvassed congressmen for support. Yet once again, no progress could be made while polygamy persisted. The obstinate prophet died while in hiding on July 25, 1887, still certain that God's commandments would eventually triumph, but unsure how. "I felt that I had lost the best friend I had on earth," Cannon recorded.[80]

Succeeding Snow and Taylor were two stalwarts whose commitment dated back to Nauvoo. Wilford Woodruff, the prolific diary keeper, took the reins of the entire church due to being senior member of the Quorum of the Twelve. Yet it took nearly two years to convince his fellow apostles, who held grudges that their voices were still not prioritized, to formally reestablish the First Presidency. Cannon felt betrayed when he learned that some "blamed" him for the Presidency constantly undervaluing the Twelve. Yet Woodruff eventually gathered requisite support to be sustained president in April 1889, the last occasion in which there was any delay between the death of one prophet and ordination of the next. He retained Taylor's counselors, Cannon and Smith, as his own.[81]

Leadership over the Relief Society fell to Zina Young, who became its next president. The zealous seeker known for spiritual gifts and a warm personality had been a plural wife to both Joseph Smith and Brigham Young. But when she left for Canada to tend to family matters in 1888, she left Emmeline Wells, the society's secretary, in charge. "Evidently my work will be more extensive in the future than it has been," Wells surmised. The assignment was another step in her growing involvement with, and eventual leadership over, the women's organization. "Responsibilities," she wrote with experience, "come thick and fast upon the women of Zion."[82]

At no point was such service as fraught as at that moment.

TERRITORIAL AND federal officials approached final victory even as saints persisted in their resistance. One territorial governor of Utah, Eli Murray, complained to Washington about the "unwarranted state of affairs." He claimed officials were "assaulted with hand grenades filled with human excrement." His successor, Caleb West, urged the federal government to cease all immigration until they could secure "a final submission and obedience to the laws." The government issued a $500 public arrest warrant for Cannon, which was $200 more than they had offered for Taylor. Meanwhile, Mormon leaders were concerned about the underground's unexpected consequences. Charles Penrose, a counselor in the Salt Lake Stake presidency, worried that "the endless subterfuges and prevarications which our present condition impose" threatened "to make our rising generation a race of deceivers." Could too stringent a commitment to one principle lead to the erosion of others?[83]

A frustrated Congress passed further legislation meant to bring finality. Senator George Edmunds worked with Congressman John Tucker to draft a bill that would dissolve all of Mormonism's remaining hopes. Among other provisions, the Edmunds-Tucker Act disincorporated the LDS church, dissolved the Perpetual Emigrating Fund, required anti-polygamy oaths for voters, jurors, and officeholders, replaced local judges with federal appointees, eliminated spousal privileges for polygamous wives, and, much to Wells's horror, revoked women's right to vote. "Woman suffrage in Utah," quipped one anti-polygamy crusader, "means only woman suffering." Wells called it "a most cruel & infamous measure" and "contrary to all sense of justice and right."[84]

The bill also reflected the era's anti-monopoly zeal. Through a series of legislative actions, Congress had become comfortable with exercising extensive federal power in governing marginalized races and combating towering corporate giants during the 1880s. Now they turned their sights on the Mormon menace. The government finally fulfilled the threat levied in the 1862 Morrill Act to confiscate any property that exceeded $50,000. The attorney general and designated receivers could bring proceedings against all LDS properties, estimated to be worth $3 million, and the revoked estates could then be sold to support public schools. Mormons appealed to the Supreme Court, but they knew their chances were slim.[85]

The government began taking control of significant sites in November 1887. That included Temple Square, which they rented back to the church for one dollar per month. John Whitaker marked the "day of gloom, and sadness" in November 1887 when he handed over keys to the Historian's Office. (But not before he and Franklin

Richards snuck away all "personal belongings" and "private records" that had been left by the "brethren who have been hiding here for months.") Whitaker himself was arrested three days later.[86]

As federal officials recognized that they approached their desired goal of full submission, they granted limited leniency to church leaders. Wilford Woodruff received informal permission to move about without fear of arrest. His appearance at the October 1887 General Conference was the first time a church president had been seen in public in over two years. Emmeline Wells reported that "the people could scarcely suppress their glad emotions." And after extensive negotiations, the government reached a compromise with George Cannon so that the faith's most prominent leader could serve a reduced sentence. As he went to jail in September 1888, Cannon claimed "a degree of pleasure that made me feel as though I was going to be married"—an ironic remark given that his imprisonment

George Q. Cannon (center) and other polygamous men while imprisoned at Utah Penitentiary, 1888.

was due to his marriages. He served five months in the Utah penitentiary among other polygamous men, who clamored for his signature
and photograph. He was finally able to live freely after his release
without the threat of further arrests.[87]

Mormon leaders, after decades of dedicated resistance, recognized
that surrender was inevitable. Woodruff proved pragmatic enough to
make compromises that his predecessors believed impossible. When
asked by a local leader for permission to solemnize a plural union in
September 1889, Woodruff responded that such marriages were "not
proper" at "the present time." The counsel shocked Cannon. "It is the
first time that anything of this kind has ever been uttered," Cannon
noted, "by one who holds the keys." He initially refused to endorse the
policy but soon understood its virtue. Cannon came to see liberty as
"so precious," both for himself and for his church, that it was wise to
avoid further conflict. As if anticipating what was coming, Woodruff
closed his 1889 diary with the prediction that "1890 will be an important year with the Latter Day Saints and the American nation."[88]

Further concessions followed. When judges and congressmen
questioned whether Mormons were eligible citizens given allegiance
to a polygamous and theocratic church, including rumors concerning
treasonous temple oaths, the First Presidency issued a direct response
in October 1889. "This Church does not claim," they declared, "to be
an independent, temporal kingdom of God, or to be an *imperium in
imperio* aiming to overthrow the United States or any other civil government." After the Supreme Court vindicated an especially restrictive test oath in Idaho, and Congress threatened to duplicate the oath
across all territories, Cannon told reporters that polygamy would die
a natural death within "a few years." The end game was clear once the
Edmunds-Tucker Act was upheld in May 1890. Refusing to give up
polygamy meant more arrests, more instability, and even the loss of
their beloved temples.[89]

Mormon leaders soon discovered a silver lining. Democrats had
been the saints' friendly, though not always consistent, allies for
decades, and Cannon collaborated with Democratic officials as late
as February 1890. But the tides were shifting. Cannon traveled to
Washington and met with a group of Republicans in June who were

pleased to hear that the Mormons were not "hopelessly Democratic," and that the saints might be willing to shift allegiances if the right opportunity arose. "If it is going to be a matter of politics," mused one Republican operative, "that changes the affair entirely." Cannon soon abandoned the Democrats, whom he denounced as "helpless," and built bridges with his former foes. "My mind leans very much to the Republican Party," he noted in July, "as being the party just now that can bring us relief." He proved the saints' worth by lobbying Mormon support for Republicans in Wyoming's elections that summer. Cannon hoped their politicking proved they could be an important bloc in the Mountain West. The only thing that stood in the way of a newfound alliance was, of course, polygamy.[90]

A final flurry of investigations in September 1890 resulted in Woodruff finally making a declaration that saints had long feared. Federal commissioners alleged that they had evidence plural marriages were still taking place in temples. Cannon viewed it as an opportunity to "officially" announce a shift that had been a year in the making. The prophet agreed. "I have arrived at the point in the history of my life as the President of the Church," wrote Woodruff in perhaps his most momentous diary entry, "where I am in the necessity of acting for the Temporal Salvation of the Church." He drafted a proclamation that dismissed the commissioners' rumors and instead claimed that no plural unions had been authorized since summer 1889. Further, he pronounced that "we are not teaching polygamy or plural marriage, nor permitting any person to enter into its practice." Cannon revised the draft, carefully recording every emendation in his journal.[91]

Woodruff gathered the First Presidency and Quorum of the Twelve the following day and shared the statement. The room was struck with "a sort of ghastly stillness." Many of their faces "became flush and then slowly pale again," and one by one they broke into tears. This was a concession that they had promised never to make. Yet it was Joseph F. Smith, nephew of the prophet who revealed the practice, who closed debate. The tall and solemn man with a fine mustache and fiery temper stood up "with a face like wax, his hands outstretched, in an intensity of passion that seemed as if it must sweep the assembly." He reaffirmed that he was prepared to fight the government tooth and nail over polygamy until death. And yet, he added, his eyes welling with tears, he had never "disobeyed" a prophet. Then, after voicing his support for the manifesto, Smith fell back into his chair, buried his face in his hands, and cried in agony. Nobody dared to oppose after that.[92]

The "manifesto," as it soon became known, was immediately released to local and national press.

NEWS OF the manifesto shocked both Utah and the world alike. It was especially difficult news for many saints who had sacrificed much for the practice. "There are some who will be very much tried over the affair," noted Emmeline Wells, whose husband had spent several years on the run. B. H. Roberts learned of the statement while traveling on a train to Salt Lake City. His earliest feelings bordered on betrayal. Given "all the saints had suffered in sustaining that doctrine," he considered the manifesto "a kind of cowardly proceeding." While Roberts eventually reconciled himself to the manifesto's necessity, the institution's about-face took many by surprise.[93]

Church leaders read the manifesto at the October General Conference to further appease government officials. John Whitaker, who had aided the brethren during the underground, recorded the tensions as thousands filled the tabernacle, overflow seating in the Assembly Hall, and the Temple Square grounds. He, like many others, worried what this meant for their decades of labor. Cannon assured the congregation that their efforts were not in vain. Just like with the failed attempt to establish Zion in Missouri, he explained, God had accepted their sacrifice.[94]

Leaders then called for a sustaining vote. The action placed congregants in an impossible dilemma. "Many of the saints seemed stunned and confused and hardly knew how to vote," observed one attendee, "feeling that if they endorsed it they would be voting against one of the most sacred and important principles of their religion." Some wept. Few dared to vocalize opposition. Others, like Roberts, who reported that his arm felt like lead, refrained from voting at all. But the motion passed. One attendee, Annie Hyde Cowley, reported that "a gloomy pall" hung over the entire tabernacle. Others tried to find hope. "To day the harts of all ware tried," Relief Society president Zina Young surmised, but they still remained "the same Latterday Saints."[95]

John W. Taylor, an apostle and son of the deceased prophet, privately despised the change. He acknowledged that the manifesto was a smart political play, but refused to believe its sincerity. Like his father, Taylor believed polygamy could never be forfeited. Nor was he alone. Only four days after the public vote, Taylor was sealed to another plural wife, Janet Woolley, in a ceremony that took place inside a carriage while riding around Salt Lake City. Francis Lyman, president of the Quorum of the Twelve, acted as officiator. The problem of polygamy continued, albeit quietly.[96]

Meanwhile, Woodruff's manifesto seemed to bring the public debate over plural marriage to a close. It also ended a national contest over religious liberty and federal control. America's Reconstruction era prompted many questions concerning the role of government, the limits of personal freedom, and the parameters of citizenship. During the underground's darkest moments, George Cannon's son, Frank, an aspiring and talented politician, wrote President Cleveland on behalf of his father, then in hiding. If the old man were to die a fugitive, the younger Cannon wrote, he would die "unreconstructed." The same could have been said about the saints at large. Their practice of polygamy, their flouting of federal laws, placed them outside America's political body. Assimilation, even when forced, "reconstructed" them as citizens, enabling them to finally achieve the rights and liberties they had long sought.[97]

Both sides, American and Mormon, continued to fight over the precise meaning of citizenship. But the question going forward was not whether the saints would have a place within America's empire, but on what grounds.

5

A Period of Progress,
1890–1920

The spirit of progress of this age [is] the work of God.
—EMMELINE B. WELLS[1]

Mormonism . . . is progressive and is destined to become the
religion of the age.

—B. H. ROBERTS[2]

IN MARCH 1897, Wilford Woodruff, who had just entered his tenth decade and suffered from a series of physical ailments, witnessed the technology of the future. He hobbled into the president's office, aided by a walking cane, and gingerly sat at his desk in front of a cutting-edge phonograph. Woodruff's voice, halting and high-pitched, was then imprinted on wax cylinders. His brief remarks, heavily emphasizing carefully chosen words, highlighted the themes of his presidency: that the LDS church was the inheritor of Joseph Smith's prophetic authority, and that "every man, woman, and child" should be allowed "the enjoyment of their religion." Here were the words of a pioneer patriarch preserved with modernity's tools.[3]

The tension at the heart of the elderly leader's recording—a firm grip on the past while embracing hope in the future—reflected a period of transition. Woodruff had broken with entrenched tradition when he publicly announced the end of polygamy, previously a cen-

Studio portrait of Wilford Woodruff, George Q. Cannon, and Joseph F. Smith, March 2, 1894. This First Presidency oversaw the church giving up polygamy and achieving Utah's statehood.

tral principle, in response to overwhelming federal pressure. Could the faith survive forfeiting a cornerstone doctrine?

Balancing the past and the future became an obsession for Woodruff, George Q. Cannon, the faith's predominant power broker, and Joseph F. Smith, the other First Presidency member and zealous nephew of Joseph Smith. It was a delicate task. In 1893, they presided over the church's dedication of the Salt Lake City Temple—an enormous neo-Gothic structure that measured 167 feet tall, 190 feet long, and 120 feet wide—a culmination of forty years of labor and sacrifice. Later that same year, they participated in the World's Columbian Exposition in Chicago, an event where the faith and its leaders, due to their surprisingly warm welcome made possible by the ecumenical work performed by Emmeline Wells and the Mormon Tabernacle Choir, achieved their first glimpse of what American belonging entailed. By the time Woodruff left for Utah, after having shaken hands "with several hundred persons from the Various Nations of the Earth untill I was tiered out," the world seemed a lot smaller.[4]

The 1890s inaugurated a period of American transition known as the Progressive Era. After a century of fracture, schism, and war, a generation of modernists envisioned a new beginning with "progress" as its clarion call. Psychologists, philosophers, and theologians argued for a new national mindset. They desired to set aside the previously entrenched, dogmatic, and foundationalist ideologies in favor of pragmatic experimentation, deliberate activism, and collaborative cooperation. Darwin's evolutionary theory chipped away at humanity's divine origins, secular higher criticism nuanced biblical interpretations, sociologists posited new solutions for worldly ills, and politicians uncoupled the state from the church.[5]

Crucial to this movement was a desire for human partnership, a social gospel based on communion and concession. Drawing on this sentiment, Cannon hoped the Chicago fair proved to the world that the Mormons were "struggling, with them, in our way, to advance the human family and to make progress." Every handshake Woodruff made with world dignitaries furthered this contemporary agenda. Latter-day Saint leaders embarked on a quest to situate the faith in better relations with its surrounding nation. The next three decades featured a series of significant compromises meant to meet modernity's new expectations, changes that were accelerated as the last of the pioneer generation passed away.[6]

Yet assimilation brought risk. What if, in their quest for acceptance, they forfeited fundamentals? External observers certainly hoped that would be the case. Mormonism was "doomed from the time the civilization of the country closed around the Mormon community in Utah," prophesied the *New York Times* in 1893. The church's decreasing majority in the state and increasing connections to broader culture seemed to spell an end to its exceptionalism. Emmeline Wells, who helped oversee the major changes in the Relief Society during these years, constantly fretted whether this was the case.[7]

Woodruff admitted at the close of 1893 that "the Greatest Changes [had] taken place Concerning the Church" that year than he had "ever known since its organization." He had participated in two major ceremonies, one sacred, the temple dedication, and one secular, the world's fair; each was serenaded by the Tabernacle Choir, and each celebrated the faith's stability. Progressive America seemed to promise a determined march into modernity—whether the Mormons were ready or not. Woodruff, at least, was hopeful. His vision was paradoxically centered on both continuity and change, a dynamic tension that would frame their church long after his death, echoing like the quivering voice found on the phonograph.[8]

WILFORD WOODRUFF's 1890 manifesto that renounced plural marriage was destined to cause ripples. But polygamy's theological draw persisted. One apostle who helped draft the document, Marriner Merrill—a stout man with seven wives and over forty children—wrote in his diary that it was merely a publicity measure taken solely to save the temples. When leaders debated a year later as to whether the manifesto held equal authority with Joseph Smith's 1843 revelation, Merrill scoffed. He could not "endorse" such an idea, because he "did not believe the Manifesto was a revelation from God," but was rather "formulated . . . for expediency to meet the present situation." He had just sealed his son, Charles, to a second wife, Chloe Hendricks, and to a third, Anna Stoddard, sometime after that. Marriner was himself sealed to Hilda Erickson, his eighth wife, eight years later. The manifesto could hardly slow the Merrill family.[9]

There also remained a question whether plural families could stay together. Many worried about continued government surveillance.

Joseph F. Smith still slept at his office most weeknights, with only short visits with his wives and children on the weekends. He went seven years without attending a public worship service to avoid arrest. Some plural families decided the best course was to split up, leaving numerous women unsupported, while others received public scorn when they lived as if nothing had changed. Things improved after Woodruff and Cannon met with federal officials and achieved limited amnesty for polygamists in December 1891. Yet government and church leaders disagreed on the new parameters: the former believed husbands would only financially support plural wives but not maintain any marital relations, while the latter taught that existing relationships could continue so long as new ones ceased.[10]

Many leaders who maintained a deep and sincere faith in polygamy refused to believe the principle had reached its end. Even Woodruff privately insisted that it remained a divine law, and might have been sealed to another plural wife himself in 1897. Mexico soon became their polygamous refuge. Leaders held private discussions with Mexican officials who were anxious for immigration to their northern regions and were therefore willing to overlook, at least publicly, the saints' marriage habits. As early as December 1890, two months after the manifesto's announcement, Woodruff dispatched couples down to their Juárez colony for plural sealings. They even created a cryptic form of written recommendations for leaders in Salt Lake City to communicate with those down south. Anthony Ivins, who oversaw the church's Mexican colonies, presided over at least forty postmanifesto plural unions.[11]

Church leaders soon addressed the other stumbling block that stood in the way of Utah statehood: their control over state politics. When Mormon leaders expressed a willingness to disband the People's Party and embrace America's two-party system, the otherwise skeptical *Salt Lake Tribune* predicted "clear sailing" toward political acceptance.[12]

The Republicans continued their surprising new coalition by guiding the Mormons on this perilous voyage. Though the Party of Lincoln had been Mormonism's foremost tormenter until 1890, it was now searching for new allies at the end of the nineteenth century. A

resurgent Democratic Party in the South, and growing disenchant-
ment over corruption charges in the North, whittled away what had
been national dominance. The GOP's best hope to regain control was
to form an impenetrable voting bloc in the West. Yet because these
western societies featured hierarchical structures and racial politics
more reflective of the antebellum South, Republicans were forced
to reconsider core principles and reevaluate previous allegiances.
Accessing Mormonism's extended reach throughout the Mountain
West was a central part of this project.[13]

Forging this new alliance posed problems. The church's People's
Party platform had closely aligned with the Democrats, as the territory's non-Mormon Liberal Party did with the Republicans. Saints had
long embraced the Democratic Party's priorities of local control and
populist governance. Yet church leaders, led by Cannon, now worried that too many saints joining the Democrats would prove "disas-
trous" in losing Republican support and perpetuating the Mormon/
gentile divide. And so this small circle of leaders labored to overcome
this half century of tradition and push the Mormon vote toward the
Republicans, as the GOP appeared more likely to deliver statehood
and further amnesty for polygamous families. It was a "wonderful
fact," Cannon explained, "that the great Republican party, who had
always been opposed to us, had now shown such friendship."[14]

Church leaders officially disbanded the People's Party in June 1891.
"We disclaim the right to control the political action of members of
our body," the First Presidency explained. But after most Mormons,
as expected, voted Democratic that fall, leaders pressed their thumbs
to the scales. Joseph F. Smith authored a pamphlet that argued that
Republican policies were "the best for Utah and the country at large,"
and apostles Anthon Lund and Francis Lyman were dispatched on
a speaking tour to, in part, urge more saints to vote Republican. The
coordinated efforts were persuasive: Republicans won surprising victories in Utah in both 1892 and 1893.[15]

The state's Democratic Party, led by several prominent Mormons,
was apoplectic. Even the Republican-leaning *Salt Lake Tribune* called
the maneuvering "a common, vulgar bargain." Most perturbed were
Moses Thatcher, a middle-aged apostle, and B. H. Roberts, who

was quickly becoming the faith's foremost historical and theological spokesman. Both had deep Democratic ties and felt the church's covert Republican support was a betrayal. They were especially angry that Lund, Lyman, and Smith were allowed to publicly support the Republicans, while they were told to hold their tongue. Thatcher publicly argued that Jesus, were he still alive, would vote Democratic due to their prioritization of the common man, just as Satan would vote Republican due to their preference for corporations. The First Presidency, however, feared that this backlash disrupted a tenuous balance, and Woodruff threatened to deny Thatcher and Roberts admission to the Salt Lake Temple's dedication if they refused to fall in line.[16]

These were novel problems for a leadership that had, for the most part, shared a singular political platform for decades. Bloc voting drew the consternation of American contemporaries, but it solidified unity within the hierarchy. When this new debate spilled into Quorum meetings, however, apostle Abraham Cannon admitted a "fear that the politics which are being introduced among us" would result in discord. Yet such division helped the church. As another apostle, Heber J. Grant, astutely put it, "the little tilt" with Roberts and Thatcher "will do more to satisfying the people of the world that we are sincere than a great amount of talk will do." America was more willing to embrace a divided Mormon hierarchy than a homogeneous one.[17]

Despite Democratic misgivings, the political calculus worked. Republican president Benjamin Harrison granted general amnesty in early 1893, and Cannon visited federal officials a few months later to successfully plead for a more lenient enforcement of the cohabitation law. Then, after Utah Republicans gained a congressional majority later that year, national officials upheld their end of the bargain and introduced a statehood bill. The Republican National Committee officially supported the measure in January 1894 and—even with newfound Democratic opposition, as the party feared statehood would result in two more Republican senators—Congress passed the highly anticipated bill. President Grover Cleveland signed it in July. Statehood would finally go into effect in 1896 as long as the Utah constitution included one proviso: "that polygamous or plural marriages are prohibited forever."[18]

Utah, long seen as America's outcast, was finally, after fifty years of struggle, admitted as a state. Mormons celebrated by hanging the largest American flag yet created, measuring 132 feet by 74 feet, from the ceiling of the tabernacle; the flag was later draped from the south end of the Salt Lake Temple, an image that had seemed impossible only a decade before. "No day in my remembrance afforded the people more pleasure," Cannon noted.[19]

Cannon hoped his efforts would result in his serving as the state's first senator, which would fulfill a dream that dated back to 1862. He publicly stated that he had "no more desire to go to Washington as a Senator than I would have to go to the Arctic Ocean," but privately he worked to secure legislative support. New political realities soon limited his hand. When it became clear there would not be enough support for a polygamous member of the First Presidency, he bowed out in favor of his son, Frank Cannon, a monogamist who had earned

To celebrate statehood, Mormons sewed the largest American flag in the nation's history. While they hung it from the tabernacle's interior for the festivities in 1896, they moved it outside and draped it from the Salt Lake City Temple in 1897.

capital with the gentile community. Further, he and Woodruff agreed to publicly support the other Republicans running for statewide elections, Clarence Allen and Arthur Brown, both non-Mormons.[20]

The Democrats who lost those races, Thatcher and Roberts, cried foul. In response, church leaders issued a new manifesto, this one political, that required any church authority running for office to first seek approval from the First Presidency. Both Thatcher and Roberts refused to sign. Roberts, however, eventually relented, apologized, and was restored to full harmony with the leadership a few weeks later. Thatcher, conversely, never budged. After several months of heated debate, Woodruff stripped him of his apostleship, a martyr to the church's new political circumstances.[21]

The unsettled political terrain brought new possibilities for Mormon women. Many who had led the suffrage cause in 1870, including Relief Society president Zina Young, were anxious to restore voting rights that had been rescinded with the Edmunds-Tucker Act in 1887. They encountered surprising resistance at the constitutional convention when none other than B. H. Roberts publicly opposed the re-enfranchisement of women. (Roberts first argued that restricting suffrage made Utah more congruent with national platforms, but subsequent speeches revealed his deeper opposition to woman suffrage, too.) Even George Q. Cannon privately supported Roberts's position, a rare bipartisan moment for the two. Yet they were defeated by politicians who were more keenly aware of their surroundings, and Utah women once again gained the vote.[22]

Cannon still tried to exert control. He advised Young to "gradually drop out of active participation in politics," likely because she, and most of the Relief Society activists, supported the Democrats. As always, however, Mormon women paved their own path. The next year, Martha Hughes Cannon, a physician, became America's first woman elected as a state senator, having defeated her own husband, Angus, George's younger brother, in the process. Mormonism's patriarchal control was always stronger in theory than practice. "Let us not waste our talents in the cauldron of modern nothingness," the senator Martha Cannon argued, but rather become women of "intellect" and "action." Martha spoke before the US House Judiciary Committee and declared that Utah's experience vindicated "the efforts of equal suffragists." To be modern, at least according to Martha Cannon and her fellow suffragists, meant a more progressive political body.[23]

Roberts once again tried his hand at campaigning three years later. Thanks to his improved relationship with church officials and prominent reputation among the saints, not to mention the Utah Democrats' resurgent popularity, he was elected in 1898 as the state's sole congressman, the same position that had previously eluded him. But as the first polygamist to represent Utah since statehood, Roberts faced steep federal opposition. Protestants viewed his election—particularly the fact that Roberts still lived with his three wives, one of whom he wed after the manifesto—as evidence of Mormonism's unrepentant status. A host of national women's organizations led coordinated opposition to Roberts's seating, including a petition that featured seven million names written on twenty-eight scrolls, each two feet in diameter, that were delivered to Congress wrapped in the American flag. (Notably, Mormon women chose not to defend Roberts, in part due to his opposition to their suffrage.) Congress officially ousted him in January 1900 by a margin of 268 to 50, stating that Roberts's election was "an explicit and offensive violation of the understanding by which Utah was admitted as a state."[24]

Mormon leaders learned their lesson. The Latter-day Saint community was now politically divided and culturally heterogeneous, as most church leaders leaned Republican while a majority of lay members leaned Democratic. It was a bargain that brought costs and benefits: Mormons had achieved statehood but lost their unity; they lost their sovereignty but achieved more credibility. It was the first of many uneven and inchoate steps toward assimilation. In a period of pragmatic bargains across the nation, the saints were prepared to make some of their own.[25]

Neither Woodruff nor Cannon lived to see the seeds they had planted come to fruition. In September 1898, while touring the West Coast, Woodruff died in San Francisco. "The event was so unexpected, so terrible, and away from home," Cannon reflected, "I could not understand it." It was a sad irony that the man who had midwifed Utah to statehood died outside of its borders. Cannon himself survived three years further, remaining a counselor to the next president, Lorenzo Snow, a petite man with a pointed, snow-white beard who had also been an apostle since 1849. Like Woodruff before him, Snow followed his imposing counselor's advice. But Cannon's final years were filled with personal, financial, and political frustrations. Shepherding the church away from prosecution, and Utah through statehood, was the culmination of his career; much of what followed was anticlimactic.[26]

Cannon's death in 1901, the dawn of a new century, marked the passing of the old. Arguably no Mormon leader would again simultaneously and successfully wield so much ecclesiastical and political power, as his theocratic legacy was buried with him in the Salt Lake Cemetery, located on a hill overlooking the city he had towered over for decades.

POLYGAMY'S END brought questions and possibilities for Mormon women. For nearly a half century, they had been told that polygamy was central to their theology, the ideal structure for the family, and the root of their identity. Many women were the principle's leading apologists, often papering over internal struggles; others were more willing to express discontent. And a growing number voted with their feet by choosing monogamy and refusing additional wives. Now they could approach marriage in much the same way as their American contemporaries.[27]

Among those eager to embrace the new age was Amy Brown. Daughter of an influential bishop in Utah County, she was one of twenty-five children born to three wives that lived together as a stereotypical polygamous family. Yet while she enjoyed an idyllic childhood, her intelligence and ambition quickly pointed further afield. In 1888, at the tender age of sixteen, she made the ten-mile voyage south to Provo in an old farm wagon to attend Brigham Young Academy, one of the church's schools that was devoted, at the time, to training teachers and preparing bright students for universities.

The school was a work in progress. Just over a decade old, the academy met in a rented warehouse next to busy railroad tracks.

Amy recalled that the noise and dust made study impossible. Yet she quickly made new friends through a lively social scene, and her "flashing eyes," chestnut-brown hair, and graceful demeanor made her the center of attention.[28]

Instruction took place under the direction of Karl Maeser, a German-born scholar whom Brigham Young appointed to head the academy soon after it opened. His intelligence impressed church officials and his care endeared him to students. But it was another man who dominated Brown's interest. Richard Lyman was six foot five, broad chested, athletic, gregarious, and possessed of a booming voice that filled the room. His chiseled looks and outgoing personality made him the most popular man in school. His pedigree was similarly impressive: he was the son of one apostle, Francis Lyman, and grandson of another, Amasa Lyman, though the latter was excommunicated for heresy shortly after Richard's birth. Amy, at five foot three, was more than a foot shorter than Richard, but was immediately smitten, and he returned the admiration. They soon started dating, the beginnings of one of Mormonism's most powerful couples.[29]

Their marriage did not happen for another seven years, however. Richard was nineteen and Amy seventeen when they met, and while those were not unusual ages to be wed, especially in Utah, there were complications. Richard's father urged them to settle down quickly, but Amy's wanted them to wait until Richard finished his education. Not that Amy minded. Like many in her generation, she was not against marriage, but her interests were not limited to it, either. After her father denied her a chance to get further education at the University of Michigan, where Richard studied civil engineering, Amy joined the Brigham Young Academy's faculty. She later secured an even better teaching job, with a raise, in Salt Lake City. She felt independent while living on her own in Utah's urban center. Amy admitted to not being "ready at all for 'the event,'" referring to her impending marriage, as she wanted "to see and hear a few more things before I sink into oblivion." She was not alone in this desire. "Oh, I wish I were a man," complained Leah Dunford, a granddaughter of Brigham Young, in 1893. "Men can do anything on

Amy Brown, sometime before her marriage to Richard Lyman. She represented a generation of Mormon women who were anxious to explore new possibilities.

earth, but if women think of anything but waiting on men, or cooking their meals, 'they are out of their sphere.'"³⁰

Mormon women were previously caught in the balance of simultaneously defending polygamy and yearning for political equality. The new generation faced a different dilemma. On the one hand, they inherited from their pioneer mothers a commitment to the public sphere and a dedication to solving societal problems; on the other, embracing the more traditional monogamous structure curtailed many opportunities that some polygamous wives had previously achieved. Amy Brown knew that she would not have a sister-wife to take care of her kids, making it difficult to receive a higher education or pursue other opportunities. Was there another way?

Brown felt so confident in exploring avenues for change because the nation was experiencing a period of reform. In the wake of Reconstruction and a series of financial recessions, activists at the end of the nineteenth century turned to progressive ideas for change. They bemoaned the shortcomings of laissez-faire capitalism and ineffectual governmental intervention, instead arguing that more education, organization, and experimentation could transform the world around them. Even western territories only recently granted statehood, and even marginalized communities like Mormons, took part in this cultural revolution.

The fusion of this reform impulse with Christianity resulted in what many termed the social gospel. Like the Second Great Awakening earlier in the century, the period in which Mormonism was born, a bevy of religious institutions fought for temperance, education reform, and poverty relief. Religious activists seemed destined to sanctify a decaying society. Mormons watched from afar, and then participated in, these national trends, finally recognizing collaborators in a redemptive mission. God's work, America's reformers argued, would take place in the slums that modern America had created. In Chicago, Jane Addams, at the vanguard of the cause, founded Hull House, a social settlement that enabled women to work and live in the city and save its citizens. Addams referred to it as the "renaissance" of "Christian humanitarianism." Within the social gospel, religious redemption, secular reform, and federal intervention merged, with women leading the way.[31]

Amy and Richard, conversant with these broader currents, finally wed on September 7, 1896. The union was performed in the Salt Lake Temple by Joseph F. Smith. Richard was soon hired as a professor of civil engineering at the University of Utah, and Amy settled into her role as housewife and, soon, mother, even as she continued her education through university classes. Thanks to a stream of nieces and nephews who helped with babysitting, she was also able to take advantage of Salt Lake City's social and intellectual opportunities. For instance, Amy was invited to join the Author's Club, a book group led by women from some of the area's elite families that debated literature and progressive ideas.[32]

Amy's real chance for growth came in 1902. On the way to New York for Richard to start a PhD program at Cornell, the couple spent a summer at the University of Chicago, where they both enrolled in classes. Amy, elated to broaden her horizons, took courses on Shakespeare and "The Bible as Literature." Her most transformative experience came in a seminar on sociology taught by George Vincent, where she learned that many of modernity's ills were rooted in societal problems that could be overcome through strategic effort. It was there that she became engulfed in the progressive quest to solve the nation's evils. She even visited Addams's Hull House on a field assignment, which allowed her to interview the famed reformer. Amy always considered these experiences a turning point in her life.[33]

After their blissful summer in Chicago, the Lymans continued to Ithaca, New York, where Richard, ever dutiful and efficient, completed his master's and then a doctorate in civil engineering within three years. They then moved back to Salt Lake City, where Richard resumed his job at the University of Utah, but Amy refused to forget all that she had learned. Still fully committed to her church, she was ready to use her skills and knowledge to build a modern future for her faith. She and her husband represented the New Mormons: educated, progressive, and acquainted with the ideas of the age.

THE CHURCH the Lymans returned to was one in the process of modernization. Just a few years earlier, in the autumn of 1901, both Lorenzo Snow, who led the church for only three years after Woodruff's death, and Zina Young, who had led the Relief Society for over a decade, passed away. They were replaced by Joseph F. Smith, the nephew and namesake of the faith's founding prophet, and Bathsheba Smith, who had been baptized in 1837 and had been a leading member of the women's organization since its early years. Bathsheba's deceased husband, George, was Joseph Smith's cousin and an apostle since 1839. Both Smiths who took control of the church in 1901, then, had deep roots within the church and firm ties to familial royalty. When their new positions were ratified in a solemn assembly held in the Salt Lake Temple, most attendees likely assumed a continuity from the faith's first century.[34]

Both Smiths, however, faced daunting tasks. External and internal disputes had left the church depleted and desperate. By 1898, the church was $2 million in debt, primarily to banks outside of Utah. Church attendance was at an all-time low, in part due to lingering traditions dating back to the underground period but also due to a lack of significance associated with local congregations. Most wards reported only 15 percent attendance. Regional Relief Societies fared no better, as participation and dues plummeted from previous decades when they were more politically active. And as the national outcry over B. H. Roberts's congressional seat had proved, a majority of Americans still distrusted the Mormons. It was no wonder that young members like the Lymans, despite their faithful heredity, were looking for new avenues for enlightenment.[35]

The faith's new leaders acted quickly. In his first sermon as church president, Joseph F. Smith admitted that, until that point, the church had been "looked upon as interlopers, as fanatics, as believers in a false religion." It was time for that to end. "The Lord designs to change this condition of things," he proclaimed, "and to make us known to the world in our true light—as true worshipers of God." To demonstrate their openness, Smith approved a new visitors' center to be constructed on Temple Square, and by 1905 the space previously blocked by imposing adobe walls was hosting two hundred thousand annual visitors.[36]

Other changes were more structural. Joseph F.'s predecessor, Lorenzo Snow, attempted to replenish their financial reserves. A coordinated effort to increase tithes led to a 50 percent boost in offerings in one year. The creation of a new auditing committee to oversee, modernize, and reform expenditures enabled the church to pay off all its debts by 1907. That consolidation, as well as its accompanying financial security, allowed leaders to restructure bureaucratic and auxiliary agencies. The organizations that oversaw children, youth, Sunday school, and priesthood quorums, as well as the Relief Society, were retooled by visionary local leaders, often without involvement from the First Presidency or apostles. Many drew from contemporary programs outside the faith in their quest to streamline and standardize activities, a subtle admission that not all truths were found within the gospel. A member's standing was now determined by participation in the local congregation. They ceased building separate halls for the Relief Society, activities, and bishop's tithing offices, instead combining them all into a central and singular structure. As a result, attendance increased, and the various institutions became much more stable.[37]

Even Mormonism's literary culture went through a transition. Leaders called for a "home literature" that fused moving prose with didactic theology. Authors borrowed from broader novelistic practices to display religious principles through fictional characters. Most popular was Nephi Anderson's 1898 novel, *Added Upon*, which followed key characters through their pre-earth, mortal, and postmortem existence, thereby exhibiting the entire plan of salvation. Also influential was Josephine Spencer, whose short stories, poetry, and novels drew from the church's historical episodes and shaped how a generation of saints understood their past. Even B. H. Roberts joined the fray when he wrote a novel, *Corianton*, which was based on a Book of Mormon character. (The work was later the inspiration for a play, *Corianton: An Aztec Romance*, and then even later for a film, *Corianton: A Story of Unholy Love*.) The home-literature movement demonstrated how Mormons were willing to engage cultural pursuits and literary genres more in line with American society.[38]

The common thread found throughout this transformative period was Mormonism's incremental movement toward American denominationalism. Throughout the nineteenth century, the church founded upon Joseph Smith's countercultural protest had defined itself in opposition to America's supposedly decaying ecclesiastical carcass by a series of institutional priorities: polygamy over monogamy, empire over state, kingdom over church. Now, at the dawn of the twentieth century, with a related yet distinct Joseph Smith in charge, the LDS faith appeared more mainstream, more traditional, more *American*. Mormonism "is solely an ecclesiastical organization," Joseph F. insisted in a public editorial in 1903, "separate and distinct from the state." Coming from a Smith, this was quite the claim.[39]

JANE MANNING JAMES, nearing seventy years old, had lost most of her sight but retained all her faith. When she first arrived in Utah nearly half a century earlier, she was one of a handful of Black pioneers, living reminders of the church's more universal origins; now she was one of that group's last survivors. Elijah Able, the most prominent Black elder, had died in 1884, and Manning's first husband, Isaac, though he returned to her household in 1890 after a long separation, passed in 1891. These losses were balanced when James's brother, also named Isaac, moved to Utah in 1892 and was rebaptized into the faith. (Unlike his sister, Isaac did not recognize Brigham Young as Joseph Smith's successor, and eventually aligned himself with the Reorganized Church.) James was likely still doing laundry for her White neighbors, necessary work to cover room and board for her brother, her children, and several grandchildren. She owned her own house, participated in local Relief Society and ward activities, paid her tithing, and gained a reputation as the beloved "Aunt Jane"—marks of a lifetime of sacrifice and, to a degree, belonging.[40]

James was finally able to enter the Salt Lake Temple in November 1894 and was baptized on behalf of her deceased niece, Mary Stebbins. This vicarious baptism was not her only temple ritual that year, however. Six months earlier, on May 18, as James stood outside the temple walls, Zina Young stood in her place to be sealed to Joseph Smith, vicariously represented by his nephew, Joseph F. Smith. Rather than being sealed to Smith as a wife, as so many women had, or as a child, as James had requested, she was instead "attached as a Servitor for eternity." It was a singular ritual, the only ordinance ever performed for someone still living but unable to participate, and the only instance in which someone was designated an eternal servant.[41]

The event came in response to James's agitation. She had petitioned for over a decade for access to temple rituals. "Is there no blessing for me?" she earnestly asked in one of many letters. Once she enlisted the help of Zina Young, president of the Relief Society, in 1894, church leaders finally relented. They attempted to reconcile, on the one hand, an inchoate if increasingly strident racial restriction and, on the other, the genuine pleadings of a faithful saint. The resulting ritual was a half measure. Neither side was satisfied, and James continued to plead her case to each new prophet as he took office. She also dictated her own autobiography, claiming her position as one of the church's most worthy believers. Her faith in Mormonism, she concluded, "is as strong today, nay it is if possible stronger than it was the day I was first baptized."[42]

James's words were a direct challenge to church leaders who wished

Portrait of "Utah Pioneers of 1847," July 24, 1905. This was a gathering of those who had been part of the faith's pioneer generation, nearly sixty years after their migration. On the far left side is Jane Manning James. She and her brother, Isaac (fourth from left), were reminders of a dwindling non-White Mormon population.

for a simpler history. They also conflicted with a country increasingly devoted to a racial divide. The decades surrounding the turn of the twentieth century featured the final failures of Reconstruction's promises and the solidifying of Jim Crow laws. In *Plessy v. Ferguson*, ruled in 1896, the Supreme Court confirmed a constitutional basis for racial segregation. Governments, institutions, and even churches hardened their segregationist policies, resulting in a nation that was no longer divided by geography but rather by race. "The problem of the twentieth century," wrote the young scholar W. E. B. Du Bois in 1903, "is the problem of the color line." This line, Du Bois explained, would determine "how far [the] differences of races" would be used to deny Blacks "the right of sharing to the utmost ability the opportunities and privileges of modern civilization."[43]

Mormonism's racial line, up until this point, had been present but blurry. Its scattered policies mostly matched the oppressive impulses of the broader nation yet were still somewhat tempered by the faith's more universalist beginnings. But as a new century beckoned, the temptation to assimilate into America's culture of White supremacy, the desire to make another kind of bargain, increased. Leaders were finally forced to settle lingering racial questions when a scant yet earnest number of Black members sought inclusion in Mormon communities throughout the nation.

Among those fighting for a place within the faith was Elijah A. Banks, a member of the newly established Minneapolis Sunday school. Banks, born enslaved in Tennessee, was part of the first trickle of Black immigration to the North that later became an overwhelming movement known as the Great Migration. Many of these newly emancipated sojourners, as part of their quest to escape oppression, embraced Christian denominations as a form of social salvation. Most joined existing Black denominations like the African Methodist Episcopal church, which exploded from twenty thousand members before the war to four hundred thousand by 1884, or created new ones, like the National Baptist Convention, which was formed in 1880 and soon boasted millions of congregants. In a society with decreasing liberties, religion was one tangible way for African Americans to exert independence.[44]

Not everyone took the route of fortifying Black denominations, however. Elijah Banks instead chose another path when he married Caroline Amelia Bailey, a White woman, in 1898, and was baptized into the Latter-day Saint faith, an almost entirely White church, in 1899. These were not easy decisions. Though attempts to outlaw mixed-race marriages at the national level had thus far failed, despite no lack of trying, many states, including Utah, had prohibited unions like Elijah and Caroline's. Further, very few denominations welcomed interracial worship, and those that did often reaffirmed the subordinate status of Black congregants.

Yet Banks tried nonetheless. He frequently participated in Sunday school discussions, and Asahel Woodruff, son of Wilford Woodruff and president of the central states mission, even dined in the Bankses' home and vouched for his worthiness. When one alarmed southern missionary expressed concern, Woodruff replied that while interracial marriage and worship might be considered bad in the South, "we of the north do not consider this any bar to their being proper candidates for admittance into the fold of Christ." A 1902 photo of the Sunday school featured Banks proudly standing in the center with an aura of confidence. He was dressed in a dark suit, white shirt, formal tie, and even a stylish mustache, the look of a man who believed that he belonged.[45]

Banks was not alone. John Wesley Harmon Jr., a nineteen-year-old Black man, for instance, was baptized in Camden, New Jersey, around the same time. He and his wife, Lilian Blanche Clark, the daughter of a Nanticoke tribal chief, embedded themselves in Delaware's Mormon community for at least a decade. They believed they had found a religion that embraced racial equality. Since "the time I was baptized," Harmon boasted, "the Lord has rested upon me in such a degree that I know the work is of God." He wanted to proclaim a message from the rooftops: " 'Mormonism' is Truth!"[46]

But the ground was shifting beneath both Banks's and Harmon's feet. LDS missionaries and leaders alike, sharing their American contemporaries' concerns over "amalgamation," increasingly embraced racial segregation. Mormonism's assimilation into White culture required a more stringent racial line. One mission president, German Ellsworth, was worried about the Bankses, and wrote that the presence of Black members and interracial couples slowed White conversions. He had instructed elders to cease working "among the colored people" around 1902, but requested clarification from Salt Lake City.[47]

Ellsworth's petition was only one of many similar inquiries regarding the church's racial policy that were rushed into church headquarters during these years. Did a White man who married a Black woman lose his right to the priesthood? If a young woman had one Black grandparent, and all the others were White, could she be sealed in the temple? Were missionaries to dedicate any time or resources to Black communities? The increasing quantity of these questions signaled the tenuous nature of existing policies. They also reaffirmed the need to introduce clarity.[48]

One of the biggest obstacles to a clear racial restriction was the presence of Black saints, like Jane Manning James, whose living memory posed complicating reminders. She wrote Joseph F. Smith once again in 1903, begging for the opportunity to "get my endowments and also finish the work I have begun for my dead." Her request included a stamped envelope for Smith's anticipated, but never composed, reply. The only thing that silenced her was death, which occurred on April 16, 1908. Smith, who never approved any of her petitions, spoke at her funeral in front of an audience that packed inside the same meetinghouse where James had worshipped for decades. He eulogized the woman whose life had been defined by her Blackness by saying that, once resurrected, she would "attain the longings of her soul and become a white and beautiful person." Only in death could James cross, but not transcend, Mormonism's color line.[49]

James's death paved the way for church leaders to finally institute a firm policy. Prompted by another mission inquiry, Smith rewrote the past to formally draw their own color line for the present. He claimed in 1908 that while Joseph Smith had indeed ordained Able to the priesthood early in the 1830s, the "ordination was declared null and void by the Prophet himself" in the 1840s. Building on a statement he made in 1907, where he described that all who possessed any trace of "negro blood," no matter "how remote a degree," were susceptible to this restriction, Joseph F. Smith now called for a "position without any reserve" regarding those with African ancestry: all "are deprived of the rights of the priesthood because of the decree of the Almighty." They could be baptized, be confirmed as members of the faith, and partake of the sacrament, but the line was drawn there.[50]

Black members were left to react to the new policy. In 1910, Elijah and Caroline Banks, who had recently moved from the urban hub of Minneapolis to the open country of Wisconsin, wrote the First Presidency requesting reassurance of their belonging. In response, the First Presidency's secretary, George Gibbs, explained that Elijah could not hold the priesthood, that he and Caroline could not be sealed in the temple, and that neither could ever be full members of the faith. Gibbs chose not to give a reason for the restriction, but promised there would be a day when "it will be revealed to you why your race is in this unfortunate state." The First Presidency wrote a similar letter the next year, though addressed to the eastern states mission president, denying Wesley Harmon's appeal for priesthood ordination. They rejected Harmon's reasoning that the New Testament promised racial equality and deflected his claims that heredity was too permeable to draw a clear line, instead invoking the "curse of Ham." Both letters urged the restriction's recipients not to be discouraged.[51]

We do not know how either family reacted. Harmon seems to have left the church shortly afterward. He went on to study religion at Howard University, where he excelled in Greek, and became a chaplain. Denied the priesthood in Mormonism, his skills found purpose elsewhere. Conversely, when the Bankses moved back to Minneapolis later that year, they remained committed members of the local Mormon community. But while Elijah could be a faithful congregant, he could never preside. Church records listed him and Caroline on their active rosters as late as 1930, shortly before their respective deaths, deep into the era of prolonged forgetfulness in which the faith's more racially inclusive past was a thing of distant memory.[52]

For many Mormons during this transition era, the proliferation of temples, standardization of worship, and synthesizing of doctrine made the faith feel more American, more stable, more welcoming. For those like Elijah Banks, Wesley Harmon, and Jane Manning James, these developments only reaffirmed their increasingly perilous place. They were denied access to temple worship, were marginalized in church practice, and were written out of the newly standardized salvific narratives. They were on the wrong side of the color line. Assimilation into American society meant assimilation into White space, an arena in which these valiant saints, who had sacrificed so much to carve out so little, were no longer citizens and saints but strangers and foreigners. They were the casualties of Mormonism's Americanization project.[53]

WHEN THE Republicans once again took control of Utah's state legislature in 1900, church leadership wondered if the time was right to nominate one of their own for the US Senate. Apostle Heber J. Grant suggested they designate Reed Smoot, a savvy businessman who had just been added to the Quorum of the Twelve. Both Joseph F. Smith and Lorenzo Snow, however, opposed the measure, fearing the backlash would outweigh any potential benefit. Two years later, when the winds seem to calm, they revisited the matter. Against the wishes of Theodore Roosevelt, who urged Utah Republicans to avoid unnecessary controversy, Smoot was elected to the Senate in January 1903 with the full support of church leadership.[54]

Smoot was born in Salt Lake City in 1862 to the city's mayor, Abraham Smoot, and his fifth wife, Anne Kristina Morrison. He possessed a tall frame, narrow torso, gangly arms, and a long mustache—the type of appearance that kept political cartoonists in business. Smith believed Smoot was the right person to act as the church's new political face because he represented, in many minds, the modern Mormon: a successful capitalist, devoted member of the Republican Party, progressive reformer, and, perhaps most importantly, monogamist.

Observers both inside and outside Utah were outraged. Many believed Smoot would be a pawn in Mormonism's pernicious agenda. At the peak of the national controversy, removal petitions garnered three million signatures, congressmen received nearly a thousand letters a day, and politicians revived talks about legislation to disenfranchise all polygamists. The Daughters of the American Revolution, one of the nation's oldest and most prestigious organizations, even called for the church's abolition. The Senate commenced public hearings that eventually dragged on for three years. While technically about Smoot, the inquisition sought to answer, in the words of one Utah delegate, whether Mormons were "unfit to hold the rights of citizenship." All the church's previous achievements at assimilation appeared at risk.[55]

Joseph F. Smith traveled to the nation's capital in early 1904 to appear before the Senate committee. He, along with eight other church leaders, had been subpoenaed as part of an investigation over whether the church still practiced polygamy. His presence was a spectacle. Newspapers obsessed over the number of his wives and chil-

"The Real Objection to Smoot." Critics accused senator-elect Reed Smoot, a Mormon apostle, of being a "puppet" for his faith. This cartoon depicts him as being controlled by the "Mormon Hierarchy," who remained committed to "polygamy," "resistance to federal authority," "Mormon rebellion," "murder of apostates," and "blood atonement."

dren, and journalists described him as if he were an Arthur Conan Doyle villain come to life. (Doyle's *A Study in Scarlet*, which featured the Mormons as kidnapping and murdering cultists, was reserialized as part of the national frenzy.) "His eyes are small and shifty," one reporter narrated, as the now long-bearded prophet allegedly chose each word carefully as he slowly, malevolently examined the room. Though that was an exaggeration, Smith did indeed hold contempt for the inquiry. He wore his anger, stemming from years of animosity toward American officials, who he believed failed to protect his community, on his sleeve—or at least on his lapel, which featured a pin with an image of his slain father.[56]

Despite the risk, and no matter the historical irony, Republican leaders hoped they could vindicate the Mormon senator and maintain their political alliance. But the party required more concessions. Not only was it readily apparent that Mormons were still cohabitating—even Smith was arrested and fined $300 when his sixth wife, Mary Schwartz Smith, gave birth to his forty-fifth, and final, child in 1906—but it became evident that new polygamous unions were still being solemnized. Investigators focused on a handful of apostles connected to the continued practice, including Marriner Merrill, John W. Taylor, and Matthias Cowley. Merrill, already in his seventies, avoided testifying due to health. The other two were bigger problems. Both Taylor, son and namesake of the prophet who spent his final years refusing compromise, and Cowley, who had replaced Moses Thatcher in the Quorum, were in their forties. Their comparative youth signified that polygamy was not merely a generational issue.[57]

Smith recognized the dilemma. Privately, he remained adamant that polygamy was central to God's law; publicly, he labored feverishly to improve the church's public standing. He could either keep allowing polygamy to covertly spread or finally achieve political assimilation, but not both.

At first, Smith tried to satisfy both desires by merely issuing another manifesto in 1904, an echo of Woodruff's in 1890, hoping it would appease the Senate. Even that decision was not without dissent, however. Abraham Woodruff, Wilford's apostolic son, opposed "anything against the principle which had given him birth." But politicians demanded further action. They specifically desired punishment for those who continued to flout the law, most notably Taylor and Cowley. The mere thought terrified many of the Twelve. "With all my heart I plead for these two brethren," argued Heber Grant. "What they have done I have also done or intended to do." Grant preferred protecting the two even if it meant Smoot "has to resign." Some openly wondered if the entire Smoot gamble had been a mistake. "It will take a magnifying glass," wrote one leader, "for us to find the good that has been done to our cause."[58]

Smith faced heat from the other side, too. Smoot, representing the opposite outlook, grew impatient with the church's duplicity. The manifesto had promised the end of polygamy, Smoot reminded Smith, and the apostle-senator refused to believe that they would "deceive" the public. It was time that church leaders finally embraced the modern world by being "honest with ourselves, with our fellow-men, and with our God." Rather than straddling the fence, they had to pick a side.[59]

The beleaguered prophet eventually asked Taylor and Cowley to compose resignation letters in October 1905. But when the move angered others in the Quorum, Smith chose not to officially accept them for another six months. He desperately hoped they could find another way out, a providential ram in the thicket. When none arrived, leadership reluctantly announced the apostles' resignations at the April 1906 conference, a disclosure that elicited audible gasps from the tabernacle's audience. Taylor and Cowley, along with Marriner Merrill, who had passed away in February of that year, were then replaced by three new apostles, all of whom appeared monogamist.[60]

These public resignations were enough to save Smoot's seat. After three years of explosive congressional hearings, Smoot's opponents had failed to persuasively connect the senator to polygamy. Though the investigating committee decided, by a small margin, to recommend removing Smoot, the Senate-wide vote was not particularly close: a 47-to-28 margin, mostly along party lines, vindicated the apostle. Republicans, encouraged by Roosevelt, came to their colleague's defense. "I think the Senate should prefer a polygamist who doesn't 'polyg,'" explained one senator, "to a monogamist who doesn't 'monog.'" The action proved that the Senate was willing to accept the nuances demanded by America's pluralist society, at least when it worked in their political interests, as well as Mormonism's commitment to meet national expectations.[61]

It is unclear whether Smith truly wished to end polygamy. There is evidence that he secretly allowed plural sealings to continue, although without official sanction. It is also clear that several devoted leaders continued to solemnize new unions. As one polygamist wife, Annie Clark Tanner, later put it, many could not give up "the capstone" of the gospel, and were therefore "going, for a time, in both directions." Many were forced to take extreme precautions: one Mormon patriarch, Judson Tolman, who officiated over at least fifteen plural unions during this time, testified that his sealing's officiator wore a mask to conceal his identity.[62]

Smith, frustrated with continued rumors, finally took the ultimate

step in 1910 to commission bishops and stake presidents to excommu-
nicate all new polygamists. Among those punished under these new
measures were John W. Taylor, who was fully cut off after he refused
to give an inch, and Matthias Cowley, whose membership was saved
when he showed a modicum of contrition.[63]

Yet plural marriage refused to die. The idea's centrality to Mormonism's origins continued to draw practitioners who were anxious to embrace the faith in its fullness, earnest believers who saw
Woodruff's and Smith's concessions as betrayal. The doctrine of plural marriage remained a fundamental for generations to come, albeit
outside official channels, even as its history and persistence became
increasingly uncomfortable for leaders and followers alike, an aggra-
vating thorn in the modern church's side.

Smith refused to look back following the first decade of his
presidency. Besides ending institutional support for polygamy, and
achieving stable relations with the national government, he instituted
other measures to modernize the faith. Following the wider Protestant movement in favor of temperance, Smith instructed local leaders
to enforce the Word of Wisdom, the faith's dietary code, more vig-
orously. The church also divested itself from numerous businesses,
with a few exceptions, allowing Utah's economy to assimilate into
America's exploding capitalistic empire. And finally, in 1907, leaders completed a decades-long process by urging Mormon converts
throughout the world to cease migrating to Utah and instead build
"Zion" in their homelands. Smith soon announced the first temples
to be built outside of Utah: Cardston, Alberta; and Laie, Hawaii.[64]

The price for these reforms was high. For political acceptance, the
church sacrificed one apostle in the 1890s, and two more a decade
later; for cultural cohesion, it forfeited some of its most cherished
doctrines and practices; for social stability, it surrendered a degree of
its long-coveted sovereignty. The faithful were now far more divided
and dispersed than ever before. America's progressive age was defined
by similar types of uneasy bargains and unexpected alliances. Mormons hoped only that the results would be worth it.

*　　*　　*

FEW FOLLOWED the Smoot hearings as closely as J. Reuben Clark, a studious and solemn man in his thirties just then breaking onto the national scene. Known as "Reube" to his close friends and family— and known for his round face and bow ties to everyone else—Clark was the eldest of ten children born in the rural town of Grantsville, Utah, in 1871. His mother, Mary Louisa, was the daughter of one of the territory's most successful businessmen and prominent bishops, a heredity that ensured connections to the faith's elites. But Clark also inherited from his father, Joshua, a devotion to the Republican Party. These twin pillars of pioneer faith and political allegiance shaped Clark's life.[65]

Clark had mixed emotions while watching Smoot's drama, and he annotated a personal copy of the proceedings. On the one hand, Clark shared with Smoot both a political party and political aspirations; he had just completed a law degree at Columbia in 1906 and was immediately appointed assistant solicitor in the nation's capital. But Clark also held a personal grudge against Smoot—the senator had denied the young student a chance to work as his secretary in 1902—as well as a discomfort with his church's entrance into politics. Clark even penned

J. Reuben Clark, 1903.
The studious Clark would become one of the most influential Mormons in the twentieth century.

an unsolicited memorandum in 1907 suggesting that no church leader "shall while holding such [ecclesiastical] office be elegible for election to a political office." In a letter to his father that same year, he denounced the church's political intervention as "un-American." Such self-confidence exemplified Clark's precocious mind.[66]

The aspiring lawyer represented a new generation of LDS intellectuals. Years earlier, after finishing at the top of his University of Utah class, Clark had fled Zion for a bigger stage. James E. Talmage, then president of the university, who served as Clark's mentor, called him "the greatest mind ever to leave Utah." His reputation grew once he arrived in the East, as his Columbia professors urged him to follow them into government appointments. He was promoted to solicitor by 1910 and helped shape the nation's policy toward Mexico, and he held the position until Woodrow Wilson and the Democrats took control of the White House in 1913. Even out of office, however, and while balancing successful law practices in Washington and New York, Clark maintained a series of federal assignments and was awarded a Distinguished Service Medal in 1920.[67]

Yet Clark's religious commitments suffered as his political star rose. He rarely attended the local LDS branches, nor did he pay a full tithing or attend the temple for over two decades. Privately, he questioned the faith's central doctrines and considered whether Joseph Smith could have "evolve[d]" his revelations "out of his own consciousness" or environment. Surrounded by the nation's intellectuals and politicians, Clark could not help but embrace their progressive spirit. "Are we not entitled," he posited, "but expected to think for ourselves?" Later in life, Clark admitted that his younger self had even flirted with atheism.[68]

Clark was part of a broader ideological wave that was pressing forward at the time. The Progressive Era witnessed an expansion of secular learning at America's top universities. Most institutions shed denominational identities and religious commitments and replaced them with new standards of academic rigor. Biblical higher criticism eroded traditional understandings of sacred texts, Charles Darwin's theory of evolution transformed biology, William James theorized religion as an expression of subjective beliefs, and Sigmund Freud (who believed religion to be a wishful delusion) and Karl Marx (who claimed it was an opiate for the masses) transformed understandings of society.

Prominent theologians responded by incorporating the emergent scientific mindset into their theologies. Protestant ministers like Charles Augustus Briggs argued that human reason was just as important as inspiration when interpreting the scriptures, that the Bible contained errors and failed prophecies, and that traditional doctrines could be cast aside. Catholics like Reverend John Augustine Zahm posited that Darwin's theories could fit within Christian belief; shortly afterward, Pope Pius X was worried enough about these developments to issue an encyclical that denounced "the doctrines of the modernists." This was the dawn of a reinvigorated debate over faith and reason. These "modernists" came to be known for their willingness to forfeit traditional, fundamental doctrines in their pursuit of truths based on scientific, rational, and secular modes of understanding. And in many cases, the label of "modernist" came with as many cultural tethers as ideological ones, as it reflected how one related to the broader society.[69]

These disputes took place just as Mormons sought to assimilate into American society, resulting in many attempting to provide their own answers. At the forefront was John A. Widtsoe, a Norwegian immigrant who possessed a serious demeanor and a distinguished goatee. Widtsoe earned degrees from Harvard and the University of Göttingen in Germany. While teaching at the Utah State Agricultural College in Logan, Utah, where he later served as president, he penned a series in the church magazine titled "Joseph Smith as Scientist." The essays sought to prove that not only could "Mormonism and science harmonize" but that "Mormonism is abreast of the most modern of the established views of science, and that it has held them many years—in some cases before science adopted them." Widtsoe even offered a tepid defense of evolution—though he separated humans from the organic process by insisting that they had not descended from animals—and argued that God directed the evolutionary process. The essays were later published by the church in a best-selling book.[70]

But perhaps the most prominent Mormon intellectual was Clark's mentor and Widtsoe's colleague, James Talmage. Born in 1862 to struggling innkeepers in Berkshire, England, Talmage had migrated with his family to Utah in 1876. He then left the region for graduate degrees in geology from Lehigh and Johns Hopkins Universities. To the young Talmage, who sported round spectacles and a rounder face, it was not Darwin that was a threat to belief but rather those ministers who "dabble[d] with matters from which their ignorance keep them at a safe distance." His scholarly breadth transcended the sciences. With Clark as his assistant, and commissioned by the First Presidency, Talmage produced a quartet of books—*Articles of Faith*, *The Great Apostasy*, *Jesus the Christ*, and *The House of the Lord*—that provided new, systematic, and rational compendiums of Mormonism's core beliefs in the wake of forfeiting the previous theological center, polygamy. Widtsoe published his own theological opus, *A Rational Theology*, which argued that any modern religion must be in "complete harmony with all knowledge." These projects reflected a willingness to draw from the era's intellectual project of professionalization and secular investigation.[71]

There were plenty trying to follow Widtsoe's and Talmage's example. The Brigham Young Academy, still only a few decades old, refined its scholarly programs. The academy succeeded in becoming the church's flagship school by changing its name to Brigham Young University, hiring faculty with graduate degrees from prestigious institutions, and offering courses like "Ecclesiastical Sociology" and "Psychology of Religion," the latter of which was taught by William H. Chamberlin, a precocious junior scholar who had studied with William James at Harvard. John Dewey, a central figure in the field of American pragmatism, visited BYU's campus and mingled with the faculty and students. Church periodicals featured editorials that argued that modern faith was to be "rational," built upon intellectual reasoning as well as belief.[72]

These journeys toward intellectual modernism did not come without obstacles. Some leaders worried that too much secular knowledge corrupted the faith. As public education became ubiquitous, and the church gave up its primary and secondary schools, more emphasis was placed on its universities. Though America's exhaustive battle over evolution was not waged until the 1920s, the first two decades of the twentieth century featured the struggle's first conflicts, and LDS leaders participated in the early skirmishes. Joseph F. Smith, hoping to reaffirm Mormonism's fundamentals, attacked the creeping secularism. Under his supervision, the General Board of Education announced a ban in 1908 on teachers using any books on the Old or New Testament written outside the church, and the next year released an official statement on "The Origin of Man" that explicitly denounced the theory that "the original human being was a development from lower orders of the animal creation." Speculative theories, Smith believed, had no place in the Kingdom of God.[73]

Uprooting these modernist ideas proved difficult. Leaders became alarmed when they learned about modernist inroads at BYU. Smith assigned Horace Cummings, superintendent of church education, to conduct an investigation in 1910. The results were disturbing: professors taught a number of modernist theories, including that the Bible was "a collection of myths, folklore, dramas, literary productions, and some inspiration." Instructors also introduced students to "the theory of evolution" as "demonstrated law," and some doubted the "objective reality" of Joseph Smith's visions. More alarming was that nearly all the students Cummings encountered "were most zealous in defending and propagating the new views." Smith's worst fears had come true: his own teachers were undermining fundamental scriptural truths.[74]

Church leaders acted swiftly. They gave the four professors who had been singled out—two sets of brothers: Joseph and Henry Peterson, and Ralph and W. H. Chamberlin—an ultimatum: renounce their heretical teachings or lose their jobs. Despite the professors' insistence that evolution could be taught in a way that was "faith promoting, not faith destroying," they were all eventually forced out. Ninety-five of the school's 114 students, livid at the tribunal, signed a petition that claimed the dismissals would be "a death-blow to our college work." But Smith doubled down and published a series of editorials that explicitly denounced the secular theories, then instructed BYU president George Brimhall to chastise the students. The General Board of Education later issued a circular that reaffirmed that "all teachers are expected to be loyal to the school, the church, and the authorities thereof, and especially to refrain from unwise criticism." Brimhall synthesized these lessons into a new slogan for the university: "The school follows the Church."[75]

This episode proved to be BYU's first major clash, the opening salvo in a long and convoluted battle between church officials and intellectuals. Smith denounced the "theological scholastic aristocracy," and even the progressive-minded B. H. Roberts scoffed at those who sided with the academics. In response to one student who claimed that higher criticism shot holes into his testimony of the Book of Mormon, Roberts proclaimed, "You have misstated the matter; you mean that the Book of Mormon shoots holes into higher criticism!" But there were still others who sought a middle way. Indeed, later that same year, in December 1911, James Talmage was ordained a member of the Quorum of the Twelve Apostles. While Talmage's successor at the University of Utah saw the move as a blatant public relations stunt, the new apostle was now in a place to shape the modern Mormon mind; a decade later, John Widtsoe joined him in the Quorum.[76]

It was around this time that J. Reuben Clark found his way back to the fold. Working in New York City and paying far more attention to his law practice than his faith, Clark felt the prodding of his church. He was also prodded by his wife, Luacine, known as "Lute," who chastised him for his inactivity. She wrote him from Utah expressing disappointment that he could not attend the baptism of their youngest child, Reuben III, and blamed him for not being around to mentor him. "I hope your work and ambitions are worth the sacrifice," she needled. At one point she noted that since he was "of age," she would "leave your religious training alone, and attend to my own."[77]

For once, Clark listened. He quit his firm and moved back to Utah, where he immersed himself in church service, frequently spoke in the tabernacle, taught Sunday school, and delivered sermons on the church's brand-new radio station. He even paid his tithes and attended the temple. Later he confessed that this was a conscious choice, a decision to "quit rationalizing" belief and instead pledge loyalty to the faith, firmly concluding that there were limits to modernity's reason. Clark forever thought poorly of those who chose otherwise.[78]

Those clashes would not come for another decade, however. In the meantime, despite the dustup in Provo, things looked promising for those hoping to assimilate Mormon and modern ideals. The apostolic ordinations of Talmage and Widtsoe seemed to portend a persistent, if faithful, engagement with secular thinking. Mormons, Talmage argued, had "pioneered the way" of integrating the "surprising progressiveness in modern views of things spiritual." Nor were Talmage and Widtsoe the only new apostles with advanced degrees. Between their appointments was that of Richard Lyman, the man with the broad mind and even broader shoulders. Like the other two, Lyman was a professor with a prestigious education, and though he was not as well known for his intellectual pursuits, he shared their progressive impulses. Yet it was his wife, Amy, who soon became the face of those efforts.[79]

A DECADE before Richard Lyman was ordained an apostle, Amy received a call that changed her life. "It becomes my duty to notify you officially," wrote the aged Emmeline Wells in 1909, "of your election to membership in the Board of Directors of the National Woman's Relief Society." Rather than looking beyond the boundaries of the society, as she and many of her generation had been considering since polygamy's end, Lyman was instead formally requested to help reform that institution. Wells's letter charted Lyman's course for the next four decades, providing her a platform for change.[80]

The society Lyman joined was one that appeared, from some perspectives, in decline. The Relief Society was decades past its activist heyday, as the battles over polygamy and suffrage, at least in Utah, faded. Still presided over by elderly women who were part of the pioneer generation, its message failed to reach the younger generations, and its relief efforts, organizational structure, and scope remained dated. Younger leaders worried the organization might not reach the children of their founding mothers. Women like Lyman preferred to be involved with societies that were more progressive, whether it be church-sponsored groups like the Young Women organization or secular clubs tied to contemporary cultural currents. Dues and attendance in most wards were in decline.[81]

The Relief Society also faced institutional pressure, as priesthood leaders no longer granted it broad latitude. The First Presidency promised the society that it could have its own building on Temple Square in 1900 if it raised $20,000; six years later, however, after saving around $14,000, the institution was told it would instead just have a suite of rooms in a new Presiding Bishopric building. Further, titles for all its local Relief Society properties, totaling nearly $150,000, were transferred to local bishops. Simultaneously, male leaders discouraged women from performing ritual healings, a slow, but not complete, erosion of their previously rich practice. Joseph F. Smith's mission to consolidate the church into a streamlined bureaucracy threatened to curtail the society's independence and relevance.[82]

Reform came slowly. When Lyman was called to the board, it was presided over by Bathsheba Smith, who worried that too much change would erode the society's spiritual foundations. After her death in 1910, however, she was succeeded by Emmeline Wells. To a degree, the new president shared Smith's commitment to their pioneer heritage; even her physical presence highlighted her antiquated aura, as her aged, petite frame was often covered in long, flowing, and lacy dresses that hearkened back to a bygone era. But Wells begrudgingly recognized that change was necessary. As one of Wells's colleagues put it, the leader was "glad to permit old truths to be dressed up in new phraseology" and "old forms modified to meet changing conditions," so long as the changes did not "disintegrate" or "destroy the institution itself." She was willing to bend the society, but not break it.[83]

Lyman, empowered by Wells, went to work merging the lessons on social reform she learned in Chicago with the commission that she received from LDS authorities. Like many modernists, Lyman believed religion's best chance at relevance came from appropriating secular modes of material restructuring. She worked with other reform-minded leaders to implement new projects and policies that spoke to contemporary concerns. They established a home for working girls in Salt Lake City and supported local officials in pushing for free kindergarten. Lyman's associates even founded their own downtown headquarters to combat urban ills, a "Neighborhood House" that was like Addams's Hull House. When Lyman accompanied Wells to a National Council of Women conference in Chicago, she shared her successes with a like-minded audience that might have included Addams herself.[84]

Lyman also transformed the society's publishing effort. Wells offered to transfer control of the *Woman's Exponent*, the newspaper that had served, for nearly a half century, as the voice of their quest for political suffrage and religious recognition. Instead, the newspaper was replaced with the *Relief Society Magazine*, a more modern format that featured content focused on "the temporal things of the Kingdom" in order to attract the "younger women who will be the future leaders." It was a clear pitch for relevance. Wells, always concerned about the institution, feared that they were "getting too far away from the spiritual side of our great work." Yet Lyman, undaunted, flooded the magazine with lessons taken from the nation's reformers and progressive leaders.[85]

Within a decade, Lyman had successfully transformed the society into an efficient and modern machine. Along with the others of her generation who were added to the society's board, and following the progressive priesthood's example, she standardized bookkeeping, correspondence, and other correlation initiatives. The result was a reformed organization that reflected contemporary bureaucracies. Lyman also widened their scope of relief: between 1917 and 1920, she trained with the Red Cross in Denver, helped create the Relief Society Social Service Department, founded new social service programs, and began teaching social work to Relief Society women during special summer schools at BYU.[86]

Lyman's efforts proved especially necessary once a world war turned the nation upside down. Though the saints supported President Woodrow Wilson's initial inclinations to stay clear of the conflict, unwilling to intercede in what appeared to be disputes between elite imperial families, the Utah region was soon swept into the war's necessity and fervor. Joseph F. Smith insisted that "God did not design or cause this," but he privately surmised that it fulfilled Joseph Smith's apocalyptic prophecies. Smith's own son, Hyrum Mack, president of the European mission, was stationed in England when the conflict began, prompting the prophet to call all missionaries home and to support military involvement. "I do not want war," he claimed, but "I would rather the oppressors should be killed, or destroyed, than to allow the oppressors to kill the innocent." Like many religious leaders across the nation who forfeited pacifist inclinations to support the war, he encouraged young men to join the conflict. Mormonism's contributions were substantial: nearly 15,000 saints served in battle, the church bought more than $1 million in liberty bonds, and Lyman oversaw over 1,000 local Relief Societies designated as Red Cross auxiliaries. Even B. H. Roberts, now in his sixties, served as a chaplain in France. "You send your sons and I will be a father to them," Roberts promised.[87]

A global pandemic brought even more tragedy. The influenza claimed nearly two hundred thousand American lives, many of the deceased in their twenties and thirties, in October 1918 alone, the deadliest month in the nation's history. The virus hit soldiers particularly hard, and over half of the LDS fighters who died in December that year did so due to the disease. The global death toll reached the tens of millions by the time the pandemic had run its course.[88]

Smith was not spared from tragedy. His eldest son, Hyrum Mack, died of a ruptured appendix on January 23, 1918, after he returned from England. This was only the latest episode in a lifetime of grief for the Smith family. Though he had nearly fifty children from six wives, Hyrum was the thirteenth he had to bury. Polygamy multiplied trauma as much as it did wives. But the death of his firstborn son, named after his own father, who was slain at Carthage, somehow stung even more. Smith, always emotional, confessed an "overwhelming burden of grief in tears" that confined him to his apartment for months. In some ways, he never recovered. Hyrum's widow, Ida Bowman Smith, gave birth nine months later to the couple's final child, whom they also called Hyrum, named after his father, named after his great-grandfather. Tragically, Ida then died, too, from heart failure. Death begat life, which begat death again.[89]

Smith spent the remainder of 1918 by himself in his bedroom contemplating life, contemplating death, and pleading for understanding. His eighty years had been filled with deep emotions and religious enthusiasm, a familial and spiritual sense of purpose. Now, as his days dimmed, he dipped once more into the prophetic legacy that flowed through his veins. On October 3, while reading the New Testament and pondering the fate of millions across the globe—dying from war, dying from flu, dying from evil—he claimed that "the Spirit of the Lord rested upon me, and I saw the hosts of the dead, both small and great." His vision included witnessing "an innumerable company of the spirits," both the just and the unjust, awaiting divine instruction. Christ, aided by his chosen messengers, including biblical prophets and Latter-day Saint leaders alike, granted the deceased both the knowledge and ordinances required for eternal rest. Nearly a century after his uncle, Joseph Smith, claimed a vision that answered the question of which church people should join, the latest Smith prophet dictated a vision that answered the question of what happened when people died. Mormonism's first century was bookended by visions that answered Americans' most pressing conundrums.[90]

Smith never had a chance to present his vision to the saints. Though he felt well enough to surprise those gathered at the Salt Lake Tabernacle for General Conference the next day, he kept his remarks brief, only hinting at what he had experienced. "I have not lived alone these five months," he volunteered, in a voice that was more breath than words, "and I have had my communications with the Spirit of the Lord continuously." Once conference was over, he dictated the vision to his son, Joseph Fielding Smith, also an apostle, who immediately recognized its significance. While the prophet was still bedridden, the First Presidency and Quorum of the Twelve unanimously "endorsed the revelation as the Word of the Lord" and slated it for immediate release.[91]

Smith, however, did not live long enough to see it published. He joined the world of the spirits, the world he was so anxious to understand, less than two weeks before the vision was printed, merely a week after an armistice signed in Germany ended the world war. Due to the ongoing pandemic, the church somberly announced they were postponing the funeral service.

Smith's death meant not only the passing of a generation but the close of Mormonism's first century. Having been born amid their bloody expulsion from Missouri, he was the last prophet who had personally known Joseph Smith, the last who had walked Nauvoo's streets, the last who remembered life before Utah—one of the few remaining bridges to the faith's pioneer origins. He viewed himself as guardian of heritage, protector of doctrine, a link between past and present. It was fitting, then, that his final act was a vision that collapsed ancient and contemporary eras, biblical and modern prophets, current anxieties and future rewards, all wrapped up in a theology of eternity that merged the entire human family into one interconnected web that would have made his prophet-uncle proud. His words, published posthumously as if uttered from the grave, urged believers to remember that the grave was not the end.

THE MAN who replaced Smith at the church's helm, Heber J. Grant, embodied much of the new era while still retaining connections to the old. Born in 1856 to Jedediah Grant, the firebrand counselor to Brigham Young, and Rachel Ivins, an early Salt Lake City Relief Society president, Heber was raised among Utah's nobility. While young, he courted, and everyone expected him to marry, Emily Wells, daughter of Salt Lake City mayor Daniel H. Wells, though through a different wife than Emmeline. But their relationship fell apart because she did not embrace polygamy; Grant then married Lucy Stringham, who did, in 1877. However, after he was ordained an apostle in 1882, Emily Wells reconsidered and was sealed to him two years later—though, by that time, she entered the Grant family as the third wife, as he was sealed to his second, Augusta Winters, the day before. To avoid arrest during the period of federal prosecutions, Grant and all three wives moved towns, states, and even countries, with Heber and Emily at one point fleeing to England.[92]

Grant had a foot in the new world, too. Raised in a different environment than his predecessor, Grant's physical appearance embodied change: where Smith's beard was long and unruly and reached to the bottom of his chest like an Old Testament prophet, Grant's was tight and trim and, combined with his well-pressed three-piece suits, made him look like a banker, which happened to be one of his occupations. Grant was much more willing to adapt to the new century and dispose of unnecessary traditions, policies birthed in a past age for reasons no longer applicable. Even though he had married plurally, he had only one surviving wife, Augusta, by the time he became president, which made him the first monogamous prophet since Joseph Smith's early years. (LDS doctrine still dictated that he was married to all three in the eternities, however.)[93]

Grant did not receive much initial pushback. The same could not be said about Amy Brown Lyman, however, who had yet to win over the Relief Society's old guard. "Let us not make fundamental changes nor alter the perfect and wise adjustment of our religious organization to match the world's," complained Susa Young Gates, a fellow society board member who frequently clashed with Lyman, "lest we fall into their mistakes and partake of their errors." Gates, a veteran of Utah's suffrage debates who had been one of the primary movers for the church's young woman organization, was as influential a voice as any in Salt Lake City. She maintained a deep devotion to the pioneer spirit of her father, Brigham Young, and was one of the founders, and the fourth president, of the Daughters of Utah Pioneers. A guardian of the past, she now feared things were moving too quickly into the future, a fear increasingly shared by Emmeline Wells, still the society's president. In Wells's mind, if the Relief Society lost its spiritual edge, it might also forfeit its autonomous identity.[94]

A turning point came in spring 1921 when the First Presidency came to meet with Wells just before the April General Conference. She expected it to be a routine discussion, but Wells was instead informed that, rather than serving as Relief Society president until death, as each of her predecessors, save Emma Smith, had done, she would instead be released and replaced. Wells was devastated. Though she suffered significant physical and intellectual decline, and the church's increasingly corporate structure required more energy, Wells saw this as an erosion of the society's independence, an encroachment that could not be reversed. After over a half century of service, she was not afforded the chance to complete her mission. Crestfallen, she cried for days, remained bedridden, and died a few weeks later, on April 25. Her passing, like that of Joseph F. Smith, marked the end of an era.[95]

Wells's tragic end was, ironically, reflective of an anxiety she felt throughout her final years. Even before the major transitions, yet after her contemporaries started passing, Wells recorded in her diary a "singular dream." The failure to interpret its meaning tortured her. "Aunts Presendia & Zina," her predecessors in the presidency, "used to interpret dreams for us," but now there was "no one to do it." She could not help but feel a sense of loss. Though she still presided over a large women's organization, had survived a lifetime of transformative experiences, and held firm to her unfailing faith, here was Wells, nearly an octogenarian living in the twentieth century, deeply concerned that she had failed. Was she—was the Relief Society, was the church, was the nation—were they all losing touch with their origins? Had she—had they—exchanged principles for accommodation? Wells, after nearly a century of dogged determination, went to the grave unsure of the answer.[96]

Lyman, conversely, was not as dour. Though she was not the new Relief Society president—that duty was given to Clarissa S. Williams, the first Utah-born woman to hold the position—Lyman retained her influential place as the organization's secretary, treasurer, and general motor. She was willing to dispense with the dross in the alchemy of progress. For Lyman, the benefits of progressive assimilation far outweighed the downsides, and the American promise pointed unwaveringly toward reform.

6

The Perils of Reform, 1920–45

Whenever an institution becomes an established, recognized, and permanent power, it becomes easy to be in sympathy with other institutional powers, and that is the seed-bed of conservatism.

—JAMES HENRY MOYLE[1]

As a young schoolteacher in 1918, Juanita Leavitt was assigned to teach in Mesquite, a small Nevada town located between Las Vegas and St. George, Utah. On her first Sunday there she met a grizzled old patriarch named Nephi Johnson. Johnson had a long beard, big brown eyes, and a wit much sharper than that of a typical man his age. He also claimed proud pioneer credentials: born in Kirtland in 1833, he had lived in Nauvoo, had crossed with the great migration train in 1848, and was among the first settlers of Southern Utah. By the early twentieth century, the aged patriarch Johnson regaled the small community with stories, and many, including Leavitt, lapped up his tales with glee.

Then, on the afternoon of a bright spring day near the end of the school year, Johnson visited Leavitt's class and refused to leave until he could speak in private. Once all the kids dispersed he approached her desk, sat down, and was ready to disclose details he had kept secret for decades. "My eyes have witnessed things that my tongue has never uttered," he said, "and before I die I want it written down." More, Johnson wanted Leavitt to do the writing.

It was not to be. Perhaps unwilling to process the depth of the occasion, and otherwise distracted, Leavitt procrastinated setting aside time to serve as scribe. However, when Johnson fell ill soon after, and frequently called for "the little school teacher" to visit his bedside, it was too late. "I've lamented and scolded myself all my life," Leavitt recalled years later, for failing to act promptly at Johnson's request. She discovered that he was a key figure in the Mountain Meadows Massacre, and was perhaps ready to reveal information he had long kept hidden. As a form of recompense, Juanita Leavitt— later, after marriage, Juanita Brooks—dedicated her life to unveiling the full story.[2]

Juanita Brooks was, in many ways, a bridge between the pioneer period she studied and the modern church she helped shape. Brooks grew up in a community that still prided itself on being isolated from the wider world, but she lived to see her faith become largely, and surprisingly, assimilated into the nation it once scorned. Indeed, her own attempts to come to grips with the past—to fulfill the promise she believed she broke to Nephi Johnson—embodied the era's cultural transformations.[3]

Reform was the age's buzzword. Growing concern over economic monopolies, distrust in corrupt government, and public debates over religious fundamentals led many to argue that it was time to redeem a decaying society. In his debut novel, *This Side of Paradise* (1920), F. Scott Fitzgerald proclaimed that the "new generation" of Americans had "grown up to find all Gods dead, all wars fought, all faiths in man shaken." Simultaneously, the traumatic results of a global war and crippling economic depression left many desperate for relief from what prominent journalist Walter Lippmann denounced as the "acids of modernity." "We can no longer treat life as something that has trickled down to us," Lippmann explained. "We have to deal with it deliberately, devise its social organization, alter its tools, formulate its method, educate and control it." These two principles—reform and relief—framed life for many Americans in the second quarter of the twentieth century.[4]

These national currents found expression within the Mormon community. At Brigham Young University, Franklin Harris attempted to tether the faith's flagship academy to the broader scholarly world; in the Relief Society, Amy Brown Lyman retooled the organization to solve the era's social problems; within leadership circles, B. H. Roberts addressed pressing theological and intellectual questions. In response, a cadre of strong-willed leaders concerned with these assimilationist strides—most notably J. Reuben Clark, who experienced a rapid and unexpected ascent—worked hard to curb them. Adherents of all stripes struggled to define the shifting boundaries of belonging and belief.

These fissures were readily apparent by 1945. In a letter to her close friend and fellow historian Dale Morgan, Juanita Brooks acknowledged the growing rift, and even admitted that some might find her "in a state of apostasy." She knew that those pushing retrenchment were reforming the faith in their image, just as she was trying to reform it in hers. But she would not go quietly. "I think it is as much my church as it is J. Reuben Clark's or anyone else's," she concluded.[5]

This battle over the faith's identity and priorities shaped modern Mormonism.

FRANKLIN HARRIS was on a mission. Born in 1884 in Benjamin, Utah, just south of Provo, he graduated from Brigham Young Academy before moving east to earn a PhD in chemistry from Cornell. His first job was teaching zoology and entomology at Utah State Agricultural College in Logan, but he jumped at the opportunity to become BYU's president in 1921. Harris was not yet forty years old and retained a boyish, clean-shaven face with a full head of hair, but his youthful demeanor did not slow his earnest desire to reform the institution. He was the first person with a PhD, as well as the first monogamist, to lead the school. Harris desired the university to follow other institutions by embracing the modern academy. "We must make of this institution a great center of religious thought," he declared, and should "have in our library the leading writings of religious subjects from all parts of the world."[6]

It was a tough task. Both Mormon and American academics viewed the campus with suspicion. But Harris, a committed pro-

gressive, was up for the challenge. He hired five professors with doctorates in his first year, granted funding for other faculty to receive
advanced degrees, provided research sabbaticals, and modernized
the curriculum. One teacher remarked that Harris had successfully
transformed the institution from a glorified high school to a university. Harris even introduced new religion courses like "Evolution and
Religion," "Philosophy and Religion," and "Comparative Religions";
of the forty-one religion courses taught in the 1920s, only seven dealt
directly with Mormonism. Harris promised that his administration
would prioritize "academic freedom without any attempt to avoid
issues." As a result of his efforts, BYU finally received university
accreditation in 1928.[7]

That Harris could accomplish so much only a decade after the
infamous battle over evolution reflected how much had changed.
This was partly due to administrative turnover. Church president
Heber J. Grant was far more pragmatic than his predecessor and
readily admitted a lack of interest in intellectual endeavors. "So far
as I am concerned, having practically no education at all," he told the
BYU Board of Trustees in 1921, "I am not as capable of understanding these necessities as some other men." This was a far cry from
Joseph F. Smith, who anxiously oversaw doctrinal teaching on campus. Charles Penrose, a First Presidency counselor who lacked formal education yet prided himself on a more progressive belief, urged
Grant to take an open stance concerning secular knowledge. They
issued a statement that admitted "it is of little significance" if the
"higher critics" were right concerning allegorical biblical passages.
With the encouragement of apostle Richard Lyman, Harris even
tried, unsuccessfully, to recruit Ralph Chamberlin back to Provo
despite Chamberlin's previous exile.[8]

Aiding Harris was Adam S. Bennion, who was named the
church's education superintendent in 1919, as well as Joseph F. Merrill, who succeeded Bennion in 1928. Just a couple of years younger
than Harris, and similarly sporting a clean-shaven face—a physical embodiment of their modern mindset—Bennion had received a
master's degree from Columbia and a doctorate in literature from the
University of Utah; Merrill, two decades their senior, boasted physics

degrees from Chicago and Johns Hopkins. Under the supervision of church leaders, Bennion and Merrill either closed most church academies and high schools or transferred them to state control, instead focusing their resources on establishing "institutes" at universities where LDS students could better learn about their faith. The first institute was located at the University of Idaho in 1926, quickly followed by Idaho Southern Branch College, the University of Utah, Utah State Agricultural College, the University of Wyoming, the University of Arizona, and the University of Southern California. Bennion hoped to place "scholarly books dealing with historical and literary analysis of the Bible" in all these institutes' libraries.[9]

These reformers hoped to staff these institutes with a generation of teachers who were able to balance faith and reason. They commenced annual summer training sessions in the Edenic setting of Aspen Grove, a BYU campground nestled on the slopes of the majestic Mount Timpanogos, whose peak towered over Utah County. LDS instructors gathered for six weeks each summer to learn about the latest developments in the scholarly world of religion. They slept in tents, hiked trails, and heard about academia's newest theories. Though apostles John Widtsoe and James Talmage were frequent lecturers, so too were Sidney Sperry, who had recently received a master's degree in Old Testament studies from the University of Chicago, and Heber Snell, who received his degree in biblical studies from the Pacific School of Religion. After a stream of visiting lecturers from the University of Chicago spoke to the gatherings, church leaders strengthened these institutional ties further: they agreed to sponsor several of their most promising teachers to travel to Chicago to earn degrees in religion. It appeared to be a new dawn for Mormon intellectualism. "Higher criticism is not [to be] feared by Latter-day Saints," Widtsoe proclaimed.[10]

What came to be known as the "Chicago experiment" was not the first tangible linkage between the Mormon world and secular academia, but it was the most daring. The eleven young men who received a half salary along with church loans were to be the core of BYU's newly revamped religion department. This was a quixotic union that, for the moment, bucked national trends. Chicago's

Divinity School was a hub for modernist thought, and the work of its dean, Shailer Mathews, a leading proponent of the social gospel, was often invoked to combat evangelical arguments. While some of the students had a hard time digesting what they were taught—one, T. Edgar Lyon, complained that all his professors were "either infidels or agnostics"—others found it refreshing. Russel Swensen, who studied with Benjamin Mays, Martin Luther King's own teacher, later reminisced that "these courses also served to correct some previous misconceptions which we had held."[11]

Some worried these changes were going too far. One parent wrote to BYU complaining that "all the professors in the university believe in the principle of evolution." It was not an unjustified fear. One editorial in the school's newspaper the next year praised Darwin as a man as great in his field as George Washington was in his. Concern continued to rise. Susa Young Gates, who desperately clung to the faith's traditional doctrines, ordered Harris to find "a new class of teachers" who were "real Latter-day Saint men instead of philosophers and theorists." When Harris demurred, Gates retorted that he was becoming too "broadminded." She had lost the battle over the Relief Society with Amy Brown Lyman, and now she was losing control of the university named after her own father.[12]

What was at stake was not just the school's curriculum but the ideological possibilities for modern Mormonism. Would the LDS tradition go the way of the modernists, who sought to transform faith in a way that matched the new, evolving era, or would it follow the path of the fundamentalists, who clung to traditional modes of knowledge and unimpeachable truth?

The modernists appeared to have the upper hand, at least for the moment. Franklin Harris proved to be a skilled administrator who could build consensus, earn trust from church leaders, and frame these advances in a way that fit the university's mission. Richard Lyman praised Harris's agenda, including the Chicago experiment. "When we have more men who can associate with great scholars," he wrote, "the work of the Church will go forward much faster." To his fellow apostles, Lyman urged that they grant "greater charity toward our church members whose views are not strictly orthodox," as it would be a tragedy if they lost their "most studious" members. Or so Lyman and his colleagues thought in the early 1930s. If they had their way, BYU and Mormonism would march proudly into the future that modernism promised.[13]

LIKE FRANKLIN HARRIS, Amy Brown Lyman saw the 1920s as full of potential. She built upon her achievements of the previous decade and continued transforming the Relief Society into a progressive agent of temporal reform. A report issued by the new Social Advisory Committee in 1921, of which Lyman was a leading figure, staked a clear vision for the Relief Society: while their agenda "does not preclude work and discussion of a theological or doctrinal nature," their focus was caring for the poor and the sick, providing resources for sex education and welfare, teaching skills for workplace and household management, and other relief efforts that mirrored contemporary secular reform. Though the church did not adopt all their proposals, Lyman implemented a more socially oriented vision for the society, in part because its president, Clarissa Williams, shared her agenda.[14]

Others remained concerned. Susa Young Gates, who resented losing full control of the *Relief Society Magazine*, complained that Lyman exhibited a "real ignorance of the fundamentals of the Gospel." Specifically, she chafed at Lyman's desire to appropriate secular approaches and merge federal and ecclesiastical relief efforts. It appeared to her that Lyman was "willing to make the Church a tail to the Gentile kite." Gates feared there was little separation between Lyman's Relief Society and the many gentile reform movements throughout the nation. Some joked that the organization could be renamed the "Club of the Church called the Relief Society."[15]

Even with her persistent detractors—who never subsided—what Lyman and her supporters accomplished during the 1920s was remarkable. Her willingness to work with government agencies, appropriate their resources, and draw on their funding empowered the Relief Society as a regional force. Like her mentor, Jane Addams, Lyman directly addressed the ills that plagued America, attempting to prove that religion could take a much more pragmatic and less dogmatic approach to the world.

Lyman was elected to the Utah State Legislature in 1923, demonstrating the overlap between government and ecclesiastical intervention. She was just one of many American women who rushed into office in the wake of the Nineteenth Amendment. While there, Lyman successfully pushed for the state's implementation of the Sheppard-Towner Act, recently passed by Congress. The first fruit of fully enfranchised women and dedicated to maternal and infant healthcare, the act was an attempt to create national health programs, steps that eventually culminated in Social Security. Lyman then worked with national and state agencies to embed the Relief Society within these efforts and established 133 health centers and 274 dental clinics and held 2,203 health conferences. She sent apprentices to train at the New York School of Philanthropy and the University of Chicago's School of Social Work.[16]

Lyman was thrilled with these efforts. She exulted that "our church," when empowered by these government tools, "has given women and girls opportunities, the like of which no other church has given." In 1929, Sylvester Cannon, the church's presiding bishop, remarked to the Relief Society, "I do not believe you really know how powerful your influence is," as they were now equipped to exert "political as well as moral influence." Federal officials knew to work with Lyman and the society, not necessarily priesthood officials, when instituting Utah relief efforts.[17]

Lyman flourished during this period because she held the full support of Heber Grant, who flattered himself as being a reformer. Some of the new policies he initiated culminated decades of changes, as when he made the Word of Wisdom a temple-recommended requirement. But other shifts were more abrupt. Starting in 1922, Grant worked with George F. Richards, president of the Salt Lake Temple, to further standardize temple liturgy, portions of which had varied by temple, and modernize garments to better align with contemporary fashion. But in codifying Mormon rituals under an increasingly formal bureaucracy, Grant and other leaders also curtailed practices that had long been part of the faith's tradition—most notably female ritual healings. The "priesthood" was now permanently associated with worthy men who held ecclesiastical offices, rather than a cosmic authority shared by believers, therefore erasing the space in which women had previously operated.[18]

Lyman agreed with these reforms so long as they matched her own progressive vision. Ritual healings were not as important to her as coordinated relief. Yet these developments crystallized the outcome that her predecessor, Emmeline B. Wells, had feared: if the Relief Society gave up its spiritual foundations in an attempt to both accommodate priesthood correlation and mirror secular reform, it risked losing the very radical mission that necessitated its autonomy. As Annie Wells Cannon, Emmeline's daughter, warned, "The spirit of the Gospel and religion seem to have disappeared" within the society, "and it seems to be a social welfare organization."[19]

Even Lyman's domestic life reflected change, albeit indirectly. While she was raised in a family with three wives and twenty-five children, her adult household included only herself, Richard, and two children, Wendell and Margaret. The small number was in part deliberate, as Lyman chose to cut off marital relations with Richard following the birth of their second child. This decision was likely rooted in health concerns—besides her own difficult pregnancies, Lyman's mother was bedridden for much of her life due to a prolapsed uterus—but that decision put her in company with contemporaries who pushed for familial options. As women envisioned careers outside the home across the country, and many limited their number of children, America's average family size dwindled. Lyman likely did not share these more radical sentiments, but her decision to forgo sex instead of expanding her family reflected a sense of bodily autonomy.[20]

Lyman presented a different image of Mormonism than that of her predecessors, just as many across the nation challenged traditional understandings of the home. The distance between the pioneer ideal and the modern reality was expanding. For the Mormon faith, where patriarchy remained a central principle, the juxtaposition was especially stark. Lyman represented loosening of domestic foundations. May Booth Talmage, wife of apostle James Talmage, playfully highlighted the tension in a poem she wrote for a social gathering in 1923:

> Now Richard loves Amy in some sort of way
> If she'd only "stay put" where he'd like her to stay.
> So retiring and modest, it breaks his heart
> To have *her* voice heard in the great public mart.
> Head drooping, pride crushed, he remembers the hour
> When she promised his word should be law. Gone is his power.
> Now in silent rebellion he grieves night and day
> To have her making laws which he's forced to obey.

While composed in jest, Talmage's words harpooned Mormon patriarchy. They may have also needled Richard. Despite his modernist leanings, he, like other contemporary men, worried things may go too far. He also felt that his physical longings were no longer being met. Richard Lyman soon looked elsewhere for satisfaction.[21]

Amy Lyman's reform efforts for the Relief Society, however, proved prescient. They were especially effective in preparing the church for Black Tuesday, October 29, 1929. When the stock markets plummeted, plunging America into the largest depression of the century, many denominations scrambled to respond. Though the social gospel movement had alerted many churches to the need to provide temporal support, the voluntary and inconsistent nature of these Depression-era efforts was inadequate for the new challenge. A sputtering federal response over the first few years eventually gave way to the landslide election of Franklin D. Roosevelt, who took the White House based on promises of vigorous government intervention. While churches worked with the president to build a permanent social safety net, many were simultaneously furious to lose their position as the nation's primary healers.[22]

The Mormon corridor was hit as hard as any region. Lyman, of course, was prepared. On the eve of Roosevelt's election, she reaffirmed in General Conference the new Democratic mantra that those in need should turn to the government before their church. Then, after Roosevelt took office, she consistently and publicly praised the

New Deal, urging members to support "the government loyally in its heroic efforts." No other government, she proclaimed, "has ever tried harder to meet a situation than has ours." Because of the shortage of trained social workers, and federal regulations that required funds to be distributed through public agencies, Lyman reorganized Salt Lake City's Relief Society as a distinct department within the county's Department of Public Welfare. They were handling thousands of cases per year by 1934. In FDR's America, where every citizen was urged to sacrifice for the common good, the Relief Society led Mormonism's relief cause.[23]

Lyman saw temporal salvation in these progressive programs. Priesthood leaders, however, feared the New Deal policies were an erosion of personal responsibility. President Grant, increasingly frustrated with Democrats, publicly opposed Roosevelt's election. Yet a majority of Utahns, agreeing with Lyman's sensibilities, supported FDR's candidacy. Lyman shared some of Grant's concerns, but also pragmatically recognized the severity of the crisis. A growing divide over political principles was forming, one that could no longer be bridged by Lyman's and Grant's shared support of progressive bureaucracy.

B. H. ROBERTS's life was consumed by words. By his death, he had accumulated at least 1,300 books, many filled with marginalia as he desperately sought truths that meshed with his vision of the gospel. His own words filled quite a few volumes, too. Since 1888, he had written nearly twenty books on historical, doctrinal, and ecclesiastical matters, edited the documentary series *History of the Church of Jesus Christ of Latter-day Saints*, and produced a string of apologetic works that responded to the age's loudest critics. When invited by the non-Mormon *Americana* magazine to write a history of the church, he produced monthly forty-two-page installments from July 1909 to July 1915; the periodical adjusted its formatting and schedule to capture all these words. Eventually, the words were compiled, edited, and published in six volumes as part of the church's centenary in 1930 to broad, if not unanimous, acclaim. ("Brother Roberts's ponderous tomes," complained Susa Young Gates, succeeded only in "studiously ignor[ing] women.") Roberts had overcome his lack of education to be seen as the faith's foremost intellectual authority.[24]

Roberts soon encountered a new challenge that even his voluminous words could not solve. William Riter, an educated Mormon residing in Washington, DC, wrote an earnest letter in 1921 to James Talmage regarding the Book of Mormon. Riter's questions were of a different stripe than previous evangelical attacks rooted in doctrinal disputes. Instead, they were drawn from sociological, linguistic, scientific, and historical reasoning. How could the Nephite people, supposedly alone when they arrived on the North American continent, result in thousands of different Indigenous tongues and tribes? How could the text refer to horses, steel, and silk prior to the European colonization? Unable to find answers, Talmage turned to Roberts, who recognized the clear stakes: "If the origin of the Book of Mormon could be proved to be other than that set forth by Joseph Smith," he reasoned, then the entire faith "must fall."[25]

Confronting these new critiques proved more difficult than previous investigations. Roberts confessed that his research resulted in only more problems. He eventually requested that the entire church leadership gather to discuss these issues, which they did on consecutive days in early January 1922. Roberts produced a 141-page document for the occasion that summarized not only Riter's questions but several more he had stumbled upon while investigating. The meetings lasted from dawn to dusk, with Roberts presenting questions and begging his brethren, any of them, to provide convincing answers. None, according to Roberts, were persuasive, so he called for a third meeting, which took place two weeks later, again to an unsatisfying conclusion. Richard Lyman asked if this line of discussion would decrease doubt, and Roberts responded that further investigation "would very greatly increase our difficulties." Lyman, then, despite his modernist sympathies, urged that they drop the issue of the Book of Mormon's authenticity, which they did.[26]

Roberts continued his digging. While presiding over the church's northeastern states mission, headquartered in New York, he encountered Ethan Smith's *View of the Hebrews*, an 1823 book that also connected Indigenous people to the House of Israel. Roberts then produced two new projects, a 284-page study and an 18-page summary, that forthrightly challenged traditional defenses of the Book of Mormon. The Twelve, however, rejected both. While it is unlikely that Roberts had lost faith in the Book of Mormon—he continued to testify to its divinity—his anxious desire to use the tools of modernism to interpret, expand, and even revise traditional truth was out of step with the LDS hierarchy's growing consensus. "What is to be our general standing," he pleaded, "before the enlightened opinion of mankind?"[27]

The discussion prompted by Roberts succeeded in softening the church's previously rigid theories concerning the Book of Mormon's geography. They removed footnotes from the scripture that identified precise locations for the scripture's events and instead posited that the Nephites and Lamanites were merely two of *many* civilizations that existed on the American continents. This idea came to be known as the "limited geography" theory. It was a concession to some of the issues raised by modern critiques while retaining traditional beliefs concerning the sacred text.[28]

Undeterred, the wordsmith sequestered himself for much of 1927 in New York City to work on his magnum opus. Staying mere blocks from the Union Theological Seminary, where the foremost debates over theological modernism were waged, Roberts worked on a systematic defense and rigorous examination of Mormonism. The result was a fifty-five-chapter tome entitled *The Way, the Truth, the Life*. It was the culmination of his apologetic career and the acme of Mormon modernism. Roberts drew from John Fiske, the American philosopher known for reconciling Christianity and evolution, and from Herbert Spencer, the social Darwinist. He cited over 150 contemporary philosophers, scientists, and theologians whose contributions were, according to Roberts, "the world's best hope" for continued progress. Roberts even attempted to answer the question of human evolution: "developmental theism," as he called it, argued that lifeforms evolved on earth for millions of years prior to Adam and Eve being transplanted from some distant planet. Though far from systematic, the theory was at least an effort to mesh his faith with the wider intellectual community.[29]

Roberts submitted the work to be adopted as a church textbook in September 1928. It immediately hit roadblocks. Although the trio of young apostles, James Talmage, Richard Lyman, and John Widtsoe, had moderated official church discourse, a move that had been tepidly approved by the pragmatic Grant, tensions during the 1920s now called these modernist reforms into question. Nationally, public debates over the rise of fundamentalism highlighted the threats of secular learning. Locally, another junior apostle who came from a privileged heritage was finding his voice and declared himself Roberts's equal.

JOSEPH FIELDING SMITH was raised convinced he was part of the faith's most important family. The first son of Julina Lambson Smith, Joseph F. Smith's second wife, the prophet's namesake was small in stature but large in confidence. He was bounced on his father's knee as a young boy while hearing stories about his grandfather's execution at the hands of a wicked mob, and much of his childhood was spent alone while his parents hid from federal prosecution. He was dedicated to preserving a knowledge of the church's persecuted past, serving as either assistant church historian or church historian from 1906 until 1970. But Smith was also the guardian of orthodoxy, an informal yet still earnest position he inherited from his father. The nation's trending ideological advances only reaffirmed his belief that eternal truths were under assault, and he warned President Grant that "there were dangers lurking in modern thought." Smith, assigned to review Roberts's new manuscript, worried he had found a Trojan horse that carried these enemies across the drawbridge.[30]

The review committee spent an entire year dissecting Roberts's manuscript and concluded that it required substantial revisions. There were "speculative" ideas, they reasoned, that "appear to be out of harmony with the revelations of the Lord and the fundamental teachings of the Church." What particularly irked Smith was Roberts's willingness to accommodate the theory of evolution. "I denounce as absolutely false the opinions of some," including "elders," Smith decried in April 1930, "that this earth was peopled with a race before Adam." Roberts, however, refused to budge. Any revisions, he believed, would destroy his "genius." Eventually, in early January 1931, both Roberts and Smith pleaded their cases before the Quorum of the Twelve. Roberts was chastised for acerbically questioning Smith's competency, and Smith denounced Roberts's "worldly philosophies" and "modernistic tendencies."[31]

The debate reflected broader intellectual currents. James Talmage, bothered by the confrontation, wondered where Smith was getting his ideas. He wrote his son, Sterling Talmage, who had followed his father's footsteps into geology, and asked about George McCready Price's *The New Geology*, a text that Smith had frequently cited. "All of Price's arguments," the younger Talmage responded, "were advanced and refuted from fifty to a hundred years ago." Price's work was neither "new," nor really "geology." Other than those "*two corrections*," Sterling snidely concluded, "the title remains the best part of the book."[32]

These biting critiques were only partly correct. Much of Price's anti-evolution apologia was indeed drawn from previous centuries, but he also embodied a new generation of dogmatists. A Canadian-born Seventh-Day Adventist, Price became famous for his fundamentalist faith and unrelenting attacks on modern scholarship. In one of his nearly fifty books, *Illogical Geology*, published in 1906, he promised $1,000 to anyone who could "show me how to prove that one kind of fossil is older than another." Plenty of scientists poked holes in his facile theories, though none to Price's satisfaction, and so he kept his pledged money until death. He could afford to spend it, however, as thousands of readers bought his books.[33]

The debate over evolution, percolating for decades, came to the nation's forefront in the 1920s. Fundamentalists linked modern scientific thought to atheism, promiscuity, and a host of social sins, and several states passed legislation banning Darwin's theory from the classroom. Henry Emerson Fosdick, one of the most prominent pastors in the nation and a chief proponent of the more modernist course, posed the most pressing question in 1922: "Shall the Fundamentalists Win?" A few years later, activists in Tennessee orchestrated the arrest of John Scopes, a high school science teacher in Dayton, for breaking the state's anti-evolution law. Mormons, like the rest of the nation, followed the public spectacle closely as reporters dispatched updates from the "trial of the century." Leading the prosecution was William Jennings Bryan, the cultural giant who was thrice the Democratic nominee for president and once the secretary of state, who drew heavily from George McCready Price in denouncing Darwinian thought.[34]

Mormon leaders had been aware of Bryan for some time prior to the Scopes trial. He had received 83 percent of Utah's votes during the 1896 election, and his populist politics and religious rhetoric had remained admired ever since. For men like Joseph Fielding Smith, Bryan's spirited defense of scriptural literalism earned devotion. Smith had previously gifted a copy of one of Bryan's fundamentalist texts to Heber J. Grant, which impressed the prophet so much that he wrote Bryan a note of appreciation. The church then published Bryan's final trial speech in its newspaper, and the First Presidency issued a statement of its own that summer reaffirming their belief that humanity originated with Adam.[35]

If the Scopes trial embodied America's division over scriptural interpretation, it also captured the same debate taking place in Mormondom. B. H. Roberts pleaded with Smith to recognize that the time had come to forgo traditional beliefs in light of modern science. Smith, in response, insisted that Latter-day Saints were "not bound to receive the theories of men," no matter "how great the weight of evidence may appear to be in favor of the theory, or how many men of world renown may accept it as established truth." William Jennings Bryan could not have said it better.[36]

President Grant finally concluded the Roberts-Smith debate in April 1931. He reviewed material from both sides and met with Roberts one last time. Then, along with the First Presidency, he announced they were going to sidestep the entire question. Church leaders were to focus on "the fundamental doctrines of the Church," and "leave Geology, Biology, Archaeology and Anthropology" alone. The decision was a blow to both Roberts and his ideological mission. Even the statement's language reflected the fundamentalist cause: members were to focus on the "fundamentals" of the gospel, most notably that "Adam is the primal parent of our race."[37]

Roberts died in September 1933, succumbing to the complications of diabetes that had slowed him in his final years, the close of a lifetime of ideological investigation tempered by circumstantial realities. Despite his voluminous works, Roberts was far from a systematic thinker. He embraced the journey of learning more than the finality of knowledge. His was the modernist voyage, the unstoppable quest to accumulate data, theories, and, above all else, words, words upon words that explored the meaning of life, society, and even the cosmos. That his last decade was his most frustrating—that his final words went unpublished—was both a testament to the faith to which he held firm and a reflection of the church he feared he could no longer shape.

THE DECADE from 1923 to 1933 proved to be the high-water mark for modernist reform within Mormonism. Franklin Harris pushed and prodded to bring BYU and its scholarly mission more in line with America's academic currents; Amy Brown Lyman paved the way for integrating the faith's charitable efforts within the larger societal vision for progressive uplift; B. H. Roberts researched, wrote, and argued his way into an LDS theology that was conversant with broader questions. Building on several decades of cultural assimilation, these reformers envisioned a Mormonism unafraid of modernity's central challenges, and unreserved in drawing from contemporary resources.

Yet their progressive attempts at social reform through secular means, if still within a faithful context, were among the few forms of the church's Americanization project that did not last.

Mormons spent much of the early twentieth century desperate to build bridges that connected them to their surrounding culture. But some bridges proved too dangerous—avenues on which too much cultural influence traveled, commerce that imported too much heterodoxy and exported too much divinity. Mormonism was, they readily confessed, destined to be an American faith. But leaders insisted it could not be *too* American, lest it lose the singularity that proved its necessity. As a result, the faith of Harris, Lyman, and Roberts was the road less traveled, and was to give way to that of another, one who entered the scene unexpectedly in 1933 yet whose impact was immediate, and whose relentless and domineering efforts came to shape the modern church.

AFTER SPENDING most of the 1920s reaffirming his commitment to the LDS faith, J. Reuben Clark, whose serious demeanor, capacious mind, and dogged determination still made him a man in demand, was once again called into public service. His previous work as solicitor had made him an expert on America's relations with Mexico, and he was appointed by President Calvin Coolidge in 1926 to help mediate business issues between the two countries. Clark was eventually promoted to ambassador and quickly became one of the most prominent Latter-day Saints in the nation.[38]

Yet his career transformed in the span of a few weeks in late 1931. Charles Nibley, a counselor in the First Presidency since 1925, passed away on December 11, leaving a vacancy in the church's most powerful governing body. President Heber Grant then said that he wanted "Clark, the ambassador to Mexico," as the deceased counselor's replacement. To Grant, Clark represented a logical step in the church's professionalization, as his expertise could help navigate the institution into the modern world. Yet it was a surprising choice. Clark had never served in any meaningful ecclesiastical position, and was known as a worldly figure—"a $100,000-a-year man," as one leader put it. But Grant, who had always been impressed by Clark's prowess, was hopeful. "We can ask him," he quipped.[39]

Grant's request arrived in Mexico City just before Christmas. Clark, intuiting what it queried, delayed opening the envelope until he was alone in his private study. The diplomat was not eager to "give up my life's work" just as he neared his profession's apex, and was worried about deserting his current ambassadorship. His initial response was to decline, and he labored for hours into the night penning a letter explaining why. But instead of mailing it off, he placed the response in a locked drawer.

Clark remained unsettled for days. After his family noticed his aloofness during Christmas celebrations, he admitted to them his conundrum. His wife, Lute, always his spiritual anchor, rejoiced. She envisioned a brighter future for him in the church than in the state. Clark, still torn, penned another letter on December 28, this time accepting the assignment. He decided to send both letters, a reflection of mixed emotions. The First Presidency could decide for him. When the hefty envelope arrived in Salt Lake City, Grant and Ivins cared only about the acceptance letter and ignored the other. Once Clark's ambassadorial duties were completed, which happened when a Democratic landslide in the 1932 election evicted all Republicans, Grant announced the new counselor at the April 1933 General Conference.[40]

Though Clark left his political post, he could not leave politics alone. This was not surprising given America's polarized response to Roosevelt's election. In his first General Conference address, Clark chastised the proposed New Deal for enabling idleness and proclaimed that America needed to return to "old time figures" of

LDS First Presidency, 1937. From left, J. Reuben Clark, Heber J. Grant, and David O. McKay. Clark's elevation to the First Presidency in 1933 marked the origins of modern Mormonism; McKay would later become prophet in 1951.

"industry, thrift, honesty, self-reliance, independence of spirit, self-discipline, and mutual helpfulness." Privately, he mused that establishing "a socialistic or communistic state" was "behind this whole propaganda." This type of animosity toward FDR was increasingly prevalent in conservative religious communities, who viewed the new president as a threat to religious and social order.[41]

Clark was especially aghast at how popular Roosevelt's policies were among Mormons. Utah residents received nearly three times the national average of federal assistance due to their vulnerable agrarian and mining economy. Further, several leaders, like Amy Brown Lyman, presiding bishop Sylvester Cannon, and First Presidency counselor Anthony Ivins, had been outspoken in supporting relief programs. Clark feared the welfare state was infiltrating Zion. Convinced saints were taking advantage of relief mechanisms, he immediately called a meeting with the Relief Society and priesthood officials and was informed that 95 percent of those who received help were in genuine need. Could the church take care of them? he asked. The question was absurd. One official scrawled the sobering truth across the top of their agenda: "If the Church were to undertake to take care of this amount, it would bankrupt us."[42]

Clark commenced a conservative push that eventually transformed the entire church. He drafted a twenty-nine-page memo detailing the federal government's overreach and how the church should take care of its own. He then reorganized auxiliary programs, particularly those serving the youth, to curtail their autonomy and align them with his conservative values. Clark finally convinced Grant to fully embrace the Republican agenda, particularly its full-throated opposition to the New Deal, once the First Presidency counselor and Democrat Anthony Ivins passed away. Grant, who was said to become physically sick whenever he spoke of FDR—"I feel almost that Roosevelt is inspired by the devil himself," he once wrote—commissioned Clark to write editorials directly opposing the president's reelection. Grant's anger at Roosevelt originated from the latter's support of repealing Prohibition, but he soon became convinced that Roosevelt's programs would result in a nation filled with immoral loafers. He and Clark overturned the *Deseret News*'s previously Democratic-leaning leadership and installed editors who supported their anti–New Deal crusade. The conservative editors at the *LA Times* even urged Clark to run against FDR as a Republican candidate.[43]

At first their work was unsuccessful: 70 percent of Utah voted for Roosevelt in 1936, and the *Deseret News*'s readership dropped precipitously. But Clark and Grant were unfazed, and they soon found a new vessel for ecclesiastical activism. Harold B. Lee, a serious man with dark brown hair, large blue eyes, and an exceptionally large and long face, had recently moved to Utah to serve on the Salt Lake City Commission. He was known for his organizational skills, which he had honed as an experienced community leader. Appointed president of Salt Lake City's Pioneer Stake at the precocious age of thirty, Lee was tasked with overlooking the welfare of several sprawling congregations struggling due to the Depression. To succeed, he drew on his farming background to renew Mormonism's communitarian spirit. Lee established bishops' storehouses at which saints could donate goods and work as well as distribute resources to those in need.

The success of Lee's initiative drew the attention of his superiors, who decided to expand the project church-wide. Grant promised that the Church Security Program, established in 1936, "set up a system under which the curse of idleness will be done away with, the evils of the dole abolished, and independence, industry, thrift, and self-respect be once more established among our people." In many ways the program mirrored the Republican Party's welfare capitalism, which argued that private organizations and corporations, not the government, should look after the well-being of citizens. The First Presidency finally had its counter to the New Deal.[44]

Soon renamed the Church Welfare Plan, the initiative drew from the faith's communitarian heritage and reaffirmed a sense of exceptionalism and patriarchal control. Amy Brown Lyman initially welcomed the program as another tool for help. But she recognized that it was not nearly large enough to replace federal assistance. After she and her husband left for England to preside over the British mission, other Relief Society leaders became demoralized that their efforts were relegated to a supporting, rather than directing, role.[45]

Clark's single-minded determination earned him his share of critics. His wife reported that he was becoming known around Salt Lake City as "nothing but a Dictator." Undeterred, Clark pressed on, and even shot back at any grumblings he heard from other leaders. The saints were to separate themselves from FDR's corrupt federal over-reach and return to pioneer principles of self-reliance. Clark bragged in 1936 to the *New York Times* that he expected 88,000 saints to be removed from government welfare by the end of the decade.[46]

The Welfare Plan, though immediately successful, never became as expansive as Clark envisioned. Only a fourth of the people Clark expected to wean off the government did so, as the New Deal remained the primary support for most members. Utah consumed the twelfth-most resources per capita in the nation, and the government spent ten times the value of church-wide Welfare Plan resources within the state. The new program ably supplemented the New Deal, but it fell far short of supplanting it. Nor did the saints immediately adopt their leaders' FDR-phobia: a majority voted for his reelection in both 1940 and 1944, each time over Grant and Clark's vocal and increasingly flustered opposition.[47]

The program's true accomplishment was its legacy. In Mormon memory, the Welfare Plan became a mythic, herculean conqueror, single-handedly pulling each and every saint out of poverty. Its heroic feats were prima facie evidence that the church could take care of itself. Even if he failed in weaning the church off federal assistance, Clark transformed the church's mindset, laying the groundwork for the community to embrace the backlash against America's liberal consensus as well as take a firm side in the political battles that ensued over the following decades.[48]

Besides Lyman, few mourned this transition more than James Henry Moyle, a tall and broad-chested septuagenarian who served in Roosevelt's government. "I am convinced that President Clark is the real cause of the political errors of the First Presidency," Moyle sighed, despondent that his own faith was rejecting the administration in which he served. Moyle had previously found his Democratic allegiance within the mainstream of Mormon political culture, but he sensed the ground shifting. He blamed Clark for ushering in a new era and was worried about the "adverse effects of the course of conservatism" that would soon follow. It would only be a matter of time, he assumed, before most believers followed suit.[49]

If J. Reuben Clark's wife, Lute, had long been the anchor for his faith, it was his uncle and cousin, John and Lorin Woolley, who caused turbulent waves. John Woolley, in whose house John Taylor spent parts of the underground, increasingly opposed church leadership over the issue of polygamy. He married his final plural wife in 1908—Woolley claimed that Joseph F. Smith officiated, a rumor that leadership denied—and was excommunicated shortly afterward. Yet Woolley refused to go quietly. He and his son commenced telling all who would listen that Taylor had ordained them, along with a handful of other trusted disciples, to a special priesthood quorum in 1886 designed to keep polygamy alive even if the church succumbed to external pressure. This small cohort of polygamists expanded during the 1920s, especially after Lorin Woolley dictated a detailed account of his experiences with John Taylor, including an alleged revelation that prophesied that their efforts would be necessary.[50]

Clark was informed of this growing threat shortly after joining the First Presidency. Around the same time that he penned his first memo denouncing the New Deal, he wrote another extended statement that similarly denounced polygamists. Both moves, he believed, were necessary. His memo, soon released as a First Presidency statement and known, to some, as the "third manifesto," rewrote the past to support the church in the present. Everyone who claimed the church had sanctioned post-1890 polygamous unions, or who married plurally, would be cut off. Clark backed up his words with actions: he coordinated with bishops to implement loyalty oaths, policemen to surveil meetings, prosecutors to bring charges, librarians to destroy books, and even the postmaster to censor mailings. One of those punished by these actions believed that Clark suffered from a "virus" known as "hysteria excommunicatus." In Clark's mind, these actions would root out polygamy's remnants once and for all.[51]

Instead of extinguishing the movement, these actions only fanned the flames. Previously an underground and loose coalition who still hoped to maintain LDS affiliation, those who believed polygamy to be a fundamental doctrine now officially organized around a set of leaders of "the priesthood." Each man who composed what they called "the Sanhedrin of God" was anointed in a hierarchical lineage that went back to John Taylor. They started their own newspaper, *The Truth*, that spread their message of "the fundamentals" to the broader Mormon public in 1935. The entire world, including Utah, was "toppling to ruin," the inaugural issue declared, as "the monogamic order of marriage, the boast of modern civilization, has failed." The only remedy was polygamy.[52]

It was the same argument made by LDS officials in the nineteenth century, only now the church was the jeremiad's target. The "priesthood" boasted hundreds of followers by the end of the decade. While a number of these "fundamentalists," as they soon became known, resided in the Salt Lake region, they also established their own isolated community, Short Creek, on the Utah and Arizona border, a replication of Mormonism's earlier colonial efforts.[53]

Nor were the fundamentalists the only challenge to church leaders during these years. Just as Clark escalated anti-polygamy efforts in 1936, the First Presidency received a petition from a group of over one hundred Mexican saints who demanded local autonomy. Mormon missionaries had boasted success in Latin America dating back to the mid-nineteenth century, and many converts in Central and South America embraced passages in the Book of Mormon that affirmed their chosen status. Now, influenced by Mexico's post-revolutionary *indigenismo* movement that overthrew all systems of colonialism and imperialism, they were anxious to take control of their own spiritual lives. They demanded that the church appoint a native Mexican as the region's presiding officer and that local saints should have a voice in the selection. Given this was the third time they had gathered to make their demands known—the first two requests were met with silence—they were called the Third Convention.[54]

Leading these efforts was Margarito Bautista, a charismatic Nahua Mexican convert who had spent over three decades moving within the church across Mexico and the United States. As a priesthood leader over Spanish-speaking congregations in Utah, as well as a missionary to Mexico, Bautista developed a theology that blended Mexican nationalism with unique Mormon teachings regarding "Lamanite" heritage and destiny. This postcolonial project, culminating in a five-hundred-page manuscript titled *La evolución de México*, rankled White LDS leaders who refused to forfeit their traditional racial hierarchy. Bautista then returned to Mexico and found an eager audience among other Hispanic saints ready to overturn all forms of subordination. "We are convinced that the ideology of the Mexican has not been understood by White people," the Convention declared, as "White people have a tendency to subjugate us in one condition or another."[55]

J. Reuben Clark's experience as Mexican ambassador made him skeptical of *indigenismo* movements in general, and his conception of an orderly church organization led him to be dismissive of this movement in particular. The First Presidency responded to the Third Convention's requests not only by reasserting its authority to appoint White priesthood leaders but by excommunicating Bautista and several of the other prominent *convencionistas*. Once again, these drastic actions backfired, as around a third of the three thousand Mexican saints left the church and followed a new schism.

Large outdoor baptism of Mexican saints who had seceded from the Latter-day Saint church following the Third Convention.

Yet Bautista could not lead them for long. Among the social circles with which he had affiliated in Utah were the fundamentalists, and he soon sought to convince fellow dissenters to embrace Mormonism in its truest form, including polygamy. Less keen on these fundamentals, Bautista's fellow *convencionistas* excommunicated him in 1937. Bautista, an embodiment of Mormonism's imaginative possibilities, was once again a man without a congregation.[56]

Clark and other church leaders treated both the Third Convention and the fundamentalists in the same manner: as serious threats to be cut off. The two movements struck at the faith's fundamental doctrines—one, the Lamanite promises in the Book of Mormon, the other, Joseph Smith's revelations on plural marriage. Could the modern church withstand such threats to core traditions? In response to these challengers who claimed a right to Mormon fundamentals, church leaders were left to reaffirm their own.

A DOWNPOUR on August 8, 1938, drenched the tents of those who attended the annual gathering for Mormon educators in Aspen Grove. These summer trainings had taken place for over a decade, and while they had previously been the nexus for introducing new and progressive theories, they had more recently become a battleground for competing ideas that echoed American disputes over modernism and fundamentalism. J. Reuben Clark was now determined to put an end to these debates. Titled "The Charted Course," Clark's address that dreary morning permanently transformed the direction of LDS intellectual life.[57]

Clark, who had long been skeptical of intellectuals, had been targeting Franklin Harris and BYU for several years. This was due to his own previous dalliance with doubt as well as his desire for a more correlated system. "I have come to deplore the fact that some of our 'literatti' as I call them," he wrote church leaders while still an ambassador, "do not spend more time on the gospel as revealed, and less on the pagan philosophy of ancient times and the near-pagan philosophy of modern times." Under Clark's influence, Heber Grant reversed his previous position of benign neglect toward BYU and instead chastised faculty for failing to prioritize sacred truths. When Harris requested funds for a new auditorium where visiting scholars could teach new philosophies, church leaders instead built a new chapel. Faculty were only to "spread revealed truth and reject worldly wisdom," Grant dictated, "as we do not care what other people believe and what their teachings are." The message of retrenchment was clear.[58]

Clark and Grant had reason to worry that these new philosophies were influencing the faith's younger generations. Confronted with an education that openly challenged traditional beliefs, a growing number of BYU students questioned core tenets of the faith. These trends were meticulously captured in 1935 by Harold T. Christensen, an inquisitive student who received school support to survey all students concerning where they stood on fundamental questions. The results were startling.

It was clear that the modern generation of saints was far removed from the church's pioneer principles. Around a quarter of the student body did not believe that modern prophets received revelation, 62 percent did not believe there was a literal devil, and 64 percent believed that humankind's creation involved biological evolution, a number that would have made Joseph Fielding Smith gasp. More ominously, these doctrinal issues paled in comparison to budding social transformations. Nearly half did not consider drinking alcohol morally wrong, 89 percent were fine with birth control, and only a half to two-thirds of students attended church every week, paid tithing, kept the Word of Wisdom, or engaged in daily prayers. When alerted to these figures, Harris immediately halted all publication plans.[59]

The crisis could not be contained for long. Several BYU professors became increasingly bold in their modernist attachments. Word reached Joseph Fielding Smith that one Chicago-trained professor taught that the Bible must be interpreted according to "external evidence," not just "mere tradition." The dogmatic apostle dashed off a letter to Harris saying that if such views "become dominant in the Church, then we may just as well close up shop and say to the world that Mormonism is a failure." Smith and Clark convinced Grant that this was a problem that required attention. "We have reached a point," Grant wrote Harris, when all professors must be judged according to "the fundamental questions." The president instructed BYU to perform a "very strict examination of all teachers to see just where they stand."[60]

Clark's address to LDS educators in August 1938 marked the end of BYU's modernist experiment. Speaking from the pulpit inside a log cabin as torrential rain pelted the exterior, Clark denounced the "newest fangled ideas" that did not square with divine truths, no matter how "backward" traditional doctrines may appear. Teachers must embrace the "essential fundamentals" of the gospel, which he defined as the infallibility of the scriptures and the divine calling of Joseph Smith. Any instructor not willing to pledge allegiance to these principles did not have a place in church education. The speech was as direct as it was partisan. The church published excerpts the next day in the *Deseret News*, proclaiming it "an official pronounce-ment of the First Presidency," and the entire remarks appeared in the church's magazine the next month. The generation-defining speech has charted church education ever since.[61]

Clark's message was not so much a faithful reconstruction of a Mormonism once lost but a selective interpretation necessitated by the modern world. This creative reimagining of the faith was in line with the broader American fundamentalist movement. Clark's ver-sion highlighted and reaffirmed principles that worked for his agenda, like scriptural literalism and prophetic authority, while overlooking others, like polygamy and theological progressivism. The domineer-ing leader followed the path of conservative evangelicals in rewriting the theological past to meet the cultural present, a movement that picked up steam in the following decades.

The ideological cleaving was immediate. One teacher offered to resign on the spot. Another, a young philosopher named Ster-ling McMurrin, later recalled that all attendees "divided ourselves up" into "liberal and conservative camps." The separate campfires reflected the diverging trajectories that stemmed from that summer morning. Ironically, the same Aspen Grove venue that, a decade ear-lier, represented the dawn of Mormon modernism, was now the site of its demise. Joseph Fielding Smith, elated, told Clark that he had "been hoping and praying for a long time for something of this kind to happen."[62]

Challenged on "fundamentals" by polygamists and *convencionistas*, Mormon leaders now reaffirmed their own fundamentalism. The anxiety caused by those who were outflanking them on what had previously been central doctrines led the First Presidency to prove theological validity and reassert dogmatic boundaries. Clark followed up his address with a memorandum to Harris reaffirming that the school should "give up indoctrinating themselves in the sectarianism of the modern 'Divinity School Theology,'" and instead embrace the core truths that would define the modern, but not modernist, church. The next year, the church's general education board, comprising the First Presidency and several apostles, took more direct control of BYU and transformed the curriculum. Courses like the one titled "Psychology of Religion" were replaced by "Restored Gospel as a Way of Life," and "Problems of Religion and Ethics" by "The Book of Mormon." Unlike the retrenchment several decades earlier, this transition proved to be permanent.[63]

Franklin Harris, though he persisted for another half decade, saw the writing on the wall. He left his beloved BYU in 1944 to become president of the Utah State Agricultural College, soon renamed Utah State University. When church leaders searched for a replacement, they prioritized the candidates' "attitude and loyalty to the Church," as well as "his faith in its doctrines." Franklin's successor, Howard McDonald, was chosen because leadership believed he was fully committed to the school's spiritual identity. One should always remember that "secular learnings [represented] the lesser value," Clark trumpeted at McDonald's inauguration, "and spiritual development, the greater."[64]

THIS DID not mean the end to Mormons performing academic scholarship. It did, however, push those who produced such work outside the establishment.

One of the most insightful observers of this transition was Juanita Brooks, the precocious schoolteacher from Mesquite, Nevada, now one of the faith's most brilliant minds. After her newlywed husband passed away in 1920—only a year after her encounter with Nephi Johnson—Brooks earned a bachelor's degree from BYU and a master's degree from Columbia, and taught English at Dixie Junior College in St. George. She still participated in the scholarly world after remarrying and having children. Brooks was hired by FDR's Works Progress Administration to find, preserve, and transcribe Mormon documents, quickly becoming a noted historian of the pioneer era. However, recognizing that her research was at odds with her community, Brooks kept a pile of clothes on the sewing table "with a threaded needle stuck to it" so that, whenever "interrupted" by visitors, she could claim she was merely performing housework.[65]

Brooks mourned what she called the "Reubenization" of Mormonism, "the writing out of every program [and] every speech" anything that was contrary to church doctrine. But while she admitted that she was "not too orthodox," and emphasized her "refus[al] to surrender my intellectual independence," Brooks maintained that "the best way to turn a herd of cattle is not to ride directly counter to them, but to travel with them and turn them gradually." As church authorities steered the faith in one direction, Brooks offered an alternative. She was not alone in this endeavor.[66]

Even before Brooks could finish her magisterial study of the Mountain Meadows Massacre, a host of other writers gained national attention for bringing Mormonism to a broader stage. Vardis Fisher's *Children of God* (1939), Maurine Whipple's *The Giant Joshua* (1941), and Virginia Sorensen's *A Little Lower Than the Angels* (1942) were all best-selling novels that used Mormon characters to tell an American saga. This generation of novelists were far from the first to draw from the faith's history, but they were the first to transcend the Mormon community. Unlike the "home literature" of earlier decades, Fisher, Whipple, and Sorensen desired to reach an audience mostly unfamiliar with the faith beyond the anti-Mormon stereotypes from the nineteenth century. They added emotional layers to Latter-day Saint characters, showed them struggling with ideals even as they yearned for perfection, and deeply ingrained the saints into the American story of grit and determination. Each author garnered widespread praise from gentile critics, who finally saw in Mormonism something of relevance to the modern world: devoted yet flawed pioneers seeking the American dream.[67]

Church leaders, conversely, were unimpressed with this new literary movement. They were especially perturbed that all three books paid considerable attention to polygamy. Official LDS periodicals either ignored the books or published dismissive reviews. After receiving a blistering letter from the director of the Deseret Book Company, Sorensen wrote across the top, "The Powers have spoken! A virtual excommunique!" Reflecting the cultural dissonance between them and their church, these authors came to be known as the Lost Generation, a label that was shared with their contemporary American writers similarly disenchanted with modern culture.[68]

No author from this generation garnered as much attention as Fawn Brodie. The niece of apostle David O. McKay, Brodie lost her faith while a graduate student at the University of Chicago. Her decision to marry a man outside the church prompted her apostolic uncle to visit and beg her—unsuccessfully—to return to the fold. McKay then became despondent when, at the age of thirty, Brodie published a new biography of Joseph Smith, *No Man Knows My History*, that depicted Mormonism's founder as a religious fraud more rooted in his environment than in divinity. The book was praised by national outlets and has long remained the primary lens through which America knows the faith's origins. Clark, conversely, called it "a veneer of pseudo-scholarship" and drafted a scathing review that appeared the next year, around the same time that Brodie was excommunicated.[69]

The debates prompted by Brodie's biography captured the community's growing fissures. Brooks, though she disagreed with Brodie's conclusion that Joseph Smith was "a conscious fraud and imposter," couldn't help but appreciate the book's "literary quality" and "patient research." She was upset, therefore, at the LDS leaders' "hysterical" reaction, and complained that their defensive stance "makes it very hard" for a historian like her "to be loyal to the church." She was particularly perturbed at the cool reception from other Mormon scholars, especially a pamphlet by Hugh Nibley, an eccentric classicist who soon became the faith's most prominent apologist. His work was condescendingly titled *No Ma'am, That's Not History*. "It seems to me that in our zeal to answer Mrs. Brodie," she wrote in a reproving letter to Nibley, "we make some statements almost as far fetched as hers." When Nibley was hired to teach at BYU, in part due to his polemic's success, Brooks feared the "Reubenization" process was nearly complete.[70]

A decade later, the Catholic sociologist Thomas O'Dea published the results of his extensive study of Mormon history, doctrine, and culture during the mid-century. "Mormonism's greatest and most significant problem," he concluded, "is its encounter with secular thought." He argued that, in the church that J. Reuben Clark built, "a questioner or critic" not only "annoys conservatives" but may also "come to threaten, or at least appear to threaten, cherished beliefs, values, and institutions." If O'Dea had conducted his study a few decades earlier, he likely would have noted less hostility between faith and intellect—a period of potential, if cautious, openness, only to be followed by backlash.[71]

LIKE THE rest of the nation, church leaders soon transferred their attention from ideological wars to military ones. J. Reuben Clark and the First Presidency reacted to Germany's imperialistic actions with simultaneous priorities that included genuine pacifism, patriotism, and the new geopolitical calculations now that they claimed members on all sides of the deadly divide. The church was especially strong in Germany due to a century of missionary work, and many regional leaders in the nation supported the Third Reich's authority. When one brave German teenager, Helmuth Hübener, was executed for publishing anti-Nazi propaganda, he was also excommunicated by the local branch president. An unexpected consequence of no longer gathering saints to America was the inability to equate a single national agenda with the church's own. Clark, long known as an Anglophobe, continued to urge peace even as war erupted.[72]

Circumstances changed in December 1941 when Japanese forces attacked Pearl Harbor. The tragedy was personal for Clark, as his own son-in-law died during the attack. The American church's next few years brought fervid military support abroad and austerity measures at home. Nearly one hundred thousand Mormon men fought in the war, and they were supported by a newly created Servicemen's Committee that provided aid and counsel. Most church auxiliaries were curtailed, missions slowed, and General Conference was transformed into a small gathering for only a few hundred priesthood leaders. The timing was especially infelicitous for the Relief Society, which was forced to indefinitely suspend centennial celebrations planned for 1942. The true tragedy, of course, was the lives lost: Utah casualties numbered 1,450, a figure higher than the national average, and nearly 6,000 Mormons died across the globe, including 600 saints in Germany who fought for the opposing side.[73]

It was during these turbulent years that Amy Brown Lyman finally took her rightful position as head of the Relief Society. After serving alongside her husband as he presided over the church's European mission from 1936 to 1938, Lyman became the Relief Society president at the start of 1940, the culmination of her three decades dedicated to the organization. In theory, it would have been the perfect time for her skill set, as years of service made her well equipped to manage wartime relief efforts.

In reality, Lyman presided over a drastically scaled-back operation, one tailored to fit an increasingly centralized church bureaucracy. Only two months into her new role, Lyman and her counselors were summoned to meet with church leaders. As Heber Grant and his other counselor, David McKay, were both frequently infirm during these years, Clark was now in charge of determining how the auxiliary organization would function. He surprised Lyman with a new memorandum that stated the society should "consolidate, cooperate, eliminate, simplify, and adjust their work so as to cooperate with the Presidency." Their social work was to be constrained to supporting the Welfare Program, and their community work to "the promotion of faith and testimony," leaving "social, cultural and educational efforts" to other groups. Clark summarized the shift several months later at General Conference: the Relief Society was to be "the handmaid to the priesthood."[74]

It was difficult to navigate these new constraints. Local Relief

Societies were instructed to work with bishoprics rather than the society's general board, and a few years later their entire charity fund, totaling $150,000, was rolled into the church's general fund, also controlled by the priesthood. The autonomy originally established by Emma Smith, expanded by Eliza R. Snow, defended by Emmeline B. Wells, and utilized by Amy Brown Lyman, was quickly evaporating into the streamlined priesthood organization.[75]

As an undaunted Lyman continued to adjust, her domestic life fell apart. The crisis was long in coming. Two decades earlier, Richard Lyman was tasked with counseling families still ensconced in extralegal plural relationships. He was specifically assigned to work with a woman named Anna Sofie Jacobsen, a Danish convert who immigrated to Utah in 1905 and, once there, became the plural wife of another Danish convert, Victor C. Hegsted. She was excommunicated in 1921 as part of the church's attempt to eradicate postmanifesto unions. Jacobsen and Lyman soon fell in love. Since a plural union was impossible, but eternal polygamy was still an option, they pledged to be sealed to each other once one of them had passed.

Church Welfare Committee, 1940. J. Reuben Clark, center, is depicted as firmly in control of the church's welfare efforts. That Amy Brown Lyman, third from left, was now the only woman included in the committee demonstrates how far the Relief Society had been marginalized in humanitarian initiatives.

Richard therefore viewed Jacobsen as "my prospective Plural Wife." Amy, however, was not consulted. After returning from his European mission in 1938, Lyman and Jacobsen's relationship evolved from spiritual to physical, and the two carried on their discreet arrangements for several years.[76]

Clark's anti-polygamy surveillance system discovered the affair in late October 1943. He tasked two of his most trusted apostles, Joseph Fielding Smith and Harold B. Lee, with investigating. When they had confirmed the rumors, they coordinated with Salt Lake City's police chief to burst in on Lyman and Jacobsen in the latter's downtown apartment on November 11. Lyman, who confessed to the relationship but insisted on its spiritual nature, was dropped from the Quorum and excommunicated the next day. But while Lyman hoped the case could remain confidential, Clark had the newspaper publish a notice that he had been excommunicated "for violation of the Christian law of chastity."[77]

Amy, who knew nothing of Richard's relationship, was devastated. "*I do not believe it,*" she initially responded, "*I do not believe it.*" She decided, however, to stay with Richard despite some urging her to leave. But her public image was shaken, and the patriarchal climate of the LDS community meant that the crisis subverted her credibility. Although it was not his primary intention—his driving focus was to stamp out all forms of polygamy—Clark's public handling of the affair undercut his most prominent and powerful rival. Clark requested Lyman to submit her resignation the following summer. War-related complications delayed the inevitable, but she was finally released in April 1945, giving up the reins of the institution she had long loved, which would now take a direction she had long feared.[78]

Amy Brown Lyman's efforts proved to be the climax of a particular period for Mormon women's activism. Hers was a vibrant movement that drew from broader cultural strains while working within the existing LDS structure, an undertaking that simultaneously challenged the status quo and carved out its own autonomous space without drawing institutional opposition. Lyman and her reformist colleagues shaped their surrounding church, state, and culture, exercising authority that matched America's progressive movement. This was what their generation of Mormon women were raised to believe was possible and perhaps even necessary.

With Lyman's fall came the end of that trajectory. The dawn of a new, corporate, and streamlined church, one poised to become a national power and global presence, meant curtailing factions that failed to align with the centralized vision of leaders like J. Reuben Clark. Just as Clark had succeeded in reasserting doctrinal orthodoxy, expelling dissenters, and abating modernist teachings, so too would he and the other priesthood leaders establish a patriarchal norm that matched America's postwar nuclear family. "Do not try to be anything else but good mothers and good homemakers," Clark urged. The Relief Society, previously a quasi-autonomous machine built on pioneer visions and dedicated to societal reform, would be subsumed into an institution that prioritized homogeneity over individuality, and patriarchy over women's rights.[79]

Lyman was not the last Mormon to push for women's empowerment and social change, of course. But those who followed her, both in time and in spirit, operated within more confined ecclesiastical spaces. Many were cast by male leaders as alternative voices, threats to the establishment. Women's activism was thereafter scandalized as external to faithful discourse.

By the end of World War II, the LDS church boasted nearly a million worldwide members, almost double the number it claimed at the end of World War I, due to their persistent and successful missionary labors. The intervening years had featured not only explosive growth but expansive organizational reform, meticulous theological retrenchment, and a reaffirmed hierarchical control. But no matter how measured and polished this new foundation appeared—the foundation upon which modern Mormonism would be built—it was the result of frequent and fervent battles, clashes over the meaning of reform in an age of progress.

7

One Family under God, 1945–70

I am thankful for this country which has given more persons opportunity to raise themselves under an individualistic, capitalistic, free enterprise system from menial to commanding positions than any other nation in the world, past or present.

—DAVID O. MCKAY[1]

LACEE HARRIS'S CONNECTION to the Latter-day Saint church was seven generations deep, dating way back to an ancestor baptized by Brigham Young himself. His family always attended church, his father had served in leadership positions, and now he was in Provo attending the faith's flagship university. Yet as he sat in a pew in a newly constructed building, surrounded by other devout Mormons, Harris could not help but feel isolated.

By 1962, the year Harris was admitted to BYU, the campus had expanded exponentially under the direction of its new president. Ernest L. Wilkinson, a dogged lawyer with a dour disposition, was as committed to growing the school as he was to rooting out any communists found within its walls. During Wilkinson's tenure, the student body, taking advantage of the postwar boom, increased six-fold to 25,000, and the school became the largest church-owned university in the nation. Wilkinson also quadrupled its faculty, grew library holdings 500 percent, and constructed dozens of buildings. The campus population became so large that the church organized student-only worship congregations in 1956, hoping that close proximity would result in more marriages.[2]

But among the tens of thousands of students, Harris stood out: he was one of only thirty-five with Indigenous heritage.

Harris had not previously experienced much friction with his White co-worshippers. Growing up, he later recalled, "my Indianness, like my Mormonness, was just there"—something crucial to his identity, but not something that marginalized him. His father, Albert Harris, a Ute, was a lifelong member who boasted generations of faithfulness, and his mother, Lucille Davis, a Northern Paiute, was an adult convert. But Harris had spent his final high school years living with a White family, James and Della Watkins, who worked for the US Army, and therefore attended mostly White schools. Nor was his educational experience unique: the church's Indian Student Placement Program (ISPP) eventually placed nearly fifty thousand Indigenous students in White Mormon homes.[3]

The mentality that led to the ISPP was one born of cultural triumphalism in the wake of World War II, an entrenched commitment to creating national unity. The trauma of global wars and economic collapse left Americans searching for harmony even as they celebrated victory. The 1950s were a decade of rapid economic growth, affluence, and prosperity for the privileged, and increased educational opportunities for many. The result was optimism that the country was approaching cultural cohesion. Citizens were confident that America was finally a "Christian nation."

Much of this new rhetoric was centered around a national ideal, the nuclear family, and decrying an external enemy, communism. "The world is divided into two camps!" pronounced Billy Graham, the nation's most popular pastor celebrity. The evil communists had "declared war" against God, religion, and the family, Graham explained, and "unless the Western world has an old-fashioned revival, we cannot last!" Victory in this eternal battle required a national conversion to bedrock principles. This was an especially important point for Mormons, who, building on the legacy of J. Reuben Clark, were increasingly committed to what were now defined as "traditional" values. "The family is a divine institution established by our Heavenly Father," declared Ezra Taft Benson, a new apostle and Clark's conservative heir; "it is basic to civilization and particularly to Christian civilization." The nuclear family swiftly became the foundation for American, and Mormon, identity.[4]

Not everyone enjoyed this new emphasis. While many Mormons, including a large number participating in the ISPP, thrived in the new setting, Lacee Harris struggled to find his footing. As he gathered in his student congregation—a congregation partially predicated on courting new families—he felt increasingly marginalized. The ward's bishop commenced the semester with a talk on the dangers of interracial dating, and later that year denounced Indian "dances and ceremonies." Harris's religion professors declared that there was no place for his Indigenous traditions, as Native Mormons "only belonged if we were Lamanites." That meant that they must conform to particular societal roles drawn from White "civilization." The chasm between his faith and his ancestry only grew from there.[5]

The dissonance that Harris experienced echoed how the optimism of 1950s unity gave way to the disillusionment of the 1960s. The civil rights movement dashed a social order based on racial inequality, a resurgent Republican Party challenged what had become a liberal consensus in national politics, and previously marginalized voices demanded substantial reform and cultural equality. Mormons came to fully embrace, and be embraced by, an American culture just as it fractured into pieces, never to be assembled again. The LDS institution witnessed remarkable and rapid growth during these decades, ballooning from just over one million members to almost three, becoming one of the most powerful churches in the nation almost overnight. But with that growth came the same problem that faced the broader nation: Could newfound prosperity result in harmony, or did massive expansion inevitably birth schism?

Harris was not optimistic. He confessed decades later that mainstream Mormon culture had "become more alien, not more familiar." After graduating BYU, Harris grew out his hair, researched and embraced his Ute culture, and when asked if he was LDS, responded, "Yes, but I'm Nuchee, Northern Ute, first, then Mormon." Choosing allegiances was a dilemma that millions of the faithful would face.[6]

* * *

IT WAS a frigid morning when Dwight Eisenhower was inaugurated the thirty-fourth president of the United States on January 19, 1953. The ceremony followed a day of exceptional fog. But David O. McKay did not mind. To the LDS president, America's future had never beamed so bright. "The fog of yesterday," which McKay believed represented "the fog that has been hanging over Washington politically for twenty years," had now vanished, and "the sunshine seems as a manifestation of divine approval." The remark failed to elicit laughs from Democrats sitting around him.

Attending Eisenhower's inaugural address was a privilege McKay would never forget. While he had publicly insisted that the church was politically neutral, and even took time at General Conference to dismiss the rumor that LDS leaders were all Republicans, he privately mused that Eisenhower's victory was "the greatest thing that has happened in a hundred years." Then, unable to stay quiet, he confessed to a journalist that "Ike's" presidency would be "the turning point in United States, if not World History."[7]

Eisenhower was known for eliciting such devotion. Due to his military success and nonpartisan reputation—he had been courted by both Republicans and Democrats to run on their tickets—Eisenhower appeared to be a benevolent and wise consensus builder. He was also beloved by evangelicals for his religious rhetoric, and had been championed by Billy Graham as the solution to America's ills. But rather than mimic fundamentalist priorities that divided opinions, Eisenhower embraced a Christian ecumenism that reflected the period's yearning for spiritual unity. "We are a religious people," he proclaimed a month before he took office, and "our form of government has no sense unless it is founded in a deeply-felt religious faith, and I don't care what it is." This desire for religion to serve as a uniting power created space for previously marginalized groups like the Mormons.[8]

No Mormon president had been as ready to take advantage of such an opening as David O. McKay. While already seventy-three when he became the church's leader in 1951, the former educator appeared

youthful and energetic. Ordained an apostle in 1906 to replace polygamist predecessors amid the Reed Smoot hearings, McKay joined the
First Presidency in 1934 and quickly became known as a moderate
voice. His extensive traveling—he was the first apostle to take a world
tour, in 1921—also gave him a more cosmopolitan background. While
previous prophets appeared "dour, dark suited figures," *Time* magazine noted, McKay was regaled for his double-breasted white suits,
perfectly coiffed hair, clean-shaven face, and gregarious personality.
Anecdotes of his modern sensibilities abounded; in one, McKay was
at a reception that served rum cake, and when asked if the dessert
would break the faith's health code, the prophet responded, "the Word
of Wisdom forbade drinking alcohol, not eating it." Even *Salt Lake
Tribune* critics admitted he was "six feet two and 199 pounds of the
kindliest, fairest and most understanding man one has the pleasure of
meeting." Some fellow church leaders, however, worried that McKay
was receiving a "celebrity status" and developing a "personality cult."⁹

McKay's time in the First Presidency had not been without
friction. Though both he and J. Reuben Clark were seen as mod-
ernizers, McKay did not share his fellow counselor's partisanship.
Some insiders later claimed that leadership was split between "Clark
men" and "McKay men," a division that was likely not as deep as
some assumed, but one that still echoed reality. When he became
president—succeeding George Albert Smith, a soft-spoken descendant of the broader Smith family—McKay demoted Clark from first
to second counselor in favor of his close friend, Stephen L. Richards.
The prophet justified the move by emphasizing Richards's seniority
among the Twelve, but it was the first time a counselor had been relegated in institutional history.

Clark, though he still presented an image of unity, privately
lamented the move. The prominent statesman spent the next decade
in McKay's shadow, even if his tedious and voluminous memos continued to shape the modern institution. The church's most influential bureaucratic titan of the twentieth century finally passed in 1961.
Those who followed his path—the "Clark men"—ensured that his
many legacies survived.¹⁰

Political disagreements between Clark and McKay often concerned degrees of conservatism. McKay, like Clark, was a lifelong Republican, and he continued to support the GOP, albeit quietly, in his new position. This included chastising the *Deseret News* editor when the paper critiqued Eisenhower. But his general approach mimicked Eisenhower's: the primary goal was cultural harmony rather than partisan triumph, and his major enemy was communism, not the Democrats. Like Ike, McKay vociferously called for a united effort in confronting the communist threat that was "moving aggressively over the face of the earth, fundamentally prompted by disbelief in the existence of God." Billy Graham could not have said it better. Mormonism's rightward march continued apace.[11]

McKay was thrilled, therefore, when one of his apostles, Ezra Taft Benson, was tapped to serve as Eisenhower's secretary of agriculture. Born in rural Idaho and educated at Iowa State College and Berkeley, Benson had served several years as the executive secretary of the National Council of Farmer Cooperatives, a position that took him to Washington to represent over two million farmers across America. His deep distrust of federal assistance meant he opposed many of Roosevelt's New Deal measures, which he denounced as "paternalistic government." Benson soon became a favorite for many Republicans who pushed back against the liberal consensus just as he was climbing the LDS ecclesiastical ladder. As a newly called apostle in 1943, Benson helped oversee the church's war-relief effort, and was sent to Europe in 1946 to help deliver nearly two hundred thousand pounds of food and clothing. His experience overseas reaffirmed what he believed were the bitter fruits of godless socialism, a theme that dominated both his religious and political agendas. A fellow apostle once remarked that "anyone who didn't agree with Brother Benson's mind was indeed a communist." It was an exaggeration, but not by much.[12]

While Eisenhower lacked Benson's partisan edge, they shared a commitment to a particular form of Christian nationalism. The decade following World War II featured simultaneous calls for recognizing America's religious core and rolling back Roosevelt's federal programs, a Christian libertarianism that merged corporate and evangelical interests. Benson declared in one of his first General

Conference addresses that America was "founded on the truth of Christian principles," ideas antithetical to socialism. Therefore, "this nation has become the world's greatest power." Eisenhower rode this cultural wave to a landslide victory in 1952 and rewarded followers with symbolic gestures like adding "under God" to the Pledge of Allegiance in 1954 and enshrining "In God We Trust" as the national motto in 1956. Benson even convinced Eisenhower to start each cabinet meeting with prayer, though other participants voted to keep the invocation "silent" due to Benson's long-winded supplications.[13]

It was easy to have such nationalist optimism when the country was experiencing so much success. America's postwar economic boom introduced prosperity to a degree rarely matched, largely due to Roosevelt's postwar recovery legislation like the GI Bill. The program, which one historian called "a veterans-only welfare state," promised a four-year college education, zero-down-payment and low-interest loans, and a "readjustment benefit" that enabled eight million White veterans to achieve financial stability. Though paying for the legislation accounted for 15 percent of the federal budget, tax revenues paid for the bill ten times over, and that generation's capitalistic achievement laid a foundation for the decades to come.[14]

The LDS church shared in this postwar growth. McKay announced that tithing receipts increased 217 percent after his first year as president. This enabled leadership to embark on an ambitious construction agenda. They built 1,350 new structures between 1946 and 1955, doubling the number of existing chapels, and erected four new temples, three of which were outside of America: Switzerland (Bern), England (London), and New Zealand (Hamilton). Out-migration from Utah, as many saints were drawn to growing economic hubs outside their home state, and successful proselytizing efforts everywhere, drawing from newly formalized missionary lessons, resulted in a growing and dispersed membership. Ecclesiastical stakes, large diocese-like units that comprised multiple local wards, grew from 180 to 319 in McKay's first decade, most of them located outside Utah. And while it had taken 117 years for the church to reach one million members in 1947, it took only 16 more to reach two million (1963), and then 8 to reach three (1971). Church membership grew by 52 percent in the 1950s alone, which included doubling its membership outside North America.[15]

This massive expansion necessitated a more bureaucratic organization. While the church had been experimental with architectural projects prior to World War II, featuring Renaissance domes, Gothic stained-glass windows, and Romanesque archways, a majority of the new structures followed a standard and banal blueprint. Buildings featured a rectangular chapel that flowed into recreational space with a basketball court, divided by a movable barrier. "I wouldn't have felt much different in the chapel had I had a basketball in my lap," quipped one observer. Surrounding these large halls were a series of classrooms and offices for ward and stake leadership.[16]

The new converts who filled these pews did not fear that joining the church meant joining America's religious outcasts. The decades-long work of assimilation had moved Mormonism's community closer to the nation's cultural mainstream. When the church celebrated its centennial for arriving in Utah in 1947, it was heralded as an example of American success. The faith's pioneers were now recognized as part of America's broader story of western settlement, religious devotion, and industry, even garnering a saccharine cover story in *Time* magazine. Three years later, a twelve-foot marble statue of Brigham Young, sculpted by his grandson Mahonri, was displayed in the US Capitol rotunda. A century earlier, Young was identified as one of the federal government's most significant critics. Now he was praised by the sitting vice president, Alben Barkley, as a "man of God" and an "advocate of justice and democracy."[17]

And now, in 1953, McKay was an invited guest at Eisenhower's inauguration, where he exulted in the privileged position in which he found his beloved people. Mormonism, like America, was on the rise. The fog was beginning to clear.

ANOTHER PARADE took place later that year across the country, only this time in the cloak of darkness. Dozens of police cars departed from their gathering point in Williams, Arizona, in the late afternoon and drove all night to Short Creek, Arizona, hoping to catch the small town by surprise. However, due to botched planning and publicity leaks, word had spread long before they reached their destination. One journalist joked that they moved with "the ponderous secrecy of an elephant on a skating rink." By the time the cars arrived in Short Creek at four o'clock the next morning, their tires kicking up enough dust to be seen from miles away, most of the town's 122 adults and 263 children were already awake and standing around their makeshift schoolhouse, singing hymns.[18]

Most residents who lived in Short Creek were Mormon fundamentalists. The small town was founded as a refuge for those who maintained the polygamous practice they believed central to Mormon belief. Despite coordinated efforts from LDS leaders and state authorities to reform the community—including synchronized raids in 1935 and 1944—Short Creek continued to grow, and its residents refused to concede. The 1953 raid was designed to be the final chapter in what the church and the state believed was a story that had lasted too long. Police carried arrest warrants for every Mormon adult. They did not plan to leave until they had "rescue[d] 263 children from vir-

Short Creek Polygamous Family, 1953. During the raid on Short Creek, families were gathered and photographed. These photos, meant to capture the "depravity" of polygamy, instead drew national sympathy.

tual bondage." Every man was arrested and jailed, while the women and children were gathered, photographed, and eventually dispersed into foster homes.[19]

The church-owned *Deseret News* proclaimed that Americans owed "a debt of gratitude" to Arizona officials. Yet in a surprising development, in view of nineteenth-century debates, the rest of the nation denounced the raid as a totalitarian repression of religious rights. Newspapers carried photographs of the women and children huddled in their doorways and crying over the loss of their imprisoned husbands and fathers. Most of the men were convicted but merely placed on probation and told to cease their polygamous unions. Once again, they refused and continued to practice the "principle."[20]

A schism now divided the group. Those who followed Rulon C. Allred moved to Bluffdale, between Provo and Salt Lake City, and became known as the Apostolic United Brethren (AUB). Conversely, those who followed Leroy S. Johnson stayed in Short Creek, soon renamed Colorado City in its Arizona portion, and Hildale in Utah. The latter body later incorporated the Fundamentalist Church of Jesus Christ of Latter-day Saints (FLDS). Despite the excommunications and arrests, plural marriage refused to die.[21]

That did not keep LDS officials from wishing polygamy would disappear. David O. McKay was only the second prophet to have never practiced polygamy, and the first who had become an apostle after the church had halted plural unions. He was therefore quite willing and anxious to place further distance between the church and its past. McKay taught that polygamy was "not a principle but a *practice*," and the doctrine of marriage revealed to Joseph Smith concerned "the eternity of the marriage covenant" rather than its plurality. This rewriting of Smith's polygamy revelation and the history that surrounded it was necessary for the church's future and soon became standard curriculum. Leaders wanted a layoff on all polygamous discussion whatsoever, going so far as to pressure the University of Utah Press to refrain from publishing a book that detailed Joseph Smith's plural unions. Juanita Brooks, still regarded as one of the faith's best historians, reported that seminary teachers were "ordered not to even mention the word *Polygamy*" to their students. A silent history was much easier to manage.[22]

The easiest way to move past polygamy was to trumpet the church's embrace of monogamy. Like most middle-class Americans during the postwar period, Mormon leaders sacralized the nuclear family as the cornerstone of civilization. This new focus replaced (and erased) a culture of multigenerational families and multiple breadwinners, and tried to roll back women's wartime vocational advances. McKay instructed that because "the family is the foundation of society," the church should no longer hire married women who had children. Gender roles were reaffirmed as crucial to national, and personal, prosperity. McKay emphasized that "the more woman becomes like man, the less he will respect her," and J. Reuben Clark's denunciation of "homosexuality" in a 1952 conference talk was the first time a church leader publicly uttered the term. By the end of the decade, McKay had assigned two apostles to solve the "homosexual problem," an institutional priority still in its infancy.[23]

Tasked with championing this domestic image was Belle S. Spafford, a woman who, ironically, had been born to a single-parent family. Her father, John Gibson Smith, died seven months before her birth in 1895, and her mother, Hester Sims, already had six children. Though her full name was Marion Isabelle Sims Smith, her "Belle" nickname embodied an approachable demeanor, and she met her husband, Earl Spafford, at BYU in 1921. She served as Amy Brown Lyman's counselor in the Relief Society presidency and, when Lyman resigned, became her successor in 1945. Though initially overwhelmed by the position, it was one she would hold for nearly thirty years, the longest leadership tenure for any woman in the church.

Much more conservative in her views on women and society than her predecessor, Spafford's agenda fit perfectly with how male leaders envisioned the society. Clark explicitly told her upon her appointment to fashion it as "a companion organization to the priesthood," hewing closely to church priorities and traditional gender roles. They solidified this reorientation later that year by changing the name from "National Woman's Relief Society" to "Relief Society of the Church of Jesus Christ of Latter-day Saints," a move that more closely and publicly aligned the institutions and reflected the faith's global reach. In return for her loyalty, Spafford achieved something previous society presidents had only wished for: the society received approval for its own building in 1945 and, after a decade of fundraising, completed it in October 1956. The society now had its own physical space, though one increasingly overseen by the First Presidency.[24]

Spafford's message as the public face for Mormon women was clear and concise. "One of the Relief Society's first concerns," she taught in 1949, was "the task of guiding, directing, and training its members in their vital role of mother and homemaker." The society abandoned Lyman's social service classes and instead focused on domesticity and spirituality. A Mormon woman's primary form of labor, they taught, was found in the home. Fulfilling spiritual callings became the hallmark of righteous living. "Ours is not necessarily the role of the campaigner against one or another of the existing community evils," Spafford instructed, but "the role of the steady, consistent builder of men and women of integrity and moral fortitude who will uphold and promote virtuous community life." Rather than social programs designed to solve urban ills, Spafford's society introduced bazaars, fundraising fairs where Mormon women raised money by selling handmade crafts.[25]

These efforts coalesced with a cultural retrenchment intrinsic to the conservative postwar patriarchy movement. However, the period also brought progressive reform movements that appeared in secular, spiritual, and domestic spaces across America. Unsatisfied with returning to the familial sphere, many women refused to forfeit wartime gains. They instead insisted on more employment opportunities. Utah's booming economy, made possible by federal stimulus and Cold War contracts, resulted in a skyrocketing number of women in the workplace. The percentage of women who labored outside the home almost doubled during the 1950s alone, and by 1970 half of adult women in Utah were employed. In 1963 Betty Friedan published *The Feminine Mystique*, a book based on interviews with White suburban housewives struggling with "the problem that has no name": a longing for success and dignity outside the home. The book sparked what came to be known as second-wave feminism, a social movement that upended traditional gender roles.[26]

Simultaneously, many denominations opened space for more leadership opportunities. Methodists, Southern Baptists, and Presbyterians started ordaining women in the 1950s, followed by the Lutherans in the next decade. Even the Catholics adjusted ritual duties following Vatican II. Women demanded equality in the pews as well as the workplace.

Helen Andelin was unimpressed with these developments. Born in 1920 to devout Arizona Mormons, Andelin, a petite woman with deep chestnut hair and wide-set eyes, feared such loosening of gender roles resulted in moral decay and societal dissolution. She struggled when her husband faced several financial setbacks and her marriage appeared to be failing around 1960. Yet rather than blaming the patriarchal structure, like housewives interviewed by Friedan, Andelin instead blamed America's progressive values and yearned for simpler fundamentals. When she encountered a series of secular pamphlets titled *Secrets of Fascinating Womanhood* that were published in 1922 to help single women attract husbands, she believed she had found God's eternal truths: that women must be more submissive and attractive to men in order to form lasting bonds. Once the lessons transformed her own marriage, she shared them with others, sparking a cultural movement that worked within and expanded from modern Mormonism's domestic ideal.[27]

Written in 1963, the same year as *The Feminine Mystique*, Andelin's *Fascinating Womanhood* was an anti-feminist manifesto. "The first law of Heaven is obedience," she repeatedly argued, "and it should be the first law of every home." A woman should become a "domestic goddess," which meant not only expert housekeeping and submitting to her husband, but also always wearing a dress and apron, mastering makeup application, minimizing personal problems, and never appearing intimidating. "A man doesn't want an intellectual woman," she cautioned. The book became a bestseller, especially in Utah. Deseret Book, the church's bookstore, ordered successive shipments of one thousand copies and advertised it with large posters. BYU's Continuing Education Program held a series of classes on the book in Salt Lake City. The text eventually sold over three million copies worldwide and transcended a Mormon audience, becoming one of the most influential publications of its era. Though Andelin's patriarchal rhetoric went beyond the church's official discourse by further sacralizing extreme female subservience, it mirrored the institution's anti-feminist retrenchment.[28]

Not all marriages were included in this new vision. Most Mormons winced at the concept of interracial unions, which J. Reuben Clark denounced as "a wicked virus." Most White Mormons either lived in areas with limited exposure to racial diversity or lacked the curiosity to consider the restriction. This changed as church membership spread throughout the nation. One LDS sociologist, Lowry Nelson, who researched the Caribbean and taught at the University of Minnesota, confessed that it was not until 1947 that he learned "there was a fixed doctrine" on priesthood and temple exclusion. Shocked, he immediately wrote church leaders hoping to dispel the rumor. But the First Presidency confirmed the policy and gave as one justification that racial integration would result in "the intermarriage of the Negro and White races." When Nelson pressed further, they threatened his membership. McKay and other leaders quietly supported state segregation policies, and the First Presidency continued to issue statements denouncing intermarriage.[29]

Yet McKay slowly, and quietly, limited the racial policy's scope. He was confronted with this problem when he visited South Africa in 1954 and met converts who could not trace their lineage and were denied ordination. (McKay had previously witnessed this issue during his mission to the South Pacific in the 1920s.) The prophet announced a subtle, yet significant, adjustment: no longer would members have to provide their genealogy so long as they had "no outward evidence of a Negro strain." Though the shift had limited impact on Mormons in America, softening the policy allowed the church to take deeper root in nations like South Africa and Brazil that featured many interracial lineages. The move also proved that the church was capable of changing. Publicly, McKay optimistically told the South Africans that "the time will come" when the restriction would disappear; privately, he nervously wrote Clark that, if the policy continued, there would soon not be "sufficient men" to run the church in the Southern Hemisphere.[30]

*   *   *

WHILE MILLIONS of families experienced economic success following World War II, Helen John's faced struggle. She was the third of
thirteen children, nine biological and four adopted. While her father
served in World War II, he was barred from the privileges enabled
by the GI Bill due to being Navajo. Familial skepticism toward the
federal government went back generations. Her ancestors were held
against their will in Bosque Redondo during the Civil War, a tragic
episode known as the Long Walk. More recently, out of fear she and
her siblings might be rounded up and taken away to boarding school,
John was told to "run and go hide up in the ravine" on their Arizona
farm whenever cars passed through their reservation. She eventually spent a few years attending school at Tuba City, where speaking
Indigenous languages was forbidden, before her father kept her home
to "learn the ways of the Navajo." John therefore accompanied her
parents when they traveled to Richfield, Utah, to work as temporary
laborers in the beet fields in the late 1940s.[31]

It was there that Helen John first encountered the Book of Mormon. Amy Avery, the farmer's wife, approached her with stories of
Joseph Smith, lost scripture, and a sacred destiny for "Lamanite"
people. They had several discussions that were limited by linguistic
barriers, but Avery provided her a copy of the Book of Mormon as a
parting gift when she left that summer, and they corresponded until
John's family returned in the fall. This time, John's interest was fully
piqued, and she desired to stay in Utah and "learn to talk like they
do and be able to understand and know more about what [Avery]
is talking about." Avery scrambled to accommodate. Eventually,
Golden Buchanan, a local businessman and LDS leader, paid John
a visit. She remembered his dark suit and "shiny shoes . . . tromping
along in the mud" as he approached her in the field. Buchanan invited
her to stay with him during the school year and return to her family
during the summers. While initially hesitant, John agreed, and soon
joined both the Buchanan household and the LDS church.[32]

John was the first of nearly fifty thousand Indigenous children to
be removed from their reservations and placed in Mormon homes
over the next few decades. During midcentury, and following centuries of dispossession, Indigenous communities outpaced the rest

of the country in terms of high rates of unemployment, infant mortality, poverty, and suicide. Legislators, overlooking colonialism as the problems' cause, concluded that forced assimilation was the only solution. Congress passed a series of bills that eliminated funding for some tribes while dissolving others altogether. Government welfare programs organized numerous adoption projects, though their numbers paled in comparison to private organizations like the Latter-day Saints.[33]

Many White Mormon leaders praised the approach. Leading the way was Spencer W. Kimball, a soft-spoken and inquisitive apostle who had been raised near Native reservations in Arizona. Kimball was ordained to the Quorum of the Twelve in October 1943, the same day as Ezra Taft Benson, and he devoted his ecclesiastical career to Indigenous members. Yet he refused to imagine a future of Native autonomy. "I firmly believe that tomorrow there will be no reservations," he once proclaimed, as "integration into our economy and community life is essential." He insisted that, based on the Book of Mormon's statement that skin color was indicative of righteousness, those who successfully assimilated would become White: "The children in the home Placement Program," he posited, "are often lighter than their brothers and sisters."[34]

Helen John was one of three Indigenous students placed by Buchanan in 1947–48. That number increased annually over the next few years. By 1954, the informal program included sixty-eight students, but the church's failure to follow state laws, and accusations of unethical practices, caused a reorganization. Belle Spafford was particularly upset with the initiative's lack of structure, and the Relief Society general board took control of the newly named Indian Student Placement Program (ISPP). The ISPP received ecclesiastical support from Kimball and other apostles, as well as resources from the Missionary Department, and White saints were sent to reservations to proselytize for the placement program. Some Native children were tricked into getting baptized, such as by being invited on a school trip or encouraged to sign up for a sports team, but these mass baptisms, which drew the ire of tribal leaders, were rare. More common were prolonged discussions between missionaries and families, with young elders and sisters introducing entire families to the Book of Mormon and then framing the ISPP as a fulfillment of the scripture's prophecies. At its peak in 1970, the ISPP placed five thousand children annually.[35]

Results were mixed. Many students spoke fondly of the practice and were grateful for their host families and educational opportunities. Others, like Lacee Harris, chafed at their marginalized place. "Rather than over-emphasize the Indian ways," Kimball told Native students at BYU, "we are going to emphasize the Lord's ways." To Lacee and others, the "Lord's ways" too often coalesced with White supremacy. Antoinette Dee, a Navajo student, recalled being referred to as an "apple": "red on the outside" but "white on the inside," an analogy that highlighted the goal for her to embrace her "true" character. One study found that over half of Navajo children who participated in the ISPP eventually rejected Mormonism altogether.[36]

The conflicts many of these students faced between Mormonism and their traditional culture mirrored those faced by Indigenous communities across the nation. Placement programs and boarding schools were envisioned as a way to "solve" the problem of Indigenous poverty and reluctant assimilation, a global phenomenon found in many settler societies. Mormons largely adopted the broader American agenda of prioritizing a united, homogeneous society built upon Anglo principles and practices, albeit one tempered with their Book of Mormon teachings concerning the "Lamanites."[37]

Helen John did not remain in school long enough to graduate, but she nevertheless lingered in the Buchanans' home for many years. She eventually went to beauty school—and even lived with Spencer Kimball while studying for her exams—served an LDS mission, married in the Salt Lake City Temple, and sent several children to BYU. Others experienced more dissonance. "It shouldn't be a conflict," Lacee Harris insisted years later, referring to the tension between his Ute and Mormon heritages; "we shouldn't have to choose." Harris's great-grandmother had been the first Indian member of the Relief Society in the Uintah Basin, but after years of faithful service, she chose to return to "the traditional ways." Now, four generations later, Harris feared the gap had only increased. The vision of unity shouted

Three Members of the Lamanite Generation, 1972. From left, Ruth Ann Brown, Ima Naranjo, and Millie Cody, Navajo students at BYU who participated in the school's Lamanite Generation program, which romanticized Indigenous culture as an extension of the Book of Mormon.

from the postwar pulpit, and embodied in the ISPP, proved to be a fragile facade.[38]

BRUCE R. MCCONKIE was a tall man with dark brown hair and a booming voice. From his father, Oscar McConkie, a judge who served in the state senate, he learned to exhibit confidence; with his father-in-law, Joseph Fielding Smith, he shared an unyielding commitment to LDS orthodoxy. His commanding presence and dogmatic persona served him well when he was called to the First Council of the Seventy, one ecclesiastical step below apostle, in 1946, at the age of thirty-one. Eight years later, on a cold November night in 1954, McConkie entered the University of Utah's Little Theatre, a cramped room in the upper floor of the student union building, to defend both family and doctrine.

The meeting he crashed was for the Swearing Elders, an informal group of Utah academics who gathered monthly to debate Mormonism's history and ideas. The ringleader was Sterling McMurrin, the same educator who had attended J. Reuben Clark's 1938 "Charted Course" address. Recognizing he no longer had a place within Clark's vision, McMurrin left church education, earned a doctorate in philosophy from the University of Southern California, and became one of the most prominent professors and administrators at the University of Utah. (He was later tapped as John F. Kennedy's commissioner of education.) Though he had given up church activity, McMurrin retained an interest in Mormon culture and authored several books on LDS philosophy and theology that remained standard treatments for decades. In his academic commitment, liberal approach, and irreverent demeanor, McMurrin was McConkie's opposite in nearly every point.[39]

The topic for the night, and the reason McConkie attended a meeting otherwise reserved for professors, was Joseph Fielding Smith's recent book, *Man: His Origin and Destiny*. The work was a distillation of Smith's fundamentalist views regarding evolution that dated back to his debates with B. H. Roberts decades earlier. "So far as the philosophy and wisdom of the world are concerned," the book trumpeted, "they mean nothing unless they conform to the revealed word of God." Defending Smith was Melvin Cook, an explosives expert and professor of metallurgy; opposing was Jennings Olson, a professor of philosophy.[40]

The debate was spirited. McMurrin, moderating the discussion, tried to wrap things up after the janitor arrived to inform them that their time had expired. But McConkie had to make his point. He stood, exceeded his two-minute allowance, and pronounced that, based on Mormon fundamentals, "what the scientists have to say about evolution and the age of the earth is false." The filibuster continued despite McMurrin furiously pointing to his watch. Finally, McMurrin stood up and commanded that he stop, and McConkie begrudgingly conceded. McMurrin later asked a graduate student to write an account because it "was the only time that I ever told one of the General Authorities to shut up and sit down[, and] I doubt I will ever have the occasion to do so in the future."[41]

McMurrin might have won the battle that November night, but the war between progressive intellectuals and conservative officials during the midcentury era continued. Joseph Fielding Smith, who characterized McMurrin's club as an "Anti-Mormon Seminar," only grew in stature as the faith's foremost doctrinal spokesman. Though the far less dogmatic McKay frequently assured inquirers that Smith's anti-evolution book "should be treated as merely the views of one man," it was impossible to slow Smith's influential ascent. (Smith at several points attempted to place McMurrin's membership on trial, only to be halted by McKay's intervention.) Now that he had outlived Roberts, James Talmage, John Widtsoe, and the other apostles with scholarly backgrounds, and their replacements were men without similar academic credentials, Smith had an unchallenged perch from which to shape modern Mormon thought. J. Reuben Clark published his own influential addition to the fundamentalist discourse, *Why the King James Version*, which squarely dismissed whole generations of academic biblical scholarship.[42]

These efforts did not keep other, more liberal saints outside official channels from creating space for critical examination. Among those leading the charge was Juanita Brooks. After a decade of dogged work, she had finally completed her magisterial history of the Mountain Meadows Massacre and was in final discussions with Stanford University Press for publication. She knew there were risks. "I do not want to be excommunicated from my church," she explained to the press's director, "but if that is the price that I must pay for intellectual honesty, I shall pay it." The publication finally appeared in 1950 to scholarly acclaim. Brooks conclusively proved that Mormon settlers masterminded the massacre and that while Brigham Young did not order the event, his actions and rhetoric made it possible. Though not as commercially successful as Fawn Brodie's biography of Joseph Smith, *Mountain Meadows Massacre* became the definitive history of the episode and a touchstone for scholarly work on Mormonism.[43]

Church leaders had learned from the Brodie saga not to make a public fight. When asked how her work was received by LDS authorities, Brooks said, "By silence, total and absolute," though she heard "via the Grapevine" that it was "severely condemned" at church headquarters. The church's chain of bookstores refused to sell it for several decades, and she often felt ostracized from the broader community. Church leaders worked quietly to quash a possible Hollywood movie based on the book. Though not the steep price she expected, it was still a cost. "I have always insisted that we not only sell ourselves short," Brooks reasoned, "but we insult our Maker when we do not use the highest faculties He has given us." Not all of her fellow congregants agreed.[44]

Brooks's call did not go fully unheralded within the community. Several Mormon scholars, the majority of whom were taking advantage of the GI Bill, became academics and composed works that followed Brooks in her critical examination. Most notable was Leonard Arrington, a short and stocky man raised in Idaho who served in World War II and received a doctorate in economics at the University of North Carolina before teaching at Utah State University. His was an unlikely journey: he evolved from "chicken farmer to agriculture major; from agriculture to economics; from regional economics to Western economic history; and finally from Western history to Mormon studies." His first book, *Great Basin Kingdom* (1958), was an economic history of the church that argued that since God's truth "cannot be apprehended" by scholars, it was necessary to offer a "naturalistic discussion" of the world in which God's people lived. He was later seen as the dean of a new scholarly movement known as New Mormon History.[45]

Whether or not church leaders were ready to trust this group of young scholars, it became necessary to marshal their support. As a new generation of leaders were added to the hierarchy, a larger percentage came from business and law backgrounds, and a smaller one from physical and social sciences. Further, an increasingly global church required leaders to act more like administrators and less like theologians. Intellectual defenses and theological expositions were therefore outsourced to trusted academics, many of whom were employed at Brigham Young University.[46]

A chance to test this new arrangement arrived in 1966. Church leaders learned that summer that several fragments of the papyri that Joseph Smith used to produce the Book of Abraham had been discovered in New York City's Metropolitan Museum of Art. (It was previously assumed that they had been destroyed in the Great Chicago Fire of 1871.) The First Presidency tasked Hugh Nibley, the BYU classicist whom Juanita Brooks had previously chastised, with investigating. A year later, it arranged to purchase the papyri and store them in the First Presidency's vault, and hoped to squelch any publicity. But Nibley, who had the look, persona, and reputation of an absent-minded professor, insisted this "momentous transaction" needed more, not less, attention. "For the first time since the angel Moroni took back the golden plates," he reasoned, there existed "a tangible link between the worlds" of sacred scripture and modern readers. He convinced the church to announce the purchase and publish images of all the papyri.[47]

Nibley, and the church, faced a problem, however: the fragments' translations did not match the text supplied by their founding prophet. Critics like Jerald and Sandra Tanner, who had left the church and were just beginning long careers dedicated to undermining the institution, immediately jumped on this fact and published the discrepancies. Nibley was forced to quickly adjust. "There is really very little new here to shed light on the Book of Abraham," he admitted. But he refused to give up ground. Instead, Nibley drew from his scholarly background and religious imagination to cultivate defenses for what he already knew was true: perhaps there were still portions of the papyri that were lost; perhaps the existing papyri hinted toward doctrines that supported LDS temple practices; perhaps the extent to which Smith's text still matched his understanding of Abrahamic lore compensated for any textual dissonance between the papyri and their translation. Regardless of the solution, Nibley promised that the Book of Abraham's historicity, as well as Mormon truth claims in general, could be salvaged.[48]

Nibley had been a prominent apologist for the church since his scathing critique of Brodie decades earlier, but his management of the Joseph Smith papyri marked a significant development in Mormon apologetics. Church leaders recognized that some modern problems exceeded the capacity of traditional responses and required rigorous engagement. After witnessing the effect of Nibley's Abraham defenses, the First Presidency devoted a substantial sum to another

BYU professor, Truman Madsen, to investigate similar issues related to church history. Academically trained apologists like Nibley and Madsen could prove useful so long as their allegiance was beyond reproach; in return for providing research support, these faithful scholars were expected to consecrate their efforts to defending God's kingdom against secular onslaughts.[49]

Sterling McMurrin, of course, saw the whole enterprise as misguided. "I am somewhat amused by those who make extensive studies of the Book of Mormon," he scoffed, which he described as "a waste of time." The issue, to him, was simple: "You don't get books from angels and translate them by miracles." Yet McMurrin also maintained a warm relationship with the "non-rationalist" Hugh Nibley; he had previously invited Nibley to speak at the Swearing Elders, and recruited him for a faculty position at the University of Utah. Leonard Arrington identified the two in 1969 as among the most prominent Mormon intellectuals of the era, as "McMurrin is concerned with ideas," while "Nibley is with the faith." They even publicly debated on at least two occasions, including once at BYU on the topic of the "Nature of Man." It was impossible to know the truth, Nibley argued, "unless you've received revelation." "Even revelation must be judged at the bar of reason," McMurrin retorted.[50]

That the two figures existed on the same spectrum of LDS thought—the same spectrum that also included Bruce R. McConkie and Juanita Brooks—demonstrated the schisms within the Mormon intellectual tradition.

LOCATED EIGHT miles southeast of church headquarters, the Mill Creek neighborhood was known as a hub for Mormonism's shrinking Black community. Many residents could trace their ancestry—the same ancestry that barred them from full membership—back several generations within the church. Few could boast a heritage as strong as Frances Leggroan Fleming, a woman small in stature but large in spirit. Her Mormon lineage went back three generations on her father's side and four generations on her mother's. Her grandmother was none other than Jane Manning James.[51]

Despite this spiritual pedigree, Fleming's faith was wavering by the mid-twentieth century. She experienced increasing hostility from White neighbors and felt her space within the church collapsing. The lack of eligible LDS Black men resulted in her marrying Monroe Fleming, the son of a Methodist minister. Even after Monroe was baptized, they decided against raising their children within the faith of her pioneer grandmother. "There wasn't anything in the Mormon Church for them," she concluded. Fleming remained close to the church—both spiritually, as she believed it was her home, and physically, as she and her husband worked at Hotel Utah, located on the same block as the Church Administration Building.[52]

The national discussion surrounding civil rights during the 1950s and 1960s prompted Mormons to confront and defend their racial restriction to an unprecedented degree. Some, like Lowry Nelson, had discovered the policy for the first time and were confused, if not outraged. Others believed that the church, now surrounded by modernizing forces, could still evolve. Sterling McMurrin, speaking to Utah's chapter of the NAACP in 1960, said there was "a great deal of evidence" that "as the Mormons have more and more experience with the Negroes, they become less and less satisfied with this Negro Doctrine and more and more liberal in their attitude." The next year, Stewart Udall, a Mormon Democrat from Arizona who served as John F. Kennedy's secretary of the interior, wrote a letter to the First Presidency arguing that "unless something is done to clarify the official position of the church," there would be "widespread public comment and controversy."[53]

Some leaders listened. Spencer Kimball, the same apostle who prioritized attention to Indigenous communities, confessed in a private letter to his son that he prayed God would "release the ban and forgive the possible error." Perhaps the apostle most anxious for change was Hugh B. Brown. Born in a Salt Lake City suburb in 1883, Brown spent most of his adult life as a lawyer and farmer in Canada until presiding over the church's British Mission before and after World War II. He then became one of the more progressive members of the Quorum of the Twelve. Brown agitated to soften the racial restriction and ordain Black men to the Aaronic priesthood, to no avail. But when McKay chose Brown for the First Presidency in 1961, and elevated him to first counselor in 1963, Brown was positioned to help steer the impressionable prophet.[54]

While Brown and others successfully convinced McKay that the policy was a "practice" and not a "doctrine"—a theological distinction that loosened its certainty—the aging president maintained that any change required revelation. There remained a fear that removing the restriction would result in interracial unions. J. Reuben Clark, who died the same year Brown joined the First Presidency, had argued that "at the end of the road" for all the civil rights battles was "intermarriage." McKay shared the concern. "We recommend that negroes marry negroes," the prophet urged, "and that whites marry whites." Like many White Americans at the time, McKay worried that loosening racial structures would destabilize society and corrupt Anglo-American purity.[55]

Some Mormons developed theologies that justified racial exclusion. Many, including Joseph Fielding Smith, argued that those born to African ancestry were "less valiant" in the pre-mortal existence and therefore rightly punished. One popular LDS book, John Stewart's *Mormonism and the Negro*, declared in 1960 that actions before this life were why some people lived in "squalor, filth, poverty, and degradation," including the "lowest classes of society in Africa" who lived in a way similar "to that of the animals." Denying them the priesthood, therefore, was "an act of mercy." Indeed, many White evangelicals responded to the civil rights movement by cultivating new theologies and practices that rejected integration.[56]

International concerns caused McKay and others to reconsider their rigid line. The church's global message reached several Nigerian communities, albeit indirectly, during the postwar period. The first petition for more information came from a man named O. J. Umordak in 1946. While the leaders did not follow through at that time, they were deluged with more requests thirteen years later. Adewole Ogunmokun, for instance, wrote that he had read a *Reader's Digest* story on the church, had visions of the Salt Lake Temple, and converted enough of his neighbors to form unofficial LDS congregations in his area of Port Harcourt. "My heart will not rest," he appealed, "for it is made up and there is no turning back for me until I [am] a baptized member of the Church of Jesus Christ of Latter-day Saints." Church leaders discovered several other informal Mormon congregations in Nigeria, most of which were unaware of the others.[57]

The situation flummoxed church leaders. They believed the conversions to be proof of the gospel's reach, and McKay wondered if the moment was like God's command to Peter to preach to the gentiles in the New Testament. Yet leaders also worried about how they could operate congregations where no men were authorized to hold ecclesiastical office or perform priesthood rituals. And there were the persistent cultural concerns. "The question of intermarriage bothers me more than anything," McKay confessed after nearly a year of deliberations on Nigeria. Brown insisted it was worth the risk, but the other First Presidency counselor, Henry D. Moyle, disagreed. "If they would stay among themselves and marry among themselves," Moyle countered, "the question will be easy, but intermarriage would be an inevitable result." Despite increasing appeals from Nigeria's would-be saints—by 1964, they numbered nearly ten thousand—McKay dragged his feet.[58]

It was domestic politics that eventually curtailed the international possibilities. Ambrose Chukwu, a Nigerian student studying in California, discovered Stewart's *Mormonism and the Negro* in 1963 and wrote home to expose the church's anti-Black policies. It caused an uproar in both Nigeria and America. Later that year, Brown admitted to national journalists that, "in light of racial revelations everywhere," the church was "looking toward the possibility of admitting Negroes." The remark infuriated McKay and other leaders. Simultaneously, several BYU professors worked with LaMar Williams, the main contact for the Nigerian mission, to bring African students to campus. This once again raised the fear of interracial mixing. When McKay learned that the NAACP planned to press the church on the Nigeria question, the prophet had seen enough. "I said that we shall make no further effort to go to Nigeria," his presidential diaries recorded, as "we shall make no concession to the NAACP." They ceased the proposed Nigerian mission altogether two years later, after another flare-up with local activists. Thousands of African converts would have to wait.[59]

The broader crisis over racial equality escalated as NAACP leaders increasingly focused on pressuring the LDS institution. They identified the church as the primary reason Utah was one of the few western states to not pass a civil rights bill by 1963. (Many saints agreed: Juanita Brooks bemoaned Utah's singular status on the issue as "a disgrace.") Utah finally lifted its anti-interracial marriage laws that year, the penultimate state in the nation to do so. Word spread about a planned protest for the church's October General Conference, a public spectacle that would have invited more negative press. Brown feverishly labored with NAACP officials to find a compromise. Working with Sterling McMurrin, Brown drafted a statement that insisted "there is in this Church no doctrine, belief, or practice, that is intended to deny the enjoyment of full civil rights by any person regardless of race, color, or creed." With McKay's begrudging approval, Brown read the statement at the conference, and the NAACP canceled its protest. It was only a temporary solution.[60]

RETRENCHMENT WAS not the only option on racial issues. During these same years, a separate community of Nigerian Christians embraced a different form of Mormonism. Dinah Tommy, writing on behalf of thirteen congregations in Abak, wrote the leaders of the Reorganized Church of Jesus Christ of Latter Day Saints requesting baptism. The RLDS church was the same institution descended from Joseph Smith's sons that had denied the existence of polygamy in Nauvoo and was now based in Independence, Missouri. Led by Smith's grandson, W. Wallace Smith, an experienced traveler with a global vision similar to McKay's, the church experienced a similar postwar boom in membership, growing to nearly 180,000 congregants by 1960. The faith had also softened on some distinctive doctrines and was trending closer toward mainstream Christianity. However, unlike the LDS tradition, the RLDS had never claimed a racial restriction. They therefore welcomed the Nigerian appeals with little hesitation. RLDS officials even assisted one of the most prominent Nigerian converts, Gobert Edet, to study at their church school, Graceland College.[61]

Further, their experience in Nigeria pushed the RLDS church to liberalize its ecclesiastical agenda. The resulting mission was based more on social projects than proselytizing. It was a subtle yet substantive shift that echoed many missions across America's mainline Christianity—humanitarian efforts abroad liberalized denominations at home.[62]

The two churches' encounters with Nigerian saints reaffirmed existing trajectories: LDS leaders viewed the episode through the prism of retaining doctrinal purity and social stability; RLDS officials amended existing structures and embraced new frameworks. The alternative courses taken after the 1960s reflected the legacies of these positions and highlight the diversity of the broader Mormon diaspora.

One man who wished the LDS church would have taken a different course was David Gillispie, a Black member in Ogden, Utah. Gillispie remembered being so excited at his baptism that he "thought [he] heard angels singing." But his enthusiasm diminished as he witnessed his White male friends being ordained to the priesthood, performing ritual duties, and serving missions. He feared he had "reached a spiritual 'dead end.'" Gillispie tried to stay committed by marrying an active Mormon woman and hoping to raise a family within the church, but the fact that he could not be sealed in the temple or bless and baptize his children was traumatic. When his young daughter passed away unexpectedly, he could not help but think that, since they were not sealed in the temple, he had no claim on her in the eternities.

In anguish, and with an admitted "spirit of bitterness," Gillispie wrote a letter to President McKay in 1967. "I begin to wonder of the justice of such things," he explained, citing the church's restrictive policies in the face of America's civil rights movement. Everything seemed like a "nightmarish day dream," a far cry from his angelic baptism. He could not help but question the racial ban. "Is this the will of God or the will of man?"[63]

It was a question increasingly difficult to answer.

*   *   *

WHEN SHANNON BYBEE attended church on Sunday, April 23, 1967, in the Redwood Second Ward, a suburb of Salt Lake City, he did not expect anything unusual. But before the opening prayer was given, and before the sacrament was blessed and passed, the bishop made an announcement: every member from all the local wards was invited to view a film that night about "the effects of communism and the role it may someday play in our lives if we do not put forth an effort to combat it." His interest piqued, Bybee attended. Present was G. Edward Griffin, the director of the film, *Anarchy U.S.A.*, who said he had received apostolic encouragement to spread his message to the saints. The film attacked the United Nations for enabling communism, claimed civil rights activists were communist pawns, and denounced both John F. Kennedy and Lyndon B. Johnson for secretly supporting America's enemies. It also featured graphic images of the blood and carnage that resulted from communist regimes.[64]

Bybee was not impressed. The film used "innuendo, implication, guilt by association, labels, and half truths if not outright falsehoods" to present a partisan message. "I do not think the Lord's House should be used as a forum for attacks on such subjects as the civil rights movement, the United Nations and federal legislation," he wrote church leaders, "nor should Church authorities lend an air of authority to such undertakings."[65]

The fear that churches were being hijacked for political messages was a common concern during the 1960s. The film Bybee's congregation watched was one produced by the John Birch Society, the national organization dedicated to exposing a communist plot that supposedly threatened the entire free world. Millions were swept up in the conspiracy. David O. McKay had met with the Birch Society's founder, Robert Welch, a week before Bybee's congregation viewed the film. Welch was determined to convince McKay to allow Ezra Taft Benson, one of the most prominent proponents of the anti-communist conspiracies, to become the society's public face. (Benson was likely the apostle who endorsed the film for an LDS audience.) Though McKay was sympathetic to the cause, he refused, fearing public outcry.[66]

Hewing too close to the Birch Society threatened the bipartisan goodwill the church had built over the past decade. Building off of Eisenhower's presidency and in the wake of Kennedy's 1960 election, a fervent sense of ecumenism swept large segments of the nation. Public figures and politicians alike believed more faiths could fit under the broad Judeo-Christian umbrella. Though McKay was not taken with Kennedy when they first met—and journalists interpreted the prophet's personal support for Richard Nixon as an official endorsement—the young American president could not help but praise the American-born faith. "As the Mormons succeeded," Kennedy once declared, "so America can succeed." His successor, Lyndon Johnson, was even more effusive with his praise, and he and McKay developed a genuine friendship. After once rerouting Air Force One to Salt Lake City for an impromptu visit, Johnson remarked, "I always feel better after I have been in [McKay's] presence." The Mormon prophet was the first religious leader invited to Johnson's White House, and the Mormon Tabernacle Choir—fresh off winning a Grammy for its rendition of the patriotic song "Battle Hymn of the Republic"—sang at his inauguration. Both invitations reflected the faith's growing stature. The church capitalized on these national victories by forming a new publicity department and embracing its clean-cut, uncontroversial image.[67]

While there were several prominent figures who helped improve the church's reputation—boxer Gene Fullmer and golfer Billy Casper among them—none took as much advantage of the positive press as George Romney. The great-grandson of Parley P. Pratt and grandson of polygamists who helped establish Mormonism's Mexican colonies, Romney was born in Colonia Dublán in 1907 but fled the country due to its revolution a few years later. A successful business career resulted in his taking over Detroit's American Motors in 1954 and leading it to new levels of success. Mostly because of his industrial prowess, but also due to his charisma and looks, Romney was named the Associated Press's Man of the Year in industry every year from 1958 to 1961. *Time* called him a "Bible-quoting broth of a man who burns brightly with the fire of missionary zeal" and featured his chiseled jaw on its cover. Such a talent could not be kept out of politics for long. He easily won Michigan's governorship as a moderate Republican in 1962, having gained support from both the state's NAACP and labor unions. No sooner did he take office in Lansing, however, than speculation arose that it was just a stepping stone to Washington, DC. "The one fellow I don't want to run against is Romney," Kennedy privately mused in 1963.[68]

But was America ready for a Mormon president? Prospects were surprisingly promising. *The Nation* identified Romney's faith as an asset for his "attractive public image," and the *New Republic* heralded him as "a kind of Billy Graham." One national poll found that 75 percent of Americans had no issue with voting for a Mormon, while only 17 percent were opposed. Romney also received high marks from the First Presidency, which frequently corresponded with him and vocalized its support. "He will have the full backing of the church," McKay admitted to journalists, even though "he will be his own man" when it came to policy. That Romney did not face anything close to the public opposition that Reed Smoot had a half century earlier demonstrated how far the church had come; that he did not even confront the same challenges as Kennedy proved that the nation had evolved, too.[69]

The major obstacle to Romney's growing ambitions was his church's position on race. The aspiring politician admitted in a private meeting that he did not want his campaign to be "hurtful to the Church by reason of the negro question," as he did not want to place his religious community in a bad light. But he also did not want to be dismissed as a bigot. Romney therefore maintained a tenuous balance by courting civil rights supporters while simultaneously refusing to critique the church for its policies. Not all his ecclesiastical leaders were pleased with the effort. One apostle, Delbert Stapley, privately reproved him for supporting equal rights, noting that previous presidents "who were very active in the Negro cause"—Abraham Lincoln and JFK—had met violent ends, possibly due to pushing policies "contrary to the teachings of the Prophet Joseph Smith." Romney, however, did not back down. "A Negro is a child of God just like I am," he told *Meet the Press*, and "our most urgent domestic problem is to wipe out human injustice and discrimination against the Negroes."[70]

Other prominent Mormons were less willing to present such a moderate image. Benson concluded his time in Eisenhower's cabinet with more, not less, distrust in government. He soon became an outspoken proponent of right-wing conspiracies. "No true Latter-day Saint could be a communist or a socialist," he declared, insisting that the "welfare state" was an unpersuasive cover for a creeping cabal. Though McKay never allowed him to officially join the Birch Society, Benson became close friends with its founder, Robert Welch, and often acted as the sounding board for conspiratorial information. When Welch published *The Politician* (1963), positing that Eisenhower was part of a global communist plot, even the soon-to-be GOP presidential nominee and partisan firebrand Barry Goldwater denounced the work; Benson, conversely, sent copies to his fellow apostles as Christmas presents. He also regaled the saints with General Conference addresses that echoed these radical theories, including the accusation that Martin Luther King Jr. and other civil rights activists were a "tool of communist deception." A few years later, he wrote the foreword for the racist diatribe *The Black Hammer: A Study of Black Power, Red Influence, and White Alternatives* (1967), one of the most extreme anti–civil rights works from the era.[71]

Benson was not alone in these efforts. During these same years, Cleon Skousen, a BYU professor and onetime Salt Lake City police

Ezra Taft Benson (center) at a speaking engagement with Robert Welch (left), founder of the John Birch Society, in 1966. Their meeting's "One Nation Under God" banner reflected how the Birch Society used Christian nationalism to push its libertarianism and anti-communism.

chief, became a popular Mormon author and speaker. His book *The Naked Communist* (1958), which classified communism as a global evil within an eternal war, was a bestseller, especially after McKay praised it in General Conference. His religious writings, like *The First Two Thousand Years* (1953), which argued for a fundamentalist reading of scripture, also became immensely influential in LDS circles. (The praise, however, was not universal: "Brother Skousen's book has been a plague," complained Joseph Fielding Smith.) While the general Mormon body had been trending in the conservative direction for a few decades, both politically and socially, Benson and Skousen cemented the course.[72]

McKay struggled with how to handle the situation. He bought into the anti-communist frenzy but did not want the church associated with partisanship. He allowed Hugh B. Brown, then an apostle, to speak at Utah's Democratic Convention in 1958 to prove LDS leadership was not "one-sided in politics." When Democratic congressman David S. King complained about Benson denouncing Mormons who supported liberal policies, McKay countered that both of his counselors in the First Presidency, including Brown, were Democrats, which he believed was message enough. When he received reports of other local leaders sharing Birch Society propaganda, McKay agreed to ask them to stop, but also insisted that "we do not want the Brethren to go out with the idea that we, as a Church, are not publicly and emphatically against Communism." After Brown told a journalist that the church opposed the Birch Society's methods, McKay instructed the church's newspaper not to publish it. The prophet was increasingly torn between his personal attachment to Republican principles and the church's institutional commitment to neutrality.[73]

The First Presidency eventually released a statement that reaffirmed its opposition to communism but also critiqued those "who pretend to fight it by casting aspersions on our elected officials or other fellow citizens." Benson complained that the statement sounded like an attack on him and Skousen—a suspicion McKay confirmed—and the church received hundreds of letters from right-wing saints upset with the message. To help avoid further conflict, at least for a while, Benson was called on a mission to Europe, though his public denunciations of socialism while in socialist countries continued to invite scorn.[74]

As the decade progressed, and partisanship grew deeper, McKay's management style became increasingly strained. His eagerness to please others and his quickly deteriorating health led him to frequently and abruptly switch courses, usually siding with whoever spoke with him last. On February 9, 1966, Benson approached McKay with the opportunity for the prophet to appear on the cover of a "patriotic" magazine, an honor placing him in the company of other men like Barry Goldwater and Edgar Hoover. McKay, flattered, agreed. Hugh B. Brown then informed McKay that the magazine was published by the Birch Society, and the prophet tried to back out. Benson, however, was persistent, and told McKay, privately, that the cover was already in production, so the prophet begrudgingly said, "They better go ahead with it." But when other church leaders discovered Benson's go-around in early March, they phoned McKay while he was at his ranch in northern Utah and convinced him to take drastic action, including threatening legal measures if they did not pull the cover. These tumultuous tug-of-wars continued for the next few years, as everyone surrounding McKay tried to sway the prophet to their side.[75]

The myth of social unity to which McKay—and America—had become attached the previous decade was coming undone, a casualty of the political wars and racial divisions that fractured the nation in the 1960s. It was impossible for the LDS church to remain neutral, let alone homogeneous, in a country riven by discord.

THERE WERE few places in America as culturally distant from Salt Lake City as California's Bay Area, and there were few figures as ideologically distinct from Ezra Taft Benson as Eugene England. Like Benson, England was raised on an Idaho farm by faithful parents committed to the church; unlike Benson, England embraced the anti-imperialist and anti-capitalist spirit of the 1960s. As a PhD English student at Stanford, he was surrounded by his activist kin. Yet England still insisted on his Mormon bona fides. His liberal or conservative credentials, he later reminisced, could "change from one to the other simply by walking across Stanford Avenue from the university to the Institute building." When surrounded by anti-war and civil rights activists, he was "that strange, non-smoking, short-haired, family-raising conservative"; when among the saints, he was "that strange liberal who renounced war and worried about fair-housing and free speech." It was a tough balance, but one he was determined to maintain.[76]

England worried that few of his fellow LDS students were willing to embark on the same struggle. As he taught institute courses, he found many young saints "overawed by their educational experience" and "finding their religious background wanting in comparison." Part of this was due to the reputation of conservative voices like Benson and Joseph Fielding Smith. But the problem was also a result of recent decisions by ecclesiastical leaders to simplify and streamline institutional messaging, a process that came to be known as correlation.[77]

Efforts to better coordinate church activities dated back several decades. David O. McKay had previously been resistant to the appeals from J. Reuben Clark and his successors, like Harold B. Lee, to formalize a system of correlation, instead hoping they could maintain a loose governing structure based on agency rather than control. Now, with a rapidly growing international body, there was a greater need to manage church lessons and practices more efficiently. Controlling disparate voices in an era of corporatization and bureaucratization was a tricky task, but one that was common in America at the time.[78]

A tipping point may have come with the publication of Bruce R. McConkie's *Mormon Doctrine* in 1958. McConkie, who never shied from proclaiming his interpretive authority, envisioned the massive volume to be the definitive overview of the faith. It was arranged by topic and ordered alphabetically, with sections as benign as "Card Playing" ("to the extent that church members play cards they are in apostasy and rebellion") and as substantial as evolution ("how scrubby and groveling the intellectual" who "finds comfort in the theoretical postulates that mortal life began in the scum of the sea"). He also detailed how "negroes" were "less valiant in pre-existence" and therefore "had certain spiritual restrictions imposed upon them," as well as identified Catholics as "the great and abominable church."[79]

J. Reuben Clark immediately recognized the problem and feared "the book would raise more trouble than anything we had in the Church for a long while." A committee was assigned to read the book and "make a list of the corrections" that could be printed as an addendum. The men eventually listed 1,067 errors within the 776 pages. To avoid public embarrassment, they decided to quietly allow the book to go out of print and instituted a rule that no church leader could publish a work without getting First Presidency approval. (McConkie had other plans, however, and convinced the impressionable McKay to let him republish a revised version a decade later.) The need for a standardized system was now clear.[80]

Apostle Lee finally received the green light to implement his correlation vision. He announced at the 1961 General Conference an "all-Church coordinating council" that would "formulate policy which will govern the planning, the writing, co-ordination, and implementation of the entire Church curriculum." Lee likened this initiative to an army consolidating its efforts to provide "the most effective possible defense" against modernity's evils. The effects were immediate. The new correlation body oversaw Sunday school lessons, church publications, and regional and local activities. It reorganized the church's international leadership structure in 1967, installing regional representatives and area authorities across the globe, and instituted standardized bishops' training programs in 1970 to ensure universal compliance. Technological developments aided this professionalization process, as the faith's financial department started using a computer in 1962; membership records were migrated to a digital system in 1968. The church was not only global but bureaucratic.[81]

Among the casualties of this streamlining effort were any shreds of Relief Society autonomy. Belle Spafford's organization, already slimmed down from Amy Brown Lyman's heyday, was firmly placed under the umbrella of priesthood correlation. The society lost control of its monthly lessons, which now focused on providing compassionate service as individuals rather than as a group. It was also no longer in charge of fundraising, as all finances were managed by local bishops. And finally, after publishing its own periodical for nearly a century—first the *Exponent*, followed by the *Relief Society*

Magazine—it now only supplied material for a single church magazine directed at adults, *The Ensign*. (But only when solicited.) Correlation not only standardized Mormonism's message and image, it cemented America's postwar patriarchal ideal as the faith's core.[82]

Esther Peterson, a consumer activist raised in Provo who served in the Kennedy and Johnson administrations, mourned this shift. "When I was at BYU" in the 1920s, she reflected, "our thinking was so broad and so big" because "our faith could encompass these things." But now she worried about "the narrowing" of opportunities for women. "Don't read it," she heard from some corners, and "don't think about that." Such limitations were inimical to her faith. "It's the broadness that we need," and Mormonism, at its heart, was "broad and big."[83]

Eugene England also worried about these developments while watching from Stanford. The correlated message might work for global expansion, but it failed to satisfy uncorrelated saints. To rectify the problem, he and four others gathered in the summer of 1965 to launch their own journal, which they hoped would "express Mormon culture and examine the relevance of religion in secular life." They envisioned a platform for members from "a variety of viewpoints" to produce robust discussion. The result was *Dialogue: A Journal of Mormon Thought*, an effort dedicated to pushing back against the church's homogeneous image. "We are active members of the church," Paul Salisbury, the journal's publisher, told journalists; "however, we seek to give voice to a growing intellectual community to open the door to a variety of viewpoints impossible to express in existing Church journals."[84]

The competing tensions of standardized doctrine and intellectual freedom only grew from there. Harold B. Lee's vision of a completely correlated church was not to be. But correlation enabled the church to continue its rapid growth through the 1960s. The vast number of members, however, meant a larger medley of beliefs and confirmed the faith's growing platform on the national stage.

JUST AS the Correlation Committee aimed to stitch the Mormon body together, the cultural tumult that surrounded America's 1968 presidential election threatened to tear the nation's social fabric apart.

The political fracturing that dissolved traditional allegiances across America left many, especially those outside party establishments, scrambling to form new unions.[85]

Benson, now seen as a political outsider who refused to mince words on socialism and civil rights, was in hot demand. In April 1966, a new Birch Society–backed political organization, styling itself the "1976 Committee," aimed to restore the nation to what members believed to be its libertarian principles during its bicentennial. They proposed running a third-party ticket with Strom Thurmond as president and Benson as vice president. Benson, ever eager to jump back into the political fray, begged McKay for approval. This was the only chance to "stem the drift toward socialism in this country," Benson urged. McKay begrudgingly agreed. The prophet became worried, however, when, six months later, Benson was moved to the top of the ticket. By January 1967, there were even bumper stickers, and Benson claimed he received hundreds of letters urging him to run.[86]

Once again, the more moderate members of the First Presidency intervened, and once again, McKay waffled. When Benson's General Conference talk in October 1966 critiqued, albeit indirectly, other apostles who lacked zeal in the cause of liberty, N. Eldon Tanner and Hugh Brown felt he had crossed a line. They opposed Benson's request to publish the talk as a stand-alone pamphlet. At first, McKay acquiesced and told Benson he could not go forward with publication; two weeks later, however, when cornered by Benson in a private meeting, McKay flipped. His counselors were livid, especially when they learned in December that McKay had approved Benson's presidential run. When confronted, the prophet denied his support; once again, he later reversed course, and even altered the meeting's minutes to hide his indecisiveness.[87]

While the 1976 Committee quietly dissolved before the primary season, a more tempting opportunity came at the dawn of 1968. The year was one of the most turbulent in American political history, as aftershocks from a decade of civil rights battles realigned political parties. The Democrats, due to their increasing support for racial equality, lost footing in what had previously been their southern strongholds; the Republicans, now fully committed to a Southern

Strategy, formed a new coalition based on racial grievance in the South and libertarianism in the West. Among the casualties of this shift was George Romney, who, due to both his moderate platform and infelicitous comments regarding "brainwashing" and Vietnam, fell from front-runner to afterthought. Both parties seemed unmoored.

Hoping to take advantage of this unsettled climate was George Wallace, the former Alabama governor who gained a national reputation for his public and stubborn opposition to racial equality. "I draw the line in the dust and toss the gauntlet before the feet of tyranny," he famously proclaimed; "segregation today, segregation tomorrow, segregation forever!" The energetic, charismatic, and uncompromising firebrand, now exiled from the national Democratic establishment, eyed a third-party run. For a running mate, he desired someone who was nationally recognized and could therefore add validity, was a Republican and could offer bipartisan support, and was outside the South and could demonstrate geographic range. Someone who was a political outsider and also known for his bombastic rhetoric. Someone like Ezra Taft Benson.

On February 12, at Wallace's request, Benson, just finished with an apostolic assignment in Wisconsin, flew to Alabama for a clandestine rendezvous in the state mansion. Wallace flattered him for over three hours, and Benson came away believing he had just spoken to the next American president. The apostle, finally seeing his chance to save the country, wanted to join the ticket. He knew that convincing McKay to give permission, however, would prove difficult, so he plotted his path carefully. Benson meticulously documented in a judiciously crafted letter why he should run, emphasizing it was the best chance to curb communism's tide once and for all. He even favorably compared Wallace's political party, the American Independent Party, to Joseph Smith's political ideals. Benson's letter was accompanied by a personal appeal from Wallace. The cause was urgent, and the timing was intricate—the deadline for getting their names on ballots was quickly approaching.[88]

Benson tried to meet with McKay the day after he returned to Salt Lake City. The nonagenarian prophet had been so sick that he had not attended any leadership meetings for months. Visits were strictly managed by his counselors and secretary. Knowing he would not receive a warm reception from either Tanner or Brown, Benson instead sidestepped them and approached Alvin Dyer, a fellow conservative who had recently been appointed an additional member of the First Presidency. The two strategized how best to approach the ailing prophet, and eventually secured a meeting at three thirty that afternoon in his Hotel Utah apartment. Dyer went in first to introduce the topic and ease McKay to the idea, after which Benson joined them. Then, after a brief discussion, both Benson and Dyer sat silent for ten minutes as McKay, sickly and bound to his office chair, perused the letters and considered the situation. The pause was poignant. Benson's entire political trajectory pointed to this exact moment.

For once, McKay was decisive. "You should turn the offer down," he said with conviction. This time, he was not willing to be swayed. Benson, hiding his disappointment, said he was willing to abide by the decision. His most promising political opportunity had effectively come to an end. McKay, likely sensing the anguish, reaffirmed his high regard for the apostle. They exchanged long handshakes and parted.

As Benson and Dyer walked back to the church's office building, only a block from McKay's apartment, Benson could not help but retrace his steps and consider where things went wrong. Was Dyer to blame? "You did not make any recommendation, did you?" he asked, referring to Dyer's preliminary chat with McKay. Dyer assured him he did not. Benson, still despondent and without someone to scapegoat, tried to accept the new reality. His opportunity to save the nation had vanished.[89]

THE REMAINDER of 1968 introduced only more drama. Church leaders' concerns over the civil rights movement evolved into fears over race riots. They hired policemen to guard Temple Square, fearing it might be the site of a protest; they stopped advertising their trips and listing their phone numbers, fearing they might become targets; they discouraged local leaders from participating in debate at all costs, fearing another firestorm. One protester threw a Molotov cocktail onto the court during a BYU basketball game against Colorado State University. America seemed on fire, and Mormon leaders were afraid they might burn with it.[90]

Other Latter-day Saints refused to stay neutral. Sterling McMurrin, growing in national prominence, declared that it was time for the church to jettison its "crude superstitions about negroes." Church leaders were incensed, and some apostles, including Joseph Fielding Smith, renewed calls for him to be "tried for his membership." McKay, again, demurred, admitting that while he was "disturbed" by McMurrin's comments, he wanted to avoid the backlash of a public excommunication. Hugh B. Brown, meanwhile, quietly gathered enough apostolic support to indeed jettison, or at least soften, the racial restriction, but his efforts were squashed by Harold B. Lee and other conservative members, who insisted it remain in place. Leaders prepared a compromise statement that reaffirmed the restriction's revelatory status while also calling for all Black Americans to receive their "full Constitutional privileges." Brown reluctantly signed, bereft that he had lost his chance at real change.[91]

The entire First Presidency soon concluded that Benson's radical politics were also a hindrance to their global message. They had received complaints from leaders in other nations—from Chile in 1962, from Britain in 1968—about how impractical it was to have a church official parrot American partisan positions. To be an international church, they decided, required dissociating from parochial politics. The First Presidency insisted that apostles should focus on "gospel principles" and "leave politics or pointed attacks on politics out of their talks." When Benson refused to comply and denounced the United Nations in an address to BYU the next year, McKay immediately sent Brown to counter the message and emphasize that the church did not have an official position on the topic. Benson, expectedly, complained; McKay, unexpectedly, held firm, and published Brown's statement for the entire church to see.[92]

No Mormon apostle would ever become as associated with partisan politics as Ezra Taft Benson was in the 1960s. The heightened anxieties over public image, especially in a global context, and the new system of correlation, which prioritized unity, neutered much of Benson's later work. But his impact remained long after his partisan career ended. His voice rang last, and it rang the longest. Mormon culture, especially in the Mountain West, was now firmly and decisively in the conservative camp. Lyndon Johnson's 1964 election was the last time Utah would ever vote Democratic for president. The region's ground had permanently shifted along with the rest of America's political geography in the wake of the era's unrest.

The two and a half decades that followed World War II featured the most explosive growth the church had ever seen. The triumph of institutional expansion, however, was matched with the difficulties of governing such a diverse community. The nearly three-million-body membership was spread across not only hundreds of nations but numerous and often diametrically opposed cultures. David O. McKay, who presided over this entire period, mirrored the transformation: he evolved from an unflappable figure optimistic in outlook and determined in vision, to a malleable figurehead shifting from one position to the other, torn between competing factions. His vision—America's vision—of a society cemented together through national pride and material success gave way to a world of schisms unwilling to grant any ground to ideological enemies. McKay died in January 1970, having barely survived the battle to maintain unity among the church's leaders, only to just miss the new confrontation with its membership.

AMONG THOSE who saw the coming conflict was Morgan D. King, a law student at the University of California at Davis. King spent the turbulent 1960s active in both his Latter-day Saint community as well as "the movement," what he and his classmates called the campus protests for civil rights. Could the two allegiances be reconciled? Could "organized religion" retain vitality "if the committed, creative young increasingly spend their passion elsewhere," and could the radical movement "sustain its positive moral quality over the long, difficult road ahead"? King hoped that both the New Left and Mormonism could adapt to the changing times. Both traditions, after all, were devoted to the well-being of society, and both traditions, in the end, were destined to exhibit "an increasingly significant influence on our national culture."[93]

8

Fault Lines, 1970–95

Our history is simply that of any group which struggles to maintain its identity as it copes with political, economic, and religious forces which seek to destroy or limit its uniqueness.

—LEONARD J. ARRINGTON[1]

W HEN A GROUP of Mormon women met at Laurel Thatcher Ulrich's Boston-area home in June 1970, they did not expect it to be a significant gathering. Attendees were merely seeking solidarity as dutiful wives, loving mothers, and dedicated believers. Many were "city-bred," with academic husbands and lots of children. But they yearned for more. The host, Ulrich, who admitted that she was well acquainted with "the problem with no name" long before she read Betty Friedan's *Feminine Mystique,* had recently started a graduate program at Simmons College. Another attendee, Claudia Bushman, who sat on a straight oak chair near the fireplace, was a doctoral student at Boston University. "The talk streamed through the room like sunshine," Ulrich recalled, as they expressed their frustrations, disappointments, and confessions.

Their discussions were prompted by a larger national movement known as second-wave feminism, in which women across the nation petitioned to expand their roles beyond motherhood and wifehood. These Boston feminists eventually embarked on a series of ambitious projects, including a new periodical. Ulrich later reminisced that if she had known they were "about to make history," they would have taken minutes, or at least passed around a roll. She also wished she knew the exact date so they could place a brass plaque outside the house to commemorate the origins of what they playfully called "the L.D.S. Cell of Women's Lib."[2]

Another gathering of faithful reformers took place the next year, once again in June, this time in Salt Lake City. Ruffin Bridgeforth, Darius Gray, and Eugene Orr, three Black converts, knelt in prayer in a vacant University of Utah classroom. The three men had very different personalities—Bridgeforth the conservative, Gray the prag- matist, and Orr the firebrand—but they were united in goal: to carve out a larger space for Black Mormons. They hoped the LDS church would reverse its racial restriction, ordain them to the priesthood, and allow their families access to temple ordinances. The men even- tually gained an audience with three apostles, Gordon B. Hinck- ley, Thomas S. Monson, and Boyd K. Packer, who approved a new church-sponsored group for Black members. No plaque marked the

Darius Gray speaks at the first Genesis Group meeting in 1971.

origins of this movement, either. But since the organization was meant to symbolize a new beginning, they called it Genesis.[3]

Both the Boston feminists and the Genesis Group loudly and repeatedly voiced their support for the institution, belief in its core doctrines, and loyalty to its leadership. But they also drew from a wider American sentiment that demanded change in the wake of the 1960s. Their activism eventually forced the church to reconsider the role of history while also controlling the future.

LDS leaders, in turn, chose a linchpin upon which the next generation could be built: the "traditional" family. Though the concept had been increasingly central to the faith for the previous few decades, it now took on even more significance as *the* defining principle.

This emphasis on the family was both a continuation of a long trajectory dating back to 1890 and a response to contemporary concerns. The saints came to unreservedly embrace a traditional definition of the family just as the concept became a political wedge. Debates over abortion, the Equal Rights Amendment, and homosexuality divided Americans into opposing factions, which left Mormons struggling to navigate an increasingly fractured environment. The conservative framework for social stability proved most appealing, but it also meant entering cultural warfare. Paul Weyrich, founder of the conservative Heritage Foundation, captured the meaning of this new battle. "It is a war of ideology, it's a war of ideas, and it's a war about our way of life," Weyrich explained. "And it has to be fought with the same intensity, I think, and dedication as you would fight in a shooting war."[4]

Leonard Arrington witnessed these profound shifts from the perspective of one of the faith's most prominent historians. "Our religion cannot avoid coming to grips with historical truth," he mused amid this transition, "because it is based on historical truth claims." Reckoning with this dynamic is a difficult, if not an impossible, task for any church, especially one with a past as layered as Mormonism's. By 1995, this confrontation with history, race, and feminism had come to the forefront.[5]

The Mormon entrance into this cacophonous dispute caused consistent angst. Leaders faced challenges both from their contested past, with historical truths challenging cherished myths, and from their diverse present, with lived realities conflicting with prized ideals.

D. MICHAEL QUINN was on a hunt in August 1972. The twenty-eight-year-old son of a Mexican-immigrant father and a seventh-generation LDS mother had brown eyes and a headful of dark hair. A graduate student at the University of Utah with a reputation for his dogged research, he had been assigned by Leonard Arrington to find missing records in the Church Administration Building's basement. A frustrated archivist finally gave up helping the anxious Quinn and instead pointed him toward a "dimly lit expanse" in the basement's corner to explore on his own. There, amid piles of boxes and books that had been restricted to academics for decades, Quinn found two stacks of material that nobody, including the church historian, knew existed.

Held in dusty cardboard and wooden boxes were "hundreds—perhaps *thousands*—of leather-bound volumes in various sizes." These included Brigham Young's office diaries, daily minutes from the First Presidency's office during the 1880s, and an assortment of nearly thirty thousand letters, speech manuscripts, and other invaluable documents. Quinn quickly lost track of time digging through the treasures. When he finally emerged from the basement, he surprised the guards, who assumed the building was empty.[6]

Quinn's discovery of foundational records embodied the spirit found among historians of the era. Joseph Fielding Smith, the dogmatic apostle dedicated to preserving the faith's orthodoxy, was released as church historian in 1970 after a fifty-year tenure. His replacement, the apostle Howard Hunter, was far less restrictive when granting researchers access. Then, in January 1972, church leaders chose Leonard Arrington, a noted scholar, to be the new church historian. Arrington, a short man with a round face and thin white hair, was the first person with a PhD to hold the position. His gregarious personality and enterprising approach won him friends in both academia and church leadership. Hunter told Arrington that they had concluded that "the Church was mature enough that our history should be honest," and that they no longer believed in "suppressing information, nor hiding documents, nor canceling or withholding minutes for possible scrutiny."[7]

Arrington was publicly sustained in General Conference that April, assembled a division of historians, and established an energetic agenda to help the faith confront its past. This included conducting research for church authorities and commencing an ambitious publication agenda. Arrington enthusiastically embraced the challenge of standing "on two legs—the leg of faith and the leg of reason." Those who participated in this "period of excitement and optimism" came to refer to Arrington's tenure as "Camelot."[8]

The plans to professionalize the historical department were part of a much larger agenda to modernize the entire church according to contemporary corporate practices. Just the previous year, leaders had hired a prominent New York consulting firm to evaluate their institutional structure and recommend changes. The final report suggested creating a corporate apparatus that relieved church officials of day-to-day operations and instead placed more responsibility on middle management. This involved hiring professionals to run various divisions, a streamlining process that coalesced with apostle Harold B. Lee's correlation movement. Arrington was immediately struck by the bureaucratic elements and "status symbols of the corporate world" that now ruled church headquarters. Persons who attained a "certain rank" were entitled to offices with rugs and adjoining bathrooms, and there were "four sizes of desks depending on rank." Even one's chair was determined by position, with "big pretentious armchairs" reserved for ecclesiastical authorities.[9]

Though Arrington and others chafed at this corporatization, it was difficult to argue with the results. The consolidation culminated in a series of organizational changes that took place in 1975. Leaders introduced a new hierarchical quorum, known as the First Quorum of the Seventy, comprising full-time general authorities with lifetime callings. A Second Quorum of the Seventy, also full-time ecclesiastical leaders, with five-year appointments, was created in 1989. To oversee global operations, they inaugurated a supervisory program with distinct geographic areas. (Explosive membership growth led them to divide the system into thirteen areas a decade later, expanded to twenty-two in 1991.) Auxiliary programs like the Relief Society were further circumscribed, as their governing boards were reduced and their annual conferences discontinued. Leaders divested the church from some of its business interests, like the fifteen hospitals it ran in the Rocky Mountain region, and moved those that remained under the purview of the Office of the Presiding Bishopric.

These developments resulted in a labyrinthine institution that matched the enormous businesses of modern America, especially other corporations led by devout owners like Hobby Lobby and Wal-Mart. It was a structure poised to capitalize on domestic and international growth. Indeed, following reforms that were pushed by First Presidency counselor N. Eldon Tanner in the wake of financial difficulties in the 1960s, largely due to overspending, leaders transformed the institution's financial management. They shifted from a save-and-spend model, hired financiers to privately grow an eventually massive investment portfolio, and ceased providing detailed accounting reports at each April General Conference. Though lacking previous generations' transparency, the new model afforded the monetary stability necessary to support the church's global efforts. Emblematic of this new age was the completion of a twenty-eight-story Church Office Building that replaced the neoclassical Administration Building as the faith's headquarters in 1972.[10]

Much of this structural transformation filtered down to the local level. In 1980, all church meetings were reduced and consolidated to weekly three-hour blocks. Ward budgets were standardized and local responsibilities for meetinghouse costs were eliminated. The goal of these initiatives was a regulated experience across all congregations. Mormonism's ability to retain consistency amid massive growth was a hallmark of its consolidation efforts.[11]

Though this corporatization began under Joseph Fielding Smith, the driving force was still Harold B. Lee, J. Reuben Clark's chief protégé. Lee took control of the global church he had long sought to shape once Smith passed away in 1972. But his long-anticipated reign proved exceptionally short. After eighteen months of whirlwind activity—Arrington suspected that "his diligence in accepting so many appointments" took a toll on his health—Lee suffered a fatal pulmonary hemorrhage the day after Christmas in 1973.

Succeeding Lee was Spencer W. Kimball, a quiet yet beloved apostle with dark-rimmed glasses, drooping cheeks, and large ears, a face that led many saints to later joke that he served as the model for Yoda in the movie *Star Wars*. Hardly anyone anticipated Kimball's becoming prophet due to his advanced age and poor health. He had suffered a series of heart attacks during his apostolic career and developed a malignancy of the throat and vocal cords that resulted in nearly losing his voice. He often had to use a miniature microphone on his cheek to be heard on television and radio. Kimball stood in stark contrast to his predecessor: whereas Lee was a firm and sober administrator who wanted control over minute decisions, Kimball was relaxed and known for wandering the halls to converse and joke. Few expected him to bring major reforms. Arrington had heard that Kimball was "a traditionalist" on the era's most pressing issues, and national journalists posited that "the new president is not likely to change Mormon views on the family or race."[12]

If Kimball was determined not to shake the foundations, he certainly built upon them. His frequent admonition for saints to "lengthen their stride," urging all young men and some young women to serve missions, continued the recent decades' massive growth. The number of missionaries sent out every year increased from 18,100 in 1974 to 29,300 in 1985, and the percentage of the missionaries serving abroad doubled from 15 to 30 percent. To accommodate this international increase, leaders built a Language Training Mission, soon renamed the Missionary Training Center, in 1976, across the street from BYU. Church membership rapidly rose from three million to nearly eight million within fifteen years of Kimball's ascension. Some scholars estimated that Mormonism was the fastest-growing global religion.[13]

Leonard Arrington celebrated these developments, but it was not long before his division ran up against the bureaucracy. Arrington soon questioned his "ability to survive in the uncertainties of church policy and practice," primarily because "every experienced bureaucrat" was afraid of running afoul of leadership. Conservative apostles were especially concerned about the new periodical *Dialogue*, founded a few years before, which they worried would lead saints astray. After Quinn became frustrated that his "commitment to full disclosure" was not welcome at church headquarters, he left Camelot for the safer confines of Yale for doctoral studies.[14]

Leading the conservative charge was newly appointed apostle Boyd K. Packer, a stern man with a steely demeanor. Packer had survived polio as a child, served as a fighter pilot during World War II, and worked for the church education system until being called into leadership at a young age. He was Joseph Fielding Smith's first choice to join the Quorum of the Twelve after the orthodox doctrinaire became president in 1970. In many ways, Packer was Smith's ideological successor, an unofficial designation he shared with Smith's son-in-law Bruce R. McConkie, the dogmatic scriptorian who also became an apostle in 1972. Packer dismissed *Dialogue* as "rak[ing] over old controversial subjects and stir[ring] up trouble and mistrust." His anxiety at times veered toward obsession. When pressed on why he despised the periodical, Packer pointed to the cover of a recent issue that he categorized as obscene: he interpreted the colorful Rorschach-style inkblots as "male and female genitals." Arrington quickly realized that whereas leaders had previously been afraid of J. Reuben Clark, and then Harold B. Lee, "now it seems to be Boyd Packer who is free to give advice and to make threats."[15]

The church's corporatization during the 1970s, while succeeding in creating an efficient global system of standards, made it more difficult for discordant voices to navigate the new maze. Diverse opinions were perceived no longer as merely a nuisance, as they were in previous generations, but as a threat.

LIKE ARRINGTON and Quinn, the Mormon feminists in Boston were attempting to carve out their own path. While walking with Eugene England across Harvard Yard, Claudia Bushman, who had short, brown, curly hair and an engrossing personality, convinced the *Dialogue* editor to allow them to edit a special issue on women's topics. The resulting volume, colloquially referred to as the "Pink" issue due to its cover, was arguably the first explicitly feminist publication in modern Mormonism. "The heritage of Mormon women is impressive in its complexity," Bushman argued in its introduction. The volume's editors argued for "the acceptance of the diversity that already exists in the life styles of Mormon women," especially a tolerance for those "not always completely satisfied with our lives as housewives." The impact was immediate. "Congratulations on your Ladies' issue of Dialogue!" wrote Juanita Brooks. However, they were critiqued both by conservative members for being too radical, and by liberals like England as too moderate—they were being "infantilized from all sides," Bushman mused.[16]

Bushman and her colleagues found a usable past from which they could draw. Nestled in the stacks of Harvard's library, Susan Kohler discovered a dusty set of the *Woman's Exponent*, the newspaper published by Emmeline Wells and other saints from 1872 to 1914. Bushman believed they had found their intellectual predecessors, "a feminist publication by definition, encouraging women to speak for and to women, speaking up against injustice and inequality of opportunity, and about the equality of the genders." This past provided clear relevance for the present. "These women were saying things in the 1870s," insisted Laurel Ulrich, "that we had only begun to think!" They eventually started their own magazine dedicated to "faithful but frank" conversations that embraced both Mormonism *and* feminism. The new periodical was titled *Exponent II*, a nod to their foremothers.[17]

Priorities determined by present Relief Society leaders soon overshadowed attempts to resurrect those from the past. After nearly three decades of leading the institution, a period in which the society's autonomy eroded, Belle Spafford was released in 1974. Her replacement was Barbara Smith, a soft-spoken woman whose kindly demeanor put people at ease. But if Smith expected her tenure to be relatively peaceful, those hopes were very quickly dashed. A harbinger of coming conflicts proved to be when one of her first official visits was from Phyllis Schlafly, the activist who did more than nearly any other American to politicize the family.

Prior to her discussion with Schlafly, and the culture war that

The founders of *Exponent II* in 1974, posing in Harvard Yard. These Boston feminists helped foment discussions concerning gender roles in the modern church as they sought a way to balance faith and equality.

followed, Smith inherited a carefully curated message. Wendell Ashton, an experienced advertising executive hired to lead the church's restructured Public Communications Department in 1972, consulted an outside research firm to study the church's current and potential image. The results were clear: most Americans were still ignorant of the faith, but one potential area for growth was its emphasis on the family. The department therefore commenced a publicity blitz titled "Homefront" that included television commercials, newspaper ads, and numerous exhibits that emphasized the church's family-centered faith and activities. Ashton was particularly successful in taking advantage of new FCC regulations that encouraged television stations to broadcast public service announcements, a category that included the "Homefront" commercials. One network observer estimated the church received $31 million worth of free airtime in just four years. Those savings then enabled the church to purchase *Reader's Digest* inserts that were read by millions of subscribers.[18]

Mormons soon became synonymous with *family*. This included their practice of "family home evening," in which parents and children gathered together every Monday night for quality time. The celebrity status of wholesome performers Donny and Marie Osmond reflected a degree of cultural acceptance. The media-darling siblings presented a traditional and fun image that was embraced by mainstream society and erased any theological distance between the two singers and the audience that embraced them. Mormonism had now completed its migration from "villains" in American popular culture to actors representative of American values.

Emblematic of the church's accepted status was the completion of a majestic temple just outside of Washington, DC, in 1974. Two years later, in July 1976, the Mormon Tabernacle Choir sang at the nation's bicentennial celebration, which Kimball enjoyed while seated right next to President Gerald Ford. When Ford's successor, Jimmy Carter, visited Utah in 1978, the church held a big event in the tabernacle with the theme "Love at Home." Carter was presented with a small statuette of two young parents playing with a child, and he delivered an address—likely written by Esther Peterson, an LDS woman who served as Carter's director of consumer affairs—praising the faith's

Spencer W. Kimball gifts President Jimmy Carter a statue of a family in the Salt Lake Tabernacle on November 27, 1978. The "family" became the church's primary message as it gained national acceptance.

family values. A national poll around this time found that 54 percent of Americans viewed Mormons in a favorable light, the highest marks such a question would ever receive.[19]

Part of this success was due to the bipartisan nature of family politics prior to the mid-1970s. Republicans like Dwight Eisenhower and Barry Goldwater held leadership positions with institutions like Planned Parenthood. The Equal Rights Amendment (ERA), which sought to end all sex-based discrimination, received support across the aisle, and seemed destined for ratification after Congress approved it in 1972. Thirty states quickly passed their support for the amendment within the next year, including conservative and Mormon-heavy states like Idaho, leaving only eight more needed. Early polling in Utah indicated there would not be any obstacles to passage there, either.[20]

The political tide quickly shifted. Phyllis Schlafly emerged as the leading anti-ERA voice in the 1970s and led a reactionary movement that suddenly reversed the amendment's momentum. She met Barbara Smith in late 1974, recognizing the LDS institution as a national force with untapped potential. Schlafly believed the saints could fit within the cross-denominational conservative coalition then being built. Smith initially demurred, insisting on the church's nonpolitical position, but Schlafly convinced her that preserving traditional gender roles was the era's most pressing moral issue. Smith's decision to back Schlafly and oppose the ERA, a move quickly supported by priesthood leaders, ultimately drafted the church into a long and bloody battle.[21]

Smith publicly announced her opposition to the ERA in December 1974, and the *Church News* cited her in its own anti-ERA editorial the next month. The First Presidency eventually released a statement that identified the ERA as "a moral issue" and urged citizens "to reject this measure on the basis of its threat to the moral climate of the future." Its passage would "strike at the family, humankind's basic institution." Shortly after the church's public statement, Utah's legislature voted overwhelmingly to reject the amendment, and Idaho soon rescinded its previous ratification.[22]

Mormon anti-ERA activism only grew from there. The federal National Commission of the Observance of International Women's Year (IWY) organized a series of state conventions in advance of a National Women's Conference set to take place in Houston in 1977. When Utah's commission initially struggled to raise enough interest in its state's event and asked the church for help, LDS leaders used priesthood channels to encourage attendance and, more importantly, defeat its more progressive resolutions like support for the ERA. An estimated 12,000 women showed up at Salt Lake City's Salt Palace, over four times the number expected and twice as many as in California, the next largest convention. The gathered women, anxious to defend their faith's traditional values and defeat encroaching liberalism, vociferously crushed every resolution on the docket. Buoyed by this success, the LDS anti-ERA efforts spread across the nation.[23]

Perhaps the most influential expression of this cultural retrenchment came in theatrical form. A play written by Mormons Douglass Stewart and Lex de Azevedo, titled *Saturday's Warrior*, premiered in Los Angeles in 1973 and soon became the most popular Mormon production in the decade. The story built on the success of other Christian theatrical performances, like *Jesus Christ Superstar* and *Godspell.* It depicted a family of eight children who promised, during their pre-mortal existence, to stay with one another after their births, only to be confronted with modern America's corruption once they were born. (The play's title was a reference to the late stage of earth's conflict.) Chief among the evils were those arguing for "zero population" measures like legalized abortion. Only when they rejected societal temptations and embraced the "traditional" family could all "spirit children" be born. Arrington, when he saw the production at BYU, called it "a delightful performance." It soon became a primary vehicle through which Latter-day Saints learned a modern adaptation of their plan of salvation, now tethered to the culture wars.[24]

Those who fell outside these newly established ideals faced immense obstacles. Carol Lynn Pearson, a fourth-generation Mormon who was a playwright, performer, and poet, wrote an essay for the church's magazine that highlighted the Relief Society's fight for women's rights in the 1870s. After it had passed the galley proof, church leaders discovered its content and were concerned that Pearson, publicly known for supporting the ERA, was a "controversial" figure. They pulled the essay at the last moment. Pearson learned about it only when she received a call from Arrington, who had heard the story from the magazine's editor. "It looks like [women] are destined to be just like a bush," she fumed, "just standing there but not allowed to express ourselves nor be regarded as human beings."[25]

Boston's feminists were aghast at these developments. Dixie Snow Huefner, a young mother with a degree in political science from Wellesley who had contributed to *Dialogue*'s "Pink" issue, moved back to Utah in time to attend the state's IWY conference. She was impressed at the church's "organizational mechanisms" in orchestrating resistance but also distraught at how unified it was at opposing reform. LDS women "did not need to be told explicitly how to vote" because "their attitudes about the conference had already been shaped." The avenue that she, Bushman, and others had worked so hard in constructing now faced a roadblock. "At the very moment Mormon women began to discover their lost history,"

Ulrich later admitted, they were "swept up" in the new world created by the anti-ERA push. "Suddenly in 1978 Mormonism and feminism seemed incompatible."[26]

THE INCREASED focus on traditional gender roles created other discontents. In his final General Conference address before his sudden death in 1973, Harold B. Lee denounced those who were delaying marriage and therefore "not doing our duty as holders of the priesthood." Present in the tabernacle was an unmarried man around forty who took Lee's words to heart. His friends elbowed him and gave knowing glances, and his bishop and stake president each called him in to chat about it a week later. Even his mother, who had long teased him about his single status, clipped out the talk from the *Deseret News* and provided a copy. The stress became so severe that he started losing his sight. When asked by his eye doctor if he was experiencing any "undue anxiety," he vocally admitted, for the first time, his secret: "The reason I'm still a bachelor is because males interest me more than females."[27]

The man soon wrote about his experience, albeit anonymously, for *Dialogue*. It may well have been the first LGBTQ perspective published in any Mormon venue. The author detailed his lifelong attempt to fit into a heteronormative culture, including his many failed attempts at dating, his faithful service as a missionary, and his consistent temple attendance. His anxiety had heightened when, as a university student, he heard Joseph Fielding Smith state that "homosexuality was so filthy and abhorrent that he would rather see his sons dead than homosexual." When he confessed his orientation to an apostle, he was told to participate in more "masculine activities" like basketball. Another leader advised him to marry a woman, but not to reveal his true sexuality or else it might "strain the relationship too severely." He finally saw a therapist who helped him work through his feelings. And though he retained a testimony of the church's truths, he could not help but conclude that "a single, much less homosexual, [individual] simply does not fit in." He titled his essay "Solus"—Latin for alone.[28]

Many religions across America confronted the question of sexuality during this era. Long forced to the margins of society, LGBTQ activists took advantage of the new space afforded by the culture wars to fight for equal rights, especially in the wake of the Stonewall riots in 1969. Troy Perry, a California pastor who had tried but failed to "cure" his homosexuality, organized the gay-friendly Metropolitan Community Church in Los Angeles. By 1971, the church had its own building and over a thousand dedicated members. These tepid steps met backlash, especially among evangelicals increasingly committed to conservative, partisan politics. Many churches warned about the growing homosexual threat. "Please remember," Jerry Falwell declared on his popular radio broadcast, "homosexuals do not reproduce! They recruit!" Though present for several generations, the question of sexuality became more pressing in the 1970s.[29]

Like their evangelical contemporaries, Mormon leaders' commitment to a conservative definition of the family meant casting alternative models as threats. The dangers of homosexuality were a particular concern for Spencer Kimball, who had been assigned two decades earlier to work with members who confessed to same-sex attraction. He instructed BYU to not admit any gay students—"I cannot imagine that this university would ever enroll a pervert knowingly," he declared to the student body in 1965—and helped formalize the church's disciplinary measures. "Homosexuality" was officially included in the list of excommunicable offenses in 1968. Kimball's most-read book, *The Miracle of Forgiveness*, published the next year, categorized homosexuality as a "crime against nature" and the "sin of the ages," just below murder as the most heinous of sins. Boyd Packer explicitly warned young men not to give in to any "temptations" that led to sexual experimentation with other men, and told the story of one missionary punching a companion who made an unwanted advance. "I am not recommending that course to you," he added, "but I am not omitting it." The threats seemed real.[30]

While LDS leaders remained consistent in their opposition to homosexuality during this era, they vacillated on the best way to deal with it. A First Presidency letter sent to local leaders in 1970 warned of an "apparent increase in homosexuality" within society and urged that the problem could be solved through "sympathetic treatment." At times they turned to methods that were more secular in nature, drawing from a growing body of literature that cast homosexuality not only as a spiritual ill that could be redeemed but also as a mental or physical problem that could be fixed. They provided pamphlets to bishops that used pastoral therapy to "cure" same-sex orientation and invoked psychotherapy methods just as the broader psychological field was distancing itself from such conversion practices. Some BYU professors even experimented with electric-shock aversion therapy. Consistent through these efforts was a commitment to reaffirming traditional gender roles—hence the author of "Solus" being counseled not only to marry a woman but also to play basketball. Leaders rejected the notion of *homosexual* as a noun altogether, instead using it only as an adjective: a person wasn't a "homosexual" but rather someone who "struggled with homosexual desires."[31]

Queer saints attempted to find a place in this constricting arena. Ina Mae Murri, the eighth of nine children born in 1935 to a Mormon family in Idaho, experienced her first lesbian relationship while in the Air Force Academy. She hoped to remain in the Mormon fold, however, and married a Mormon man in 1960. (Her husband, Jim, did not mind her previous dalliances; he, too, suppressed homosexual feelings.) But when their marriage fell apart a decade later, Murri joined other activists fighting for equal rights. Most heartening was her discovery of Affirmation: Gay Mormons United, an organization founded in Salt Lake City in 1977 by both current and former LDS members. Participants attempted to reconcile their Mormon faith and their sexual identity. "My belief [is] that since I am an eternal being," one member wrote for Affirmation's newsletter, "I have always been gay, and [I] will be gay after I die." Rather than being "a punishment from a loving God" to be "overcome," or even a "test" he had to pass in mortality, his queerness was intrinsic to his eternal identity.[32]

Among those who tried paving a workable path was Gerald Pearson, who married poet and author Carol Lynn after they met working in theater. Yet like many mixed-orientation relationships during the era, the union dissipated once Gerald determined he could no longer live a lie. He fled to San Francisco to join its gay community, but returned six years later after being diagnosed with AIDS. Carol Lynn accepted him back into the family and cared for him until his death.[33]

Michael Quinn related to the Pearsons' story. His own first "sexual stirring" came when his uncle baptized him as a child, forever linking spiritual and sexual identities. He later admitted to "struggl[ing] against my suicidal feelings and homosexual attractions" throughout his entire life. Quinn concluded that the only way he could survive was to "fulfill a Mormon boy's sense of duty," which included marrying a woman. His wife, Jan, was initially shocked when he revealed his orientation, but they both determined to make it work. The Quinns returned to Utah when Michael was hired to teach history at BYU after completing his PhD at Yale. For a time they succeeded in playing the part of the "perfect Mormon couple" by holding daily prayer, weekly family home evenings, morning scripture study, and regular temple attendance.[34]

The efforts were unsustainable. Michael and Jan's relationship soon deteriorated and they divorced in 1985. By then, Quinn's scholarship had also invited conflict. But regardless of the ensuing debates over historical truths and intellectual freedom, it was the church's teachings on marriage and gender that first shattered Quinn's sense of belonging.

DURING THE fall of 1972, Lester Bush found himself about as far from LDS headquarters as possible. Bush was born in Atlanta to Mormon parents in 1942 and trained as a doctor for the US military. He had already served a six-month navy deployment to the Indian Ocean as well as a two-year assignment at the American embassy in Cyprus. Now he was stationed in Saigon as the Vietnam War ended. At one point a nearby explosion blew out all his windows. Bush tried to find a sense of normalcy in his busy medical work while also serving in the presidency for the local LDS branch.[35]

Much of Bush's limited free time was spent writing, mostly in response to the groundbreaking work of someone else. Two years earlier, a graduate student at Cornell named Stephen Taggart wrote an article on the origins of Mormonism's racial restriction. Though he initially submitted the manuscript to *Dialogue*, his sudden and unexpected death resulted in his family publishing Taggart's project as a book instead. The work argued that the racial policy was not present at Mormonism's founding but instead originated after its sojourn in Missouri. The *Salt Lake Tribune* noted that the "weight of the evidence suggests that God did not place a curse upon the Negro—that his children did." Even the *New York Times* mused on the book's implications.[36]

Bush, for whom the topic had become an "obsession," was not convinced that the restriction's roots were in Missouri. Instead, his own research demonstrated that the policy came even later, likely after Joseph Smith's death. He dashed off a review of Taggart's book for *Dialogue* shortly after leaving on one of his assignments—he did not receive a physical copy of the publication until his ship docked in Bombay, India—and kept working on the topic until he had a four-hundred-page, single-spaced anthology filled with over a thousand items of documentary evidence.[37]

Encouraged by *Dialogue*'s editors, Bush transformed this work into an article. He labored on it during the winter of 1972–73, surrounded by Saigon's chaos, and submitted the full manuscript in March. He knew the radical impact his work could have, as the article "had undermined virtually the entire traditional case for the [restriction's] inspired origins." He decided to send the work to church authorities, including Boyd Packer, who in turn urged him not to publish the material until after the Quorum of the Twelve could discuss it. Packer indirectly encouraged Bush to pull the article, first on the phone and then in person when Bush traveled to America in summer 1973. But Packer, knowing how such an edict would appear, refused to command the publication's halt. (Church leaders did, however, apply enough pressure for at least two other LDS scholars to pull out of writing responses for the issue.) Bush told Arrington that the apostles insisted the "Negro doctrine" was "solved and settled," and Bush left Utah convinced that "there appears to be no possibility of a change."[38]

When "Mormonism's Negro Doctrine: An Historical Overview"

appeared a few months later, spanning fifty-seven pages and 219 footnotes, it made an immediate impact. Besides sparking scholarly discussion, the essay was read by many church leaders who reconsidered the historical origins of one of the faith's most distinctive practices. One general authority, Marion D. Hanks, later admitted that Bush's scholarship "started to foment the pot." The reaction from Bruce R. McConkie, whose popular book *Mormon Doctrine* tethered the restriction to Blacks' less-valiant service in the preexistence, was more visceral: "CRAP!" he declared as he allegedly slammed the *Dialogue* issue onto his desk.[39]

One individual who expressed a keen interest in the topic, however, was Spencer W. Kimball. Though he was otherwise traditional by inclination, his pastoral approach and his background working with racial minorities made him open to reconsidering the restriction. He told journalists at his first press conference as president that he had given the issue "a great deal of thought, a great deal of prayer," and that while any change would require a revelation, he quickly added, "but we believe in revelation." He kept a notebook full of correspondence and news clippings related to the policy and was known for asking many people about their opinions on it.[40]

External pressure on the church's racial restriction had simmered since the raucous 1960s. The formation of the Genesis Group in 1971 appeased many internal and external critics, and the church often deployed one of its founders, Darius Gray, to ease tensions. Though BYU officials worried about federal intervention, especially in the wake of Bob Jones University losing its tax-exempt status over its refusal to desegregate in 1975, they had done enough to at least temporarily satisfy civil rights standards. The university had even elected a Black man, Robert Stevenson, as student body president in 1977. Progressive saints continued to protest the policy, but with decreasing efficiency and attention. Most merely expected incremental changes. In his New Year's predictions for 1978, Arrington hoped "the Church will take a small step toward recognizing the dignity and worthiness of members of the Church of the black race."[41]

International concerns soon overtook domestic priorities. Though missionary work to Africa remained paused, the church witnessed an explosion of converts in South America, which drew much of the leadership's resources and attention. As with the Polynesian islands, with which Kimball's predecessors had dealt in previous decades, Brazil's growing LDS membership posed a pressing dilemma: generations of intermarriage resulted in the impossibility of tracing racial lineages. Missionaries were instructed to teach potential members a "lineage lesson" that walked them through the policy, culminating in the question, "If in the future you discover that one of your ancestors was Negro[,] will you tell your Branch President?"[42]

Kimball effectively announced the restriction's expiration date when he declared in 1975 that a temple would be built in São Paulo. Kimball's focus on building temples throughout the globe represented the church's new international reach. Though scarcely more than a dozen temples were in operation when Kimball took office, he oversaw the completion or announcement of thirty more during his tenure. "We will continue to build temples," he declared, "and there will be hundreds, possibly thousands, of temples built to the Lord our God." But given the makeup of Brazil's residents, the proposed São Paulo Temple brought the church's racial policy to the forefront. "All those people with Negro blood in them have been raising money to build that temple," observed one apostle, LeGrand Richards, and "if we don't change, then they can't even use it."[43]

After decades of resistance, movement came remarkably quick. Kimball assigned several authorities, including McConkie, to investigate the scriptural and historical basis of the restriction. They all failed to find firm justification for the policy. Meanwhile, James E. Faust, an apostle in charge of global missions, frequently brought Kimball stacks of letters from potential converts in Africa, and the question of Brazil continued to hover. Kimball spent much of the early months of 1978 in prayer, often alone in the temple, sometimes disturbed only by cleaning crews who assumed the building was vacant. By March, with the Brazil temple only months from completion, he concluded it was time to finally remove the racial restriction.

Kimball broached the topic with the Quorum of the Twelve on Thursday, June 1, at their weekly meeting. Those involved later referred to the two-hour gathering as a spiritual Pentecost. All present provided unanimous approval for Kimball's proposal. (Two of the apostles who had been outspoken in defending the restriction were absent: Mark Petersen was on assignment in South America, and Delbert Stapley was in the hospital.) They drafted a statement to announce the change.[44]

The news flooded the globe a week later. Leaders finalized an official declaration, dated June 8, that explained how "the expansion of the work of the Lord over the earth" had given them "a desire to extend to every worthy member of the Church all of the privileges and blessings which the gospel affords." All men could now be "ordained to the priesthood without regard for race and color," a policy shift that, while not expressly stated, also allowed women of all races access to temple rituals. Though they did not refer to it, leaders took advantage of historical scholarship that had undercut the notion that the racial restriction was always present, and now framed the saga as pointing toward a "long-promised day" of racial universalism. The announcement immediately made national and international news. Both *Time* and *Newsweek* halted their presses to squeeze in coverage, and the story made the front cover of the *New York Times*. Sterling McMurrin called it "the most important day of the church in this century."[45]

Members sustained the statement, soon canonized as Official Declaration 2 in LDS scriptures, at October's General Conference. Kimball dedicated the São Paulo Temple a month later. Leaders hoped that this was the end of the dispute and that they could merely move forward. "Forget everything that I have said," McConkie pronounced later that year. "We spoke with a limited understanding and without the light and knowledge that has now come into the world." The new revelation, he explained, "erases all the darkness, and all the views and all the thoughts of the past. They don't matter any more."[46]

Nobody was more surprised than Darius Gray. After helping found the Genesis Group, he worried that no change would come. He had scaled back his service and fallen into what he called "a walkabout" from the church. Then, on that fateful morning, while he worked in his downtown Salt Lake City office, an assistant walked in and said, "Hey Darius, I hear they're gonna give negroes the priesthood." Gray, who assumed it to be a mean joke, told her to "get the hell out of here." But he decided to investigate for himself and called Kimball's office. When a secretary confirmed the news, Gray broke down and wept. "I always knew," he told someone else when he was found looking out the window at the Salt Lake City Temple, the building he had frequently seen but could never enter. "God is good."[47]

SOME HISTORY was more difficult to erase. Shortly after the racial restriction was revoked, two "little old women" walked into the *Salt Lake Tribune*'s office with enough "old crumbly $50 bills" to purchase a full-page advertisement. (The money was "obviously out of somebody's sock," one observer quipped.) The five-thousand-word ad, titled "LDS Soon to Repudiate a Portion of Their Pearl of Great Price?" accused church leaders of forfeiting divine truths by rescinding a racial practice based on scripture. "Will Latter-day Saints remain true to their former revelations," the manifesto charged, "or will they yield to the pressures of this crucial day?" The authors were identified as "Concerned Latter-day Saints," chaired by one Joseph Jensen.[48]

National reporters soon identified "Joseph Jensen" as J. LaMoine Jenson, a leader in the Apostolic United Brethren (AUB). The AUB was a fundamentalist group headquartered in the southern part of Salt Lake County that claimed over two thousand members and was led by Rulon Allred, a chiropractor with over a dozen wives and nearly fifty children. Then, on May 10, 1977, two women disguised with sunglasses and wigs walked into Allred's office and shot him dead. The killing was one of several ordered that decade by Ervil LeBaron, leader of another rival, radical, and deadly fundamentalist sect.[49]

The string of murders resurrected national attention on Mormonism's polygamous past just as the LDS church was finally achieving cultural acceptance. LDS leaders were simultaneously terrified of the growing number of members joining the fundamentalist ranks. One apostle, Mark E. Petersen, led a committee to investigate the problem. But despite appeals from Leonard Arrington to directly confront the issue, they decided to deny legitimacy to the fundamentalists' claims of post-manifesto sealings and to downplay polygamy's historical significance. Their phobia at times verged on the comical: at one point, Arrington was assigned to write an essay on Brigham Young's family but instructed not to mention polygamy—a tall order when the man's family included fifty-six wives.[50]

Michael Quinn, however, decided it was time to investigate the full story. He wrote a letter to the First Presidency pleading for access to restricted sources, explaining that "one of the reasons why the so-called 'Fundamentalists' have made such inroads among our young people was because we had failed to teach them the truth." Lacking a full and honest history, "tens of thousands of Latter-day Saints will be increasingly vulnerable targets for polygamist cultists." But even Quinn was shocked by what he found in the records. He knew that if he compiled his notes into a research article, which he planned to submit to *Dialogue*, "there is no power on earth that will spare me from excommunication."[51]

EVEN AS LDS leaders were fleeing any mention of one form of culture war, they were soon eyeing another. Though always a significant force in American history, evangelicals catapulted back to national power during the 1970s. White evangelical leaders, especially those of a more fundamentalist bent, had for several decades segregated themselves from the allegedly corrupt spheres of politics and culture. But now they recognized that their potential to mobilize could shape both. Figures like Jerry Falwell and Pat Robertson urged that it was time to fill public spaces and shape the national discourse. *Newsweek* declared 1976 "the Year of the Evangelical," in part due to the election of President Jimmy Carter, a born-again Christian. But when Carter's politics proved unpopular with the religious base, most efforts moved to solidifying a religious right coalition, which soon dominated the national scene.

Simultaneous with this rise of White evangelicalism's political power was a resurgent skepticism toward Mormonism's place within the Christian community. Part of this animosity was rooted in a newly resurrected fear of "cults" that followed the mass murder-suicide at Jim Jones's People's Temple in 1978. A wave of books, pamphlets, and movies dredged up old stereotypes of conniving Mormon leaders and duped LDS followers. Mormons could not be trusted because they were theologically heretical and socially "weird." Most successful was the film *The God Makers*, which was shown across America in the early 1980s and climaxed with around a million monthly viewers in 1984. But also feeding evangelical fears was concern over LDS missionary success: "Mormons are winning over Baptist souls at a rate of 231 every single day," complained one Baptist pastor in 1985. The church had recently built temples in Dallas and Atlanta, monuments to their inroads into evangelical regions. Both theological squabbles and sectarian rivalry, therefore, threatened to overturn many of Mormonism's gains over the past century. A continued focus on the features that made Mormons distinctive promised to fuel the conflict.[52]

While finding a way to maintain a tenuous collaboration between Mormons and evangelicals seemed difficult, there were leaders on both sides anxious to pave a path forward. Falwell, for instance, hoped to count the Mormons in his new Moral Majority coalition, both to increase its reach but also to prove its inclusivity. Robertson, similarly, refused to show portions of *The God Makers* on his influential Christian Broadcasting Network. The Mormons were too numerous and powerful to merely cast aside. Along with Paul Weyrich, these evangelical leaders crafted a new political coalition that transcended denominational boundaries and ignored theological purity, instead focusing on carefully chosen moral issues and pragmatic cooperation.[53]

Mormonism had to be packaged correctly to take advantage of this outreach. This involved two priorities. First, the church had to prove its ability to deliver on key social issues, including those deemed crucial to the religious right's political agenda. Second, it had to quiet theological and historical disputes that threatened its correlated message and exaggerated its ideological distance from contemporary evangelicals. It had to appear, in other words, less "weird." Both initiatives involved choosing a side in the partisan battle then fracturing America.

Overseeing the effort to find a respectable balance that preserved the church's conservative path but avoided the perils of extremes was Gordon B. Hinckley. The mild-mannered, publicity-savvy administrator with penetrating blue eyes was known for his quick wit and pragmatic approach. Leonard Arrington noted that he was "pleasant, if not charming" and often exhibited "a twinkle and [a] smile." Hinckley had been an apostle since 1961 and was taking on increasingly significant ecclesiastical assignments as more senior leaders succumbed to deteriorating health. "Elder Hinckley clearly is a voice of the Church in policy affairs," Arrington concluded as early as 1973. He was soon tasked with managing both the church's opposition to the ERA and its handling of historians and intellectuals.[54]

THE SAGA of Sonia Johnson, perhaps more than that of any other individual, embodied the ensuing culture war. Johnson was an unlikely political martyr. Born in a small Idaho town in 1936, she had short curly hair and a warm smile. Johnson met her husband while they were students at Utah State University, and his job took them to Samoa, Minnesota, Nigeria, California, Malawi, Korea, and Malaysia before they finally settled in Virginia with their four children. Though she had a doctorate in education from Rutgers, Johnson was a latecomer to feminist scholarship. But once converted, she was fully committed. Johnson later narrated her own First Vision–like account of praying to God and hearing a clear answer: "Patriarchy is a sham."[55]

Johnson joined a group of Mormon feminists in Virginia who rallied around the "Mormons for ERA" banner. (Sometimes literally: they hired a plane to fly an actual banner with that slogan over Salt Lake City during General Conference.) She and her collaborators genuinely believed that supporting the amendment squared with their religious belief. But if Johnson was chosen as a public figure due to her benign background, her words and actions quickly vaulted her to the center of a heated debate. She told a US Senate hearing that though "early Mormon feminists demonstrated that the movement for equal rights could be compatible with Mormon doctrine," now LDS authorities were trying "to tamper with our agency." Her verbal sparring with the conservative Utah senator, and faithful Mormon, Orrin Hatch gained national attention. When the church escalated its activities in her home state—one estimate reported that while Mormons made up 0.5 percent of Virginia's population, they accounted for over 85 percent of the anti-ERA mail—she refused to back down. Mormonism was "the Last Unmitigated Western Patriarchy," she declared in a blistering address to the American Psychological Association in New York City.[56]

The ERA, and the gender issues it represented, became a wedge that divided most Americans. Even the pragmatist George Romney called ERA supporters "moral perverts." Helen Andelin also joined the fray. Though the author of *Fascinating Womanhood* had previously eschewed politics, she came to embrace the anti-ERA, anti-homosexual, and anti-abortion cause with gusto. Her failure to achieve a public ecclesiastical endorsement for her activities, culminating in a frosty meeting with Gordon Hinckley in 1977, however, left her disillusioned, and she eventually left public life altogether.[57]

Most Mormons, including most women, supported the church's stance. They believed that the faith's emphasis on the family, and practice of benevolent patriarchy, offered stability in a world of tumult. Arrington estimated that less than 10 percent of the church's American membership backed the ERA. However, he also noted that many of the feminists who worked with him disapproved of the leadership's position, albeit quietly. One woman researcher successfully compelled the church to change its policy of not employing women once they had children. Elsewhere, those who wrote for *Exponent II* and *Dialogue* attempted to pave a middle way that embraced women's rights without directly opposing LDS authorities.

Johnson, conversely, refused to acquiesce, even in the face of church discipline. Her ensuing membership trial in late 1979 became a public spectacle. The fact that the bishop worked for the CIA excited salivating journalists who depicted her as a brave heroine standing up to the male hierarchy. While Johnson was too radical for Arrington's taste, he admitted that "the Church cannot gain from this entire incident" and that "any bishop would be stupid to initiate a trial like this." A large group of "Supporters of Sonia" took out full-page advertisements in both the *Salt Lake Tribune* and *Deseret News* that urged LDS authorities to intervene on her behalf. Watching from New England, Laurel Ulrich bemoaned the larger implications. "I resented the excommunication because I resented what it taught me about the priesthood," she wrote. "The vision of that all-male council trying a woman's membership was more revealing than any of the rhetoric on either side."[58]

Johnson's formal excommunication made her an immediate martyr. In January 1980 she appeared on Phil Donahue's show, which

Sonia Johnson arrested after protesting outside the Latter-day Saint temple in Seattle, Washington, on November 17, 1980.

then also hosted Beverly Campbell, an LDS spokesperson. To counter the national attention, the church initiated a media blitz that emphasized its belief in family values and domestic harmony. Hinckley oversaw a last-minute anti-ERA pamphlet, which was inserted into the March issue of the church's magazine, that taught members how to explain their stance to their neighbors. When a reporter asked Hinckley why he was not willing to talk with Johnson, the media-savvy apostle responded, "We'd be delighted to meet with her." Yet their private conversation resulted in little, as Hinckley "was not in the mood to listen," and Johnson was "not in a mood to tearfully express repentance."[59]

The trial of Sonia Johnson was the church's Rubicon. It inaugurated nearly two decades of cultural clashes fought in the public sphere to preserve traditional authority. Several conservative leaders, like Boyd K. Packer and Ezra Taft Benson, capitalized on a power vacuum once Spencer W. Kimball's health declined due to three minor strokes and a subdural hematoma in 1979, followed by more crippling complications two years later. Because the other two members of the First Presidency were also in poor shape, Hinckley was called as an additional counselor in 1981, his entrance into the faith's highest echelon. But though he tried, he could not contain his colleagues who took part in the wider partisan debates that engulfed the nation.[60]

THREE EXPLOSIONS rocked Salt Lake City over two days in October 1985. The first two bombs killed one victim each, and the third severely burned Mark Hofmann, a documents dealer known for discovering manuscripts that challenged traditional Mormon narratives. Most controversial of Hofmann's findings was an early letter that alleged Joseph Smith was led to the gold plates by a white salamander, a story that squarely placed the scripture's origins within America's magic culture. Steven Christensen, one of the deceased victims, had purchased some of Hofmann's findings. Speculation arose that the murders were an attempt to silence these revisionist histories. But the investigation soon shifted to Hofmann himself, who eventually confessed to forging most of his documents and then building the bombs to cover his tracks. (The third explosion, in his car, was an accident.) Hofmann, who was sentenced to life in prison, remains the most successful forger in American history.[61]

The 1970s and 1980s witnessed heated debates over the nature of history across the nation. America's bicentennial prompted partisans on all sides to fight over the authority to interpret the past, especially considering the divided present. The fight reached Leonard Arrington's History Division well before Hofmann entered the scene. After his team published *Story of the Latter-day Saints*, a devotional yet rigorous social history of the church, apostles Boyd K. Packer and Ezra Taft Benson commissioned a report that denounced it for "not bringing God into the picture," highlighting "bad stories," and "basically [being] a secular history." Refusing to back down, a despondent Arrington met with the apostles, as well as the First Presidency, in a fateful meeting on September 21, 1976. Benson and Packer argued the "new history" caused "young people to lose faith" and "tended to degrade or demean Joseph Smith." Arrington responded that an honest history would build, not tarnish, belief. The heated debate lasted for nearly two hours. Spencer Kimball, who presided over the discussion, reassured Arrington that he still had the leadership's support, but the historian feared his end was approaching.[62]

Kimball's declining health allowed the more conservative apostles to further erode Arrington's autonomy. Leaders eventually transferred Arrington's division to Brigham Young University in 1980, a move orchestrated by Gordon Hinckley to, in part, distance scholarly projects from apostolic oversight. Arrington identified it as "a demotion, an expression of lack of confidence," and confessed that he was "angry, hurt, [and] heartsick" that credible history could not be produced from church headquarters.[63]

BYU proved to be no safer ground. In 1981, Packer again publicly railed against historians, including BYU professors, who judged the church according to academic standards rather than "the revealed word of the Lord." It was imperative for saints to demonstrate God's hand "in every hour and in every moment of the existence of the Church, from its beginning until now." Historical work could never be "neutral," because "there is a war going on, and we are engaged in it." These arguments closely mirrored those made by evangelical historians during the period, who dismissed secular scholarship in favor of spiritual hagiography, like Peter Marshall and David Manuel's best-selling *The Light and the Glory*. When it came to unflattering or controversial truths, Packer's counsel was clear: "Some things that are true are not very useful." He closed on an ominous note: "Those who have carefully purged their work of any religious faith in the name of academic freedom" should not "expect to be accommodated."[64]

Michael Quinn, now a tenured professor in BYU's history department, was so offended by Packer's remarks that he offered a public rebuttal. Historians could write a humanistic story, he argued, without denigrating "the actuality of divine revelations." Indeed, Mormon historians had a "professional obligation" to tell the truth, no matter how it meshed with cherished myths. He used post-manifesto polygamy as one example. Though Quinn provided his bishop an advance copy of his remarks and agreed not to publish them, the conflict garnered national attention, culminating in a *Newsweek* feature. Hinckley summoned Quinn to meet with him in Salt Lake City, and while Quinn persuasively demonstrated his case—Hinckley was "visibly stunned" when hearing the truth about post-manifesto polygamy—the moderate apostle expressed grave concern "that you have publicly criticized living members of the Quorum of the Twelve."[65]

Quinn and Arrington were far from the only scholars facing apostolic resistance. Just the previous year, Eugene England, who had finally secured a position at BYU after he agreed to distance himself from *Dialogue*, had delivered an address on campus in which he defended one of Joseph Smith's more audacious, and controversial, doctrines: that God continued to progress in knowledge and power, an idea that rejected classical Christian arguments of omnipotence and omnipresence. The speech prompted an acerbic rebuke from Bruce R. McConkie in a university-wide devotional in which the apostle identified it as one of seven "deadly heresies." When England continued the conversation through correspondence, McConkie's response was blunt: "It is my province to teach to the Church what the doctrine is," he trumpeted; "it is your province to echo what I say or to remain silent." Soon afterward, Benson and Packer hatched a plan to closely surveil all scholars associated with *Dialogue*, and over a dozen were summoned to meet with their local bishops. Hinckley, when he discovered the ploy, ceased the inquisition and reprimanded its proponents.[66]

Then, in 1985, Quinn finally published the article based on his decade-long post-manifesto-polygamy research. The essay filled ninety-seven pages, boasted 383 footnotes, and definitively dispelled the traditional LDS narrative that no polygamous unions were authorized after Woodruff's manifesto. The impact was immediate. Packer publicly denounced Quinn and privately labored with apostles to orchestrate his firing. They instructed his stake president, Hugh West, to revoke Quinn's temple recommend, the small paper that represented one's worthiness and was required for church employment. West, however, balked, instead opting to physically take Quinn's recommend but not change his official status. If BYU authorities asked Quinn if he had a recommend, Quinn was to respond in the affirmative, but not to "volunteer that it's in my desk-drawer." The work-around bought Quinn time. But he was finally forced to resign two years later after he published a book on early Mormonism and magic that was in part prompted by the Hofmann saga. Quinn's only solace was an unflinching confidence that he had done "everything I had thought God wanted me to do."[67]

Meanwhile, in part in response to Quinn's work, LDS authorities placed severe restrictions on archival research. Any historian who wished to publish something based on archival sources had to receive written permission by submitting "sufficient text before and after the quotation to show its context." Arrington was mortified. He consoled himself by envisioning a political cartoon: Packer and Dallin H. Oaks, a newly called apostle known for conservative views, are admiring a little dog. Packer gushes about the pooch's obedience— "He sits, he heels, he rolls over. He never gives you any trouble"—to which Oaks responds, "The perfect historian!" The bright optimism of Arrington's Camelot years was a distant memory.[68]

*   *   *

THE MOST daring forms of intellectual experimentation during the era came from Mormon women. Starting in the 1960s, and building off second-wave feminism, religious women throughout America pushed for more rights in their congregations and institutional hierarchies. The most divisive issue was ordination. By 1965, northern and southern Presbyterians, Southern Baptists, and a portion of the Methodists had approved of women ministers, a move followed by some Lutherans and the Episcopal church. Not all reform attempts were successful. In 1976, after hundreds of Catholic women agitated for ordination, the Vatican released a statement reaffirming the male-only priesthood, arguing that masculinity was integral to the priesthood practice. And in 1984, the Southern Baptist Convention rescinded its previous practice of allowing women ministers, instead embracing the traditional gender roles now politicized by the culture wars.[69]

As with Catholics and evangelicals, the culture wars convinced Mormon authorities of the dangers of even modest gender reforms. While the 1978 revelation that rescinded their racial restriction seemed to highlight the possibility that any ingrained tradition could be overturned, leaders did all they could to dismiss similarities. When the Quorum of the Twelve discovered that a Boston bishop had called a woman to the position of Sunday school president—something not explicitly forbidden in the ever-growing *Handbook of Instructions*—they forced him to reverse the decision, and then revised the handbook accordingly. An insider told Arrington that this was to "avoid the impression that we are about to turn over certain leadership positions to women." To Alice Smith, a longtime member of the Relief Society board, Arrington soon raised the possibility of writing a new history of the Relief Society; he was shocked that she urged him not to proceed. "This would be too damaging to the testimonies of LDS women who would read it," she reasoned, because "if it tells the truth, it will relate the deterioration of the power and position of women in the Church and will be very depressing to women who care." If anything, Smith explained, women were losing prestige, as Relief Society leaders no longer had direct access to the First Presidency.[70]

A new wave of Mormon women willing to go beyond their

predecessors challenged the foundational doctrine of a male-only priesthood in the 1980s. Nadine McCombs Hansen, for instance, published an article in 1981 that wondered why so many were willing to acknowledge that the racial restriction was a mistake but refused "to see a denial of priesthood to women as a similar injustice." Others turned to history to buttress their arguments. An essay by Linda King Newell, also published in 1981, uncovered the forgotten history of Mormon women giving blessings. In 1984, Margaret Toscano, an instructor at BYU, delivered a public address that drew from gender theory and ancient studies to deconstruct the notion of hierarchical and patriarchal authorities altogether.[71]

New venues enabled the promulgation of these feminist arguments. Starting in 1979, Mormon liberals gathered at an annual Sunstone Symposium in Salt Lake City, and soon started their own magazine. The next year, BYU organized its own women's conference, which was managed by the more moderate, yet still scholarly, women's studies program. Only a decade removed from Harold B. Lee's attempt to correlate messaging through a priesthood prism, there were now more avenues for ideological diversity than ever before.[72]

Whereas LDS women faced a barrier in their attempts for reform, their distant ecclesiastical cousins prompted a watershed. In early 1984, a group of RLDS women gathered in a Benedictine abbey located in northern Missouri. Attendees were part of the feminist advocacy organization named AWARE, which had agitated for equal rights since 1976. Activists employed at Graceland College, the RLDS equivalent of BYU, had already founded the liberal periodical *Courage: A Journal of History, Thought and Action*, the RLDS equivalent of *Dialogue*. The Reorganized tradition had continued its slow but steady assimilation with mainline Protestantism, and these reformers took advantage of the progressive impulse. Now, huddled in an abbey and led by Sharon Welch, an RLDS-raised theology scholar recently hired by Harvard Divinity School, these women violated institutional policies by blessing and passing their own communion.[73]

Rather than being denounced and punished, this activism prompted change. RLDS president Wallace B. Smith, the great-grandson of Joseph Smith, presented before the church's World

Conference shortly afterward a revelation that removed all gender restrictions for priesthood ordination. It was just the latest, but was perhaps the most substantial, institutional shift for a church that understood progressive accommodation as the fulfillment, rather than the betrayal, of Mormonism's foundations. The chasm between LDS and RLDS trajectories, each crafted in conjunction with and in response to broader cultural currents, only widened.[74]

LDS retrenchment around gender issues solidified when Ezra Taft Benson succeeded Spencer Kimball as president in 1985. Benson, though mellowed from his anti-communism heyday, intensified opposition to any attempts to redefine gender roles. "Contrary to conventional wisdom," he taught in 1987, "a mother's calling is in the home." Women scholars who presented alternative research were on shaky ground. Linda King Newell and Valeen Tippetts Avery, who authored a groundbreaking biography of Emma Smith that depicted her as a reform-minded activist, were forbidden from speaking in any church setting. Others, especially those who wrote in defense of worshipping a divine feminine or explored the concept of a Heavenly Mother, were threatened with excommunication. But the feminists refused to back down. When asked if she considered leaving the faith, Newell responded, "No, why would I leave? It's my church. I chose it."[75]

These debates over ordination laid the foundation for the LDS church's next all-consuming fight. In April 1984, Dallin H. Oaks, a conservative justice on the Utah Supreme Court, was called as a new apostle. Previously, as president of BYU, he had supervised an institute that worked on anti-homosexuality research and had authored a defense of anti-sodomy laws. Some speculated that he would be Ronald Reagan's next pick for the Supreme Court, before his being appointed to the LDS hierarchy instead. Then, only several months into his apostleship, he authored a memo that shaped much of the church's political activities for the next three decades.

Oaks urged his colleagues to look beyond the current disputes over gender and antidiscrimination laws and instead focus on one key target: same-sex marriage. "The interests at stake in the proposed legalization of so-called homosexual marriages," he reasoned, "are sufficient to justify a formal Church position and significant efforts in opposition." Oaks highlighted their moral obligation to defend a particular vision of the family that rested on procreation. "One generation of homosexual 'marriages' would depopulate a nation," he warned, and "our marriage laws should not abet national suicide." His memo asked the church to strategically prioritize this approach, even if it meant conceding on other measures, because it solidified their family-centered message and could rest on moral authority.[76]

Oaks's counsel proved prescient. Though only one mainstream denomination, the Unitarian Universalists, had accepted gay marriage by 1984, the legal-minded apostle knew the topic would soon consume the nation. Perhaps just as importantly, Oaks's arguments solidified the church's approach to the policy sphere, now safely framed by its commitment to "moral," rather than explicitly "political," issues. This distinction, at least in Oaks's eyes, validated policy involvement. It also helped to place the church in step with the broader religious right movement so long as the faith could avoid being cast as a heretical cult. If it was no longer seen as a threat, the Mormon political body could instead be classified as an asset.

FEW MOURNED the passing of Spencer W. Kimball as much as George P. Lee. Born to a Navajo family in Towaoc, Colorado, Lee was one of the first children placed in the church's Indian Student Placement Program (ISPP). He later received degrees from BYU, including a doctorate in education, and became president of the College of Ganado, located in Navajo Nation, Arizona. Lee and his wife, Katherine Hettick, a Comanche, presided over the Arizona Holbrook Mission in 1975 when he received a call from Kimball appointing him to the First Quorum of the Seventy. He was the first "child of the Book of Mormon people," as he put it, to become a general authority. Lee opened his first General Conference address with a joke concerning his minority status. Looking out at the tabernacle filled with White faces, he quipped, "Brothers and sisters, I finally realized how General Custer must have felt."[77]

Lee's call as a Seventy was the climax of the "Day of the Lamanite," a decades-long push by Kimball to "redeem" Native Americans. By the mid-1970s, the church claimed to have 500 missionaries serving in Native-focused missions, over 5,000 students placed in the ISPP, more than 15,000 Indian high school seminary students, and a total of 35,000 members spread across 152 Indian wards and branches. Many, like Lee, took advantage of the church's promise of an education at BYU, and the school enrolled over 500 Indigenous students in 1978, more than any other university in the nation. Native students at BYU published their own newspaper, *Eagle's Eye*, and participated in a performance group, the Lamanite Generation, that depicted a romanticized, and Mormonized, version of Indian cultures.[78]

A number of Indigenous Mormons merged these promises of a chosen heritage with arguments for autonomy championed by civil rights activists. The American Indian Movement (AIM), founded in 1968 to pressure governments and leaders, provided a blueprint for recognizing Native sovereignty and addressing systemic inequality. These debates bled into the religious sphere, especially in denominations that marginalized Indigenous members. AIM picketed Temple Square during General Conference in 1973, and soon Indigenous Mormons were echoing their appeals for more representation, a desire that was partly satisfied with Lee's appointment. One BYU student, Stanley Snake (Ponca), called for "a new awakening of Indians all over North and South America," starting with those inside the church.[79]

Other leaders did not share Kimball's commitment to the Lamanite mission, especially in the wake of the Red Power movement. Boyd K. Packer, in particular, was unimpressed with the limited results after the church dedicated substantial resources on Indigenous communities. When he spoke to Native students in 1979, he juxtaposed their expectations for conversion and retention to the reality, noting that the predicted explosion of Indigenous membership never came. "If it sounds like I'm scolding you a little," he noted, "it will be because I am." He then made an ominous comparison that reflected a bigger shift. While there were just over 1 million Native Americans in the United States, he reasoned, there were over 75 million people in Central and South America "who share in your birthright," and "have an equal claim on that destiny spoken of in the revelations." Why should so much attention be paid to North America's Indigenous community?[80]

The church's international growth made it impractical and illogical to retain such a traditional focus on literal lineages. As Packer's remarks implied, conversion trends in Central and South America forced leaders to reassess priorities, as did the rising Hispanic population in American cities. Throughout the 1970s, stakes across the nation created new Spanish-speaking wards and branches, especially in intercultural hubs like Los Angeles. This was even the case in Utah, where the Spanish-speaking population grew tenfold from 6,850 in 1960 to 60,045 by 1980. Many Hispanic converts found in Mormonism a sense of prophetic destiny, communal belonging, and social stability. Some quickly latched onto the "Lamanite" identity marker, though in a much broader sense than had been invoked when discussing Indigenous members. Further, by identifying "Lamanites" hemispherically, Latter-day Saint leaders could erase tribal distinctions or Indigenous concerns from the issue altogether, a crucial step in not having to engage Indigenous land claims, language, and sovereignty.[81]

This rhetorical shift also reflected a subtle, yet significant, theological transition. The previous emphasis on the Book of Mormon's mission to "redeem the Lamanites" was an awkward fit for an era that drew heavily from evangelical discourse. Mormonism's integration into American culture included echoing a Protestant lexicon centered on grace, repentance, and Christ's atonement. One of the hallmarks of Ezra Taft Benson's tenure as president was his frequent and emphatic emphasis on the Book of Mormon's significance, as when he urged members to "flood the earth" with copies. While this move might have jeopardized the desired alliance with the evangelical culture that always viewed the book as heresy, the church now packaged it in a way that made the text more palatable. It published the Book of Mormon together with the Bible, along with other Restoration scripture, in a single "standard works" volume to reaffirm its codependence with Christianity's foundational text. The church also announced a subtitle to the Book of Mormon meant to cement its Christian affiliation: "*Another* Testament of Jesus Christ."

At the dawn of their coalition with evangelical conservatives, LDS leaders neutralized arguments concerning their founding, and heretofore controversial, scripture. Later, in 1988, to further emphasize their standing in Christian circles, they encouraged journalists to avoid the *Mormon* nickname and refined their logo to make *Jesus Christ* larger than all the other words.[82]

George Lee was not happy with the church turning its attention away from the "Lamanites." He argued that leaders were forfeiting the faith's divine mission. After several years of increasing criticism, the First Presidency excommunicated Lee in September 1989 for apostasy and "conduct unbecoming a member." A few years later, Lee confessed to molesting a twelve-year-old girl, though it is unclear whether church leaders were aware of it at the time. Lee was eager to suggest that his excommunication was political, and he provided the press with letters he had written that condemned leadership for neglecting the Native population. "I speak unto you not just for myself," he wrote, "but for all of my people the Lamanites." To soothe any discontent prompted by the episode, the church dispatched authorities to several Navajo communities in Arizona and New Mexico to address concerns, with limited success.[83]

The shift in resources was substantial. By the end of the 1980s, the church closed or consolidated its Indian missions, abolished the Indian youth seminaries, and shuttered the ISPP. The number of Native students at BYU dropped by half. Though there still existed some hope for a "Lamanite redemption," Mormons mostly appropriated racial stereotypes from the wider culture. "As long as native Americans remain a voiceless minority," wrote P. Jane Hafen, a Taos Pueblo Mormon and literature scholar, they will be "a subordinate nation even as they are sentimentally draped in noble savage rhetoric and admired." Simultaneously, as in Catholic parishes across America, the number of Spanish-speaking congregants continued to grow and shape the church's future. A multicultural Mormonism that balanced exceptional scriptural mandates with contemporary Christian discourse produced any number of unexpected paradoxes.[84]

*   *   *

WHEN FIFTEEN hundred progressive Mormons attended Sunstone Symposium in August 1992, they did so in protest. The symposium had become a center point in the growing battle between leaders and activists, especially as apostles grew increasingly outspoken in denouncing what Dallin Oaks called "alternative voices." Church authorities decided to finally draw a line. They issued a "Statement on Symposia" after the 1991 conference that condemned gatherings in which speakers explicitly criticized the faith. Members were warned by local leaders not to present in future Sunstone events, and BYU professors were forbidden to even attend. But instead of dampening participation, the statement escalated the activists' resolve.[85]

This yearlong tension culminated in a presentation by Lavina Fielding Anderson. A literary scholar who had previously edited church magazines, Anderson had recently cofounded the Mormon Alliance, an organization dedicated to documenting ecclesiastical and spiritual abuse within the institution. Her presentation, which balanced a genuine devotion to the faith with unflinching commitment to accountability, meticulously detailed dozens of actions taken by local and general leaders intended to suppress free thought. The accusations closed with a bombshell: she alleged the existence of "an internal espionage system that creates and maintains secret files on members of the church."[86]

Eugene England, who defied his BYU superiors' orders by attending the Sunstone meeting, stood up and declared, with his finger violently stabbing the air, "I accuse that committee of undermining our Church." An AP reporter who witnessed the spectacle soon ran the story, prompting an immediate media uproar. The church soon confirmed the existence of the Strengthening Church Members Committee, which a spokesperson said provided local leaders with "information designed to help them counsel with members who, however well-meaning, may hinder the progress of the Church through public criticism." It was even chaired by two apostles, James E. Faust and Russell M. Nelson.[87]

The agitation continued to grow. That December, Maxine Hanks, a feminist theologian, published an explosive volume, *Women and Authority: Re-emerging Mormon Feminism*. It included chapters on controversial issues ranging from Heavenly Mother to women's ordination. "Feminism has always existed in Mormonism," Hanks declared, and the faith's future depended on restoring fundamental doctrines of gender equality. Among the volume's authors was Michael Quinn, who had just returned to Utah after spending the past five years in exile hoping to avoid excommunication. His chapter argued that Mormon women were ordained to the priesthood through Nauvoo rituals in 1843.[88]

A few months later, in early 1993, Lavina Anderson published her extensive article on ecclesiastical abuse in *Dialogue*. "We must speak up," she insisted, because "if we silence ourselves or allow others to silence us, we will deny the validity of our experience." Anderson promised that the Mormon Alliance would continue documenting and publicizing these abusive episodes. It was clear the activists were not standing down.[89]

After a decade of fighting the culture war over gender, church leaders, led by Packer, were no longer willing to exhibit patience. It

Cal Grondahl, cartoon, 1993. Progressive Mormons accused church leaders of stifling intellectual critique and faithful dissent. Latter-day Saint authorities, conversely, believed "Sunstone" Mormons were disloyal and dangerous to the church.

was time to root out the three "major invasion[s]" that had infiltrated the church, Packer declared in May 1993: "the gay-lesbian movement, the feminist movement[, and] the so-called scholars or intellectuals." He then met with local ecclesiastical leaders to orchestrate a purge.[90]

The coordinated expulsion took place that fall. A half dozen prominent intellectuals were either excommunicated or disfellowshipped, most due to their scholarship or feminist agitation, in what came to be known as the September Six. The first was Lynne Whitesides, the president of the Salt Lake Mormon Women's Forum, who was disfellowshipped on Tuesday, September 14, due to her writings on Heavenly Mother. Hanks was then excommunicated the following Sunday, and Anderson the Thursday after that. Arrington called the latter "one of the saddest days in my life," due to Anderson being "one of the most devout, believing Mormons" he had ever met. Local leaders started proceedings against Margaret Toscano, the feminist scholar who had written on women and the priesthood, but instead turned their attention to her husband and coauthor, Paul, who criticized church officials. He was excommunicated on the same day as Hanks.[91]

Then, on Sunday, September 26, a disciplinary council excommunicated Michael Quinn. The move concluded a long and painful trajectory that had begun with his employment in Arrington's Camelot two decades before. When Quinn dined at Arrington's home a few days later, his former boss recorded that the now ex-Mormon seemed resigned to a fate that had long been scripted. Arrington, already retired from BYU, worried that he could be next.

The summons never arrived for Arrington, but others were not as fortunate. Margaret Toscano's sister, Janice Allred, a theologian whom Arrington described as "more orthodox than half the men in [his] High Priests Group," was excommunicated a year later for her *Dialogue* essay "Toward a Mormon Theology of God the Mother." Also in 1994, BYU denied tenure to feminist scholar and pro-choice supporter Cecilia Konchar Farr, among several other liberal professors. Eugene England, who had dedicated his life to demonstrating the potential for dialogue, was forced to resign in 1997 from the only university he ever loved. Finally, Toscano herself was excommunicated in 2000.[92]

Near the beginning of this chaotic whirlwind, BYU's board of trustees, mostly consisting of apostles, quietly rescinded the university's invitation for Laurel Ulrich to speak at their women's conference. (The church had recently taken over the yearly event, transforming it from a secular symposium to a devotional one.) Ulrich, who had just received the Pulitzer Prize for her work on gender in early American history, was still known in Mormon circles for cofounding Boston's feminist movement. She had begun the era helping rediscover Mormon women's voices, only to see her own silenced by church leaders. Arrington expressed shock at the decision to "cut down intellectuals who are honest and splendid writers." Fortunately, he later added, "historians always have the last word." For her part, Ulrich refused to forfeit either the Mormon or the feminist label. She hoped "feminism may be larger than [others] imagined," and Mormonism "more flexible."[93]

LDS LEADERS shifted from fighting the battle over orthodoxy to planting their flag on national discussions surrounding the family. But first there was a change in leadership. Ezra Taft Benson was infirm for much of his later presidency, and he passed away in May 1994. He was followed by Howard Hunter, an Idaho-born lawyer who spent much of his pre-leadership life in California, but he, too, suffered severe age-related health problems and died in March 1995. (Hunter's nine-month tenure was the shortest in LDS history.) Finally, the global church's reins came to Gordon Hinckley, who had spent much of the past fourteen years as the only healthy member of the First Presidency and the moderate voice in the hierarchy. Though nearly eighty-five at the time he became president, his bustling energy and exuberant optimism made him appear much younger.

Hinckley's first major move came that September. At the women's session of General Conference, he read a statement signed by the entire First Presidency and Quorum of the Twelve titled "The Family: A Proclamation to the World." The text "solemnly proclaim[ed] that marriage between a man and a woman is ordained of God," and that "the family is central to the Creator's plan for the eternal destiny of His children." While fathers and mothers were to "help one another as equal partners," the proclamation reaffirmed traditional gender roles: "Fathers are to preside over their families" and "provide the necessities of life and protection," while mothers "are primarily responsible for the nurture of their children." They called on government leaders to promote laws and principles that "strengthen the family as the fundamental unit of society."[94]

Though LDS leaders had taught many of these ideas for decades, the proclamation crystallized them in a far more cohesive form than existing scripture. It was the fulfillment of a century-long trajectory that dated back to the initial renunciation of polygamy in 1890. Refined in the post–World War II period of social and domestic prosperity, it was now distilled in a quasi-canonical document that sacralized the nuclear family and extended traditional gender norms into the eternities.

There was an immediate context for the proclamation, too. Following the blueprint that Oaks had outlined a decade before, the First Presidency had recently taken an active interest in the bubbling issue of same-sex marriage. It issued a letter in February 1994 that urged members to "appeal to legislators, judges, and other government officials" to defend laws that preserved the "sanctity of marriage between man and a woman." It then attempted to intervene in Hawaii's legal case over same-sex marriage by adding the church's name to the denominations that would be harmed by any change in law, using the same family-centric arguments that had been previously outlined in Oaks's memo.[95]

Amid these new circumstances, Boyd Packer, then acting president of the Quorum of the Twelve, assigned Oaks, Russell M. Nelson, and James E. Faust in late 1994 to draft "a scripture-based proclamation to set forth the Church's doctrinal position on the family." Oaks later identified Nelson as the primary author, but rumors circulated that they had also consulted lawyers to craft a document that reflected contemporary legal disputes. They did not consult Relief Society leaders at all. This decision miffed Chieko Okazaki, a beloved and tenacious Asian American counselor in the Relief Society presidency who was the first person of color to hold any church-wide leadership position. When an apostle remarked, "Isn't it wonderful that [Hinckley] made the choice to present [the proclamation] at the Relief Society meeting?" Okazaki retorted, "That was fine, but as I read it I thought that we could have made a few changes in it."[96]

The proclamation was the result of battles over gender that were sparked in the 1970s with the rise of second-wave feminism and fights over the ERA, escalated in the 1980s with debates over women's ordination and feminist scholarship, and now cured through the legal disputes over same-sex marriage and association with the Moral Majority. The same era that witnessed the LDS church yielding on one of its foundational cultural touchstones, racial restriction, also saw it retrench on the other, patriarchal rule.

This orientation brought instant benefits. Evangelicals, Catholics, and other groups who made up the religious right were soon working with the Mormons in defense of traditional marriage. Just as Phyllis Schlafly had convinced the Relief Society to join the anti-ERA movement, Mormons were now linked with the conservative cavalry. The Christian Coalition presented its "Contract with the American Family" just months before the LDS proclamation, and the Southern Baptist Convention adopted its own article on "the Family" a few years later. Framing these political debates as "moral issues" carved out space for dominant religions to impact the political marketplace, exerting a force seemingly axiomatic for a secular republic.[97]

There was always a possibility that the increasingly powerful religious right might identify the Mormons as targets, rather than partners, in its crusade. There was plenty of evidence that the Mormons did not fit its religious worldview and that it would continue the longer historical trajectory of denominational resentment. Instead, Mormons and evangelicals exited the twentieth century more in line with each other than ever before. Part of this surprising alliance was due to LDS leaders' success in framing their history, doctrine, and even their scripture in ways that were not threatening to mainstream Christianity. But just as significant was American evangelicalism's shift to prioritize conservative culture over dogma, creating a political coalition that sought power at the expense of doctrinal purity.

Mormons were now deeply enmeshed in the Christian Right movement that sought to shape modern America in its own likeness and image. Yet this same alliance that ensured cultural assimilation also embedded within the faith the very societal fissures that fractured the rest of the nation.

9

Showtime, 1995–2012

We're fighting for a cause,
But we're really nice!
We are the army of the Church
Of Jesus Christ!
    . . . Of Latter-day Saints!
                —*THE BOOK OF MORMON* MUSICAL[1]

MORMONS ACROSS AMERICA eagerly anticipated April 7, 1996. Many were either watching or listening to a broadcast of General Conference, their biannual chance to hear the men—and some women—they sustained as church leaders. The real fascination, however, was to take place later that night: CBS's *60 Minutes*, watched by more than twenty million Americans every week, was dedicating an entire program to the faith. This included a one-on-one interview between host Mike Wallace and LDS president Gordon Hinckley. It was the first sit-down, substantial, and televised interview with a Mormon prophet in the church's existence. In his address to the faithful that afternoon, only hours before the CBS broadcast, Hinckley confessed that it was a risk. The show would undoubtedly feature "critics and detractors," and there was no expectation that the program would be "entirely positive."

But after a decade of media stories focused on internal crises, Hinckley had decided "it was better to lean into the stiff wind of opportunity than to simply hunker down and do nothing." If the program went awry, Hinckley pledged to "never get my foot in that kind of trap again." The saints had to wait and see.[2]

They need not have worried. While *60 Minutes* did feature some critical voices, much of the program focused on the church's positives. Prominent members like businessman Bill Marriott, Senator Orrin Hatch, and quarterback Steve Young spoke of their faith in glowing terms that succeeded in humanizing even their more exotic features. (Young quipped that when teammates ask where he got his "sacred underwear," he would reply, with a grin, "Oh, they're way too expensive.") Nobody shined more than Hinckley, however. The aged prophet had a way of defusing any critical question with his quick wit and gregarious smile. Lingering problems with racism? "Don't worry about those little flicks of history." Accusations that the church was a gerontocracy run by old men? "Isn't it wonderful to have a man of maturity at the head," someone "who isn't blown about by every wind of doctrine?" Hinckley's message could be summarized with a single soundbite: "We are not a weird people."[3]

Hinckley was the best person to right the church's course after several years of obstacles. His fervent optimism and considerable openness enabled the community to continue its long and uneven march toward cultural acceptance. The faith's future seemed to demand a steady hand, as Mormonism became much larger, more international, and quite politically powerful. A year after Hinckley took office in 1995, the church announced that it now had more members living outside America than inside. Of the church's 1.7 million baptisms during the first few years of the twenty-first century, three-quarters were adult converts. Mormonism was quite literally becoming a new community, even if it could not escape its inherent tensions.[4]

After a century of slow, uneasy, but consistent cultural assimilation, the Mormon tradition was on the verge of becoming a national obsession. CBS's feature presaged nearly two decades of constant media attention, an at-times-overbearing spotlight that illuminated both its triumphs and its lingering problems. As America became fascinated with its homegrown religion, the faith served as a flashpoint for broader questions that plagued modern denominations, questions regarding the integration of minority races, marginalized genders, and dissenting activists. These debates took place across media blitzes, presidential campaigns, Hollywood screens, and even Broadway theaters, touching nearly all portions of a community that was becoming as diverse and fragmented as it was global.

By 2012, the church cemented important political allies through its devotion to conservative values. But doing so meant disappointing those who wished the tradition would move in alternative directions. Indeed, to secure this new position of prestige and power, church leaders further solidified a cultural coalition that comfortably fit within America's political landscape.

Hinckley's nerves that April Sunday ably captured the anxiety of a community ready for a new era. Achieving maturity is difficult for any denomination, but to do so while also on a national stage seemed a near-impossible task. Yet in Hinckley's vision, having faith meant moving forward.

ONE OF Hinckley's first initiatives as president was to oversee a major shift in the church's public relations. He was the first LDS leader to allow questions in his inaugural press conference, a move that pleased but surprised journalists. The decision set a tone for his entire tenure. An internal study concluded that the church would do well to transition from mass marketing toward targeted relationships, and Hinckley worked to form friendships with leading cultural influencers. Just eight months into his presidency, he organized a lunch at New York City's Harvard Club with thirty opinion leaders and emphasized the church's openness. It was there that Hinckley befriended Wallace and organized the landmark interview. But *60 Minutes* was just the start: other in-depth dialogues soon followed, with the *New York Times*, *Wall Street Journal*, and two appearances on *Larry King Live*. Another feature with *Time* magazine pronounced that Hinckley was successfully steering the church toward the mainstream.[5]

Hinckley's Mormonism was one not afraid of the public spotlight. He emphasized the faith's optimistic outlook, community alliances, and inoffensive posture. "Bring with you all the good that you can," he pronounced to potential converts, "and then let us see if we can add to it." After a half century of leading the church's public affairs, and surviving several prominent controversies, Hinckley was anxious to put a new face on the faith tradition. The American media, despite being only a few years removed from digging into the church's many internal divisions, lapped up this new friendly, assimilationist vision. Even the sesquicentennial celebration of the saints' 1847 migration to Utah—a trek initiated to *escape* America—was recast in 1997 as a triumph of American pioneer spirit. Journalists and onlookers alike followed as up to ten thousand saints reenacted the harrowing voyage.[6]

The apex of Mormonism's new cultural acceptance came when Salt Lake City was chosen to host the 2002 Winter Olympics. Skeptics worried that the event would be short on alcohol and high on proselytizing. But Hinckley reassured a curious press that the faith would not enlist missionaries, and the city promised potential guests that there would be plenty of drinks. When planning got off to a rocky start with the leak of details concerning a bid scandal and financial shortfall, the organizing committee hired successful Latter-day Saint businessman Mitt Romney to correct their path. The son of the former Michigan governor and presidential candidate George Romney, and an inheritor of his father's firm jawline and full head of hair, Mitt gained national acclaim when he quickly turned around the event's financing. He capitalized on that success by winning the Massachusetts governorship in 2002, thereby setting himself up for a run at even higher offices.[7]

If Romney took advantage of the Olympic Games, he was only following his church's example. LDS leaders kept their promise not to proselytize and invested massive resources into playing the gregarious host. Their public affairs team prepared polished press kits for the media, including a ten-minute clip with Steve Young and former Miss America Sharlene Wells, titled "Myths and Reality," that challenged traditional stereotypes: Mormons were not polygamists, but devoted to conservative family values; the church did not only help their own but operated global humanitarian initiatives; and rather than exotic and distinct, their beliefs were deeply Christian.[8]

The praise was near universal. "After years of fear that these would be the Mormon Games," the *Chicago Tribune* summarized, "the church's contribution turned into a plus." A series of surveys conducted after 2002 showed American opinion of the church slowly climbing and demonstrated a growing awareness of the institution's family- and Christ-centric teachings. Hinckley could not help but celebrate. Visitors that "came with suspicion and hesitancy," he boasted, instead "found something they never expected": a transnational, uncontroversial, welcoming faith.[9]

Coupled with the church's extensive worldwide humanitarian efforts and continued global growth—membership grew from 9 million when Hinckley took office to nearly 13 million just a decade later—it was difficult not to share the new prophet's optimism. Particularly influential was his decision in 1997 to build smaller temples that served saints in more "remote" locations. While there were just under 50 temples in operation that year, the number would more than double to 124 by 2006. Among the new structures was the Nauvoo Temple, which was rebuilt in 2002 to appear just like the original from the 1840s. This rapid increase in Mormonism's most sacred

Gordon B. Hinckley, who ascended to the LDS presidency in 1995, meets with President George W. Bush on August 31, 2006. Hinckley's tenure as president was notable for his kind relations with the press and conservative politicians.

structures, most of which were outside of the United States, demonstrated the faith's increasingly international reach.[10]

President George W. Bush awarded Hinckley the Presidential Medal of Freedom on the prophet's ninety-fourth birthday in 2004. "He has inspired millions," Bush pronounced, "and has led efforts to improve humanitarian aid, disaster relief, and education funding across the globe." The honor reflected Hinckley's glowing reputation as well as his church's continued assimilationist march. (Also receiving a Medal of Freedom from Bush that year was Pope John Paul II.) It was apparent that the LDS church's positive media approach was working, at least for the time being.[11]

As HINCKLEY looked unflinchingly to the future, others struggled with lingering legacies of the past. David and Betty Jackson were Black Baptists who joined the church in California during the early 1990s but grew frustrated with racist ideas still circulating in their congregation and in print. When they pressed their home teacher, Dennis Gladwell, about how the now-discarded racial restriction had lasted until 1978, Gladwell cited Bruce McConkie's still-influential encyclopedic work, *Mormon Doctrine*. The Jacksons were unpersuaded. Finally, after a long and tearful discussion, Gladwell realized the harm these racist teachings inflicted long after the policy had been erased. He helped the Jacksons pen a twelve-page letter to Hinckley pleading with him to publicly repudiate these beliefs and remove *Mormon Doctrine* from print. They even drafted a new Official Declaration that pronounced these anti-Black doctrines "false."[12]

Hinckley was reluctant to respond. He had hoped that the 1978 revelation would have definitively closed the race question. Directly addressing prophetic statements that had justified the ban in the past meant highlighting the possibility of prophetic fallibility in the present. It was simpler to just turn the page. But refusing to engage with the racial ideas that created and perpetuated the restriction in the first place allowed those same biases to continue. Upon receiving the Jacksons' letter, Hinckley wrote a letter to their bishop that reaffirmed the church's present position.

The Jacksons refused to respond to a letter that was not directly addressed to them. Working with Armand Mauss, a sociologist who had published extensively on Mormonism and race, they composed a thirty-four-page survey of LDS teachings on Blacks that they sent to Marlin K. Jensen, a church authority in Salt Lake City known for his sympathetic demeanor and pragmatic approach. Jensen, in turn, recognized the issue's severity and organized an ad hoc committee composed of the Jacksons, Gladwell, Mauss, and a public affairs official tasked with summarizing the problems for the First Presidency. They hoped Hinckley might issue a public repudiation of racist "folklore" in June 1998, just in time for the twentieth anniversary of Spencer Kimball's revelation.[13]

The hope soon faded. Rumors of the committee's work leaked to the press, and the *Los Angeles Times* published a major story revealing that church leaders were "debating a proposal to repudiate historic church doctrines that were used to bolster claims of black inferiority." Angered, and anxious to not appear conducive to external pressure, church authorities dismissed the report as "totally erroneous." Hinckley maintained his position that "the 1978 official declaration continues to speak for itself." When he returned from a trip to Nigeria later that year, he reemphasized that there was no need for further action, as "the reception he received in Africa convinced him that the church is on the right track." Directly addressing the faith's past racism would have to wait.[14]

Hinckley felt justified in this decision due to the church's fast growth both in Africa and in African American communities. He had recently announced plans to build a temple in Accra, Ghana, and the church had worked with the African Methodist Episcopal church in Los Angeles to run a series of successful and well-publicized food drives. Darius Gray, the former Genesis leader, helped spearhead a collaboration that resulted in the digitized Freedman's Bank Records, an essential source for genealogists and historians interested in African American history. Hinckley was honored with a distinguished service award from the NAACP in April 1998. "The black family in this nation has been a tremendous institution," he declared at the organization's national meeting, connecting the church's familial focus with its racial outreach. Hinckley's ninetieth-birthday gala was later headlined by Gladys Knight, the famed "empress of soul" who was the faith's most prominent recent convert.[15]

It was often left to Mormonism's members of color, many of them first-generation congregants, to carve out their own space. One 1998 survey found that of the nearly forty thousand saints in New York City, about 20 percent were Black, and another quarter were Hispanic. The *New York Times* reported that the church's Harlem congregation featured "one of the most racially integrated [gatherings]" in the region. One recent convert said that he was initially skeptical when approached by missionaries because he feared "it was going to be a one-sided race thing," but soon felt that he "belong[ed] here," something he had not sensed at primarily Black denominations. This interracial worship was especially the case in the American Southwest, where a flood of Hispanic members transformed the lived reality of local worship. Like many Catholic and evangelical churches across America, Mormonism's missionary success was increasingly tethered to its ability to court marginalized communities. "I love walking into a Hispanic meetinghouse," wrote Nelda McAllister, a self-identified "LDS Latina." "I love to hear their voices loud and strong and never ashamed."[16]

The transition was far from seamless for everyone. Though as much as 40 percent of the global LDS membership could be characterized as Hispanic, Latino/a, or Latinx at the start of the twenty-first century, these groups remain vastly underrepresented in leadership positions, especially at the highest levels. Many continued to face racialized stereotypes and theological barriers. Some members proved willing to speak out. Darron Smith, a Black convert and sociologist who taught for a time at BYU, urged the church to root out racialized biases inherent in many church settings. Others were anxious to take action. When Arizona passed new legislation in 2007 that required immigrants to carry official documentation at all times—a bill authored by Latter-day Saint Russell Pearce—more than one hundred LDS Latinos signed a petition to Mexican authorities requesting that they deny visas to Mormon missionaries until the church took formal action opposing the new law.[17]

Church leaders took note of rising racism within the ranks even before the events in Arizona. Speaking in General Conference in 2006, Hinckley confessed alarm that "racial slurs and denigrating remarks are sometimes heard among us." Racism, he insisted, had no place "among the priesthood of this Church." Leaders and members alike wrestled with the legacies that remained from the since-extinguished policy, including the ideas and biases that both instigated and perpetuated it. Finally, in 2010, the church ceased the printing of McConkie's *Mormon Doctrine*. Leaders claimed it was due to low sales, an assertion disputed by booksellers. The decision was an important milestone, but plenty of lingering questions remained. A continued unwillingness to directly address past prophetic fallibility, in part to buttress current ecclesiastical authority, left some Black converts like the Jacksons feeling as if they did not fully belong. Meanwhile, other members of color found their way in what was still a White-majority faith.[18]

AMID THE Olympics media blitz, NBC's *Saturday Night Live* opened its show with a skit that captured America's fascination with Mormonism. Comedian Amy Poehler portrayed an Olympic skier hurtling down the slopes only to be surrounded by two LDS missionaries, both named Young, played by Dan Aykroyd and Will Ferrell. After several failed attempts to convert her to the faith—"What do you think, you in?" Ferrell asks—they raise a topic that the public imagination never fully forgot. "I know what you're thinking," Ferrell reassures; "polygamy is over. . . . We simply don't do it." Ackroyd, smiling, interjects: "I do it." Ferrell begrudgingly nods and concedes, "A few of us still do it. But mainly no."[19]

Polygamy was never far from the surface in discussions concerning the Mormons. An internal poll a few years earlier discovered that plural marriage remained the second-most-common thing associated with the church, behind only Salt Lake City. International fascination surged around the case of fourteen-year-old Elizabeth Smart. Abducted from her Salt Lake City home in June 2002, she was saved ten months later from an excommunicated man named Brian David Mitchell who had made her his plural wife. Then, mere months after

Smart's reappearance, Jon Krakauer's *Under the Banner of Heaven: A Story of Violent Faith* became an immediate bestseller. The book focused on the 1984 murder of Brenda Lafferty and her daughter, Erica, by two polygamist brothers-in-law, in order to explore the violent aspects of fundamentalism, Mormonism, and religion writ large. LDS authorities, aghast at the renewed attention, released no fewer than three tedious statements denouncing the work. (Two decades later, *Under the Banner of Heaven* remains America's best-selling book on Mormonism; it was eventually adapted into a television series.) Both the Smart tragedy and the Krakauer story fed into popular narratives of an ever-present and always-dangerous vestige of polygamy.[20]

Journalists did not have to look far to find more recent and relevant ties to polygamy's legacies. The fundamentalist community had further splintered in recent decades, and the more conservative faction was most recently led by Rulon Jeffs, a devoted purist born in 1909 and married to as many as seventy-five women. (His first wife, Zola Brown, the daughter of LDS leader Hugh B. Brown, divorced him when he embraced the principle in the 1940s.) Jeffs led the Fundamentalist Church of Jesus Christ of Latter-Day Saints (FLDS) into a retrenchment of their own. Women and men were now expected to don pioneer clothing, and Jeffs banned them from wearing anything red, a color reserved for Jesus. Members were even forbidden to speak the word *fun*. While a third of the flock had been previously scattered across the Utah region, Jeffs ordered that all ten thousand members gather back to Short Creek and withdraw from public schools. He prophesied that Utah's 2002 Olympics marked the end of the world.[21]

While the world survived 2002, Jeffs did not. He passed away that September, leaving behind his many wives and over sixty children. One of his offspring, Warren, a gaunt and spindly man, maneuvered his way to become the next FLDS leader despite never serving on the governing priesthood counsel. Warren Jeffs then presided in a way that fulfilled external stereotypes of a polygamous autocrat, proclaiming a slew of revelations that exposed his competitors and rearranged existing families. He took on many women himself, including several child brides. His ambitions and actions, including child sexual abuse, placed him on the FBI's Most Wanted List. He was forced into hiding within the first year of his prophetic tenure. Jeffs was finally captured outside Las Vegas in 2006 in a bright red Cadillac Escalade with one of his wives, a portrait of his father, twenty-seven bound stacks of $2,500 cash, two wigs, fourteen cell phones, and two navigation units. A jury convicted him of assaulting minors and sentenced him to multiple prison terms.[22]

The revitalized federal hunt for polygamists did not end there. Prompted by an alleged call from a sixteen-year-old girl, federal authorities raided the FLDS Yearning for Zion Ranch near Eldorado, Texas. The rural compound was built as a refuge for the faith while Jeffs was on the run. A total of four hundred children were taken from their mothers and placed with foster families, the largest single act of its kind in American history. As with the Short Creek raid over fifty years earlier, many Americans denounced the gov-

Women residing in the FLDS compound in Eldorado, Texas, meet with an attorney to discuss how to regain custody of their children. Media coverage of the raid on the Yearning for Zion Ranch mostly skewered the government's overreach, a repeat of what had happened in Short Creek a half century before. PHOTOGRAPH BY BY TRENT NELSON

ernment's intervention into domestic choices. The 1993 Waco siege, where authorities had botched a raid on the Branch Davidians, had soured many citizens on the idea of forcibly punishing unpopular religions. While documents found in the raid were the basis for charging many men, including Jeffs, with marrying minors, a Texas Court of Appeals determined that the state had not met the threshold of proof for separating families, and most children were returned to their mothers.[23]

Another reason Americans were more sympathetic to previously marginalized polygamists was their increased presence on television. HBO launched a dramatic series in 2003 titled *Big Love* that traced the lives of Bill Henrickson and his wives Barbara, Nicolette, and Margene, modern polygamists who lived in Salt Lake City. LDS officials, terrified of the association, released a statement days before its premiere that expressed displeasure in the network glorifying the "deceptive life of a fringe world of polygamy." They claimed the show would minimize the problems inherent in these communities and cause "confusion over the continued practice of polygamy." "Polygamous communities," the statement argued, "should never be referred to as 'Mormon' polygamists or 'Mormon' fundamentalists." In part as a result of these protests, HBO added a disclaimer at the start of the show clarifying that its central characters were not part of the LDS church.[24]

Despite the church's opposition—or perhaps because of it—*Big Love* became a popular and critical success. It also spawned a new era of public enthrallment with modern polygamists who did not fit the Warren Jeffs mold. TLC developed a reality series titled *Sister Wives* based on Kody Brown and his three wives Meri, Janelle, and Christine, as well as their courtship of a fourth, Robyn. These media portrayals of the fictional Henricksons and nonfictional Browns challenged traditional stereotypes by depicting modern families with fashionable clothes, materialistic ambitions, and contemporary sensibilities. They also reflected the growing number of polygamists outside the FLDS community, like the Apostolic United Brethren. (One scholar estimated that an average of six LDS families converted to the AUB every month during the 1990s.) The Brown family, who belonged to

Kody Brown and his family, who became famous through the television series *Sister Wives*, protest to decriminalize polygamy in 2017.
PHOTOGRAPH BY SCOTT SOMMERDORF

the AUB, eventually sued Utah and claimed their marriages were protected under religious-liberty laws, the first move toward successfully decriminalizing plural marriage in the state, which happened in 2020.[25]

While modern polygamists celebrated this rise in positive awareness, LDS leaders winced at the constant reminders of their uncomfortable past. "There are no Mormon fundamentalists," Gordon Hinckley told CNN's Larry King in an effort to differentiate the denominations. Many complained when a 2007 PBS documentary devoted to the church, *The Mormons*, dedicated thirty minutes of its four-hour running time to the past and present of plural marriage. To modern Latter-day Saints, polygamy was an unfortunate artifact that could not be disposed of quickly enough.[26]

Another Mormon community was similarly willing to break tradition. The RLDS church's decision to acknowledge that Joseph Smith practiced polygamy, as well as its revelation to ordain women in 1984, initiated a transitional era. Many of its purist members, disillusioned with this new direction, defected and formed their own denomination, the Remnant Church of Jesus Christ of Latter Day Saints. Meanwhile, RLDS leadership, emboldened by missionary success across the globe, felt increasingly called to embrace a more mainstream, progressive mission. Wallace B. Smith, the president who oversaw most of these changes during the 1980s and 1990s, decided to disrupt the faith's iconic lineal-succession model and instead appointed W. Grant McMurray as his successor.

McMurray, who took over in 1996, was the first RLDS president to not be a descendant of Joseph Smith. He continued the faith's trajectory. McMurray openly downplayed whether believing members had to accept the Book of Mormon's historicity, questioned the traditional narrative that priesthood authority had been unavailable until 1829, and moved the church from a closed community to open communion, decisions that reflected general practices of liberal creeds. Then, in 2000, the church adopted McMurray's proposal to formally change its name to the Community of Christ. The new title echoed the 1830 "Church of Christ" name, and exemplified what McMurray termed a commitment to "zionic communities." Though McMurray resigned four years later, his successor, Stephen M. Veazey, as well as the church's racially and gender-diverse governing body, have further cemented its status as a denomination deeply enmeshed in mainline Protestant Christianity, albeit with remnants of its unique heritage. Many members even refuse the nickname "Mormon."[27]

LDS leaders have often found themselves between these two poles: anxious to distance themselves from the extreme fundamentalism of polygamists, but also reluctant to follow the religious liberalism of the Community of Christ. (Unlike with fundamentalist sects, though, the LDS church has recently developed a warm relationship with the Community of Christ.) This broader restorationist diaspora, present since the faith's founding, reflects divergent trajectories that, in turn, both build upon and separate from their shared past.[28]

BY 2003, Peggy Fletcher Stack had seen nearly everything. The great-granddaughter of a prophet, Heber Grant, and granddaughter of a senator, Wallace Bennett, Stack studied at Graduate Theological

Union in Berkeley before becoming a founder of *Sunstone*, the popular countercultural magazine, which she edited from 1978 to 1986. She was then hired by the *Salt Lake Tribune* in 1991 and became the premier reporter of Utah's dominant religion. Her coverage ranged from the institution's clashes with intellectuals in the 1990s to the church's involvement with the Olympic Games in 2002. But she noticed one previously central facet of the Mormon scene was becoming less visible, and in October 2003 published a long column titled "Where Have All the Mormon Feminists Gone?"

It was a fair question. The previous decade's divisive conflicts resulted in many women either seeking refuge outside the faith or censoring themselves within it. The activist organization Mormon Alliance no longer drew large crowds, and the heralded feminist magazine *Exponent II* was currently avoiding topics like women's ordination and Heavenly Mother. Claudia Bushman, who had helped found the influential Boston movement in the 1970s, worried that Mormon feminism "is dead or dying with our generation," as even the word has "been expunged from our vocabulary." Though all was not lost. Stack interviewed several women who were hopeful that a new generation could better navigate patriarchal spaces through less confrontational means, even if the "f word" was off-limits.[29]

There were still individuals trying to create more opportunities for faithful women. At the forefront was the same Relief Society presidency that Gordon Hinckley surprised with the family proclamation in October 1995. Before being instructed to focus the women's General Conference session on the traditional family to support the new quasi-canonical document, the society's leadership had planned to center their remarks on the diversity of Mormon women, a diversity reflected within the presidency itself. Elaine Jack, the first Relief Society president born outside America, had a successful business career; for counselors, she chose Chieko Okazaki, a Japanese Hawaiian who converted from Buddhism and held two graduate degrees, and Aileen Clark, who had chaired the Utah Task Force on Gender and Justice. Hinckley's intervention changed their plans, but they continued to find ways to better reflect the lived realities of LDS women throughout the globe.[30]

The 1995 proclamation on the family contained mixed language on the doctrine of gender. It firmly denounced same-sex unions, and said that men must "preside" in the home. But it also emphasized equal partnership and shared governance, which in turn reflected a broader anxiety among American evangelicals, who couched patriarchy in the language of service. Even the Southern Baptist Convention's contemporaneous resolution on "the Family" called for "servant leadership" and stated that women stood "equal to [husbands]" in authority. In part as a concession to women leaders and reformers, LDS officials now presented a discourse that framed the family in companionship terms, relegating strict "presiding" duties to religious functions. (Even the terms *patriarch* and *patriarchy* abated, except in temple ordinances.) "There is not a president and Vice President in a family," declared apostle L. Tom Perry, as "we have co-presidents working together." Authorities retreated from their previous stance that urged large, "traditional" families, first removing a restriction on birth control and then stating that couples possessed the right to choose their number of children.[31]

Some women took advantage of this opportunity by presenting an innovative, if still conservative, theological defense of complementarianism, or shared familial governance. Valerie Hudson, an academic and specialist on gender and international justice, delivered an influential address titled "The Two Trees." She argued that the Garden of Eden provided an empowering narrative of separate but collaborative gender roles, and that "relationships of gender equality are the bricks of Zion." Eve, though relegated to hearkening to her husband, was just as central to the eternal plan of salvation as Adam. "Priesthood is a man's apprenticeship to become a Heavenly Father," she argued, "and I believe that women have their own apprenticeship to become like their heavenly mother."[32]

While many feminists agreed on the language of empowerment, some still critiqued the corollary between motherhood and priesthood. (Not all women had children, they responded, and men were both priesthood holders *and* fathers.) Further, others critiqued the increasingly strained rhetoric that used the language of equality to defend patriarchal institutions. "Chicken patriarchy," as one critic framed the rhetoric, "never allows itself to be pinned down to a single perspective," as it is "too chicken to stand up for what it believes" but also unwilling to mean what it says.[33]

One arena in which women were able to stake out more ground was the mission field. Starting in the 1990s, young women made up a larger, though still minority, percentage of those sent out across the globe. And when Gordon Hinckley oversaw a new missionary program in 2004 that emphasized conversations and building relationships, titled "Preach My Gospel," sister missionaries embraced a process that better meshed with their own experience. A later decision to lower the age for missionary service for women from twenty-one to nineteen, and for men from nineteen to eighteen, resulted in a flood of women in the field. Previously assumed to be a fallback option for women who did not marry within a few years of high school, missionary work was now nearly as common for women as it was for men. Before the age change, only one in six missionaries was a woman; afterward, it was closer to one in three, and 45 percent of active Mormon women who identify as millennial served a mission.[34]

The digital age provided more opportunities for expression. Many women turned to blogging as a creative outlet to demonstrate their domestic values, deeply held faith, and attachment to consumerism. One Salon writer became engrossed in the plethora of "Hipster Mommy Blogger[s]" who had "bangs like Zooey Deschanel and closets full of vintage dresses." Their children looked like "Baby Gap models," and their husbands like "young graphic designers, all cute lumberjack shirts and square-framed glasses." Beyond modeling chic domesticity, however, they were also fulfilling the church's injunction to smartly share the gospel in unobtrusive ways. Many interwove their commitment to modern fashion with their commitment to Mormon beliefs, interspersing tales of parenting comedy with lessons of genuine faith.[35]

Not all blogging voices were as faith-promoting. After reading Stack's coverage of the disappearance of Mormon feminists, Lisa Butterworth, a stay-at-home mother of three in Boise, Idaho, who felt increasingly marginalized due to her liberal politics, decided it was time for a new call to action. "I wanted to find something that could be faithful, liberal, and feminist," she told the *New York Times*; when she could not discover any, she created one herself. Butterworth and her cadre of writers titled the blog *Feminist Mormon Housewives*, a label that reflected their multiple identities. Their devotion to dealing with serious issues, but with an irreverent smirk, was reflected in the blog's first tagline: "Angry Activists with Diapers to Change." The blog launched in 2005 and soon exploded in popularity, a testament to the ever-present questions of gender equality that never fully disappeared.[36]

FEMINISM WAS not the only controversial issue resurrected in 2005. That spring, hundreds of academics and interested observers gathered at the Library of Congress in honor of the bicentennial of Joseph Smith's birth. The event was cosponsored by the library as well as Brigham Young University, and featured several of the leading academics who studied Smith, his scriptural texts, and his historical legacies. It also included an address from apostle Dallin H. Oaks, which provided a degree of ecclesiastical approval. That the event took place only a dozen years after the September Six crisis indicated a growing comfort on the part of both the academy and the church that scholarly discourse was possible. Though not all were as impressed: "Is this an academic or an evangelistic conference?" asked one non-Mormon professor, Douglas Davies, when he felt some comments verged on apologetics.[37]

One of the keynote speakers at the event was Richard Bushman, husband of the activist Claudia Bushman and accomplished scholar of early America. Recently retired from Columbia University, Bushman had spent the previous decade with two projects. First, a comprehensive and cultural biography of Joseph Smith that immediately became a bestseller and watershed within the faith. And second, starting in 1997, Bushman had cultivated a new generation of Mormon scholars who could navigate the politics of faith and scholarship in the wake of the prominent excommunications, disfellowships, and dismissals. Through summer seminars and semi-regular conferences, Bushman demonstrated that the church need not fear critical investigation, and that LDS academics could take advantage of Gordon B. Hinckley's era of optimism and openness. The results were slow but clear: a conference on Mormon theology held at Yale Divinity School in 2003, a National Endowment for the Humanities–sponsored seminar held at BYU in 2005, as well as the Library of Congress conference. Claudia even led her own seminar focused on Mormon women, once again plumbing the depths of the faith's gendered past. Each event succeeded at building bridges that just the previous decade had appeared to be burnt.[38]

These external efforts were matched by internal reform. Richard E. Turley, who became managing director of the LDS historical department in 1989, and Marlin K. Jensen, who was the department's executive director from 1996 to 1998 and then named church historian in 2005, worked to soften the headquarters' animosity toward any and all academic scholarship. Though they lacked Leonard Arrington's academic credentials, they fulfilled his vision of granting more access to researchers and producing more accurate and transparent historical accounts. One obstacle was Arrington's own ghost: when Utah State University's archives opened the Arrington papers in 2001, two years after his death, some of the first visitors were church employees who scoured the collection and demanded that the university sequester 148 boxes and censor forty journal entries. (Those demands were eventually reduced to only the most controversial documents.)[39]

These new church historians responded to calls for more transparency by releasing a digital collection of significant archival sources in 2002 that filled seventy-four DVDs. They also announced the formation of the Joseph Smith Papers Project, which aimed to publish and analyze all known writings of the faith's founding prophet according to the highest documentary standards. Leaders authorized and supported a new and unflinching account of the Mountain Meadows Massacre that went beyond Juanita Brooks's half-century-old book in disrupting traditional and apologetic myths just after the tragedy's sesquicentennial in 2007. Then, in 2009, the church completed a massive 250,000-square-foot, five-floor library across the street from Temple Square, the physical embodiment of a new optimistic era that would have made Arrington envious.[40]

The combination of this academic interest with institutional collaboration resulted in a new wave of scholarship known as Mormon studies. One of the field's key figures was a familiar face. Eugene England, fresh from his forced resignation from BYU, was hired to teach Mormon literature at nearby Utah Valley State College. From there, outside ecclesiastical control, he secured National Endowment for the Humanities funding for a new Mormon studies program, an initiative to support and promote scholars investigating Mormonism's cultural meanings. The movement quickly spread, as universities ranging from those in the Wasatch Front to Harvard "scrambled" to offer courses on one of America's most notorious religions.[41]

This curricular interest transformed into permanent faculty positions. Endowed chairs funded by wealthy LDS donors were created at a handful of institutions inside and outside of Utah. The first was located at Utah State University and appropriately named after Leonard Arrington, while the second was founded at Claremont Graduate University in Southern California and named after LDS leader Howard Hunter. The tensions between Mormon and academic interests were often on display with these new hybrid positions. Claremont's donor body demanded that the chair holder be on good-enough terms with the church to have "access to LDS Church archives," a designation controlled by church authorities. But the chair's early success signified a cordial relationship. Bushman, often a bridge figure in these discussions, played a key role: after he served as the inaugural holder of Claremont's chair, another chair was endowed in his name at the University of Virginia. Meanwhile, when D. Michael Quinn, long exiled from BYU, was considered for another academic job, LDS donors opposed his hire. The new period of academic openness did not welcome everyone.[42]

The improved relationship between scholars and church leaders was a subtle yet necessary step for Mormonism's public relations agenda during Hinckley's tenure. Soon, due to presidential campaigns and media fascination, Mormonism would be everywhere, requiring skilled analysts to address uncomfortable conversations. The end goal, as always, was the long-promised dream of societal assimilation and acceptance.

* * *

SURROUNDED BY American flags and wearing a dark suit, white shirt, and blue tie, Mitt Romney stepped up to a podium in the George H. W. Bush Presidential Library to address a topic he had heretofore studiously avoided: his faith. Romney, after four years as Massachusetts's pragmatic and mostly popular governor, was vying for the Republican Party's presidential nomination within a crowded field. And while he had led in several polls for much of 2017, a recent surge from evangelical Mike Huckabee, Arkansas's governor, raised questions regarding whether the GOP's religious base would back a Mormon. The sectarian skepticism surprised Romney's camp. Religion had rarely come up during his gubernatorial run, and many assumed that Mormons had safely embedded themselves within the Republican base enough that they were immune from such questioning.

Decades after his father, George, did not face much religious backlash for his 1968 presidential campaign, signs that Mitt Romney's Mormonism would be a factor arrived as soon as he was a rumored candidate. Two major polls in December 2006 discovered a majority of Americans were "very uncomfortable" supporting a Mormon. The animosity was multifaceted. For some progressives already skeptical of religion, LDS faith represented an ideological failing. "Someone who truly believed in the founding whoppers of Mormonism," wrote an editor at Slate, exhibited "a basic failure to think for himself or see the world as it is." Liberal media highlighted the "secret" and "outlandish" elements of the faith, often mocking the intellectual capabilities of any believer. The very label that Hinckley had worked so hard to vanquish—"weird"—was once again predominant.[43]

Even the religious right seemed uneasy. While evangelicals were happy to work with Mormons on conservative political and social issues, electing one as president was another matter. Unlike Catholics, Latter-day Saints had not yet proved their loyalty through decades of collaboration. Many evangelical leaders voiced a fear that a Romney victory would validate a faith to a susceptible public. The Pew Research Center released a survey in September 2007 that found

36 percent of White conservative evangelicals had serious reservations about Romney's religion. Ted Haggard, the president of the National Association of Evangelicals, explained this hesitancy by noting that many in their sphere continued to view Mormonism "as a Christian cult group." The outspoken Reverend Bill Keller went so far as to say that a vote for Romney was "a vote for Satan."[44]

Anxiety grew as Romney retained his lead among Republican hopefuls throughout 2007. Huckabee was ready to take advantage of this uncertainty. "Don't Mormons believe that Jesus and the devil are brothers?" Huckabee wryly asked one reporter in early December. Though he later walked back the remark, his coded language signaled to evangelical voters that there remained a theological chasm.[45]

It was in this context that Mitt Romney decided to explain his faith to an eager American audience. His choices regarding what to highlight and what to avoid reflected the new circumstances. Like Hinckley, Romney emphasized his Christian affiliation and left unsaid any unique elements of the Mormon faith. He only mentioned the word *Mormon* once, and the only reference to the faith's past was in declaring his pioneer heritage. Indeed, Romney's address was a stronger defense of the religious right than of Mormonism. "Freedom requires religion just as religion requires freedom," he argued. He denounced the "religion of secularism" that was threatening to separate church and state. Romney deemed questions concerning his faith appropriate because politicians should not run away from their belief. Like John F. Kennedy in his famous speech in 1960 addressing his Catholicism, Romney insisted that he would not hearken to ecclesiastical commands; unlike Kennedy, he refused to acknowledge any distance between faith and politics. The difference between how these two presidential candidates from minority religions framed the topic demonstrated how much had changed in American politics during the intervening five decades. The religious right's coalition embraced the idea that one's belief should dictate one's partisanship.[46]

The speech helped quell the rising anti-Mormon tide but was not enough to save Romney's candidacy. He continued to struggle in evangelical-dominated states during the primaries, which typically went for Huckabee, and failed to muster a following in more moderate states, which backed eventual nominee John McCain. Romney pulled from the race in early March 2008, only months after he was the clear front-runner. He would not be gone from the national stage for long.

Months before Romney's campaign fell apart, another prominent Mormon politician made headlines. Speaking before BYU students, Harry Reid, US Senate majority leader and a committed member from Nevada, emphasized that Romney's conservative path was not the only one available to devout believers. "I am a Democrat because I am a Mormon," he pronounced, "not in spite of it." Reid invoked the tradition's previous affiliation with progressive politics during the early twentieth century and expressed a hope that Mormon Democrats had a bright future given the party's stance on healthcare, global warming, and income inequality.[47]

Reid faced intense headwinds, however. The same rightward trends that had been readily apparent for several generations became only more pronounced by the beginning of the twenty-first century. When pressed by journalists in 1998 about the church's Republican dominance, Gordon Hinckley assigned Marlin Jensen, the popular general authority who happened to be Democrat, to address the issue. "It's not in our interest to be known as a one-party church," Jensen insisted. Jan Graham, Utah's attorney general and the only Democrat to hold statewide office, predicted that Jensen's statement would "cut the church umbilical cord to the Republican Party."[48]

Graham and Jensen were fighting a losing battle. By 2008, only 22 percent of American Mormons identified as Democrat. And unlike those in most other denominations, Mormonism's younger generations were more likely to favor the Republican Party than older ones. The lone issue on which American Latter-day Saints did not squarely align with conservatives was their embrace of immigration; this cultural preference was a result of the faith's own history and global presence, as well as the foreign mission experiences of many of the adults. But a liberal stance on immigration was the exception that proved the rule. At the national level, where influential Mormon politicians used to be found in both parties, soon Reid was the only prominent Mormon Democrat, the last lingering reminder of a bygone era when saints were split between both parties.[49]

EVEN AS Romney's national chances faded, the church remained the focus of a great deal of popular attention. Not all of it was positive. On a Thursday night in November 2008, thousands of Californians gathered outside the Los Angeles temple and shouted "Bigots" and "Shame on you" at the suited men who stood behind the locked gates. The protesters were gay rights advocates upset at that week's passage of Proposition 8, a state amendment that defined marriage as between a man and a woman. The proposition had been heavily backed by the LDS church. Demonstrators' signs included "Keep Your Magic Undies off My Civil Rights" and "You Have Two Wives,

Protestors supporting gay rights gathered at the Los Angeles Temple following the passage of Proposition 8 in 2008. The Latter-day Saint church played a crucial role in the amendment's passage, and was then blamed accordingly.

I Want One Husband." One ex-Mormon gay man, Benjamin Wiser, attended the rally dressed in a white shirt, a tie, and his own missionary name tag. He told journalists that he had been raised in the church, had served a mission, but then left over its anti-LGBTQ stance. He, along with thousands of others, expressed outrage over the church's political involvement.[50]

Protesters were right that Mormons had played a disproportionate role in the campaign. By 2008, the LDS church already had over a decade of experience in mobilizing against gay marriage. The church's success in Hawaii during the 1990s had provided a blueprint: collaborating with other conservative denominations, cultivating the appearance of grassroots coordination, and framing the question as moral instead of political. "This is not a matter of civil rights," Hinckley said ahead of the church's support of California's anti-gay-marriage statute in 2000, "it is a matter of morality." Officials in Salt Lake City sent detailed letters of instructions to local leaders in California that encouraged all members to donate what they could but for bishops to target "more affluent members" when soliciting funds. Thanks to support from Mormons and other conservative groups, thirty-seven states passed bans against gay marriage by 2003.[51]

LDS mobilization held firm even as the national discourse shifted. When California's Supreme Court ruled in 2008 that the 2000 statute was unconstitutional, church leaders resorted to time-proven methods. The First Presidency issued a letter to all California members urging them to "do all you can to support the proposed constitutional amendment by donating of your means and time." They launched a new website and issued a pamphlet that pleaded their case in non-denominational rhetoric. "We are pro-marriage," one training document explained to volunteers, "not anti-gay." While hardly surprising, the results were staggering. The church made up only 2 percent of California's population, but observers estimated that members contributed around half of the total $40 million in donations and 80–90 percent of the volunteer work. When the amendment passed by only a few points, Mormons were therefore frequently and loudly blamed.[52]

Yet amid the national ridicule, LDS leaders learned an important lesson and gained influential friends. One prominent evangelical pastor noted that while "our theological differences with Mormonism are, frankly, unbridgeable," the attacks on the faith "are unacceptable." Many conservative leaders spoke out in defense of the church for publicly supporting measures with which they sympathized. That Mormon members were willing to stand up for one of the culture war's most prominent battles forged their alliance with the religious right, embedding them within a societal coalition that ensured mutual support even as it courted liberal antipathy. Antagonism toward the faith would not disappear, but the church would no longer face these battles alone.[53]

Some within the faith still hoped for reform. LGBTQ members continued to seek a middle path between, according to John Gustav-Wrathall, "on the one hand, embracing the Church and rejecting the love I share with my partner and, on the other, rejecting the Church and embracing my sexuality." For Gustav-Wrathall, the same spiritual impressions that initially bound him to the church were also prompting him "to continue to nurture my love for my partner." Other queer Mormons, both those in mixed-orientation marriages and those not, spoke about their experiences and worked to carve out a more welcoming space. Some posited that accepting homosexuality was the faith's next frontier.[54]

The chorus became so strong that LDS authorities softened their rhetoric, though not their policies. It was a tenuous balance. One solution was found in separating "orientation" from "action," classifying the former as natural while the latter was sinful. Dallin H. Oaks, for instance, admitted as early as 1995 that "same-gender attraction" could be an "inborn" trait "acquired from a complex interaction of 'nature and nurture.'" Even as they pressed forward with supporting anti-gay-marriage legislation—or, perhaps, because of it—they emphasized compassion for homosexuals by validating their orientation as natural, albeit sinful if acted upon. The language of "same-sex attraction" therefore enabled them to concede internal inclinations but retain the right to punish the "choice" of fulfilling the "temptation." LGBTQ members were left in a sexual limbo, with their desires deemed natural but their activities still suspect. To reflect this shift, the church's revised handbook in 2010 officially separated attraction from action.[55]

The years that followed 2008 included further evolution in the church's stance against homosexuality. Apostle Boyd Packer, long an orthodox stalwart, attempted to reaffirm the faith's absolute rejection of same-sex attraction. He denounced the push to legalize gay marriage as doomed to fail because the legislation would "alter the designs" of divine law as outlined in the family proclamation. "Do you think a vote to repeal the law of gravity would do any good?" he asked in a General Conference address. He scoffed at the idea that homosexuality was rooted in "inborn tendencies toward the impure and unnatural." That could not be the case, because "why would our Heavenly Father do that to anyone?" Yet Packer was fighting a losing battle. When a transcript was posted online, the address was edited to reflect new circumstances. Gone was the explicit harangue against "inborn tendencies." By excising his "Why would our Heavenly Father do that to anyone?" remark, the church unofficially forfeited its belief that homosexuality was solely a social construct.[56]

BYU proved to be, once again, a testing ground for change. Students formed a new campus organization in 2012 to support the LGBTQ community, Understanding Same Gender Attraction. Twenty-two of its members put together an "It Gets Better" video in which they spoke about their experiences and expressed hope for the future. They also received permission to host a forum that would address, as one advertisement pronounced, "everything you wanted to know about being gay at BYU but were too afraid to ask." Six hundred students crammed into an auditorium that fit 260 to hear students like Bridey Jensen explain how being gay and LDS "was just a fundamental part of me that I never chose." Another student, Adam White, clarified that queer members were trying to "create new spaces for us to be gay and Mormon and be active in the church." One study found that while 69 percent of BYU students opposed gay marriage in 2004, that number had dwindled to 38 percent only a decade later. Outside BYU, members formed the Mormons Building Bridges organization that marched at the state's Pride parade without institutional pushback. Even the church published a new sympathetic website, mormonandgay.lds.org, that attempted to build its own bridges.[57]

California's anti-gay-marriage amendment did not last two years

Mormons participating in a Salt Lake City Gay Pride parade in 2013. Mormons Building Bridges was an unofficial Latter-day Saint group organized to provide more support for queer members.

before it was overturned by a district court in 2010. Though the LDS newsroom issued a statement expressing regret at the decision and maintaining that "marriage between a man and a woman is the bedrock of society," leaders recognized the battle was lost. The church did not get involved in any state referendum or proposition efforts in 2012, an election cycle in which every bill in favor of gay marriage won. Utah's own law on marriage was overturned in December 2013. Oaks bemoaned how homosexual unions were now "becoming popular in our particular time and place." But instead of exiting the battle, church leaders redefined the battle lines. Externally, they shifted their efforts from directly opposing gay marriage to instead carving out religious exemptions under the umbrella of "religious liberty." And internally, they dedicated more attention to reaffirming cultural standards for their members even as they keenly felt their surrounding society slipping away.[58]

*   *   *

AFTER LEADING the church for a dozen publicity-filled years, Gordon Hinckley passed away in January 2008 at the age of ninety-seven. He had been a church employee since 1935, a church apostle since 1961, and still active and earnest in his later years. Hinckley's passing marked both the end of one era and the creation of another, as his management of media attention set a standard for the modern institution. (Some openly wondered whether the church would have handled Proposition 8 more deftly had Hinckley still been at the helm.) But ironically, it was not until his death that Mormonism received the most cultural attention in the faith's history.

The June 2011 double issue of *Newsweek* featured Mitt Romney's smiling head pasted on an LDS missionary's body jumping in the air while holding the Book of Mormon. In multiple colors, the title read, "The Mormon Moment: How the Outsider Faith Creates Winners," and the issue's feature story focused on the media frenzy then circling the faith. Romney's second presidential campaign had just officially launched days before, and he was immediately considered the front-runner. The missionary body to which he was photoshopped was from the *Book of Mormon* musical, which was the hot ticket on Broadway and on its way to setting new records for sales. But beyond the presidential hopeful and theatrical hit, the American public seemed desperate to learn more about the homegrown religion, an appetite met by a surprisingly amiable and now-experienced LDS public relations machine.[59]

The musical had been in development for seven years. Produced by Trey Parker and Matt Stone, who had previously skewered Mormonism in their popular TV show *South Park*, and Robert Lopez, a Broadway veteran, the show focused on Mormon missionaries attempting to preach the gospel in rural Uganda. However, the earnest yet naïve elders struggle with a host of obstacles ranging from violent warlords to infectious diseases. One of the elders sings about suppressing homosexual inclinations in a song titled "Turn It Off," which made light of how many saints were advised to deal with intellectual, mental, and spiritual challenges by merely avoiding them. ("My hetero side just won!" Elder McKinley exclaims. "I'm all better now.") But even as the musical targeted the ignorance of Mormon beliefs, Mormons themselves were depicted as lovable, albeit gullible, characters.[60]

The church's reaction to the raunchy, irreverent, but acclaimed musical was remarkably restrained. "The production may attempt to entertain audiences for an evening," their one-line statement needled, "but the Book of Mormon as a volume of scripture will change people's lives forever." It even purchased a one-page advertisement in the Playbill that said, "You've seen the play . . . Now read the book." Stone and Parker admitted that the institution's response was "just brilliant."[61]

The same month *Newsweek*'s "Mormon Moment" issue hit shelves, and months after *The Book of Mormon* premiered, an innovative church media campaign appeared in Times Square. Titled "I'm a Mormon," the campaign was predicated on the belief that most people gave up their suspicions that Mormons were "weird" once they knew them. Billboards, posters, and videos depicted members of the faith from divergent races, jobs, and backgrounds. They featured professional athletes, acclaimed chefs, accomplished surfers, and popular musicians, all exhibiting their hobbies and dreams before closing with the catchphrase, "And I'm a Mormon."

These advertisements demonstrated the variety of Mormon lives even as they downplayed distinctive Mormon doctrines. Rather than depicting the faith as a homogeneous group tied together through unique beliefs and complete obedience, this new public relations effort displayed Mormons as hip, modern, and independent. "Previous campaigns focused on what we believe," explained LDS spokesman Michael Purdy, "and we also want people to know who we are because of what we believe." Leaders tepidly tested the approach in nine markets in late 2010, and then seized on the "Mormon Moment" attention by expanding into twenty more, including New York City, the next year.[62]

The campaign was perfectly tailored to an American culture increasingly rooted in personal expression. It was also an immediate success, as national polls showed a growing number of Americans comfortable with the previously marginalized faith. Comedian Stephen Colbert captured this perspective when responding to a media statement that Romney appeared "weird"—a formerly common but indirect reference to his religion. Colbert's outlandish character sarcastically explained how Romney was obviously one of those "weird" kids in high school who "had lots of friends and led the football team to one of those weird state championships." Similarly, Mormon beliefs that "Joseph Smith received golden plates from an angel on a hill" could be classified as "weird" only because "everyone knows that Moses got stone tablets from a burning bush on a mountain." Colbert even poked fun at the "I'm a Mormon" campaign by creating his own spoof: an "I'm a Catholic" commercial in which he rode a skateboard while playing guitar, beckoning a falcon, and high-fiving a tiger. "In your face, Mormons," he triumphantly declared.[63]

Both Romney's and the church's campaigns added to an already flourishing media moment. Americans were especially fascinated with the homegrown faith's economic success, the fruits of financial efforts that leaders had initiated a half century earlier. "If Harvard Business School were a religion," wrote Harvard professor, and LDS leader, Clayton Christensen, "it could be Mormonism." The church's investment portfolio and financial holdings were especially striking to an audience who typically associated the faith with modest homes and pioneer clothing. A new and massive mixed-use development titled City Creek Center, in part financed by the church and located across the street from its headquarters, opened in March 2012. It featured an upscale mall and high-end apartments, including a tower that cast a shadow over the neighboring Temple Square. LDS leaders attended the grand opening and joined in the chant of "Let's go shopping!" As one financial journalist summarized, "Watching a religious leader celebrate a mall may seem surreal," but the billion-dollar investment reflected "the spirit of enterprise that animates modern-day Mormonism." While critics were skeptical of this sprawling corporate empire, and believers viewed it as the product of wise stewardship and divine blessings, many observers were merely aghast at its enormity.[64]

The new wave of publicity was not all positive. One investigation resulted in the church readdressing an issue it had hoped was dead. A *Washington Post* reporter visited Brigham Young University's religion department in February 2012 to learn more about the church's historic teachings concerning race, but instead learned that some of the ideas were still being taught. Religion professor Randy Bott repeated past Mormon doctrines that Blacks were "the descendants of Cain," and defended the previous restriction by noting that denying African Americans the priesthood "protected them from the lowest rungs of hell reserved for those who abuse their priesthood powers." Bott, a popular teacher who taught hundreds of students each semester, defended the ban as "the greatest blessing God could give them."[65]

The resulting outcry was immediate, and church leaders were left scrambling. They issued a statement the next day that explained that Bott's teachings "absolutely do not represent the teachings and doctrines" of the church, and condemned all forms of racism, "including any and all past racism by individuals both inside and outside the Church." More significantly, the statement was accompanied by a new document titled "Race and the Church: All Are Alike unto God." This text admitted that the racial restriction originated after Joseph Smith, though hedged by saying, "It is not known precisely why." The church then issued a new introduction to the 1978 revelation, which had been canonized as part of Latter-day Saint scripture, with the same historical information, as well as published another statement that disavowed "the theories advanced in the past." These repudiations of past "speculation" were precisely what David and Betty Jackson had requested fourteen years earlier.[66]

The Bott episode proved to be a blip in an otherwise overwhelmingly positive period of media attention. Journalists covered Mormon presence in mainstream music, the faith's influence on Stephenie Meyer (bestselling author of the Twilight series), the pervasiveness of Mormon mommy bloggers, and the surprising success of collegiate basketball sensation Jimmer Fredette. One reporter jested that the 2012 presidential campaign could also be termed a "Polygamist Moment," as both Romney and Barack Obama were descendants of polygamist ancestry. (Romney had two polygamist great-great-grandfathers, including Parley Pratt, and Obama's Kenyan grandfather had four wives.) Not that Utah's polygamists supported either candidate—most rooted for libertarians who were more likely to rescind anti-polygamy laws. But the common thread throughout most of this media coverage was the assumption that Mormons reflected mainstream American values.[67]

The person who most benefited from this path to normalization was Mitt Romney. Whether by choice or by necessity, the same evangelicals who expressed skepticism about his 2008 candidacy now came around to his defense. Baptist pastor Robert Jeffress said that while Mormonism was obviously a "cult," he clarified that it was a "theological" cult, not a "sociological" one—a distinction that reflected the new political calculus that underwrote the religious right. Others were even willing to shed the label altogether. After Romney received Billy Graham's endorsement during a personal visit, the Graham Evangelistic Association removed "Mormons" from its website's listing of "cults." Romney was soon invited to deliver the commencement address at Liberty University.

The "Mormon moment" appeared to have successfully defanged the "Mormon question." Even when facing Barack Obama in the general election, when many assumed liberals would directly attack Romney's religious connections, at least its conservative tendencies, Mormonism rarely came up. The Pew Research Center estimated that only 1 percent of campaign coverage from major news outlets focused on the candidates' faith. America's theological chasm was no longer insurmountable. Nearly 80 percent of evangelicals ended up supporting Romney, a higher total than had supported John McCain in 2008.[68]

It was still not enough. Obama carried twenty-six states and 332 electoral votes compared to Romney's twenty-four and 206. It was the closest a Mormon had ever come to holding America's highest office, a margin that Joseph Smith likely could not have fathomed during his own ill-fated and long-shot run in 1844.

THE DEATH of Romney's campaign birthed a new phase for his faith. A journalist for the *Boston Globe* declared that November 6, 2012, the day that Romney lost to Obama, was "the most important day—ever—in Mormons' history." The next week, the Associated Press ran a story titled "And the Winner Is . . . the Mormon Church." The LDS tradition, this common sentiment implied, had finally reached mainstream status, a validation Mormons had sought for over a century. If anything, journalists seemed bored with the religion. McKay Coppins, a Mormon who covered the campaign for BuzzFeed, noted how reporters assigned to accompany Romney to his church increasingly saw it "less as a tantalizing peek into the candidate's strange religion," and more as the way that most Mormons, as well as most Americans, view their faith: "A dull chore to be fulfilled out of obligation." Romney's campaign had lost, but his religion was here to stay.[69]

The dawn of the twenty-first century brought a national platform for a community that had never been quite sure what to do with attention. Previously reluctant to emphasize commonalities, even as the saints yearned for cultural acceptance, Gordon Hinckley now led them down the path of embracing labels of "normal" and "mainstream." In his vision, "Mormons" were simultaneously proud of their heritage and nonthreatening to their contemporaries. They were not afraid of the spotlight nor ashamed of their relevance. "A Mormon boy, a Mormon boy, / I am a Mormon boy," went one of Hinckley's favorite children's songs, "I might be envied by a king, / For I am a Mormon boy." Now nearing 15 million members worldwide in 2012, there were plenty of Mormons to share that pride, even if internal divisions threatened the repeated calls for unity.[70]

10

Latter-day Legacies,
2012–Present

My people were Mormon pioneers.
Is the blood still good?
They stood in awe as truth
Flew by like a dove
And dropped a feather in the West.
Where truth flies you follow
If you are a pioneer.

—CAROL LYNN PEARSON[1]

THERE ARE FEW members of the Church of Jesus Christ of Latter-day Saints more famous than David Archuleta. Born in Miami in 1990 to a mother who had immigrated from Honduras, Archuleta was raised with four siblings in a Spanish-speaking household that moved to Utah when he was six. His singing talent earned him attention, awards, and an appearance on *Star Search*. He then achieved national acclaim by taking second place on *American Idol*, and immediately became a pop music icon. But Archuleta shocked the nation and endeared himself to fellow Latter-day Saints when he took a break from his career in 2012 to serve a two-year mission to Chile. In a tradition that has produced no shortage of celebrities, Archuleta's fame held few rivals.[2]

Over three hundred thousand fans therefore watched when Archuleta bared his soul during a fifty-one-minute Instagram live post in January 2022. Wearing a plain black T-shirt and unkempt hair while sitting in a modest bedroom with only a white lamp in the background, the singer said he needed to "let out some of the steam inside of me that's building up." Archuleta had publicly announced that he belonged to the "LGBTQIA+ community" the previous summer, identifying himself as both bisexual and asexual. At that time he expressed a desire to still embrace his Latter-day Saint faith, including its prohibition on homosexual relationships. But now, only six months later, he wondered whether a balance between his faith and sexuality was even possible. His public confession was raw and emotional. "I can no longer pretend," he shared between tears, "like everything's fine."

After years of anguish, Archuleta had decided to explore his sexuality despite the church's policies. There was now a "greater likelihood" that he would marry a man than a woman. He knew the consequences, too. Archuleta likened his situation to Mark Twain's Huckleberry Finn, specifically when the fictional character was forced to choose between doing the "Christian" thing by turning in Jim, who was fleeing slavery, to authorities, or defying society's expectations and letting him go free. "All right then," Finn concluded as he chose the latter, "I'll go to hell." Archuleta's narrative climax was no less dramatic: "I'm choosing damnation."[3]

Archuleta's journey represents much of the modern Latter-day Saint church's central tensions. He is part of a younger generation that combines a deep personal religiosity with a willingness to challenge traditional standards. He is the son of an immigrant and part of the growing number of non-White members. His decision to serve a mission mirrored the deep devotion of his fellow congregants. And finally, his struggle to reconcile the church's teachings with broader societal changes, particularly debates in favor of LGBTQ rights, took place within a wider series of faith crises within the community. Questions of identity, race, gender, freedom—these are the battlefields on which modern Mormonism, just like modern America, is contested, all taking place in a digital sphere that makes everyone both intimately connected and inherently vulnerable.

The Latter-day Saint church claimed nearly 15 million worldwide members at the dawn of 2013. Though a majority were located outside the United States, the faith's leaders were still enmeshed in American politics, culture, and society. America's homegrown religion continues to be shaped by its first and most prominent context, despite its increasingly global reach. And American culture has become increasingly fractured into generational, political, and cultural divides, a society of partisans who view their rivals with scorn and suspicion.[4]

As had always been the case, there was no singular Mormon culture, no undisputed answer to Mormon questions, no universal Mormon identity. The Latter-day Saint community's cohesion, already under siege, has splintered into a cacophonous chorus of diverse expressions at the turn of the twenty-first century. Examining the contemporary church means peering into a kaleidoscope of disparate experiences and ideas, all attempting to address foundational concerns, while still connected to an institutional system desperately trying to manage a community that could never truly be controlled.

LIFE FOR an average Mormon revolves around church activity. Sunday meetings last several hours and include a sacrament service, Sunday school, priesthood meetings for men, Relief Society lessons for women, and smaller classes for youth and children divided by age and gender. Families dedicate at least one weeknight, typically on Monday, for "family home evening," in which parents and children spend quality time together with both a spiritual lesson and wholesome recreation. Youth return to the chapel on another weeknight for "mutual" activities that could be as basic as sports or as elaborate as pageants. High schoolers attend seminary during the academic calendar, which takes place either during school, if they live in Mormon-heavy regions, or at an early morning hour before school starts if they do not. Families share rotating assignments to clean church buildings every Saturday morning, and occasional firesides take place Sunday evenings. It is no surprise that one's standing is described as whether one is "active" or not.

The faithful routinely acknowledge a connection between their worthiness and priesthood authority. Individual members meet with their bishop every year to declare that they are full tithe payers, which implies donating 10 percent of their income. There are also successive interviews with bishops and stake presidents every other year to answer a set list of questions to gain the recommendation required for temple attendance—which they are expected to do several times a year, depending on proximity to the nearest temple. Saints hear from the faith's highest authorities, including the First Presidency and Quorum of the Twelve Apostles, every April and October at General Conference. The conference consists of five meetings that total ten hours over two days; at one of those meetings, all members are asked to sustain the leaders as prophets, seers, and revelators. Local officials are sustained biennially in stake, ward, or regional conferences. It is impossible to overlook the modern church's hierarchical structure.

There is a series of benchmarks for members from cradle to grave, many of which are dictated by gender. Infants are blessed in a sacrament meeting, typically by their father while surrounded by other men who hold the priesthood. While some women have petitioned to hold their child during the blessing, such allowances are infrequent. Both boys and girls are baptized and confirmed as members of the church at the age of eight. Boys are then ordained to the Aaronic priesthood around the age of twelve and advance to different offices within that priesthood—deacon, teacher, priest—in two-year intervals. Each office plays a public role in worship services. Those ordained as teachers are tasked with preparing the sacrament, priests with blessing it, and deacons with passing it to all congregants. The young women have their own classes with similar age groups but are not granted an equivalent public role in church meetings.

This dynamic and rigorous structure has succeeded in committing many youths to the church and its standards. Mormon millennials are more likely to believe in God than their contemporaries, more likely to attend church, pray, and read the scriptures, and more likely to follow rules of chastity and refrain from drugs and alcohol; they even claim more spiritual experiences than their parents' generation. In an age when their peers are increasingly skeptical of both dogma and institutions, Mormon millennials have retained a commitment to unique truth claims and to local officials, though in more nuanced ways than their predecessors.

While not matching the high missionary numbers of the 1990s and early 2000s, young LDS men and women continue to serve missions at an astonishing rate, given the sacrifice of two years (for men) or eighteen months (for women). During 2021, after recovering from a COVID lull, nearly 55,000 saints served proselytizing missions and 37,000 served service missions. Returned missionaries are expected to find a partner while attending singles-only congregations, marry in the temple, have children, and then, in the twilight of their careers, volunteer for yet another mission. Mormonism is a lifelong commitment.[5]

Local wards and stakes, which typically comprise eight to twelve wards, are entirely staffed by volunteers. Men are called to serve as bishops, the ward's presiding officer, for an average of five years, and as stake presidents for an average of ten. Other men within each congregation are assigned to preside over priesthood quorums and Sunday schools, while women oversee Relief Societies, young women, and children's primary. A recent emphasis seeks to amplify women's voices in ward governing councils, though final decisions are still reserved for bishops. All congregants are given chances to deliver sermons in sacrament meetings and teach lessons in classes, and most hold some formal assignment. Weekly curriculum is prepared by a correlation committee in Salt Lake City and is standardized throughout the globe. This multilayered, highly structured, and intricately overseen system enables a rotating host of amateur participants at all levels who are simultaneously integral to the faith's success and also unmistakably replaceable at any moment.

Overseeing such a sprawling system predicated on volunteer labor involves inevitable complications. Sometimes that includes tragedy. Investigators have highlighted a series of instances in which priesthood leaders either abused or overlooked the abuse of children and youth. One particularly egregious case in Arizona prompted an investigation that uncovered a "helpline" that bishops can call when managing abuse cases. Details concerning that reporting system raised questions concerning whether its priority was to defend the church or help the victims. Like many other large institutions, both religious and secular, the Latter-day Saint church has had to determine how best to reform problems without confessing culpability. Church leaders joined Catholics in defending clergy confidentiality when it comes to child-abuse reporting, to the chagrin of many members. While Mormon millennials are less anti-institution than their contemporaries, they are still less likely to fully trust their hierarchical authorities than previous generations.[6]

Many of the church's current structures, standards, and experiences have been crafted over the past century. But few leaders brought as many reforms as Russell M. Nelson. The retired doctor became the faith's seventeenth prophet in January 2018 when Thomas S. Monson, who was medically incapacitated for much of his ten-year term, passed away. Raised in a family that was not particularly active in the faith nor embedded within the church's elite society, Nelson became a successful heart surgeon, and even performed surgery on one of his prophetic predecessors, Spencer Kimball. His final bypass operation, which took place just after being called as an apostle in 1984, was on none other than Leonard Arrington. After "thousands of these bypasses," Nelson told Arrington, he was thrilled that his last "historic operation [was] on a historian!" As an apostle, he was known for his serious demeanor, somber sermons, and willingness to engage divisive cultural and doctrinal issues like abortion and evolution, in each case with a conservative angle. Then, ordained as president, Nelson, though ninety-three, exuded both an energy for disruption and an appreciation for the spotlight that had not been rivaled since David O. McKay seventy years before.[7]

Nelson wasted no time in implementing a series of changes. He condensed Sunday meetings from three hours to two; ended the church's affiliation with Boy Scouts of America; reformed the member-to-member ministering program; revised the handbook, dress code, and communication roles for missionaries; adjusted ceremonial temple clothing and temple-recommend questions; and consolidated church magazines, among dozens of other changes. Nelson announced plans to build over one hundred temples across the globe, an audacious goal that surpassed even Hinckley's construction agenda. His wife, Wendy Nelson, frequently told stories of Nelson rising in the middle of the night to record a stream of further ideas.

"Take your vitamin pills," the prophet told one journalist, as there was "much more to come."[8]

This level of change, and the attention that came with it, heightened Nelson's reputation as a consequential leader. He is referenced by other general authorities at rates far higher than his predecessors. When Spencer Kimball was first ordained prophet, for example, authorities at the following General Conference mentioned his name 95 times; since Nelson achieved that position, he is mentioned an average of 118 times each conference, with a high of 133 in October 2021.[9]

Perhaps because of his lack of ties to Mormonism's cultural heritage, Nelson has been willing to forgo long-held traditions. He is, in some ways, the first post-pioneer prophet. He announced the end of the famous Hill Cumorah Pageant, which took place on the mound where Joseph Smith alleged to receive the plates and had been performed every summer for nearly a century. He approved the removal of historic murals from the Salt Lake City and Manti temples, though agreed to leave the latter in place following public outcry. Most consequential was his proclamation that saints and media alike should refrain from using the *Mormon* name altogether. Only six years following the massive "I'm a Mormon" campaign, Nelson declared that using *Mormon*, rather than the church's full name, was a "major victory for satan," because it downplays Jesus Christ's centrality. The institution went through a colossal rebranding to remove the forbidden term from sponsored material. Even the famed Mormon Tabernacle Choir would now be called the Tabernacle Choir at Temple Square.[10]

On the one hand, this emphasis on names was a natural end point of the faith's long path toward cultural assimilation. *Mormon*, the marker of uniqueness, held no place in a church that emphasized its commonalities within the Christian mainstream. Yet Nelson has simultaneously reaffirmed other facets of the tradition's singularity that he deems bedrock. The faith's latest prophet acts like the hybrid of a market strategist and venture capitalist: willing to strip down assets to bare essentials, modernize bureaucratic systems, and forfeit unnecessary practices or appendages, no matter how previously beloved, in order to lay foundations for anticipated long-term gains. For Nelson, the church's core foundations are the belief in Jesus Christ, the expansion of temple worship, the authority of apostolic leaders, and the defense of traditional families. Everything else is transient.[11]

The modern Latter-day Saint church also reflects the broader corporate world in successfully accumulating massive amounts of wealth and property. Following N. Eldon Tanner's fiscal reforms in the 1960s, leaders had empowered financial managers to grow a portfolio rarely matched in world history. Reports based on limited data estimate that the church's various investments total more than $100 billion. It owns at least 1.7 million acres of land valued at $16 billion in America alone. That includes meetinghouses, temples, office towers, shopping centers, residential skyscrapers, cattle ranches, and high-mountain timberlands. It holds over $100 million in asset valuation in at least fifteen urban centers, and an excess of $25 million in another sixty-six.[12]

The church's attempts to avoid disclosing details concerning its financial portfolio eventually courted trouble. It was charged by the US Securities and Exchange Commission in 2023 for failing to file forms that would have revealed the institution's stock holdings. The church blamed bad legal counsel but agreed to pay a settlement: its primary investment arm, Ensign Peak, agreed to a $4 million fine, while the church paid its own $1 million resolution. A whistleblower who previously worked for Ensign Peak claimed the lack of disclosure was due to the church's fear that, if its wealth was made known, it would result in fewer members being willing to pay tithing. Regardless of the reason, the church's half-century-long tradition of keeping its finances fully confidential will receive increasing scrutiny in an American culture that places such a premium on transparency. Yet the permanency associated with these reserves may be necessary for a church whose future is increasingly tethered to growth in the Southern Hemisphere, where expenditures will likely outpace incoming tithing revenue.[13]

Emblematic of the blending between material and spiritual in the modern church is a new church-owned skyscraper built in downtown Salt Lake City. The tower was erected on the same ground where a modest two-story pioneer social hall had previously stood. It houses a four-story meetinghouse and twenty-one stories of high-end business space, as well as a large grocery store to the side. Presiding Bishopric counselor Todd Budge quipped that if Brigham Young "were to come up that escalator now, I think he'd be quite surprised at what's on this piece of land."[14]

Young's consistent and fervent opposition to materialism, and fear that the saints were becoming obsessed with consumer goods, might have made him squirm at the gaudy sight. Yet the modern church now possesses financial resources necessary for the long-term stability he had long craved. The reserves also enable the faith to be among the globe's most powerful humanitarian givers. In 2022, for instance, the church donated over $1 billion worldwide to various efforts, including $32 million to the World Food Programme to address famine in Africa.[15]

Further institutional decisions on how to use that wealth, prioritize the faith's principles, and engage its members, however, have proved to be more difficult.

IN EARLY 2012, Elder Marlin Jensen, the church historian who already helped inaugurate a new era of scholarly transparency, spoke to a gathering of Utah State University students. The mild-mannered leader discussed a growing wave of younger saints who were fleeing the church due to encountering "difficult" topics or "troublesome" history on the internet. "Everything [is] out there for them to consume," he noted; all they had to do was "Google it." The church could no longer control the flow of information. A year later Hans Mattsson, previously one of the faith's leading authorities in Europe, gave an exclusive interview to the *New York Times* about his personal faith crisis. Jensen posited that "not since Kirtland have we seen an exodus of the Church's best and brightest leaders."[16]

A variety of websites, blogs, and podcasts had appeared over the previous decade that challenged Mormon orthodoxy. Some were more neutral in terms of attacking or supporting the church, while others were explicitly critical. One podcaster, John Dehlin, gained popularity by drawing both prominent and common members alike onto his show to discuss thornier topics. He published a collection of testimonials in March 2012 on a website that featured 3,086 participants narrating why they lost faith in traditional teachings. The topics included, among others, the history of polygamy, multiple accounts of Joseph Smith's First Vision, the Book of Mormon's historicity, and the racial restriction. This and other data were eventually presented to leadership. The threat was far from new, however: church authorities had been briefed as early as 2008 that as much as three-quarters of their young single adult population was no longer active.[17]

Leaders were divided on how to act. Some pleaded for members not to, as apostle Quentin Cook put it, become "immersed" in "internet materials that magnify, exaggerate, and, in some cases, invent shortcomings of early Church leaders." The church had long been the target of misrepresentation and malice, they argued, so it was best to just ignore derisive attacks. Another apostle, Jeffrey Holland, urged saints not to "hyperventilate" over information that could be easily discredited. The hope was that the ideological threat could merely be avoided. Such an approach had mostly worked for nearly two centuries.[18]

Yet others believed that the new circumstances required a different response. A group of leaders and historians, drawing on various projects that had been in progress for over a decade, focused on a new initiative in May 2012 to stem the tide: a series of essays, each focused on a difficult topic, that could acknowledge complexity while also reaffirming faith. They commissioned several trusted scholars to write initial drafts that were then edited by church historians and vetted by Latter-day Saint leaders. The first two essays, one of which was on the First Vision accounts, were released in November 2013; the thirteenth and final essay, on women and the priesthood, appeared in October 2015. Others in the series covered polygamy, Book of Mormon and DNA studies, the racial restriction, and Brigham Young's teachings concerning blood atonement.[19]

One of the driving forces behind the project was Dieter Uchtdorf, a German-born apostle and former pilot who had been in the First Presidency since 2008. He prepared saints for the essays' release by preaching that, "to be perfectly frank, there have been times when members or leaders in the Church have simply made mistakes," and that "there may have been things said or done that were not in harmony with our values, principles, or doctrine." The best way to deal with the issues, he counseled, was to confront them head-on. Uchtdorf urged that "truth and transparency complement each other," and that one could not exist without the other.[20]

The essays were a watershed in the church's good-faith engagement with historical and theological issues. Though critics claimed that they did not go far enough—and some scholars disputed particular arguments—they demonstrated an unprecedented willingness to tackle previously avoided issues. The essays also prompted a national stir. "It's Official: Mormon Founder Had up to 40 Wives," read a *New York Times* headline covering the essay on Joseph Smith's polygamy. Many members were shocked to discover that facts that had previously been dismissed as "anti-Mormon" were in fact true. Some refused to believe the essays were authorized, instead insisting they were merely a public relations measure. Nor were all Latter-day Saint leaders thrilled with the results: because of internal disputes among the hierarchy, the essays were never publicly announced over General Conference, printed in church magazines, or given extensive publicity. It was not until a few years later that they became more interwoven with Sunday school, institute, and seminary curricula.[21]

These debates over spiritual truth took place against a broader backdrop of disaffiliation. A growing number of the nation's millennials have chosen private and malleable forms of devotion divorced from institutional alliance. They are rejecting not necessarily religion but religious structures they find stifling and oppressive. This movement has been nicknamed "spiritual but not religious"; the category loosely defined as "nones" is the largest-growing religious movement in the nation. Whereas America was previously beset with interdenominational competition, in which churches fought over converts, seekers now withhold their allegiance and instead chart their own course.[22]

These cultural currents have seeped into the Mormon community. A 2016 survey of over 1,600 self-identified Mormons and former Mormons revealed stark generational divides on crucial social and doctrinal issues. Like their contemporaries, Latter-day Saint millennials have proved adept at forging their own form of religiosity. Most are more spiritual than their predecessors but are not as certain on unique Mormon beliefs like priesthood authority and prophetic fallibility. They are less likely to attend the temple or always wear their temple undergarments, and more likely to drink coffee and skip Sunday meetings. The most important factors for those who go inactive are social or personal matters, like policies on gender and sexuality. And when young Mormons leave the church, most of them choose not to affiliate with another denomination. Instead, they join the congregation of the nones.[23]

Another group of saints were becoming concerned the faith was growing *too* distant from its past. Denver Snuffer Jr., a Utah lawyer with a short grey beard and deliberate speaking tone, published a series of books urging saints to recover a lost spirituality. He criticized officials for forfeiting foundational doctrines in an attempt to gain cultural acceptance. Polygamy, Snuffer argued, commenced after Joseph Smith's death, and he denied that Mormonism's first prophet had anything to do with the practice. Thousands of saints, many of whom shared misgivings about the new historical "facts," embraced his message.

Snuffer was excommunicated in September 2013 when he refused to rescind his publications. A few months later, he announced that God had revoked the church's priesthood authority and he began baptizing followers into "the Remnant." Congregations, which believers called "fellowships," cropped up across the Mountain West along with large gatherings held in massive meeting halls. Followers compiled Snuffer's revelations into a new book of scripture. The Remnant movement represented a more conservative alternative to the mainstream church, only the latest schism in a tradition filled with divergent trajectories.[24]

The church's boundaries for tolerance and exclusion continued to simultaneously expand and constrict. In 2015, leaders excommunicated John Dehlin, the podcaster who built a financially successful podcast network predicated on critiquing traditional narratives, and disciplined or threatened to discipline many others. But they also supported faithful scholars who modeled a nuanced approach to asking questions. Deseret Book, the church's publishing imprint, produced a stream of titles that emphasized the benefits of doubt and critical thinking. Even the terrors of 1993's September Six continued to cast an inconsistent shadow: Maxine Hanks, who was excommunicated for her feminist scholarship, was rebaptized in 2012, insistent that both her and the church's arc had bent back together; however, when Lavina Fielding Anderson, who was excommunicated for exposing ecclesiastical abuse, applied for rebaptism in 2018, the First Presidency denied her petition.[25]

There have been other signs of retrenchment in recent years. When Russell Nelson ascended to the presidency, he removed Dieter Uchtdorf, a favorite among more progressive saints for his stance on transparency, from the First Presidency; Uchtdorf was replaced with Dallin Oaks, the cultural warrior who previously chastised historians for not supporting traditional narratives. BYU professors soon reported more oversight concerning their public scholarship and private views, an imposing surveillance that hearkened back to Michael Quinn's and Eugene England's conflicts in the 1980s and 1990s. Disputes over religious freedom within the faith appear cyclical.[26]

The contests between faith and doubt, belief and intellect, and obedience and dissent will likely never dissipate. Mormonism's religious imagination—originating with Joseph Smith, synthesized through Eliza Snow, challenged by B. H. Roberts, refined by Juanita Brooks, and polished by the likes of Sterling McMurrin, Carol Pearson, Richard Bushman, and a myriad of others—remains as unsettled as ever, a sign of an open canon of truth that is as sweeping and audacious as the tradition from which it sprang.

QUESTIONS CONCERNING women's issues have similarly never been fully settled. The Relief Society remains a crucial but auxiliary body within the increasingly correlated church. The frequent rotation of Relief Society presidencies, which change every five years, has meant that no leader has approached a stature and influence like Eliza Snow, Emmeline Wells, or Amy Brown Lyman. At the local level, however, Relief Societies remain the engine that makes wards function by providing aid, support, and lessons throughout the week and no matter the circumstances. Kitschy Mormon films often depict these women as always ready with a casserole and spiritual thought, typically with several children at their hip, and rarely seeking the spotlight or pushing for reform. This image of domestic, silent, and supportive labor was the fulfillment of J. Reuben Clark's vision that they be a "handmaid to the priesthood."

Modern America's circumstances make such an ideal impossible, however. The number of women with careers grows with every generation, as does the average age for marriage and childbirth, and family sizes continue to shrink. The idea of a "traditional" family, always more a myth than reality, appears increasingly incongruous with lived experiences. Three-quarters of Mormon millennials were raised by mothers who worked outside the home, and the younger generation of saints prefer a more egalitarian form of marriage. While the average Latter-day Saint woman who chooses to get married does so in her early twenties, there is a growing number who remain unmarried. Single saints therefore feel out of place in a religion that places so much significance on nuclear families. The wide spectrum of lived realities rarely falls within the prescribed "handmaid" vision. Yet many conservative religions, like the Latter-day Saints, have chosen not to forfeit their ideals but rather to tweak existing orthodoxy, as when the proclamation merged both patriarchal and companionate rhetoric when describing marriages.[27]

Several women used digital tools to help agitate for gender reforms in 2012. Activists built on the existing blogging communities, like Feminist Mormon Housewives, to coordinate a successful campaign against a policy that forbade menstruating girls from participating in temple baptisms. Then, later that year, they organized a mass show of resistance through the mildest of measures. Stephanie Lauritzen, a twenty-six-year-old mother of two, was tired of feeling like she was alone in her dissatisfaction. What if there was a way to show solidarity? She called for a "Wear Pants to Church" day that December, where women could express a desire to reform the patriarchy by choosing not to wear dresses, the symbol of traditional gender roles, and instead don slacks, the dress code for progress. Thousands of women participated, and the episode drew national attention. To some, however, it was a blatant challenge to social order, and a handful of online critics even threatened violence. But the event's success, followed by another campaign the following spring to have women deliver a prayer in General Conference, proved the power of online organizing.[28]

Emboldened, some Mormon feminists were ready to take the next step. To Kate Kelly, a fiery human-rights attorney and BYU graduate, that meant finally granting women the priesthood. She formed a new organization, Ordain Women, in March 2013. When addressing the frequent rebuttal that Mormon women already "feel equal," Kelly was resolute: "Equality is not a feeling." They built a website where both men and women contributed testimonials to women's ordination. Kelly staged an event at the October 2013 General Conference by requesting 150 tickets for the priesthood session, a portion of the conference reserved for men and teenage boys. The church declined the tickets and instead announced that the broadcast would be available to everyone. Kelly pressed on. She and 130 supporters stood in line for standby tickets on the night of the session and were denied, one by one, by a church representative. The spectacle of tearful women pleading for a seat appeared on websites across the nation. Kelly's continued agitation eventually resulted in excommunication in June 2014, a clear echo of Sonia Johnson's story back in 1979. "I am not an apostate," Kelly told journalists, "unless every single person who has questions to ask out loud is an apostate."[29]

Moderate reformers sought a middle ground. The same week Ordain Women protested at General Conference, Neylan McBaine, a marketing executive and brand strategist, published an essay titled "A Moderate Mormon Manifesto." She called for tweaks within the system that empowered women and spotlighted their talents. She started the Mormon Women Project, an online repository of women's stories of how they balanced work, faith, and family. McBaine eventually published a book on the topic, *Women at Church*, that offered practical counsel for how to grant women more leadership duties and provide girls more visibility. "I didn't start with the goal

Kate Kelly, founder of the Ordain Women movement, led a group of protestors to attend the men-only priesthood session of General Conference in October 2013. All women were denied entry.

of being a spokeswoman for a particular vein of thought on Mormon women," she insisted, but she felt "thrust into this position."[30]

Any attempt at reform still had to be measured against scripture. Russell Nelson, at his inaugural press conference as the faith's new president, was asked about gender roles in the church. His response cited a scriptural verse that explained how women were created "before the foundations of the world" to birth and raise children as a way to "glorify God." Though Nelson did not specify it, this passage came from Doctrine & Covenants 132, the revelation Joseph Smith had dictated on polygamy in response to Emma Smith's protest. It was a reminder that the faith's polygamous past continued to shape the modern institution's gendered expectations.[31]

Indeed, polygamy is still technically present within the Latter-day Saint faith. Faithful men are allowed to be sealed to more than one spouse in the event that their first wife is deceased. The expectation is that the husband will be united with both wives in the eternities. Nelson, for instance, is sealed to both Dantzel White, who passed away in 2005, and Wendy Watson, whom he married the next year. When Dallin Oaks courted Kristen McMain in 2000 after his first wife, June Dixon, passed in 1998, he confirmed that she "felt comfortable becoming a 'second wife.'" As poet and playwright Carol Lynn Pearson later demonstrated, the anxiety accompanying this ongoing reality continues to impact many women. Among the eight thousand responses Pearson gathered on the topic, one saint said she genuinely felt "bludgeoned by polygamy," even in the present.[32]

Other traditional doctrines have proved more generative for feminist thinking. A number of women in recent years have speculated on how a more robust theology of Heavenly Mother could produce a sense of empowerment and belonging among the faithful. Rachel Hunt Steenblik, a poet and philosopher, wrote two best-selling volumes of poetry that found the power of female divinity in the quotidian of everyday life. Concerned leaders, in turn, cautioned members to avoid all "speculation" on Heavenly Mother. This did not slow agitation, of course, and some feminists took the movement in novel directions. A number worried that too much focus on Heavenly Mother might perpetuate heteronormative systems and therefore urged more innovative theological seeking. Womanists and feminists of color, similarly, have criticized the focus on women's ordination when the priesthood structure has itself been based on racial privilege. The future of Mormon feminism, many argued, was in more diverse and intersectional avenues.[33]

One of Joseph Smith's earliest revelations concerned the duties of his wife, Emma. Mormonism's first lady was commanded to be both a comforting spouse and an expounder of scriptures; she was to serve both husband and God. Emma's roles changed over the following fourteen years—she later became a hymnist, a host, an organizer, an activist—and the roles for all Mormon women, both leading and common, evolved even more over the following two centuries. The plight of dealing with polygamy, the reforms associated with the progressive age, the sacralization of postwar domesticity, the protests of second-wave feminism—each era inaugurated novel questions and tentative solutions. A woman's place in both Mormon homes and

Mormon pews has transformed with each generation even as authorities insist that it remains eternally stable.

JULIE BECK was no stranger to the podium. She had served as Relief Society general president from 2007 to 2012 and came from a family of prominent businessmen, politicians, and church leaders. Among her addresses to the millions of Latter-day Saints was a controversial "Mothers Who Know" sermon in 2009 that reaffirmed the idea that women were natural nurturers and belonged in the home. Her remarks renewed a vociferous debate over the role of women in the modern church. Yet none of her actions were as overtly partisan as when, donning a full-length blue overcoat, she offered the opening prayer for a Donald Trump campaign rally in October 2016.[34]

Utah had not been considered a presidential swing state since the 1960s. Yet Donald Trump, the thrice-married real estate investor and raunchy reality-television celebrity, whose reputation seemed to eschew Mormonism's foundational morals, tested the region's Republican attachment. Mitt Romney, still the most prominent Latter-day Saint politician, was one of Trump's most consistent critics. Some journalists predicted that the Republican nominee had a "Mormon problem." Thousands of Utahns turned to Evan McMullin, a moderate running an independent campaign, who also happened to be Mormon. When media reported on the *Access Hollywood* tape, in which Trump was recorded bragging about sexually assaulting women, many assumed the saints could never vote for such a depraved man. The church-owned newspaper called on Trump to resign from the ticket. Polling on October 12 showed that Trump and Clinton were tied with 26 percent of the vote, McMullin close by with 22 percent, and Libertarian Gary Johnson earning 14 percent. Utah, for once, seemed up for grabs. Republicans therefore sent the more palatable vice-presidential candidate Mike Pence to shore up support.[35]

Observers were aghast at how religious conservatives throughout the nation rushed to sacralize a man that many had previously considered a disgrace. Trump's history of filthy language, dalliances with women, and deceitful business practices, along with his penchant for lying and his abject disregard for religion, made him an odd hero for evangelical worship. Yet the support also fulfilled several cultural priorities that came to dominate evangelical society even more than theological or moral principles: a message of White solidarity, unflinching masculinity, cultural grievance, and outright war with liberals. For those still uncomfortable with Trump's persona, his ability to appoint Supreme Court justice seats—with the hope of overturning cases like *Roe v. Wade*—was enough to plug their nose. To much of the nation's surprise, then, Trump became the religious right's messiah.[36]

Pence's trip to Utah reminded Mormons that they were part of this coalition. It was significant that Pence, an evangelical, was inviting saints to "come home" to the Republican Party. The gesture demonstrated both how far Mormon culture had come and how embedded it now was within the religious right. Julie Beck's presence and prayer provided absolution for those who worried that supporting Trump was inherently sinful. Idaho representative Raúl Labrador, a BYU graduate, reminded attendees that they were electing a "president," not "a bishop." Another Mormon, Layne Bangerter, who was a bishop as well as a Trump campaigner, was more resolute. Trump, Bangerter explained, was like "Paul on the road to Damascus": a sinful man who had been called of God to change his ways and lead a divine mission.[37]

The event, coupled with the GOP rallying around its candidate, worked. Utah voted 45 percent for Trump, compared to just 27 percent for Clinton and 21 percent for McMullin. Surveys showed that 61 percent of Mormons nationwide supported the Republican victor. While that figure was seventeen points lower than Romney's performance in 2012, the difference was mostly due to the large numbers who voted for McMullin, the Mormon independent candidate. And Julie Beck proved quite representative: bucking nationwide trends, Mormon women voted for Trump at the same rate as Mormon men.[38]

Latter-day Saint support for Trump, both during and after the 2016 election, marked the faith tradition's firm place within the modern Republican coalition. The GOP was "home," no matter the name on the ticket. Even the church's nonpartisan biannual letter encouraging members to vote subtly reflected this change: following Bill Clinton's scandals, the church's letter, a version of which is released every election year, had added the statement that members should "seek out and then uphold leaders who will act with integrity and are wise, good, and honest"; starting in 2016, however, that statement was removed, replaced with the more tepid admonition to seek candidates who support "principles compatible with the gospel." As a visual embodiment of this alliance, the church sent the Mormon Tabernacle Choir, as it was still known at the time, to Trump's inauguration. It was their fifth consecutive Republican inaugural performance, while they had not sung for a Democrat since Lyndon Johnson.[39]

Trump's reelection campaign in 2020 proved the alliance's resiliency. Without the benefit of an independent candidate who happened to be Mormon, and despite four years of Trump's controversies, an estimated 71 percent of Mormons voted for Trump to remain in office, a ten-point increase from 2016. White Mormons were nearly

The Mormon Tabernacle Choir performs at Donald Trump's presidential inauguration on January 20, 2017.

as likely to support Trump as White evangelicals. This support did not fizzle following Joe Biden's victory or the insurrection at the Capitol. A Public Religion Research Institute study the following spring determined that 46 percent of Mormons believed Trump's lie that the election was stolen, which placed them only behind White Evangelicals, at 61 percent. Among those who stormed the Capitol on January 6 was Nathan Entrekin, a Mormon from Arizona who dressed as Captain Moroni and waved a "Banner of Liberty"; he associated the Democrats with the evil "Kingmen" in the Book of Mormon, deceivers devoted to destroying democracy.[40]

Political violence was not entirely new to the Mormon tradition. Several Latter-day Saints with radical libertarian leanings in the West had challenged federal authorities in recent years. In 2014 rancher Cliven Bundy led an armed standoff with troops in southeastern Nevada due to a dispute over grazing fees. Two years later his son, Ammon, named for a Book of Mormon figure, occupied

Among those who participated in the insurrection at the US Capitol was Nathan Wayne Entrekin, a Latter-day Saint from Arizona. Entrekin dressed up as Captain Moroni, a character from the Book of Mormon. He eventually pleaded guilty to disorderly conduct, among other charges, and was sentenced to forty-five days in jail.

the Malheur National Wildlife Refuge in rural Oregon. The conflict lasted for over a month, and one of Bundy's followers, Robert LaVoy Finicum, was killed by federal authorities while resisting arrest. There are also a growing number of Mormon survivalist communities, especially in Idaho, who are preparing for a coming apocalypse, both political and biblical. Many cite the teachings of Ezra Taft Benson as evidence for a global cabal seeking to destroy their liberties. These extreme right-wing groups claim to be the "true" Mormons even as they operate on the institution's fringe.[41]

Many saints have pushed back against these libertarian factions as well as the Make America Great Again coalition. A group of women formed Mormon Women for Ethical Government, an echo of the nineteenth-century Mormon feminists who addressed issues they felt were both moral and urgent. Even Latter-day Saint leaders decried the extremes emblematic of the Trump era. Dallin H. Oaks indirectly denounced the Capitol insurrection in General Conference three months after it took place. "Sovereign power of the people," he chastised, "does not mean that mobs and other groups of people can intervene to intimidate or force government action."[42]

Mormon politicians have been divided on how to handle the moment. Some have modeled a so-called "Utah way," a "compassionate" conservatism more reminiscent of a George W. Bush–led GOP. Mitt Romney, elected a Utah senator in 2018, was the only Republican to vote for Trump's impeachment in 2020; he has remained one of the former president's most vocal and consistent critics. Yet Utah's other Mormon senator, Mike Lee, fully embraced Trump's claims and policies, and urged saints in 2020 to support the modern "Captain Moroni." Rusty Bowers, a Mormon Republican who served as Arizona's House Speaker, refused to support Trump's attempt to overturn the state's electoral results. When called to testify before the US House Select Committee to Investigate the January 6th Attack, his defense cited Mormon lore of saving the "divine" Constitution from its opponents. "The funny thing is," Bowers quipped, "I always thought it would be the other guys." Members from his own party protested at his home for weeks. Bowers was unseated in the next primary election by David Farnsworth. Like Bowers,

Farnsworth was a Mormon; unlike Bowers, Farnsworth supported Trump's "big lie."[43]

Deeper political divisions are found between generations. A 2020 survey revealed that while 80 percent of Mormons over the age of forty voted for Trump, only 43 percent of those below forty did. Indeed, Mormon millennials exhibited much more progressive views than their predecessors, with only 46 percent leaning Republican, a figure that paled in comparison to young Mormon voters only a decade earlier. Animated by issues like social justice, racial equality, and gender rights—and building on long-standing Mormon support for immigration—the rising generation of saints appears anxious to take the "Mormon vote" in new directions. Digital technologies and social media have enabled Latter-day Saint liberals to organize as a minority faction within a minority religion. And yet the very topic that appears most animating among Mormon millennials— gender and sexuality—is increasingly the hill on which the modern LDS institution is willing to fight, making their long-term prospects within the faith an open question.[44]

The long road that led to the seemingly irreversible Mormon-Republican alliance was built over a century. It was made possible by a series of pragmatic compromises and cultural shifts. George Q. Cannon set the process in motion, J. Reuben Clark solidified its direction, Ezra Taft Benson shepherded its fulfillment, and Mitt Romney reaped its benefits. Not even Donald Trump could fracture its foundations. Yet while America's conservative coalition appears to have been predetermined from the start, it was always historically contingent on particular personalities and cultural influences.

The Latter-day Saint church's Conference Center, a massive theater-style auditorium that houses 21,000 people, had likely never seen a performance like that given on June 1, 2018. A multiracial choir dressed in blue, purple, green, maroon, and orange sang African spirituals as they swayed side by side and were accompanied by drums. Speakers from America, Africa, Brazil, and Haiti shared stories of God's influence and narrated the history of Black saints.

Though Mormon worship services typically prioritize reverence, this gathering's audience shouted and clapped. The climax came when Gladys Knight performed her own rendition of *West Side Story*'s "Somewhere," belting out, "We'll find a new way of living, we'll find a way of forgiving." President Nelson delivered the final marks, promising that "differences in culture, language, gender, race and nationality fade into insignificance as the faithful enter the covenant path and come unto our beloved redeemer." The audience offered a hearty "amen."[45]

The occasion was a fortieth-anniversary gala celebrating the end of the church's racial restriction. It was meant to represent how far the community had come since those with African heritage were barred from the faith's most sacred rituals. Zyon Smiley, a Black BYU alum, was thrilled with the "acknowledgement of historic black saints who were faithful in the gospel despite opposition from some members." Seeing their history on such a prominent stage was the fruition of decades of labor.[46]

Some could not help but highlight what was missing, however. Ever since Spencer W. Kimball announced the end to the policy, church officials have refused to offer an apology for the pain it had caused. For some leaders it is a matter of principle. "The history of the church is not to seek apologies or to give them," Dallin H. Oaks remarked. He insisted that the word *apology* does not even appear in scripture. His position is rooted in a broader anxiety among White Americans. Many refuse to address the historic problem of racism because it shatters the myth of an idyllic past and highlights how some have benefited from a system of privilege. Instead of facing these terrible truths, James Baldwin frequently argued, White Americans cling to the "lie" of national innocence. These tensions are especially acute in the Latter-day Saint context. Acknowledging the racism inherent in past institutional policies opens the question of prophetic fallibility and undercuts authority in the present hierarchy.[47]

Choosing not to account for past racism has left significant theological questions unsettled. Despite one of the thirteen Gospel Topics essays documenting the historic, and human, origins of the restriction, three-quarters of Mormons polled in 2016 believed the ban was divinely inspired. Janan Graham-Russell, a Black scholar and convert raised by a Protestant mother and Muslim father, feared this lack of frank discussion perpetuated harm. "The seeming reluctance by some Mormon leaders to speak about the violence faced by its black members in the United States," she wrote, "has brought many black Mormons to points of frustration." Yet the institution's philosophy remains the same: look forward, build new relationships, and fulfill God's commands, but do not become enmeshed in the past.[48]

Lingering internal conflicts persist. Alice Faulkner Burch, Relief Society president for Genesis, the Black organization dating back to 1971, confessed in 2016 that "racism still exists and still has a tight grip within the LDS Church." Things became worse after Trump's election. One of the speakers at Charlottesville's deadly Unite the Right rally in August 2017, the most notorious gathering of White supremacists in modern American history, was Ayla Stewart, a Mormon blogger. Stewart was part of a growing chorus of Mormon alt-right figures who wedded the racism of Trump's movement with Latter-day Saint beliefs. They called themselves #DezNat, short for Deseret Nationalism, on Twitter. Darius Gray, one of Genesis's founders, in 2022 bemoaned having witnessed a "resurgence of insensitive comments and attitudes the likes of which I have never experienced before." The Public Religion Research Institute's Structural Racism Index in 2022 found that Mormons ranked only behind White evangelicals in perpetuating White supremacy and racial inequality.[49]

Religious leaders throughout the nation were forced to do more to reckon with America's racist history after a series of protests during the summer of 2020. The Latter-day Saint church was not immune. The First Presidency had already released a statement following the Charlottesville rally denouncing members "who promote or pursue a 'white culture' or white supremacy agenda." Then, in the October 2020 conference following the Black Lives Matter demonstrations, Nelson delivered one of the most pointed anti-racism addresses ever delivered by a Latter-day Saint president. He expressed grief that "our Black brothers and sisters the world over are enduring the pains of racism and prejudice," and he urged saints to help heal the world from racist ills. Speaking at BYU a few weeks later, Oaks proclaimed that all forms of racism must be "rooted out," and even endorsed "Black Lives Matter" as a "universally acceptable message." Notably, neither Oaks nor other leaders have walked back these messages following the conservative backlash against the Black Lives Matter movement. Indeed, Morehouse College awarded Nelson its inaugural Gandhi-King-Mandela Peace Prize in 2023 for his efforts toward "universal justice."[50]

It was saints of color, of course, who exerted the most effort for reform. "I have found solidarity among the often-weary voices of African American Mormons," Graham-Russell wrote, "who must work to affirm their spiritual and physical lives in a Church where those lives didn't always matter." Black students at BYU became especially bold in their agitation for change. Some highlighted how one of the school's founders, Abraham Smoot, owned enslaved people. Melodie Jackson, who served in BYU's Black Student Union, said that their administration building being still named after Smoot "meant that there was no place for blackness at that school." This sentiment mirrored a broader national discussion that saw numerous universities being forced to address their historic ties to slavery. Another group of social media–savvy students created a TikTok account titled "Black Menaces" that went viral for exposing entrenched racist, bigoted, and homophobic beliefs still prevalent among their classmates. "We know what's really happening here," said Kylee Shepherd, president of the Black Student Union in 2022, including "the names we've been called."[51]

Nor were African Americans the only non-White group making inroads. Though the church does not release demographic data, Latino Americans have likely made up a majority of Latter-day Saint converts in the past few decades. Hispanic immigrants often find solidarity within Latter-day Saint communities. Reyna Aburto, for instance, was born in Nicaragua in 1963 and immigrated to California in 1984 to escape violent unrest. Five years later, while struggling as a single mother with a three-year-old son, she felt warmth and joy when meeting members of the Mormon community. Aburto was soon baptized and moved to Utah to work as a translator. She became the first Hispanic woman to serve in the Relief Society presidency in 2017. The society was not "a Sunday lesson, an activity, or a presidency at the local or general level," she preached after five years of traveling the globe fulfilling numerous diplomatic missions, but "the covenant women of the Church." For hundreds of thousands of Latinx converts, Mormonism provided the covenant community needed to withstand life's trials.[52]

Aburto's call was just one example of recent moves to diversify church leadership. The higher levels of the Latter-day Saint hierarchy remained predominantly White and American for much of the church's existence, despite the faith's global reach. That began to change in the final decades of the twentieth century and first decade of the twenty-first when an increasing number of authorities were called from the Southern Hemisphere. But representation lagged behind for diverse members within the United States. Finally, in April 2019, Gerrit Gong, an Oxford-educated scholar of international relations, became the first Asian American and non-White apostle. Then, six months later, Peter Johnson became the first Black man born in the United States to speak in General Conference. Johnson, a convert from the Nation of Islam, taught accounting before becoming a General Authority Seventy, a leadership body just below the Quorum of the Twelve. Black saints were thrilled merely to hear his voice from the pulpit. Three years later Tracy Browning was appointed second counselor in the General Primary Presidency, the first Black woman to serve in any of the church's general presidencies.[53]

Indigenous saints also continue to seek ways of blending their faith with that of their ancestors. A group of BYU faculty, students, and alumni organized a roundtable in 2019 to address lingering Mormon theologies of colonialism in the form of Latter-day Saint reverence toward Columbus. While much of America fought over the colonist's bloody legacy, saints had a particularly complicated attachment: one Book of Mormon passage refers to a man being led by the "Spirit of God" to travel "upon the many waters." Many saints therefore believed Columbus fulfilled a divine mission. Yet this "doctrine of discovery," according to Diné scholar Farina King, is antithetical to the true gospel. Sacralizing stories of colonialism and conquest "have blinded and misled" members about "the complexities and realities of the past and their constant relevance to our present and future." Roni

Jo Draper, a Yurok professor at BYU, accused these ideas of providing a prophetic veneer to "an expression of white supremacy."[54]

The label that continued to symbolize cultural disconnect, however, was "Lamanite." As Lacee Harris had written decades before, Indigenous saints struggled to reconcile pride in their heritage with stereotypes prevalent within Mormon culture. Monika Brown Crowfoot, Navajo, recalled frequently being told by teachers that she must "forsake the incorrect traditions of our forefathers." While on a temple trip, her Navajo youth leader rubbed her arms and said, "I'm going to miss my brown skin when we get to the celestial kingdom." Crowfoot eventually determined that she could no longer be ashamed of her Indigenous ancestry. "I am not a Lamanite," she concluded, just as Harris had. Others chose to embrace ambiguity. Daniel Glenn Call, Aymara, said that while some interpret his being "Lamanite or Aymara or person of color as confusion," to him they were all parts of an intricate puzzle that comprised his life and faith. "Like Walt Whitman," Call posited, "I can lean into being a walking contradiction, happy with the multitudes of generations, lives, and longings that I carry in me." Mormonism often means embracing competing allegiances.[55]

That quest for shared burdens and full belonging has been around ever since the faith's founding. It was exhibited in Black Pete's ecstatic visions in Kirtland, Jane Manning James's pleading for temple rituals in Salt Lake City, and Lacee Harris's attempts at assimilation at BYU. It will likely persist, too, as the church becomes increasingly non-White and non-American. Deciphering the faith's doctrinal core while shedding its racial baggage remains a constant part of the Mormon experience.

CHELSEA GIBBS attended BYU from 2008 to 2012, the very years the campus hosted its early LGBTQ-organization efforts. She cheered the protests and events, but did not feel comfortable coming out as a lesbian herself. Nor did she live openly once at the University of Southern California studying film and surrounded by more queer students. It was not until after the summer of 2015, when the Supreme Court legalized same-sex marriages nationwide, that Gibbs felt an "optimistic wave of change" that seemed "inevitable even for the LDS Church." That September she attended the international meeting for Affirmation, the support institution for LGBTQ Mormons, and reveled in the solidarity. "The rainbow ceiling felt shattered and we didn't have to be quiet anymore," she recalled, as "everyone at the conference felt like pioneers whose time had come." It was a fair assumption: one study found that in the year following the Supreme Court decision, Mormon opposition to same-sex marriage dropped precipitously.[56]

The moment of joy was almost immediately followed by devastation. Less than two months later, on November 5, news leaked that Latter-day Saint leadership had updated their policies regarding same-sex unions. The church handbook now specified "same-gender marriage" as an act of "apostasy" that necessitated a disciplinary council. Further, it included a new section stating that any "natural or adopted child of a parent living in a same-gender relationship" would not be eligible to be blessed as an infant or baptized as an eight-year-old.[57]

These new policies were immediately decried by the faith's LGBTQ community and its allies. Gibbs, "unable to wrap my head around the fact that it could possibly be true," numbly scrolled through social media reactions. The same friends she had met just two months earlier were now announcing their resignations. Gibbs could not blame them. Suddenly the church in which she had gained comfort throughout her life "felt inherently distancing," and the members with whom she had worshipped "like another species." She eventually decided there was no longer any space for her, either.[58]

The origins of these policies, some of the most controversial in modern Mormonism, are difficult to determine. There had previously been inconsistency in how bishops and stake presidents handled homosexual families, and some wondered if same-sex relations might be treated differently once legally recognized. Churches across the nation scrambled to adapt to a new reality in which homosexuality was not only legal but firmly embraced by younger generations. Recognizing that banning homosexual unions was no longer possible, LDS leaders, like many conservative churches, turned their attention to two fronts. First, they ceased opposing laws that granted gay rights in return for securing legal privileges that afforded religious institutions to govern their own members' sexuality. This resulted in what came to be known as the "Utah Compromise," legislation that was, at least initially, believed to balance LGBTQ liberties and religious freedom. Dallin Oaks became particularly vociferous in claiming that the one cannot be achieved without the other.[59]

The second emphasis was on reaffirming boundaries within the church. If the "world" was going to embrace the queer community, it was even more important to draw a stark contrast. Some senior leaders pushed to draw a clear line of exclusion, crafting policies that mimicked how they handled modern-day fundamentalists. It has never been precisely determined who pushed this extreme approach. Some speculation, however, pointed to Russell M. Nelson, who had just become president of the Quorum of the Twelve following Boyd K. Packer's death earlier that year; Nelson certainly became the policies' most adamant defender in the years following. Several reports even claimed that the changes were pushed through so quickly that other leaders could not offer revisions, let alone express discomfort.[60]

Regardless of the policies' origins, their release proved exceptionally slapdash. The Public Affairs Department, which carefully choreographs every major announcement, was caught off guard. Many in the department first learned about the changes through news reports. They hastily organized an interview between Todd Christofferson, an apostle, and Michael Otterson, the managing director of public affairs. Christofferson, whose brother is a prominent gay member of the faith, was visibly uncomfortable while defending the actions.[61]

The backlash was immediate and urgent. Thousands of members attended a mass resignation event the next week, and national media reported a large wave of young saints fleeing the faith. Polling the next year determined that only 40 percent of millennial members backed the new policies. In response, Nelson felt it necessary a few months later to reaffirm that the changes came through "revelation"; yet the fact that Nelson's address was removed from the church's website shortly thereafter hinted at lingering ambivalence.[62]

The extreme policies eventually proved too controversial. Oaks announced less than four years later that they were walking back the provision that treated same-sex couples as "apostasy" as well as the prohibition on their children being baptized. In a rare concession to the broader culture, Oaks admitted that the retraction was in part "to reduce the hate and contention so common today." Nelson later defended the original policies' revelatory status while also celebrating their reversal by claiming that both actions were "motivated by love."[63]

LGBTQ saints continued to agitate for a more welcoming space within the church. Matt Easton, a BYU valedictorian, made national headlines in April 2019 when he came out as "proud to be a gay son of God" in his commencement speech. He wanted to let other queer members know that they, too, were worthy of divine love. The message was personal for Easton. A classmate of his, Harry Fisher, had committed suicide just a few years earlier when unable to reconcile his faith and sexuality. Indeed, a string of studies showed that LGBTQ Mormons suffered a higher risk of depression and suicide. The group Mama Dragons, a collection of Mormon mothers with gay children, claimed that at least thirty-two young LGBTQ saints had taken

Matt Easton participating in a protest supporting queer students at BYU on April 12, 2019. Two weeks later, at BYU's graduation ceremony, Easton declared he was proud to be a "gay son of God" in his valedictory address. PHOTOGRAPH BY RICK EGAN

their lives in the months following the November 2015 policies. In response, the church released a new website focused on mental health resources. Several other initiatives, like Encircle, which focused on providing shelter for evicted LGBTQ youth, and the LoveLoud Festival, a music event hosted by Dan Reynolds, delivered additional support. Both groups received church approval and funding. Still, many gay saints concluded that their future was outside the fold.[64]

These tensions have been exceptionally poignant for those who identify as transgender. Oaks confessed in 2015 that "while we have been acquainted with lesbians and homosexuals for some time," the "unique problems of a transgender situation" were not something they had yet codified. This was not completely true—the church's handbook already stipulated that transgender men could not be ordained to the priesthood—but it did reflect a growing concern across American culture. As gay rights were increasingly protected in the nation, many activists, religious leaders, and politicians turned their attention to transsexuality. Pope Francis, for instance, caused news in early 2015 when he embraced a transgender man whom he had invited to the Vatican.[65]

Yet if homosexual unions were seen as a challenge to Latter-day Saint theologies of the family, the gender fluidity associated with transgender identities was even more of a threat. The family proclamation insisted that "gender is eternal," a concept that, in many Mormon minds, appeared at odds with attempts to disrupt a gender binary. The topic soon became a divisive one in the culture wars, with many conservatives denouncing actions ranging from multigender bathrooms to identifying pronouns. Finally, in 2019, Oaks addressed the same question he previously left unanswered when he closed the door on any form of acceptance. "The intended meaning of 'gender' in the family proclamation," he told a gathering of leaders, is "biological sex at birth."[66]

The statement angered the growing number of transgender Mormons. Laurie Hall, who had previously been a stake president and was the architect of several temples, was excommunicated when she refused to stop living as a woman. She believed that gender was eternal but insisted that she was born in the wrong body. Hall accused Oaks of "warp[ing] the family proclamation" to his political bias. Other saints offered their own solutions. Naji Haska Runs Through, born the fifth child to an Assiniboine family, rejected both the labels "transsexual" and "gay," instead identifying as *wikita*, an Indigenous term for "two-spirit." They mixed both ancestral and religious ideas into a usable solution. "I am taught that a man and a woman complete each other," Runs Through mused, so "if I already have both a male and female spirit inside me," then have they already fulfilled their destiny? Despite not feeling welcome in the church's culture, their spirituality made it difficult to leave entirely. So they remained uncertain about their future in a faith that seemed to provide some tools for understanding gender's complexities but a culture that circumscribed answers.[67]

And still some transgender pioneers continued to blaze a trail. Kris Irvin, who admitted that anguish over sexual identity had caused suicidal ideation since the age of five, pleaded with leaders to consider a more expansive theology and inclusive policy. "President Oaks," they wrote in a *Salt Lake Tribune* editorial, "we stand outside the door to the Church and knock. Will you let us in?" About eight months before their untimely death, Irvin authored a poem that tied transgender issues to Heavenly Mother, the same theological concept that has so often served as a cultural touchstone:

> Do you think
> our Mother
> held Her nonbinary children
> for just a moment longer as we said
> goodbye?
> Do you think She wept
> to know that like Her,
> We, too, would be forgotten
> Pushed to the fringes of doctrine?
> Does She sigh
> Knowing that
> Her identity, and ours,
> Are intrinsically misunderstood?
> Do you think our Mother
> walks a little closer

to those unchained by gender?
Whispering to us
"It's all right, my child,
I understand.
Men have hidden me too."

From Eliza R. Snow's ruminations in the 1840s to Kris Irvin's pleading in the 2020s, Heavenly Mother remained a platform for exploring
Mormonism's gendered imagination.[68]

JEFFREY R. HOLLAND, a Yale-credentialed educator who had been
an apostle since 1994, stood before BYU's faculty and staff on August
23, 2021. The stage was set in the sprawling Marriott Center, home to
the university's basketball teams. He expressed his love for the school,
over which he had presided during the 1980s, but voiced a warning
that it was losing its way. Some in the community, he warned, felt
"abandoned and betrayed" by professors who were "supporting ideas
that many of us feel are contradictory to gospel principles." He specifically disapproved of how a student had "commandeer[ed]" the
graduation podium to "announce his personal sexual orientation,"
and denounced "language, symbols, and situations that are more
divisive than unifying." The former reference was to Matt Easton's
2019 valedictory address, and the latter was to objects like rainbow
stickers and other signals for LGBTQ support. BYU professors were
expected to not only support but champion "the doctrine of the family and defending marriage as the union of a man and a woman."

The apostle, otherwise known for his compassionate rhetoric,
then invoked a surprising analogy. While drawn from the Latter-day
Saint tradition, it bordered on dangerous for an era of rising right-
wing violence and anti-LGBTQ bigotry. Holland recalled how those
who built the Nauvoo Temple did so "with a trowel in one hand and
a musket in the other," a core memory of when the faith was in an
armed conflict with its Illinois neighbors. He hoped modern saints
would resurrect that devoted allegiance: "I would like to hear a little
more musket fire from this temple of learning." In the same address

On the one-year anniversary of BYU students lighting up the famous *Y* on Provo's mountainside in rainbow colors, BYU officials blocked off the area to prevent further demonstrations. PHOTOGRAPH BY CORTNEY HUBER

that discouraged "divisive" language, Holland used the rhetoric of war to call for reinforcements.

While many members circled the wagons, others chose another route. A little over a year after Holland's address, David Archuleta, the famous pop singer who had been vocal about his attempt to reconcile his faith and his sexuality, announced he had left the church. When apostles and other church leaders failed to adequately address his concerns, the resulting "faith crisis" led him to new sources for truth and spirituality.[69]

One of the reasons the Church of Jesus Christ of Latter-day Saints has proved to be so resilient and successful is its ability to provide a narrative of continuity while constantly adapting to new circumstances. Religions thrive when they transform with time but still convince followers they never change. Latter-day Saint leaders have been able to forfeit previously central doctrines—polygamy, theocracy, racial restriction—while simultaneously proclaiming compliance with eternal laws that never bend. Many observers wonder, then, if the faith will once again shift away from cultural allegiances that currently appear unshakable: right-wing politics, theological ortho-doxy, and social conservatism, particularly in matters concerning gender and sexuality. History has shown that even the most unlikely outcomes can eventually become possible.

Some elements for change are indeed present. Just as Mormonism faced intense pressure in the 1880s over polygamy and in the 1970s over the racial restriction, the church now faces pressure in the 2020s to change its stance on same-sex marriage. This push comes from external forces, with LGBTQ organizations labeling the Latter-day Saint church as a hate group, as well as internal: BYU students in 2021 protested the school's LGBTQ policies by lighting the *Y* with rainbow colors; a year later, a *Deseret News* study found that 58 per-cent of active saints, including 89 percent of Utah residents in the eighteen-to-twenty-four-year-old range, believed same-sex unions should be legal. Whether leaders recognize it or not, the war over preserving "traditional" marriage has already been lost.[70]

Yet the Latter-day Saint church is in a novel position compared to previous points of crisis. While it certainly has a growing number of critics, it also has a firm coalition of allies. The groups who make up the modern religious right are similarly fighting against LGBTQ acceptance, women's equality, social reform, racial justice, and sec-ular truths. Latter-day Saint authorities will see no need to surren-der the fight as long as they are not fighting alone. The battle they are waging is not between Mormons and America, as the dividing lines are now *within* America. Their temples are not under threat of being seized, their tax exemptions are not at risk of being revoked, and they are not vulnerable to being cast as a pariah. The same cul-tural currents that launched Latter-day Saint society on this trajec-tory have also made it nearly impossible—or at least difficult—to change directions.

So long as the church is ensconced within a powerful cultural bloc that enables the stability, privileges, and backing indicative of an assimilated and sanctioned community—indeed, the benefits that the Latter-day Saint tradition has long sought—they will be unlikely to reach the tipping point necessary for change.

EPILOGUE

Longing for Zion

And Enoch and all his people walked with God and he dwellt in the midst of Zion and it came to pass that Zion was not for God received it up into his own bosom and from thence went forth the saying Zion is fled.

—JOSEPH SMITH'S REVISION TO
THE BOOK OF GENESIS[1]

"ZION," AS AN IDEAL, has been a central principle for the Church of Jesus Christ of Latter-day Saints since its inception. God's people were called to establish Zion, a celestial community too pure for the earth and therefore worthy of exaltation. Zion required sanctification; Zion's people were of one heart and one mind. Enoch's people achieved Zion in the Old Testament, and the Nephites nearly did so in the Book of Mormon. Joseph Smith's followers made building Zion their primary goal, joining the biblical Israelites gathered near the "rivers of Babylon" who "wept" as they "remembered Zion" (Psalm 137:1).

Latter-day Saints still weep for Zion.

The story of Mormonism in America is the story of the changing parameters of American religion. The faith founded by Joseph Smith tested the boundaries of religious liberty socially, as when his followers were evicted by a state-licensed mob, legally, as when polygamy clarified the judicial limits for religious practice, and politically, as when modern saints worked with the religious right to define national values in an age of partisan fracture. Their history reveals the deep and persisting power that religion wields in American culture, for good and ill. Conversely, this drama also reveals the many ways, both subtle and explicit, that American culture creates and shapes the religion, a tradition reliant on both secular and spiritual influences as it evolves with each generation, always bearing the marks of its surroundings while simultaneously appealing for transcendence.

The Mormon faith was born from a desire to address problems that society seemed unable to solve. Scripture, revelation, prophetic pronouncements, priesthood authority—these are testaments to a yearning for divine finality. For Zion. Democracy provides a license for freedom but also produces an anarchy of possibilities. Believers find strength in the doctrine that God cuts through the morass of opinions to reveal truth, to uncover bedrock. "Lo here," cried the ministers of Joseph Smith's day; "lo there," cry the competing factions today. Mormonism is an attempt to find facts in a world of fictions, certainty in a realm of distrust, belonging in a sphere of disunion, permanence in an age of transience, a longing to slay the demon of emptiness and confusion as if the adversary were reachable and could be killed.[2]

ACKNOWLEDGMENTS

THIS BOOK WOULD not have happened were it not for Bob Weil and Dan Gerstle having enough faith in me to pitch the project in the first place. Giles Anderson, as always, made sure the deal worked in my favor. Dan then lived up to his reputation as the best editor in the field. Sarah Johnson was a phenomenal copyeditor. I also appreciate Zeba Arora and the production and marketing teams. Liveright has proved to be an author's dream, and I remain both surprised and grateful to be part of their literary family.

The fact that there is an Atlantic-sized ocean of scholarship on Mormon history is both the field's strength and what makes it so daunting. So many historians have produced articles and books that are crucial to understanding the faith's past that it is impossible to list even a fraction of them. While word restrictions meant that only those works upon which I directly drew are cited in the endnotes, I could have cited hundreds, if not thousands, more. I am therefore thankful to the community of scholars who are hopefully as forgiving as they are brilliant.

Attempting to cover such a broad chronology in so few pages is a fool's quest, but it is made less egregious only with the help of specialists who provide feedback, suggestions, and needed corrections. The following individuals read at least one chapter and offered critiques based on their expertise: Gary Bergera, Barbara Jones Brown, Calvin Burke, Sarah Barringer Gordon, Dave Hall, Robin Jensen, Janiece Johnson, Adam Jortner, Hannah Jung, Patrick Mason, Spencer McBride, Jessica Nelson, Lindsay Hansen Park, Ardis Parshall, Sara Patterson, Taylor Petrey, Paul Reeve, Brent Rogers, Cristina Rosetti, Kerry Spencer, Joey Stuart, Lisa Tait, and Colby Townsend. Elise Boxer and Jane Hafen kindly helped me understand important Indigenous elements. Participants in the best writing group never to be named—Rick Bell, Lindsay Chervinski, Robert Elder, and Megan Kate Nelson—tore apart my prose and assumptions to make this a more readable and understandable book. And above everyone else, Christopher Jones and Jenny Reeder deserve the highest honors for reading and critiquing the entire manuscript. As much as I'd like to blame any of these individuals for mistakes that remained in the manuscript, those faults are more likely due to my own stubbornness.

Writing a book during a pandemic provided both obstacles and opportunities. Unable to visit archives for over a year, I was fortunate to enlist the help of Ardis Parshall, the best researcher Mormonism has ever claimed. Her supplemental mining was crucial to broadening my scope and fleshing out the narrative. Once the archives opened again, I was benefited by the help of the LDS Church History Library, especially Jennifer Barkdull, who responded to my numerous requests and assisted me on an extended research trip. I later sent a complete manuscript to Bryan Buchanan, the community's foremost antiquarian, to spot any errors, both substantive and benign. This book would have been much worse without the help of these devoted diggers.

Several scholars have helped teach me, through both mentorship and example, how to be a historian. I will always be grateful to Grant Underwood, Paul Kerry, Stewart Brown, Frank Cogliano, Sarah Pearsall, Jeffrey Pasley, Joanna Brooks, Laurie Maffly-Kipp, Sally Gordon, Annette Gordon-Reed, Richard Bushman, and the late Michael O'Brien for sticking with me through the years. And the *Juvenile Instructor* team continues to be my favorite circle of overspecialized nerds.

Serving as coeditor of *Mormon Studies Review* has been the perfect perch from which to view the field, for two reasons. First, I have learned from so many brilliant scholars who are pushing our community in new directions. And second, I have labored with one of academia's best, Quincy Newell, who is not only a gifted historian but a magnificent person.

Sam Houston State University has been a wonderful academic home due to the people with whom I get to work. Brian Jordan is the best chair, colleague, and friend I could ask for. Chien-pin Li has been a very supportive dean. A department fund, enabled by the legendary James Olson, made it possible to include so many images. It has truly been an honor—albeit a taxing one—to serve as director of graduate studies and get to know all our wonderful students. And my fellow faculty continue to inspire me with their wit and generosity.

I first learned to love Mormon history from my mother, Melanie, who taught me how to appreciate my heritage while also accounting for any shortcomings. My father, Richard, demonstrated the virtues of an indomitable work ethic and insatiable curiosity. I look up to my brothers, Spencer, Jared, and Abe, more than they know. My grandmother, Arlene, has always demonstrated the best of the Mormon tradition. Catherine, as always, has been both supportive and a reminder of what matters. And finally, this book is dedicated to my two children, Sara and Curtis, who continually inspire me to be a better person and fight for a better world.

APPENDIX:
KEY CHARACTERS

Helen Andelin (1920–2009): housewife whose best-selling book *Fascinating Womanhood* both drew from and shaped Latter-day Saint ideas of domesticity.

Leonard Arrington (1917–99): historian who taught at Utah State University before becoming church historian in 1972. He led a new generation of scholars intent on digging into the faith's past.

Ezra Taft Benson (1899–1994): apostle (1943–85) and president (1985–94) of the Latter-day Saint church. Known for his strong anti-communist views, he was influential in shaping modern Mormon conservatism.

Juanita Brooks (1898–1989): historian and author who challenged the church's traditional history while remaining firmly committed to the faith.

George Q. Cannon (1827–1901): apostle (1860–1901) who served both as a counselor in the First Presidency (1873–1901) and as delegate for Utah Territory (1873–82). One of the church's foremost spokesmen and most influential politicians in its entire history.

J. Reuben Clark (1871–1961): lawyer and civil servant with a successful diplomatic career, including as US ambassador to Mexico (1930–33), before becoming a member of the LDS First Presidency (1933–61). Did more to shape the modern church as leader than any other figure.

Oliver Cowdery (1806–50): clerk and school teacher who became Joseph Smith's primary scribe for the Book of Mormon. Served in various leadership positions before being excommunicated in 1838. Was rebaptized in 1848 but never joined the church in Utah.

Eugene England (1933–2001): literature scholar who taught at BYU from 1976 until his forced resignation in 1998. Cofounder of *Dialogue: A Journal of Mormon Thought* in 1966.

Darius Gray (1945–): Black writer and speaker. One of the founding leaders of Genesis Group, a group designed to help fellowship Black saints in 1971.

Franklin Harris (1884–1960): agronomy professor who became president of Brigham Young University in 1921, which he tried to reform before leaving to be president of Utah State University in 1945.

Lacee Harris (1944–2020): community leader and descendant of several generations of Ute Mormons. Wrote about attempts to reconcile Mormon and Native cultures.

Martin Harris (1783–1875): upstate New York farmer who volunteered to be scribe for the Book of Mormon and finance its publication. He was excommunicated in 1837 but was rebaptized in 1870.

Gordon B. Hinckley (1910–2008): apostle (1961–95) and president (1995–2008) of Latter-day Saint church. Helped usher in a more media-friendly era for the faith.

Zina Diantha Huntington (1821–1901): midwife and early convert to the church. Was first married to Henry B. Jacobs, but then became a plural wife of Joseph Smith and then, after Smith's death, a plural wife of Brigham Young. Held various leadership positions in the Relief Society before becoming its president (1888–1901).

Jane Manning James (1822–1908): early Black convert to Mormonism who migrated to Nauvoo in 1843 and lived in Joseph Smith's home. Later migrated with the saints to Utah. Remained faithful her entire life, though her appeals for access to temple rituals remained unheeded.

Sonia Johnson (1936–): feminist activist and writer who supported the Equal Rights Amendment. Was excommunicated by the church in 1979 for her public opposition to church leaders.

Amy Brown Lyman (1872–1959): reformer who, after joining the Relief Society board in 1909, was a key figure in the organization for three decades. Later served as a state legislator (1923) as well as the Relief Society's general president (1940–45). Wife of apostle Richard Lyman.

Bruce R. McConkie (1915–85): prominent author, speaker, and apostle (1972–85). Son-in-law of Joseph Fielding Smith, and outspoken advocate for a conservative Mormon theology and culture.

David O. McKay (1873–1970): educator and administrator who served as an apostle (1906–51), counselor in the First Presidency (1934–51), and church president (1951–70). His tenure as leader marked massive growth for the faith worldwide and influence in America.

Sterling McMurrin (1914–96): liberal theologian and philosopher who taught at the University of Utah and served as John F. Kennedy's commissioner of education (1961–62). Mourned and denounced the church's conservative move during the mid-twentieth century.

Russell M. Nelson (1924–): accomplished surgeon who served as apostle (1984–2018) and is currently president (2018–) of the church.

Dallin H. Oaks (1932–): law professor, Utah Supreme Court justice, and apostle (1984–) who is known for conservative social views.

Boyd K. Packer (1924–2015): educator and administrator who served as an apostle (1970–2015). Known for his conservative social views and dogmatic beliefs, he frequently and vociferously denounced progressive ideas and activists.

Emily Dow Partridge (1824–99): daughter of early converts and leaders Edward and Lydia Partridge. Became a plural wife of Joseph Smith and then, after Smith's death, Brigham Young. Her daughter, Caroline, became a plural wife to George Q. Cannon.

Phebe Pendleton (1797–1868): convert who left her adult children when she moved to Utah in 1851. Became a plural wife to Jeremiah Woodbury. Her letters to her children offer an unrivaled view of Utah during the mid-nineteenth century.

Parley Parker Pratt (1807–57): prominent author, missionary, and apostle (1835–55) who was the faith's most prominent minister for its first three decades.

D. Michael Quinn (1944–2021): historian and professor who taught at BYU and hid his homosexuality. His historical research caused friction with church leaders, resulting in his forced resignation in 1988 and excommunication in 1993.

Sidney Rigdon (1793–1876): popular minister whose baptism in 1830 brought an entire congregation into the new faith. Served as either assistant president or counselor in First Presidency (1832–44). Challenged Brigham Young as chief successor to Joseph Smith.

B. H. Roberts (1857–1933): author, politician, and church leader whose historical and theological works helped shape Progressive Era Mormonism more than anyone else.

Emma Hale Smith (1804–79): wife of Joseph Smith who supported the faith's development even as she rejected certain elements, most notably polygamy. After her husband's death, supported rivals to Brigham Young's authority, eventually endorsing her son, Joseph Smith III, as the tradition's rightful president.

Hyrum Smith (1800–44): brother of Joseph Smith and son of Joseph Sr. and Lucy Mack Smith. Served as assistant president or counselor in First Presidency (1837–44). After his first wife, Jerusha Barden, died, married Mary Fielding Smith, who gave birth to Joseph F. Smith. Died with Joseph Smith at Carthage Jail.

Joseph F. Smith (1838–1918): son of Hyrum and Mary Fielding Smith, father of Joseph Fielding Smith, served as apostle (1866–1901) and president (1901–18) of Latter-day Saint church. Oversaw the faith's initial assimilation into American culture, including the end of post-manifesto polygamy and the election of Senator Reed Smoot.

Joseph Fielding Smith (1876–1972): son of Joseph F. Smith, served as apostle (1910–70) and church historian (1921–70) before becoming church president (1970–72). His conservative views on theology and history influenced many in the modern church.

Joseph Smith Jr. (1804–44): son of Joseph Sr. and Lucy Mack Smith. First elder of the Church of Christ, translator of the Book of Mormon, founding prophet of the Mormon tradition. Husband to Emma Smith, father of Joseph Smith III.

Joseph Smith Sr. (1771–1840): farmer, teacher, and cooper. Husband of Lucy Mack Smith, father of Joseph and Hyrum Smith. After being a spiritual wanderer for most of his life, embraced his son's church and became its first patriarch.

Joseph Smith III (1832–1914): son of Joseph Jr. and Emma Hale Smith. Became president of the Reorganized Church of Jesus Christ of Latter Day Saints in 1860, which, among other foundational beliefs, rejected the notion that Joseph Jr. practiced polygamy.

Lucy Mack Smith (1775–1856): wife of Joseph Sr. and mother of Joseph Jr. and Hyrum Smith. Earnest religious seeker who later dictated a memoir that remains one of the most important records for the church's earliest years.

Mary Fielding Smith (1801–52): wife of Hyrum Smith and mother of Joseph F. Smith. Her pioneer spirt exemplified the faith's sacrifice during the era and influenced her son's later leadership.

Reed Smoot (1862–1941): politician, businessman, and apostle (1900–41). His election to the US Senate in 1903 sparked a national debate over whether Mormons could ever be trusted as loyal Americans.

Eliza R. Snow (1804–87): poet, author, and most prominent Mormon woman for most of the nineteenth century. Was a plural wife to both Joseph Smith and then, after Smith's death, Brigham Young. Served as general president of the Relief Society (1866–87).

Belle Spafford (1895–1982): longest-serving president of the Relief Society (1945–74) in the church's history. Helped reframe the society as an "appendage to the priesthood," and reinforced women's domestic duties.

John Taylor (1808–87): English-born convert who served as apostle (1838–80) and president (1880–87) of the church. Taylor's devotion to the principle of plural marriage led to a conflict between the church and the federal government.

Laurel Thatcher Ulrich (1938–): historian and professor who was part of a feminist movement starting in the 1970s to challenge patriarchal ideas and practices.

Emmeline Wells (1828–1921): author, journalist, and women's rights advocate who edited the pro-suffrage *Woman's Exponent* for nearly four decades. Her simultaneous support for polygamy and woman suffrage bewildered contemporary observers. She later served as general president of the Relief Society (1910–21).

Wilford Woodruff (1807–98): early convert who served as an apostle (1839–89) and president (1889–98) of the church. As president, made the decision to publicly forfeit polygamy in order to halt federal prosecutions. His voluminous diaries are among the most important records for nineteenth-century Mormonism.

NOTES

Abbreviations

A1H: Joseph Smith, draft history 1838–39, H1.

AP: Associated Press (New York), 1917–.

APP: Parley Pratt, *The Autobiography of Parley Parker Pratt* (New York: self-pub., 1874).

ATP: Jennifer Reeder and Kate Holbrook, *At the Pulpit: 185 Years of Discourses by Latter-day Saint Women* (Salt Lake City: Church Historian's Press, 2017).

BoM: The Book of Mormon (Palmyra, NY: Joseph Smith Jr., 1830).

BoMET: Royal Skousen, ed., *The Book of Mormon: The Earliest Text* (New Haven: Yale University Press, 2009).

BY: Brigham Young.

BYCD: Richard S. Van Wagoner, *The Complete Discourses of Brigham Young*, 5 vols. (Salt Lake City: Signature Books, 2009).

BYD: George D. Smith, ed. *Brigham Young: Colonizer of the American West; Diaries and Office Journals, 1832–1871*, 2 vols. (Salt Lake City: Signature Books, 2021).

BYOF: Brigham Young Office Files, CHL.

BYP: Brigham Young Papers Collection, CHL.

BYU: L. Tom Perry Special Collections, Harold B. Lee Library, Brigham Young University, Provo, UT.

BYUSQ: *Brigham Young University Studies Quarterly*, 1959–.

CBM: Century of Black Mormons, "Discover the Many Histories of Black Mormons," J. Willard Marriott Library, University of Utah, https://exhibits.lib.utah.edu/s/century-of-black-mormons.

CCLA: Community of Christ Library and Archives, Independence, MO.

CHL: LDS Church History Library, Salt Lake City, UT.

CN: *Church News* (Salt Lake City), 1931–.

CoC: Community of Christ Library and Archives, Independence, MO.

CR: *Conference Report* (Salt Lake City, UT), 1880–1970.

D&C: *The Doctrine and Covenants of the Church of Jesus Christ of Latter-day Saints.* (Salt Lake City: The Church of Jesus Christ of Latter-day Saints, 1981).

Dialogue: *Dialogue: A Journal of Mormon Thought.* Quarterly, 1966–.

DN: *Deseret News* (Salt Lake City), 1850–. (Names varied over years.)

DOMD: Harvard Heath, ed., *Confidence amid Change: The Presidential Diaries of David O. McKay, 1951–1970* (Salt Lake City: Signature Books, 2019).

EBW: Emmeline B. Wells.

EBWD: Emmeline B. Wells Diaries (Salt Lake City: Church Historian's Press), https://churchhistorianspress.org/emmeline-b -wells.

EMD: Dan Vogel, ed., *Early Mormon Documents*, 5 vols. (Salt Lake City: Signature Books, 1996–2003).

EMS: *The Evening and the Morning Star* (Independence, MO), 1832–34.

ERS: Eliza R. Snow.

ERSCP: Jill Mulvay Derr and Karen Lynn Davidson, eds., *Eliza R. Snow: The Complete Poetry* (Provo, UT: Brigham Young University Press, 2009).

ERSD: *The Discourses of Eliza R. Snow* (Salt Lake City: Church Historian's Press), https://churchhistorianspress.org/eliza-r-snow.

ERSJ: Eliza R. Snow Journals, CHL.

FPC: First Presidency Correspondence, 1847–77, 1877–87, CHL.

GASP: George Albert Smith Papers, CHL.

GCM: General Church Minutes, CHL.

GCP: Grover Cleveland Papers, CHL.

GQC: George Q. Cannon.

GQCD: *The Journal of George Q. Cannon* (Salt Lake City: Church Historian's Press), https://churchhistorianspress.org/george-q-cannon.

HFoF: Laurel Thatcher Ulrich, *A House Full of Females: Plural Marriage and Women's Rights in Early Mormonism, 1835–1870* (New York: Knopf, 2017).

HL: Huntington Library, Art Museum, and Botanical Gardens, San Marino, CA.

HOYP: Mark Staker, *Hearken, O Ye People: The Historical Setting of Joseph Smith's Ohio Revelations* (Salt Lake City: Kofford Books, 2009).

IE: *Improvement Era* (Salt Lake City), 1897–1970.

JB: Juanita Brooks.

JETJ: James E. Talmage Journals, BYU.

JFSP: Joseph F. Smith Papers, CHL.

JI: *Juvenile Instructor* (Salt Lake City), 1901–30.

JMH: *Journal of Mormon History.* Quarterly, 1974–.

JRC: J. Reuben Clark.

JRCP: J. Reuben Clark Papers, BYU.

JS: Joseph Smith.

JSP: Matthew C. Godfrey, R. Eric Smith, and Ronald K. Esplin, eds., *Joseph Smith Papers Project*, 27 vols. (Salt Lake City: Church Historian's Press, 2009–23). Volumes are referred to as Series:Volume, as in D:1 for "Documents: Volume 1." Series include Documents (D), Revelations and Translations (R), Histories (H), Administration (A). If unspecified, reference is to documents found on https://www.josephsmithpapers.org.

JWHAJ: *John Whitmer Historical Association Journal.* Biennial, 1981–.

LAT: *Los Angeles Times*, 1881–.

LB: Lavina Fielding Anderson, ed., *Lucy's Book: A Critical Edition of Lucy Mack Smith's Memoir* (Salt Lake City: Signature Books, 2001).

LDSGC: LDS General Conference database, https://www.churchof jesuschrist.org/study/general-conference.

LJAD: Gary Bergera, ed., *Confessions of a Mormon Historian: The Diaries of Leonard J. Arrington, 1971–1997* (Salt Lake City: Smith-Pettit, 2018).

M&A: *Messenger & Advocate* (Kirtland, OH), 1834–37.

ME: Linda King Newell and Valeen Tippets Avery, *Mormon Enigma: Emma Hale Smith*, 2nd ed. (Urbana: University of Illinois Press, 1994).

MF: Joanna Brooks, Rachel Hunt Steenblik, and Hannah Wheelwright, eds., *Mormon Feminism: Essential Writings* (New York: Oxford University Press, 2015).

MIAM: J. B. Haws, *The Mormon Image in the American Mind: Fifty Years of Public Perceptions* (New York: Oxford University Press, 2013).

MSR: *Mormon Studies Review*, 2013–.

MSS: Colleen McDannell, *Sister Saints: Mormon Women since the End of Polygamy* (New York: Oxford University Press, 2019).

MU: Eber D. Howe, *Mormonism Unvailed* (Painesville, OH: self-pub., 1834).

Newsroom: LDS Church Newsroom, https://www.newsroom.church ofjesuschrist.org.

NYT: *New York Times*, 1851–.

PP: John G. Turner, *Brigham Young: Pioneer Prophet* (Cambridge: Harvard University Press, 2012).

PPWL: Phebe Pendleton Woodbury Letters, 1851–67, CHL.

QCP: D. Michael Quinn, "Chosen Path," unpublished manuscript in Signature Books collection. Later published as *Chosen Path: A Memoir* (Salt Lake City: Signature Books, 2023).

RSD: Jill Mulvay Derr et al., eds., *The First Fifty Years of Relief Society: Key Documents in Latter-day Saint Women's History* (Salt Lake City: Church Historian's Press, 2016).

RSM: *Relief Society Magazine* (Salt Lake City), 1915–70.

RSR: Richard Lyman Bushman, *Joseph Smith: Rough Stone Rolling* (New York: Knopf, 2005).

S: *Saints: The Story of the Church of Jesus Christ in the Latter Days.* 3 vols. to date (Salt Lake City: Church Historian's Press, 2018–).

SGKC: Scott G. Kenney Collection, UofU.

SLJB: Craig S. Smith, ed., *The Selected Letters of Juanita Brooks* (Salt Lake City: University of Utah Press, 2019).

SLT: *Salt Lake Tribune* (Salt Lake City), 1870–. (Names varied over years.)

SoTLDS: James Allen and Glen Leonard, *The Story of the Latter-day Saints*, 2nd ed. (Salt Lake City: Deseret Book, 1992).

TNM: Jana Riess, *The Next Mormons: How Millennials Are Changing the LDS Church* (New York: Oxford University Press, 2019).

UofU: J. Willard Marriott Library Special Collections, University of Utah, Salt Lake City, UT.

USU: Special Collections and Archives, Utah State University, Logan, UT.

WoC: Jill Mulvay Derr, Janath Russell Cannon, and Maureen Ursenbach Beecher, *Women of Covenant: The Story of Relief Society* (Salt Lake City: Deseret Book, 1992).

WP: *Washington Post*, 1877–.

WWD: Wilford Woodruff Diaries, CHL online collection.

Epigraph

1. Edward Tullidge, "Views of Mormondom," *Galaxy* 2 (1866): 214.

A Note on Names and Narratives

1. Joseph Smith, discourse, July 23, 1843, in D12:493.
2. Newsroom, August 16, 2018.

Prologue: Faith and History

1. Trey Parker, Robert Lopez, and Matt Stone, "All American Prophet," track 7 on *The Book of Mormon: Original Broadway Cast Recording*, Ghostlight Records, 2011.
2. Joseph Smith, revelation, April 6, 1830, D1:129 [D&C 21:1].
3. Joseph Smith, revelation, March 8, 1831, D1:286 [D&C 47:1]. John Whitmer, "The Book of John, Whitmer kept by Comma[n]d," ca. 1838–ca. 1847, CCLA.
4. See Dan Vogel, ed., *History of Joseph Smith and the Church of Jesus Christ of Latter-day Saints: A Source and Text-Critical Edition*, 8 vols. (Salt Lake City: Smith-Pettit, 2015); "Introduction to History, 1838–1856 (Manuscript History of the Church)," JSP.
5. Joseph Fielding Smith, *Essentials in Church History: A History of the Church from the Birth of Joseph Smith until the Present Time* (Salt Lake City: Deseret News Press, 1922).
6. LJAD, August 9, 1982, 1:230. SoTLDS.
7. S1, S2, S3. As of this writing, the fourth and final volume was still in production.
8. Among the prominent leaders whose records have only recently been made available are Joseph Smith, George Q. Cannon, Eliza R. Snow, Emmeline B. Wells, Amy Brown Lyman, David O. McKay, Spencer W. Kimball, and Leonard J. Arrington.
9. One-volume histories include SoTLDS; Leonard J. Arrington and Davis Bitton, *The Mormon Experience: A History of the Latter-day Saints*, 2nd ed. (Urbana: University of Illinois Press, 1992); Richard Ostling and Joan Ostling, *Mormon America: The Promise and the Power*, rev. and updated ed. (New York: HarperOne, 2007); Matthew Bowman, *The Mormon People: The Making of an American Faith* (New York: Random House, 2012); K. Mohrman, *Exceptionally Queer: Mormon Peculiarity and U.S. Nationalism* (Minneapolis: University of Minnesota Press, 2022).
10. See Gordon Shepherd et al., *The Palgrave Handbook of Global Mormonism* (New York: Palgrave Macmillan, 2020); Melissa Wei-Tsing Inouye, "Busting the Silos of 'Global' Scholarship," MSR 10 (2023): 54–66. An important

intervention will be Laurie Maffly-Kipp, *Making Zion: A History of Global Mormonism* (New York: Basic Books, forthcoming).

11. Steven Shields, *Divergent Paths of the Restoration: An Encyclopedia of the Smith-Rigdon Movement*, 5th ed. (Salt Lake City: Signature Books, 2022).

12. JS to Israel Daniel Rupp, June 5, 1844, JSP.

Chapter 1: A Visionary Nation, 1775–1830

1. *Millennial Harbinger* (Bethany, WV), February 1831.

2. JS, revelation, April 6, 1830, D1:129 [D&C 21:1]. Citations for Joseph Smith's revelations will be to earliest sources as reproduced in JSP, with modern scriptural references in brackets.

3. LB, 477. Dean C. Jessee, "Joseph Knight's Recollection of Early Mormon History," BYUSQ 17, no. 1 (1976): 11.

4. Ralph Waldo Emerson, "The Present Age" (1840), in Robert Richardson, *Emerson: The Mind on Fire* (Berkeley: University of California Press, 1995), 333. Francis Trollope, *Domestic Manners of the Americans* (London: Whittaker, Treacher, & Co., 1832), 99.

5. Ralph Waldo Emerson, *The Collected Works of Ralph Waldo Emerson*, 5 vols., ed. Robert Spiller and Alfred Ferguson (Cambridge: Harvard University Press, 1971–94), 2:166.

6. LB, 277–78. Smith's dating of this event is somewhat unclear, and it may have been 1803.

7. Solomon Mack, *Narrative of the Life of Solomon Mack* (Windsor, VT: self-pub., 1811), 19. LB, 51, 230–31, 236–39.

8. Thomas Jefferson to Benjamin Waterhouse, June 26, 1822, in *Jefferson: Writings* (New York: Library of America, 1984), 1459.

9. For general surveys of the era, see Nathan Hatch, *The Democratization of American Christianity* (New Haven: Yale University Press, 1989); Jon Butler, *Awash in a Sea of Faith: Christianizing the American People* (Cambridge: Harvard University Press, 1990); Amanda Porterfield, *Conceived in Doubt: Religion and Politics in the New American Nation* (Chicago: University of Chicago Press, 2012).

10. LB, 291. Tunbridge (VT) Universalist Society record, December 6, 1797, in EMD, 1:633–34. RSR, 14, 17.

11. LB, 292–94, 295–98, 319–20, 324–25, 330.

12. LB, 275, 280–86. RSR, 18–19. See Mark L. Staker and Donald Enders, "Joseph Smith Sr.'s China Adventure," JMH 48, no. 22 (2022): 79–105.

13. LB, 329.

14. LB, 303–12. RSR, 19, 21, 26.

15. "Smith Family Warning out of Norwich, VT," March 15, 1816, in EMD, 1:666–68. Cornelia Dayton and Sharon Salinger, *Robert Love's Warnings: Searching for Strangers in Colonial Boston* (Philadelphia: University of Pennsylvania Press, 2014).

16. RSR, 32–33, 42. Dan Vogel, *Joseph Smith: The Making of a Prophet* (Salt Lake City: Signature Books, 2004), 27–28.

17. LB, 330–31. See Spencer W. McBride and Jennifer Hull Dorsey, eds., *New York's Burned-Over District: A History in 70 Documents* (Ithaca, NY: Cornell University Press, 2023).

18. LB, 330–31. Charles G. Finney, *Memoirs of Rev. Charles G. Finney* (New York: A. S. Barnes, 1876), 19–20. Jarena Lee, *Religious Experience and Journal of Mrs. Jarena Lee* (Philadelphia, 1849), 6–7. *Wayne Sentinel* (Palmyra, NY), October 22, 1823. For the evolving threat of visions and prophecy, see Susan Juster, *Doomsayers: Anglo-American Prophecy in the Age of Revolution* (Philadelphia: University of Pennsylvania Press, 2003); Richard Bushman, "The Visionary World of Joseph Smith," BYUSQ 37, no. 1 (1997–98): 183–204; Adam Jortner, *Blood from the Sky: Miracles and Politics in the Early American Republic* (Charlottesville: University of Virginia Press, 2017), 67–87.

19. LB, 335. Pomeroy Tucker, *Origin, Rise, and Progress of Mormonism* (New York: Appleton, 1867), 16–17.

20. JS, 1832 history, H1:11. Alexander Neibaur, journal, May 24, 1844, JSP. JS, A1H, H1:210–12.

21. JS, 1832 history, H1:12–13. There is dispute over Smith's age when he experienced his vision. His earliest account (JS, 1832 history, H1:12) reported "the 16th year of my age," while his later, and authoritative, account said he was fourteen (JS, A1H, H1:208). Some critics have claimed that Smith backdated a later experience that coincided with another series of Palmyra revivals in 1824–25. However, as will be discussed below, Smith's visionary and conversion experience should be best understood as a process, likely commencing in his early teenage years and then reignited several years later.

22. For the Methodist context for Smith's earliest accounts, see Christopher C. Jones, "The Power and Form of Godliness: Methodist Conversion Narratives and Joseph Smith's First Vision," JMH 37, no. 2 (2011): 88–114. For an analysis of the various accounts and their evolving interpretations, see Steven C. Harper, *First Vision: Memory and Mormon Origins* (New York: Oxford University Press, 2019).

23. JS, A1H, H1:215–16.

24. Fee Bill, for Albert Neely, ca. November 9, 1826, JSP. The details regarding this case are difficult to decipher, and will perhaps never be fully determined, due to a lack of contemporary documents and inconsistent reminiscences. See "Introduction to *State of New York v. JS-A*," JSP.

25. JS, 1832 history, H1:13. JS to Oliver Cowdery, December 1834, M&A, December 1834. For histories of Joseph Smith and magic culture, see John L. Brooke, *The Refiner's Fire: The Making of Mormon Cosmology, 1644–1844* (New York: Cambridge University Press, 1994), 149–83; D. Michael Quinn, *Early Mormonism and the Magic World View*, rev. ed. (Salt Lake City: Signature Books, 1998); Mark Ashurst-McGee, "A Pathway to Prophethood: Joseph Smith Junior as Rodman, Village Seer, and Judeo-Christian Prophet" (master's thesis, Utah State University, 2000); Vogel, *Making*, 35–52; RSR, 48–52; Adam

Jortner, *No Place for Saints: Mobs and Mormons in Jacksonian America* (Baltimore: Johns Hopkins University Press, 2021), 11–33.

26. Joseph Smith Sr., interview with Fayette Lapham, 1830, in EMD, 1:456. Daniel Woodward, 1870, in EMD, 1:624–25. James Brewster, 1843, in EMD, 3:316–18. LB 323. Mark Twain, *The Adventures of Tom Sawyer* (Toronto: Belford Brothers, 1876), 232. See David D. Hall, *Worlds of Wonder, Days of Judgment: Popular Religious Belief in Early New England* (New York: Knopf, 1989); Alan Taylor, "The Early Republic's Supernatural Economy: Treasure Seeking in the American Northeast, 1780–1830," *American Quarterly* 38, no. 1 (1986): 6–34.

27. Willard Chase, statement, December 11, 1833, in MU, 241. William Kelley, statement, September 17, 1884, EMD, 2:130. W. Wafford, affidavit, December 8, 1833, in MU, 239. Martin Harris, interview, August 1859, in EMD, 2:303. Michael MacKay and Nicholas Frederick, *Joseph Smith's Seer Stones* (Provo, UT: BYU Religious Studies Center, 2016), 29–44.

28. LB, 335. JS, A1H, H1:220–31. For Smith's previous treasure-seeking on the hill, see John A. Clark to Dear Brethren, August 24, 1840, in EMD, 2:264.

29. JS, A1H, H1:232–34. JS, 1832 history, H1:14. LB, 342.

30. Quinn, *Magic*, 136–39.

31. LB, 345. Elizabeth Fenton, *Old Canaan in a New World: Native Americans and the Lost Tribes of Israel* (New York: New York University Press, 2020); Matthew Dougherty, *Lost Tribes Found: Israelite Indians and Religious Nationalism in Early America* (Norman: University of Oklahoma Press, 2021).

32. LB, 343. Quinn, *Magic*, 139–53. Vogel, *Making*, 48–49.

33. LB, 345.

34. JS, A1H, H1:235–36. LB, 360. Agreement of Josiah Stowell and Others, November 1, 1825, in D1:350. RSR, 46–48.

35. LB, 371. Vogel, *Making*, 75–79.

36. *Utah Christian Advocate* (Salt Lake City), January 1886, JSP. EMD, 4:249–50, 253, 260. For the broader context of this trial, see Manuel W. Padro, "Cunning and Disorderly: Early Nineteenth-Century Witch Trials of Joseph Smith," *Dialogue* 54, no. 4 (2021): 35–70; Jortner, *No Place*, 29–33.

37. *Evangelical Magazine and Gospel Advocate* (Utica, NY), April 9, 1831, in EMD, 4:96. See Vogel, *Making*, 85–86; RSR, 51–52; Gordon Madsen, "Being Acquitted of a 'Disorderly Person' Charge in 1826," in Madsen et al., *Sustaining the Law: Joseph Smith's Legal Encounters* (Provo, UT: BYU Studies, 2014): 71–92.

38. William R. Hine, statement, circa March 1885, in EMD, 4:184. ME, 1–6; Jennifer Reeder, *First: The Life and Faith of Emma Smith* (Salt Lake City: Deseret Book, 2021), 8–9.

39. Isaac Hale, statement, 1834, in EMD, 4:285. Willard Chase, statement, December 11, 1833, in MU, 243–44.

40. Orsamus Turner, 1849, in EMD, 3:50. Tucker, *Origin*, 18. LB, 357.

41. *Saints Herald* (Plano, IL), October 1, 1879. ME, 117–18. Reeder, *First*, 16–18.

42. Isaac Hale, statement, March 20, 1834, in EMD, 4:286. Alva Hale, statement, 1834, in MU, 268.

43. LB, 375. Willard Chase, statement, December 11, 1833, in MU, 243. Jessee, "Recollection," 4–5.

44. LB, 367–79, 385. Jessee, "Recollection," 7. The physicality of the plates has caused problems for historians since Joseph Smith's days, as it forces one to decide whether Smith was a fraud, genuine, or something in between. RSR, 58–61. For the argument that Smith was a pious fraud who manufactured plates out of tin, see Vogel, *Making*, 98–99. For arguments asserting that Smith did not make fraudulent plates but rejecting the notion that the plates were ancient, see Ann Taves, "History and the Claims of Revelation: Joseph Smith and the Materialization of the Golden Plates," *Numen: International Review for the History of Religion* 61, no. 2–3 (2014): 182–207; Sonia Hazard, "How Joseph Smith Encountered Printing Plates and Founded Mormonism," *Religion & American Culture* 31, no. 2 (2021): 137–92. For the broader debate, see Richard Bushman, "Reading the Gold Plates," JMH 41, no. 1 (2015): 64–76.

45. Jessee, "Recollection," 7–8. JS, H1:236–37. Martin Harris, interview, August 1859, in EMD, 2:307. LB, 391–92.

46. LB, 400–403.

47. Hale, statement, March 20, 1834, in EMD 4:286. *Saints' Herald* (Plano, IL), October 1, 1879.

48. Jessee, "Recollection," 7. BoM, 538 [Mormon 9:32]. *Saints' Herald*, October 1, 1879. *Journal of History*, October 1916. See Michael MacKay, "Performing the Translation: Character Transcripts and Joseph Smith's Earliest Translating Practices," in *Producing Ancient Scripture: Joseph Smith's Translation Projects in the Development of Mormon Christianity*, ed. Michael MacKay et al., 81–104 (Salt Lake City: University of Utah Press, 2020).

49. JS, 1832 history, H1:15. Anthon to Eber Howe, February 17, 1834, in MU, 270–72. JS, A1H, H1:240–44.

50. Jessee, "Recollection," 8. *Palmyra* (NY) *Reflector*, March 19, 1831. DN, December 13, 1881. For an overview of the translation process, see R5, xi–xxvi.

51. LB, 409–19, 423. JS, revelation, July 1828, D1:8 [D&C 3:4–7]. JS, 1832 history, H1:16. JS, A-1 history, H1:252–53.

52. LB, 432–34. M&A, October 1834. JS, A-1 history, H1:276–77. JS, revelation, April 1829-D, D1:50 [D&C 9:8].

53. JS, A-1 history, H1:307–9.

54. LB, 453. Twain, *Roughing It* (Hartford, CT: American Publishing Company, 1872), 130. BoM, 589–90.

55. *Wayne Sentinel* (Palmyra, NY), June 26, 1829. JS, A-1 history, H1:254–55. John Gilbert to James Cobb, February 10, 1879, in EMD, 2:522–23. Gilbert, memorandum, September 8, 1892, in EMD, 2:543.

56. See David F. Holland, *Sacred Borders: Continuing Revelation and Canonical Restraint in Early America* (New York: Oxford University Press, 2011), 89–170.

57. *Palmyra* (NY) *Freeman*, August 11, 1829. See Grant Hardy, *Understanding the Book of Mormon: A Reader's Guide* (New York: Oxford University Press, 2010); Elizabeth Fenton and Jared Hickman, eds., *Americanist Approaches to*

The Book of Mormon (New York: Oxford University Press, 2019); William Davis, *Visions in a Seer Stone: Joseph Smith and the Making of the Book of Mormon* (Chapel Hill: University of North Carolina Press, 2020); R5; Terryl L. Givens, *By the Hand of Mormon: The American Scripture That Launched a New World Religion* (New York: Oxford University Press, 2002).

58. BoMET, 89 [2 Nephi 5:10], 644–45 [4 Nephi 1:24–28]. When engaging the Book of Mormon itself, this book cites Royal Skousen's "Earliest Text" edition, which is based on reconstructing the text as Smith would have dictated it. When engaging how the book was read and interpreted, it will cite the relevant published edition. LDS scriptural citations are found in brackets.

59. Fenton, *Old Canaan*, 113–41.

60. BoMET, 3 [Title Page], 619–20 [3 Nephi 20:14–17]. See Jared Hickman, "*The Book of Mormon* as Amerindian Apocalypse," *American Literature* 86, no. 3 (2014): 429–61.

61. BoMET, 18 [1 Nephi 5:21]. William Apess, *A Son of the Forest: The Experience of William Apes . . . Written by Himself* (New York: self-pub., 1829). See Max Perry Mueller, *Race and the Making of the Mormon People* (Chapel Hill: University of North Carolina Press, 2017), 31–91; Elise Boxer, "The Book of Mormon as Mormon Settler Colonialism," in *Essays on American Indian and Mormon History*, ed. Jane Hafen and Brenden Rensink (Salt Lake City: University of Utah Press, 2019), 3–22; Peter Coviello, "How the Mormons Became White: Scripture, Sex, Sovereignty," in Fenton and Hickman, *Approaches*, 259–76.

62. BoMET, 137 [2 Nephi 26:33]. See Carol Lynn Pearson, "Could Feminism Have Saved the Nephites?," *Sunstone*, March 1996; Hardy, *Understanding*, 288; Kimberly Berkey and Joseph Spencer, "'Great Cause to Mourn': The Complexity of *The Book of Mormon*'s Presentation of Gender and Race," in Fenton and Hickman, *Approaches*, 298–320.

63. BoMET, 79 [2 Nephi 2:19–25].

64. BoMET, 90 [2 Nephi 5:18–19, 26], 254 [Mosiah 23:6–8], 273–75 [Mosiah 29:13, 26–27]. See Richard L. Bushman, "The Book of Mormon and the American Revolution," BYUSQ 17, no. 1 (1976): 3–28; Eran Shalev, *American Zion: The Old Testament as a Political Text from the Revolution to the Civil War* (New Haven: Yale University Press, 2013), 84–117.

65. BoMET, 145–47 [2 Nephi 29:3–14]. See Holland, *Sacred Borders*, 141–48; Grant Hardy, "*The Book of Mormon* and the Bible," in Fenton and Hickman, *Approaches*, 107–35.

66. BoMET, 176–79 [Jacob 7:1–23], 278–79 [Alma 1:2–16], 382–89 [Alma 30:6–60].

67. BoMET, 7:34 [Moroni 10:27].

68. *The Gem* (Rochester, NY), May 15, 1830. *Millennial Harbinger*, February 7, 1831.

69. Lucy Mack Smith to Solomon Mack Jr., January 6, 1831, CHL. APP, 38. See Grant Underwood, "Book of Mormon Usage in Early LDS Theology," *Dialogue* 17, no. 3 (Autumn 1984): 35–74; Janiece Johnson, "Becoming a People of the Books: Toward an Understanding of Early Mormon Converts and the New Word of the Lord," *Journal of Book of Mormon Studies* 27 (2018): 1–43.

70. Jesse, "Recollection," 10.

71. JS, A1H, H1:364–66.

72. JS, revelation, March 1829, D1:17 [D&C 5:14]. See Butler, *Awash*, 225–56; Richard Hughes, "Two Restoration Traditions: Mormons and Churches of Christ in the Nineteenth Century," JMH 19, no. 1 (1993): 34–51.

73. BoMET 266 [Mosiah 27:5], 280 [Alma 1:26]. See Hatch, *Democratization*, 113–22.

74. JS, 1832 history, H1:10. Jessee, "Recollection, 10. See D. Michael Quinn, *The Mormon Hierarchy: Origins of Power* (Salt Lake City: Signature Books, 1994), 1–26; Michael MacKay, *Prophetic Authority: Democratic Hierarchy and the Mormon Priesthood* (Urbana: University of Illinois Press, 2020), 24–36. The dating of the second angelic visitation is disputed among believers, and is best understood as just one part of a multilayered development. See Michael MacKay, "Event or Process? How 'The Chamber of Old Father Whitmer' Helps Us Understand Priesthood Restoration," BYUSQ 60, no. 1 (2021): 73–102.

75. "Articles and Covenants," circa April 1830, D1:123 [D&C 20:39]. JS, revelation, April 6, 1830, D1:129 [D&C 21:1]. JS, A1H, H1:364–66. See Michael MacKay, *Sacred Space: Exploring the Birthplace of Mormonism* (Salt Lake City: Deseret Book, 2016).

76. *Ensign of Liberty* (Kirtland, OH), August 1849. APP, 65–66. Whitmer, history, H2:36. JS, revelation, March 8, 1831-B, D1:286. RSR, 128–30; Robin Scott Jensen, "'Rely upon the Things Which Are Written': Text, Context, and the Creation of Mormon Revelatory Records" (master's thesis, University of Wisconsin–Milwaukee, 2009).

77. JS, Visions of Moses, June 1830, D1:152–56 [Moses 1:4]. See Philip L. Barlow, *Mormons and the Bible: The Place of Latter-day Saints in American Religion*, updated ed. (New York: Oxford University Press, 2013), 46–61; Terryl L. Givens, *The Pearl of Greatest Price: Mormonism's Most Controversial Scripture* (New York: Oxford University Press, 2019), 37–41.

78. LB, 499–500. PP, 23–27.

79. Mark L. Staker, "Joseph and Emma Smith's Susquehanna Home: Expanding Mormonism's First Headquarters," *Mormon Historical Studies* 16, no. 2 (2015): 100, 106–7. Reeder, *First*, 57–58.

80. JS, revelation, April 16, 1830, D1:138 [D&C 22:1]. ME, 31–33.

81. Jessee, "Recollection," 11–12. Michael Hubbard MacKay and William G. Hartley, eds., *The Rise of the Latter-day Saints: The Journals and Histories of Newel Knight* (Provo, UT: BYU Religious Studies Center, 2019), 11–14. RSR, 116–18.

82. The twins, if born premature in April 1831, may have been conceived shortly after the Colesville trip. ME, 39.

83. JS, revelation, July 1830-C, D1:162–64 [D&C 25:3–11]. ME, 33–34. Reeder, *First*, 60–64.

84. Catherine A. Brekus, *Strangers and Pilgrims: Female Preaching in America, 1740–1845* (Chapel Hill: University of North Carolina Press, 1998), 249–50.

85. Ingersoll, statement, in MU, 234–35. LB, 486–87.

86. JS to Newel Knight, August 28, 1830, D1:174. JS, revelation, September 1830-A, D1:179 [D&C 29:8].

87. JS, A1H, H1:426. MacKay and Hartley, *Rise*, 21.

88. JS, revelation, September 1830-B, D1:185–86 [D&C 28:2–3, 13]. See RSR, 118–22; MacKay, *Authority*, 68–70.

89. JS, revelation, September 1830-B, D1:185 [D&C 28:8]. Covenant of Oliver Cowdery and Others, October 17, 1830, D1:204. See Kathryn Gin Lum, *Heathen: Religion and Race in American History* (Cambridge: Harvard University Press, 2022), 97–123.

90. JS, revelation, December 30, 1830, D1:227 [D&C 37:1]. JS, revelation, January 2, 1831, D1:231–32 [D&C 38:32]. David Whitmer, history, H2:21.

91. MacKay and Hartley, *Rise*, 32. ME, 37. LB, 502.

92. Lucy Mack Smith to Solomon Mack Jr., January 6, 1831, CHL.

93. LB, 477–78. JSJ, December 18, 1835, J1:134.

94. "Life Sketch of Solomon Chamberlain" (1856), 4–11, BYU. Larry C. Porter, "Solomon Chamberlin's Missing Pamphlet: Dreams, Visions and Angelic Ministrants," BYUSQ 37, no. 2 (1997): 113–40. Bushman, "Visionary World."

Chapter 2: The Voice of the People, 1831–46

1. C50 Minutes, April 5, 1844, A1H:84.

2. JS, revelation, July 20, 1831, D2:7–8 [D&C 57:2–3].

3. Charles Latrobe, *The Rambler in North America*, vol. 1 (New York: Harper and Brothers, 1835), 104. RSR, 162–63; Jortner, *No Place*, 94–96.

4. MU, 198–99. JS, revelation, July 20, 1831, D2:7–8 [D&C 57:4].

5. Alexis de Tocqueville, *Democracy in America*, trans. and ed. Harvey C. Mansfield and Delba Winthrop (1835; Chicago: University of Chicago Press, 2000), 236–37. Nancy Towle, *Vicissitudes Illustrated*, 2nd ed. (Portsmouth, NH: John Caldwell, 1833), 157.

6. Richard S. Van Wagoner, *Sidney Rigdon: A Portrait of Religious Excess* (Salt Lake City: Signature Books, 1994), 5. HOYP, 47.

7. JS, revelation, December 7, 1830, D1:221–23 (D&C 35:4–5). APP, 50. *Painesville (OH) Telegraph*, November 30, 1830.

8. *Painesville Telegraph*, February 15, 1831. MU, 107, 216. APP, 65. HOYP, 74–86, 111–12.

9. See Sam Haselby, *The Origins of American Religious Nationalism* (New York: Oxford University Press, 2015); David Sehat, *The Myth of American Religious Freedom* (New York: Oxford University Press, 2011), 13–70.

10. JS, revelation, February 1831-A, D1:258 [D&C 43:4]. HOYP, 111–14, 156–62. See Spencer Fluhman, *"A Peculiar People": Anti-Mormonism and the Making of Religion in Nineteenth-Century America* (Chapel Hill: University of North Carolina Press, 2012), 21–48.

11. Lyndon Cook, ed., *David Whitmer Interviews: A Restoration Witness* (Salt Lake City: Grandin Book Co., 1991), 154. John Whitmer, history, 1831–circa 1847, 10–18, JSP.

12. Elizabeth Ann Whitney, "Leaf from My Autobiography," WE, August 1, 1878. ME, 38–39.

13. JS, revelation, February 9, 1831, D1:251–52 [D&C 42:30, 32].

14. Robert Owen, *Discourses on a New System of Society* (London: Whiting & Branston, 1825), 11. Oliver Wendell Holmes, *Ralph Waldo Emerson* (Boston: Houghton, Mifflin, 1884), 164. See Daniel Walker Howe, *What Hath God Wrought: The Transformation of America, 1815–1848* (New York: Oxford University Press, 2007), 292–304.

15. Whitney, "Leaf," WE, October 1, November 1, 1878. JS, blessing to Newel Whitney, October 7, 1835, D5:20–21. HOYP, 230–35. Geographic wards were not established until a decade later in Nauvoo.

16. Levi Hancock, autobiography, 22, CHL. Orson Hyde and Hyrum Smith to Edward Partridge and Others, January 14, 1833, JSP. HOYP, 243–44. Leonard J. Arrington et al., *Building the City of God: Community and Cooperation among the Mormons* (Salt Lake City: Deseret Book, 1976), 1–43.

17. JS, revelation, February 27, 1833, D3:20–24 [D&C 89]. See Lester Bush, "The Word of Wisdom in Early Nineteenth-Century Perspective," *Dialogue* 14, no. 3 (1981): 46–65. Jed Dannenbaum, "The Origins of Temperance Activism and Militancy among American Women," *Journal of Social History* 15, no. 2 (1981): 235–36.

18. Philo Dibble, "Recollections of the Prophet," JI, May 15, 1892. JS, revelation, February 16, 1832, D2:183–92 [D&C 76].

19. JS, A1H, 192, JSP. RSR, 196–202. HOYP, 322–26. See Kathryn Gin Lum, *Damned Nation: Hell in America, from the Revolution to Reconstruction* (New York: Oxford University Press, 2014), esp. 126–63.

20. Brigham Young, discourse, August 29, 1852, JD, 6:281. Orson Pratt, diary, December 29, 1832, CHL.

21. Luke Johnson, "History of Luke Johnson, by Himself," 834–35, BYU. HOYP, 345–53. Later historians speculated that the incident, especially the attempted castration, was prompted by Joseph Smith's having an affair with a young woman in town, likely due to Smith's later practice of polygamy. However, all contemporary accounts point toward other instigators.

22. RSR, 178–80. Van Wagoner, *Rigdon*, 114–18.

23. Towle, *Vicissitudes*, 155, 158.

24. ME, 38–39.

25. Emily Dow Partridge Young, "What I Remember," 1–7, CHL. APP, 76. Phoebe Lott to Anna Pratt, August 10, 1832, CHL.

26. "Explanation of the Plat of the City of Zion," circa June 25, 1833, D3:124–46. See Richard Jackson, "The City of Zion Plat," in *Mapping Mormonism: An Atlas of Latter-day Saint History*, ed. Brandon S. Plewe (Provo, UT: BYU Studies, 2012), 38–39; Benjamin E. Park, "To Fill up the World: Joseph Smith as Urban Planner," *Mormon Historical Studies* 14, no. 1 (2013): 1–27.

27. See Brett Malcolm Grainger, *Church in the Wild: Evangelicals in Antebellum America* (Cambridge: Harvard University Press, 2019).

28. Cowdery to JS, May 7, 1831, D1:296. MU, 178. Jortner, *No Place*, 107–9. Paul Reeve, *Religion of a Different Color: Race and the Mormon Struggle for Whiteness* (New York: Oxford University Press, 2015), 116–19.

29. *Richmond Whig*, quoted in Howe, *Wrought*, 431. Lincoln, "Address to the Young Men's Lyceum of Springfield, Illinois, January 27, 1838," in *Lincoln: Speeches and Writings, 1832–1858*, ed. Don E. Fehrenbacher (New York: Modern Library, 1989), 28–36. See Joanne Freeman, *the Field of Blood: Violence in Congress and the Road to the Civil War* (New York: Farrar, Straus and Giroux, 2018), 4–5; Alan Taylor, *American Republics: A Continental History of the United States, 1783–1850* (New York: Norton, 2021), 240–45.

30. Young, "Remember," 7. EMS, December 1833. APP, 103. Josiah Gregg, *Commerce on the Prairies*, 2 vols. (New York: Henry Langley, 1844), 1:316. Jortner, *No Place*, 113–16.

31. Young, "Remember," 15.

32. JS, revelation, December 16–17, 1833, D3:395 [D&C 101:80]. T&S, December 1, 1845. Cass to Gilbert et al., May 2, 1834, CHL. *Columbia* (MO) *Intelligencer*, November 30, 1833.

33. JS, revelation, February 24, 1834, D3:460 [D&C 103:15]. See Andrea G. Radke, "We Also Marched: The Women and Children of Zion's Camp, 1834," BYUSQ 39, no. 1 (2000): 147–65; Matthew Godfrey, "'The Redemption of Zion Must Needs Come by Power': Insights into the Camp of Israel Expedition, 1834," BYUSQ 53, no. 4 (2014): 125–46; Jortner, *No Place*, 125–46.

34. *Missouri Republican* (St. Louis), May 17, 1836. M&A, August 1836. JS et al. to William Phelps, July 25, 1836, D5:269–71. See Samantha Seeley, *Race, Removal, and the Right to Remain: Migration and the Making of the United States* (Chapel Hill: University of North Carolina Press, 2021).

35. See Craig Campbell, *Images of the New Jerusalem: Latter Day Saint Faction Interpretations of Independence, Missouri* (Knoxville: University of Tennessee Press, 2004).

36. B. G. Ferris, *The Mormons at Home* (New York: Dix & Edwards, 1856), 157–58. ERS, "Sketch of My Life," in *Personal Writings of Eliza Roxcy Snow*, ed. Maureen Beecher (Logan: Utah State University, 2000), 6–10. ERS, "Praise Ye the Lord," in ERSCP, 68. WE, December 15, 1887.

37. Esaias Edwards, autobiography, BYU. Steven C. Harper, "Infallible Proofs, Both Human and Divine: The Persuasiveness of Mormonism for Early Converts," *Religion and American Culture* 10, no. 1 (2000): 99–118.

38. LB, 583–85. HOYP, 436–37. ME, 55–60.

39. JS, sermon, February 17, 1834, in D4:437–38. See D. Michael Quinn, *Mormon Hierarchy: Origins of Power* (Salt Lake City: Signature Books, 1994), 39–77; MacKay, *Authority*, 71–84.

40. JS, sermon, February 12, 1834, and Oliver Cowdery remarks, February 21, 1835, D3:429, D4:243. Cook, *Whitmer Interviews*, 154. PP, 40.

41. R4, xxiv–xxvi. Givens, *Pearl*, 118–21.

42. WE, November 1, 1878. ATP, 7–9. JSJ, February 23, 1836, J1:189. WoC, 15–17.

43. JSJ, March 27, 1836, J1:200–11. Stephen Post, journal, March 27, 1836, CHL.

ERS, in Edward Tullidge, *The Women of Mormondom* (New York: Tullidge and Crandall, 1877), 95. RSR, 315–19.

44. JSJ, April 3, 1836, J1:219–20 [D&C 110].

45. Mary Fielding to Mercy Thompson, June 15, 1837, CHL.

46. See Howe, *Wrought*, 375–76; Jessica Lepler, *The Many Panics of 1837: People, Politics, and the Creation of a Transatlantic Financial Crisis* (New York: Cambridge University Press, 2013), 8–42.

47. For overviews of the society, see HOYP, 391–550; Jeffrey Walker, "The Kirtland Safety Society and the Fraud of Grandison Newell," BYUSQ 54, no. 3 (2015): 33–59; D5:xxxvii–xxxii.

48. Articles of Agreement, January 2, 1837, D5:324–31.

49. WWJ, January 24, 1837. Lepler, *Panics*, 197–223.

50. Emma to JS, April 25, 1837, D5:376. Mortgage, July 11, 1837, D5:404–7. On financial and legal issues, see D5:290–91; Walker, "Fraud," 59–98.

51. M&A, June 1837. Pratt to JS, May 23, 1837, D5:389–91. M&A, July 1837. Terryl L. Givens and Matthew J. Grow, *Parley P. Pratt: The Apostle Paul of Mormonism* (New York: Oxford University Press, 2011), 90–102.

52. Jay Parry, "Called to Drink Deep of the Butter Cup: Mary Fielding Smith (1801–1853)," in *Women of Faith in the Latter Days*, ed. Richard Turley Jr. and Brittany Chapman, vol. 1, *1775–1820* (Salt Lake City: Deseret Book, 2011): 380.

53. Minutes, September 3, 1837, D5:420–25. LB, 603. John and Clarissa Smith to George Smith, January 1 and January 15, 1838, CHL.

54. JS, revelations, April 26, May 19, 1838, in D6:114–15 [D&C 115:4, 7; 116]. Capitalization and hyphenation for the name evolved over the following years.

55. Cowdery to Warren Cowdery, January 21, 1838, HL. D&C reference. M&A, May 1837. *Elder's Journal* (Far West, MO), November 1837. Minutes, April 12, 1838, D6:87–89. See Don Bradley, "Mormon Polygamy before Nauvoo? The Relationship of Joseph Smith and Fanny Alger," in *The Persistence of Polygamy: Joseph Smith and the Origins of Mormon Polygamy*, Newell G. Bringhurst and Craig L. Foster, eds. (Independence, MO: John Whitmer Books, 2010): 14–58. Alger was twenty at the time of the alleged relationship. The word *affair* in Cowdery's letter was written over the word *scrape*, leading some to claim Cowdery's initial accusation was not regarding sex. However, his excommunication trial made clear that Cowdery was accusing Smith of "committing adultery," and narrating what they called "the adultery scrape."

56. JS to John Corrill, September 4, 1837, D5:426–31. Minutes, November 6 and 7, 1837, D5:446–49. Cowdery to JS, January 21, 1838, in D5:504–5. Minutes, April 12, 1838, D6:88–90. JSJ, July 4, 1838, J1:276. "Minutes and Testimonies, 12–29 November 1838 [State of Missouri v. Gates et al. for Treason]," 17, JSP.

57. Sidney Rigdon, *Oration Delivered by Mr. S. Rigdon* (Far West, MO: Journal Office, 1838), 12. JSJ, July 4, 1838, J1:276. "Minutes and Testimonies," 10.

58. LB, 630. Lilburn Boggs, executive order, October 27, 1838, Missouri State Archives, Jefferson City, MO. For overviews of the Mormon-Missouri War, see Stephen LeSueur, *The 1838 Mormon War in Missouri* (Columbia: University of Missouri Press, 1987); Leland Gentry and Todd Compton, *Fire and Sword:*

A History of Latter-day Saints in Northern Missouri, 1836–39 (Salt Lake City: Kofford Books, 2010), 169–394.

59. David Lewis, in Clark Johnson, ed., *Mormon Redress Petitions: Documents of the 1833–1838 Missouri Conflict* (Provo, UT: BYU Religious Studies Center, 1992), 276. For the Hawn's Mill Massacre (previously known as "Haun's Mill"), see Thomas Spencer, "'Was This Really Missouri Civilization?': The Haun's Mill Massacre in Missouri and Mormon History," in *The Missouri Mormon Experience*, ed. Thomas M. Spencer (Columbia: University of Missouri Press, 2010), 100–118; Alexander Baugh, *Tragedy and Truth: What Happened at Hawn's Mill* (Salt Lake City: Covenant Communications, 2014).

60. ERS, "The Slaughter on Shoal Creek," ERSCP, 105. Johnson, *Petitions*, 512–15. See Andrea Radke-Moss, "Silent Memories of Missouri: Mormon Women and Men and Sexual Assault in Group Memory and Religious Identity," in *Mormon Women's History: Beyond Biography*, ed. Rachel Cope et al. (Madison, NJ: Fairleigh Dickinson University Press, 2017), 49–82.

61. Mary Fielding Smith to Joseph Fielding, June 1839, CHL. LB, 676. ERS to Isaac Streator, February 22, 1839, CHL. ERS, "Missouri," ERSCP, 278.

62. "Far West Committee Minutes, January–April 1839," January 26, 1839, CHL.

63. T&S, January 15, 1841. See Glen Leonard, *Nauvoo: A Place of Peace, a People of Promise*, 41–61. Benjamin E. Park, *Kingdom of Nauvoo: The Rise and Fall of a Religious Empire on the American Frontier* (New York: Liveright, 2020).

64. LB, 706. JS and Elias Higbee to Hyrum Smith, December 5, 1839, D7:69. See Spencer W. McBride, *Joseph Smith for President: The Prophet, the Assassins, and the Fight for American Religious Freedom* (New York: Oxford University Press, 2021), 7–22.

65. See James Simeone, *The Saints and the State: The Mormon Troubles in Illinois* (Athens: Ohio University Press, 2021).

66. See Park, *Kingdom*, 53–56.

67. T&S, September 1, 1841. PP, 66–84.

68. See Lori Ginzberg, *Women in Antebellum Reform* (New York: Wiley-Blackwell, 2000); Robert Gross, *The Transcendentalists and Their World* (New York: Macmillan, 2021), 452–55.

69. Minutes, March 17, 31, April 19, 1842, RSD:28–37, 42–46, 49–52. See WoC, 26–50; HFoF, 62–70; Jonathan Stapley, "Mormon Women and Authority," in *Women and Mormonism: Historical and Contemporary Perspectives*, ed. Kate Holbrook and Matthew Bowman (Salt Lake City: University of Utah Press, 2016), 101–20.

70. See "Elijah Able," CBM. Quincy D. Newell, *Your Sister in the Gospel: The Life of Jane Manning James, a Nineteenth-Century Black Mormon* (New York: Oxford University Press, 2019), 23–55.

71. Patriarchal Blessing of Elijah Able, circa 1836, in *Early Patriarchal Blessings of the Church of Jesus Christ of Latter-day Saints*, ed. Michael Marquardt (Salt Lake City: Smith-Pettit Foundation, 2007), 99. Patriarchal Blessing of Jane Manning, in Newell, *Sister*, 140. See Mueller, *Race*, 135–37. Reeve, *Different*, 125–28.

72. LB, 714. JS, revelation, January 19, 1841, D7:517–18 [D&C 124]. See Ryan G.

Tobler, "'Saviors on Mount Zion': Mormon Sacramentalism, Mortality, and the Baptism for the Dead," JMH 39, no. 4 (2013): 182–238.

73. Willard Richards, draft notes, May 4, 1842, quoted in J2:54, fn.198. For Masonry and the Mormon endowment, see Michael W. Homer, *Joseph's Temples: The Dynamic Relationship between Freemasonry and Mormonism* (Salt Lake City: University of Utah Press, 2014); Cheryl Bruno et al., *Method Infinite: Freemasonry and the Mormon Restoration* (Salt Lake City: Kofford Books, 2022).

74. WE, December 15, 1878. JS, revelation, July 27, 1842, CHL.

75. ERSJ, June 29, 1842. For general overviews of Nauvoo polygamy, see Todd Compton, *In Sacred Loneliness: The Plural Wives of Joseph Smith* (Salt Lake City: Signature Books, 1997); Brian Hales, *Joseph Smith's Polygamy*, 3 vols. (Draper, UT: Kofford Books, 2013); HFoF, 70–107.

76. See Lawrence Foster, *Religion and Sexuality: The Shakers, the Mormons, and the Oneida Community* (Urbana: University of Illinois Press, 1984); Stewart Davenport, *Sex and Sects: The Story of Mormon Polygamy, Shaker Celibacy, and Oneida Complex Marriage* (Charlottesville: University of Virginia Press, 2022).

77. Emily Dow Partridge Young, "Diary and Reminiscences, 1874–1899," BYU. See Park, *Kingdom*, 146–54.

78. William Clayton, diary, July 12–13, 1843, AI, 110. JS, revelation, July 12, 1843, D12: 470, 476 [D&C 132:19–20, 54].

79. ERSJ, September 23, 1842. See George D. Smith, *Nauvoo Polygamy: ". . . But We Called It Celestial Marriage"* (Salt Lake City: Signature Books, 2008), 181–82.

80. *Nauvoo Neighbor* (IL), April 17, 1844. ERS, "My Father in Heaven," ERSCP, 314. *The Prophet* (New York), May 24, 1845.

81. T&S, January 1, 1842. *Quincy* (IL) *Whig*, January 22, 1842. *Peoria* (IA) *Register and Northwestern Gazetteer*, January 21, 1842. *New York Herald*, August 27, 1841.

82. Thomas Ford, *A History of Illinois* (Chicago: S. C. Griggs & Co., 1854), 319. Alex D. Smith, "Untouchable: Joseph Smith's Use of the Law as Catalyst for Assassination," *Journal of the Illinois State Historical Society* 112, no. 1 (2019): 8–42; Park, *Kingdom*, 154–60.

83. JS to Calhoun, December 2, 1843, D13:306–7.

84. McBride, *President*, 75–106.

85. Minutes, March 11, 14, April 11, 18, 1844, A1:40, 48, 95–96, 110. Park, *Kingdom*, 198–207.

86. Nauvoo City Council Minutes, June 10, 1844, JSP. Though the Smiths had initially expected to be charged with destroying the press, Ford changed the charge to treason based on Joseph's declaring martial law in Nauvoo.

87. Warsaw Committee of Safety, "To His Excellency Thomas Ford," broadside, Beinecke Library, Yale University, New Haven, CT.

88. Richards to Nauvoo, June 27, 1844, CHL. Leonard, *Nauvoo*, 396–404.

89. LB, 748–49. Richard Holzapfel and David Whitchurch, *My Dear Sister: Letters between Joseph F. Smith and His Sister Martha Ann Smith Harris* (Provo, UT: BYU Religious Studies Center, 2018), xvi. ERS, "The Assassination," ERSCP, 298.

90. WWD, August 7, 1844.

91. WWD, August 8, 1844. T&S, September 15, 1844. William Clayton, diary, August 8, 1844, A1:207. See D. Michael Quinn, "The Mormon Succession Crisis of 1844," BYUSQ 16, no. 2 (1976): 1–44.

92. T&S, October 15, 1844. See ME, 199–209; PP, 132–40.

93. LB, 747. See Sharalyn Howcroft, "A Textual and Archival Reexamination of Lucy Mack Smith's History," in *Foundational Texts of Mormonism: Examining Major Early Sources*, ed. Mark Ashurst-McGee et al. (New York: Oxford University Press, 2018), 298–335; Janiece Johnson, "Lucy Mack Smith and Her Sacred Text," in *Open Canon: Scriptures of the Latter Day Saint Tradition*, ed. Christine Blythe et al. (Salt Lake City: University of Utah Press, 2022), 149–68.

94. Dean C. Jesse, *John Taylor's Nauvoo Journal* (Provo, UT: Grandin Books, 1996), 73–77. Heber C. Kimball, diary, June 30, 1845, CHL. T&S, June 1, 1845. *Warsaw* (IL) *Signal*, October 29, 1845. Kyle Walker, *William B. Smith: In the Shadow of a Prophet* (Salt Lake City: Kofford Books, 2015), 209–306. Johnson, "Sacred Text," 156–57.

95. See Robin Scott Jensen, "Mormons Seeking Mormonism: Strangite Success and the Conceptualization of Mormon Ideology, 1844–50," in *Scattering of the Saints: Schism Within Mormonism*, ed. Newell G. Bringhurst and John C. Hamer (Independence, MO: John Whitmer Books, 2007), 115–40.

96. BY, March 9, 1845, RSD:171. See Park, *Kingdom*, 260–61.

97. *Warsaw Signal*, September 17, 1845. *Alton* (IL) *Telegraph and Democratic Review*, October 11, 1845. Ford to J. B. Backenstos, October 29, 1845, CHL.

98. T&S, November 1, 1845. William G. Hartley, "The Nauvoo Exodus and Crossing the Ice Myths," JMH 43, no. 1 (2017): 30–33.

99. Smith, *Polygamy*, 573–656. PP, 134–35. Jonathan Stapley, "Adoptive Sealing Ritual in Mormonism," JMH 37, no. 3 (2011): 53–117.

100. *Utah Genealogical and Historical Magazine* (Salt Lake City), April 1916. Holzapfel and Whitchurch, *Sister*, xix.

Chapter 3: Of Empires and Wars, 1846–69

1. ERS, "National Song," ERSCP:397.

2. John Brown, reminiscences and journals, April 3–7, CHL. SLT, May 21, 1897. "Green Flake," CBM.

3. WWD, August 8, 1847.

4. *The United States Magazine and Democratic Review* (New York City), July 1845. See Ned Blackhawk, *Violence over the Land: Indians and Empires in the Early American West* (Cambridge: Harvard University Press, 2006).

5. Walter Nugent, "The Mormons and America's Empires," JMH 36, no. 2 (2010): 1–27; Brent Rogers, *Unpopular Sovereignty: Mormons and the Federal Management of Early Utah Territory* (Lincoln: University of Nebraska Press, 2017), 6–8.

6. Hosea Stout, diary, May 25, 1847, in *On the Mormon Frontier: The Diary of Hosea Stout, 1884–1889*, ed. Juanita Brooks (Salt Lake City: University of Utah

Press, 2009), 256–57. Richard Burton, *The City of the Saints* (New York: Harper & Brothers, 1862), 240.

7. PPW to children, February 22, 1852, PPWL.

8. DN, October 22, 1903.

9. BY to Addison Pratt, August 28, 1845, BYP. PP, 144–45.

10. EBWD, March 6, 9, 1846. ERSJ, August 9/10, 1846. Eliza Partridge Lyman, diary, April 9, 1846, CHL. Carol Madsen, *Emmeline B. Wells: An Intimate History* (Salt Lake City: University of Utah Press, 2017), 74–87. Richard E. Bennett, *We'll Find the Place: The Mormon Exodus, 1846–48* (Norman: University of Oklahoma Press, 1997), 31–66. Emily Partridge Young, diary, February 15, 1846. HFoF, 141.

11. See Amy Greenberg, *A Wicked War: Polk, Clay, Lincoln, and the 1846 Invasion of Mexico* (New York: Knopf, 2012).

12. James K. Polk, diary, June 3, 1846, in *The Diary of James K. Polk*, ed. Milo Quaife (Chicago: A. C. McClurg, 1910), 445–46. BY to Polk, August 9, 1847, BYP. Matthew J. Grow, *"Liberty to the Downtrodden": Thomas L. Kane, Romantic Reformer* (New Haven: Yale University Press, 2009), 52–60.

13. Zina to Mary Huntington, December 29, 1846, CHL. ERSJ, January 1, 26, March 14, June 6, 1847. Abigail Abbott to Brigham Young, June 28, 1852, BYP. PP, 152–60. HFoF, 178–82. Richard E. Bennett, *Mormons at the Missouri, 1846–1852* (Norman: University of Oklahoma Press, 1987); HFoF, 160.

14. Willard Richards, diary, March 14, 1847, CHL. PP, 162–64.

15. WWD, April 3, 1847.

16. WWD, July 24, 1847. Levi Jackman, journal, July 28, 1847, CHL.

17. Bennett, *Place*, 251–99 (quote on 269); Jared Farmer, *On Zion's Mount: Mormons, Indians, and the American Landscape* (Cambridge: Harvard University Press, 2008), 42–50.

18. HFoF, 185–208 (quote on 202). Bennett, *Place*, 300–333.

19. Amanda Hendrix-Komoto, *Imperial Zions: Religion, Race, and Family in the American West and the Pacific* (Lincoln: University of Nebraska Press, 2022), 110–11. Stephen C. Taysom, *Like a Fiery Meteor: The Life of Joseph F. Smith* (Salt Lake City: University of Utah Press, 2023), 60–66.

20. WWD, August 25, 1847. ERS, "Hail to the Twelve and Pioneers," ERSCP:364.

21. GCM, December 5, 27, 1847, CHL. PP, 171–74.

22. GCM, July 24, 1849. Ronald Walker, "'A Banner is Unfurled': Mormonism's Ensign Peak," *Dialogue* 26, no. 4 (1993): 71–91.

23. GCM, October 14, 1849. Taylor, discourse, November 1, 1857, JD 6:18–20. PP, 184–88.

24. BY, address, December 3, 1849, Deseret Papers, CHL. Peter Crawley, "The Constitution of the State of Deseret," BYUSQ (Fall 1989): 7–22; Sarah Barringer Gordon, *The Mormon Question: Polygamy and Constitutional Conflict in Nineteenth-Century America* (Chapel Hill: University of North Carolina Press, 2002), 26, 74, 94–95.

25. Steven Hahn, *A Nation without Borders: The United States and Its World in an Age of Civil Wars, 1830–1910* (New York: Penguin, 2016), 200–204.

26. Rogers, *Unpopular*, 41–46.
27. *New York Herald*, January 10, 1852. ERS, "Celebration Song," ERSCP:433. Ronald Walker and Matthew Grow, "The People Are 'Hogaffed or Humbugged': The 1851–52 National Reaction to Utah's 'Runaway' Officers," JMH 40, no. 21 (2014): 1–52.
28. ERS, "The New Year 1852," ERSCP:421–22. WoC, 69–71. HFoF, 289–97.
29. PPW to children, August 19, 1851, February 22, 1852, March 1, 1855, PPWL. Joseph Smith Sr., patriarchal blessing, May 18, 1836, PPWL. Everett Hall Pendleton, *Brian Pendleton and His Descendants, 1599–1910* (self-pub., 1911), 329.
30. Lucy Meserve Smith, "Historical Sketches," June 12, 1889, RSD:217. DN, November 12, 1856. PP, 248–49.
31. William Hartley, "Brigham Young's Overland Trails Revolution: The Creation of the 'Down-and-Back' Wagon Train System, 1860–61," JMH 28, no. 21 (2002): 1–30.
32. BY to Luke Lea, August 13, 1851, BYP. Pratt to Orson Pratt, September 5, 1848, in *Millennial Star* (Liverpool, UK), January 15, 1849. BY to Chief Walker, May 14, 1849, BYP. Farmer, *Mount*, 77–80. PP, 211–12. For Wakara and the Mormons generally, see Mueller, *Race*, 153–80.
33. "Meeting with Utes in Utah," May 22, 1850, BYP. Reeve, *Different*, 78–79.
34. BY to Luke Lea, June 8, 1852, BYP. GCM, April 8, 1855. PPW to children, March 1, 1855, PPWL. Farmer, *Mount*, 81–82. PP, 208–18.
35. BY to "Indian Chiefs," May 6, 1850, BYP. Leonard J. Arrington, *Great Basin Kingdom: An Economic History of the Latter-day Saints, 1830–1900* (1958; Urbana: University of Illinois Press, 2004), 96–130.
36. Rogers, *Unpopular*, 106–9.
37. Great Salt Lake Relief Society, Minutes, January 24, 1854, RSD:190. BY, discourse, June 4, 1854, BYCD, 2:804. WWD, June 17, 1857. WoC, 75–80. HFoF, 297–305.
38. *National Intelligencer* (Washington, DC), April 20, 1857. Reeve, *Different*, 75–76. Rogers, *Unpopular*, 120–30.
39. MS, April 28, 1855. Mueller, *Race*, 198–99.
40. Paul Dahl, "'All Is Well . . . ': The Story of 'the Hymn That Went around the World,'" BYUSQ 21, no. 4 (1981): 515–27.
41. Lewis's given name is spelled in several variations, including Quak, Quaku, and Kwaku. Connell O'Donovan, "The Mormon Priesthood Ban and Elder Q. Walker Lewis: 'An Example for His More Whiter Brethren to Follow,'" JWHAJ 26 (2006): 48–99.
42. *The Prophet*, May 20, 1844. WW to BY, November 16, 1844, BYP. GCM, March 26, 1847.
43. William I. Appleby to BY, May 31, 1847, BYP. Autobiography and Journal of William Appleby, June 16, 1847, CHL. O'Donovan, "Priesthood Ban," 82. See Martha Hodes, *White Women, Black Men: Illicit Sex in the 19th-Century South* (New Haven: Yale University Press, 1997).
44. GCM, December 3, 1847. Reeve, *Different*, 128–39 (quotes from 129); PP,

218–28. Angela Hudson, *Real Native Genius: How an Ex-Slave and a White Mormon Became Famous Indians* (Chapel Hill: University of North Carolina Press, 2015).

45. WWD, March 4, 1850, states he received a letter from Lewis, which, given the context, likely stated his intent to gather. O'Donovan, "Priesthood Ban," 90.

46. For slavery in Utah, see Amy Thiriot, *Slavery in Zion: A Documentary and Genealogical History of Black Lives and Black Servitude in Utah Territory, 1847–1862* (Salt Lake City: University of Utah Press, 2022).

47. Reeve, *Different*, 148–152 (quotes from 149). Utah's bill specified that children born to parents who were enslaved would not inherit the status, and that those who were forcibly moved to the territory could not be transferred or removed without their consent. However, these moderating principles had little impact on those who were currently in bondage in the territory, nor is it clear if these restrictions were enforced.

48. Reeve, *Different*, 152–61 (quotes from 154). Young's and Pratt's sermons, previously unavailable due to being written in shorthand, are reproduced in Paul Reeve, Christopher Rich Jr., and LaJean Carruth, *This Abominable Slavery: Race, Religion, and the Battle over Human Bondage in Antebellum Utah* (New York: Oxford University Press, forthcoming).

49. BY, "Message to the Joint Session of the Legislature," December 13, 1852, BYP.

50. *Lowell* (MA) *Advertiser*, November 9, 1852.

51. Ellen Bishop to Lucretia Bishop, May 28, 1854, CHL. (Emphasis in original.)

52. DN, September 18, 1852. BY, discourse, August 29, 1852, BYCD, 1:582. David Whittaker, "The Bone in the Throat: Orson Pratt and the Public Announcement of Plural Marriage," *Western Historical Quarterly* 18, no. 3 (1987): 293–314.

53. Stout, diary, August 29, 1852, 449–50. Christopher C. Jones, "'A Very Poor Place for Our Doctrine': Religion and Race in the 1853 Mormon Mission to Jamaica," *Religion & American Culture* 31, no. 2 (2021): 262–95.

54. Taysom, *Smith*, chap. 4.

55. Augusta Cobb Young to BY, January 31, 1851, BYOF. (Emphasis in original.) Belinda Pratt, *Defence of Polygamy, by a Lady in Utah* (Salt Lake City, 1854). HFoF, 339–42; Sarah M. S. Pearsall, *Polygamy: An Early American History* (New Haven: Yale University Press, 2019), 249–94.

56. *The Seer* (Washington, DC), January 1853. N. Slater, *Fruits of Mormonism* (Coloma, CA: Harmon & Springer, 1851), 86–87. Gordon, *Question*, 29–49; Christine Talbot, *A Foreign Kingdom: Mormons and Polygamy in American Political Culture, 1852–1890* (Urbana: University of Illinois Press, 2013), 34–62.

57. WWD, January 18, 1847. Jeffery Johnson, "Determining and Defining 'Wife': The Brigham Young Households," *Dialogue* 20, no. 3 (1987): 57–70. PP, 236–37.

58. Eliza Partridge to BY, February 24, 1853, BYP. HFoF, 280. PP, 190–92. See also Gordon, *Question*, 172–78.

59. EBW to Daniel Wells, March 4, 1852, Wells Papers, CHL. EBWD, January 7, 1878. Madsen, *Wells*, 105–9.

60. Marie Cornwall et al., "How Common Was the Principle? Women as Plural Wives in 1860," *Dialogue* 26, no. 2 (1993): 101, 139–53; Kathryn Daynes, *More*

Wives Than One: Transformation of the Mormon Marriage System, 1840–1910 (Urbana: University of Illinois Press, 2001), 119–27; HFoF, 366.

61. Elizabeth MacDonald, autobiography, CHL, 38–40, 44.

62. WWD, March 2, 1856. Harriet Doremus to Henry Doremus, December 24, 1856, CHL. Bowman, *Mormon People*, 138–41.

63. WWD, September 21, 1856. GCM, March 17, 1848. Ardis Parshall, "'Pursue, Retake & Punish': The 1857 Santa Clara Ambush," *Utah Historical Quarterly* 73, no. 1 (2005): 64–86; Ronald Walker et al., *Massacre at Mountain Meadows* (New York: Oxford University Press, 2008), 24–27; PP, 254–63.

64. Woodruff to George Albert Smith, April 1, 1857, Church Historian's Office-book, CHL. BY to Uriah Butt, February 17, 1857, BYP. Daynes, *More Wives*, 119–27.

65. BY to Douglas, April 28, 1854, Stephen Douglas Papers, University of Chicago, Chicago, IL. Bernhisel to BY, January 13, 1854, BYP. See Rogers, *Unpopular*, 135–81.

66. Donald Johnson, ed., *National Party Platforms*, vol. 1, *1840–1956* (Urbana: University of Illinois Press, 1957), 27–28. *New York Daily Times*, June 23, July 4, 1857. WWD, August 30, 1857. Gordon, *Question*, 55–84.

67. PPW to children, March 5, 1858, PPWL.

68. NYT, April 21, May 11, 1857. WWD, May 20, 1857. Utah Memorial, January 6, 1857, BYP. John Bernhisel to BY, April 2, 1857, BYP. William MacKinnon, *A Documentary History of the Utah War, to 1858*, volume 1 of *At Sword's Point* (Norman: University of Oklahoma Press, 2008); Rogers, *Unpopular*, 152–62.

69. WWD, August 15, 1857. DN, October 14, 1857. BYD, August 11, 1857, 1:577. Givens and Grow, *Pratt*, 366–91.

70. BY, proclamation, September 15, 1857, BYP. George Bailey, diary, August 22, September 28, 1857, CHL. PPW to children, July 22, 1858, PPWL. Will Bagley, *Blood of the Prophets: Brigham Young and the Massacre at Mountain Meadows* (Norman: University of Oklahoma Press, 2002), 112–14; Walker et al., *Massacre*, 145–47.

71. Walker et al., *Massacre*, 51–53. Richard Turley and Barbara Jones Brown, *Vengeance Is Mine: The Mountain Meadows Massacre and Its Aftermath* (New York: Oxford University Press, 2023), chap. 3.

72. Walker et al., *Massacre*, 187–209. Sarah Barringer Gordon and Jan Shipps, "Fatal Convergence in the Kingdom of God: The Mountain Meadows Massacre in American History," *Journal of the Early Republic* 37, no. 3 (2017): 307–47. The degree of Indian participation is disputed. Any involvement, however, should be considered coaxed given the Paiute's dependence on Mormon aid.

73. WWD, September 29, 1857. On the degree of Young's knowledge concerning the cover-up, see Bagley, *Blood*, 242–47; PP, 275–82; Turley and Brown, *Vengeance*.

74. Walker et al., *Massacre*, 5.

75. Lewis Barney, diary, BYU, 78. Lucy Smith, "Historical Sketches," RSD:218. PPW to children, March 5, 1858, PPWL. Rogers, *Unpopular*, 195.

76. PPW to children, March 5, 1858, PPWL.

77. George Bailey, diary, April 6, 1858, CHL. PPW to children, July 1858, PPWL. EBW to "Dear absent sisters," April 15, 1858, Wells Papers, CHL. Madsen, *Wells*, 116–22.

78. Buchanan, proclamation, April 6, in William MacKinnon, "A Documentary History of the Utah War, 1858–1859," part 2 in *At Sword's Point* (Norman: University of Oklahoma Press, 2016), 398–99. BY to Warren Snow, June 26, 1858, BYP. PPW to children, July 1858, PPWL. PP, 290–300. Grow, *Reformer*, 149–206. Rogers, *Unpopular*, 224–49.

79. BYD, July 9, 28, 1861, 2:316, 322. DN, October 18, 1861.

80. PPW to children, January 31, 1861, July 8, 1862, PPWL. WWD, December 11, 1861. BY to Abraham Lincoln, March 7, 1863, LOC. See E. B. Long, *The Saints and the Union: Utah Territory during the Civil War* (Urbana: University of Illinois Press, 1981).

81. The best biography of Cannon is Davis Bitton, *George Q. Cannon: A Biography* (Salt Lake City: Deseret Book, 1999).

82. GQCD, May 5, 1862. See Rogers, *Unpopular*, 287.

83. Stephen Foster, *Republican Land Policy* (Washington, DC: Buell & Blanchard, 1860), 5. Gordon, *Question*, 55–84.

84. GQCD, June 10–14, 18, 24, July 1, 6, 1862.

85. Hahn, *Nation*, 237–43.

86. BY, discourse, July 6, 1856, BYCD, 4:2031. *New York Daily Times*, June 23, 1857.

87. Thomas Stenhouse to BY, June 7, 1863, BYP. Gordon, *Question*, 81–83. PP, 325.

88. GQCD, June 30, July 4, 16, 1862.

89. Hahn, *Nation*, 281–85. Gary Anderson, *Massacre in Minnesota: The Dakota War of 1862* (Norman: University of Oklahoma Press, 2019).

90. Brigham Madsen, *The Shoshoni Frontier and the Bear River Massacre* (Salt Lake City: University of Utah Press, 1985); Darren Parry, *The Bear River Massacre: A Shoshone History* (Salt Lake City: BCC Press, 2019).

91. Rogers, *Unpopular*, 251–58; Scott Christensen, *Sagwitch: Shoshone Chieftain, Mormon Elder* (Logan: Utah State University Press, 1999); John Peterson, *Utah's Black Hawk War* (Salt Lake City: University of Utah Press, 1998).

92. BY, discourse, May 8, 1865, BYCD 4:2272. LB, 129–32.

93. See Vickie Speek, *"God Has Made Us a Kingdom": James Strang and the Midwest Mormons* (Salt Lake City: Signature Books, 2006); Miles Harvey, *The King of Confidence: A Tale of Utopian Dreamers, Frontier Schemers, True Believers, False Prophets, and the Murder of an American Monarch* (New York: Little, Brown, 2020).

94. See Roger Launius, *Joseph Smith III: Pragmatic Prophet* (Urbana: University of Illinois Press, 1988), 77–189. They called themselves the Church of Jesus Christ of Latter Day Saints. Unlike the Utah branch, their church's name lacked the hyphen and capitalized the *D*.

95. BY, discourse, October 7, 1863, BYCD 4:2159. GQCD, February 6, 1863. See Hales, *Polygamy*, 1:356–60. HFoF, 366–67.

96. Launius, *Pragmatic*, 217–72.

97. See Valeen Tippets Avery, *From Mission to Madness: The Last Son of the Mormon Prophet* (Urbana: University of Illinois Press, 1998).

98. Henry David Thoreau, *Walden* (Boston: Houghton, Mifflin, 1854), 146. *Atlantic Monthly*, May 1859. David Walker, *Railroading Religion: Mormons, Tourists, and the Corporate Spirit of the West* (Chapel Hill: University of North Carolina Press, 2019), 33–38.

99. BY, discourse, May 26, 1867, BYCD, 4:2442. GQC, discourse, October 7, 1868, JD 12:290. Walker, *Railroading*, 67–69.

100. GQCD, December 23, 1866. PP, 351–55.

101. BY, discourses, December 8, 1867; April 8, 1868, RSD:249–52, 263–65. ERS, discourse, May 12, 1868, ERSD. WoC, 86–94.

102. ERS, discourses, March 12, June 4, 1868; March 4, 1869, ERSD. ERS to Augusta Smith, May 7, 1858, RSD:281–83. (Emphasis in original.) ERSJ, October 3, 1843.

103. WoC, 95–88; HFoF, 372–76 (Kimball quote on 375). Madsen, *Wells*, 127–28.

104. Walker, *Railroading*, 44–48.

105. Walker, *Railroading*, 80–82.

106. PPW to children, January 12, 1864; July 30, 1865, PPWL.

107. PPW to children, October 20, 1867, PPWL. Ronald W. Walker, "The Salt Lake Tabernacle in the Nineteenth Century: A Glimpse of Early Mormonism," JMH 32, no. 23 (2005): 198–240.

108. PPW to children, January 22, October 20, 1867, PPWL.

Chapter 4: The Boundaries of Citizenship, 1870–90

1. GQCD, March 8, 1887.

2. SoTLDS, 351–52.

3. ERS, discourse, January 6, 1870, ERSCD. Mrs. Frank Leslie, *California: A Pleasure Trip from Gotham to the Golden Gate, April, May, June* (1877; Nieuwkoop, Netherlands: B. De Graaf, 1972), 78.

4. ERS, discourse, January 13, 1870, ERSD. WoC, 111–12; HFoF, 377–82.

5. Jill Lepore, *These Truths: A History of the United States* (New York: W. W. Norton, 2018), 311–16 (quote on 311–12).

6. See Richard White, *The Republic for Which It Stands: The United States during Reconstruction and the Gilded Age, 1865–1896* (New York: Oxford University Press, 2017), esp. 4–8. Clyde A. Milner II and Brian Q. Cannon, eds., *Reconstruction and Mormon America* (Norman: University of Oklahoma Press, 2019).

7. *New York Tribune*, November 22, 1871. GQCD, January 4, 1873. *Ainslee's Magazine*, January 1900.

8. Katherine Kitterman, "First to Vote: Utah's Unique Place in the Suffrage Movement," BYUSQ 59, no. 3 (Fall 2020): 17–43. A small segment of landowning women in New Jersey were able to vote during the early republic.

9. NYT, December 17, 1867.

10. Bathsheba Smith, January 6, 1870, RSD, 308. DN, March 24, 1869. William

H. Hooper, "The Utah Delegate and Female Suffrage Advocate," *Phrenological Journal* 51, no. 5 (November 1870): 328. Indigenous women living on reservations were still deprived of the vote in Utah until 1957.

11. SLT, July 1, 1871.
12. ERS, discourse, July 24, 1871, ERSD. See Jill Derr, "Eliza R. Snow and the Woman Question," BYUSQ 16, no. 2 (1976): 250–64.
13. WE, July 1, 1877. See Carol Madsen, *An Advocate for Women: The Public Life of Emmeline B. Wells, 1870–1920* (Provo, UT: BYU Press, 2005).
14. EBWD, March 24, June 3, 1875. Madsen, *Wells*, 130–34.
15. Fanny Stenhouse, *Exposé of Polygamy in Utah: A Lady's Life among the Mormons* (1872; London: George Routledge, 1873), 165.
16. Madsen, *Wells*, 163–66.
17. SLT, December 23, 1877. *Utah Magazine* (Salt Lake City), October 16, 1869. Ronald W. Walker, *Wayward Saints: The Godbeites and Brigham Young* (Urbana: University of Illinois Press, 1998); PP, 355–60. The *Tribune*'s name evolved at various points over the following decades.
18. Schuyler Colfax, *The Mormon Question* (Salt Lake City: Deseret News, 1870), 3–5. Eric Foner, *Reconstruction: America's Unfinished Revolution, 1863–77*, updated ed. (New York: Harper, 2014), 346–411.
19. William Nebeker to Theodore McKean, February 12, 1870, HL.
20. DN, January 12, 1870. GQC to George Albert Smith, GASP. SoTLDS, 353–55.
21. WP, February 6, 1878. SoTLDS, 351. Bitton, *Cannon*, 172–73. Lepore, *These Truths*, 339–48.
22. *Baltimore* (MD) *Evening Bulletin*, January 17, 1880. GQCD, February 4, 1873. Bitton, *Cannon*, 187–91. PP, 368–71.
23. See Terryl L. Givens, *The Viper on the Hearth: Mormons, Myths, and the Construction of Heresy* (New York: Oxford University Press, 1997), 97–120.
24. GQC to BY, April 18, 1874, BYP. GQCD, April 28, June 2, 1874. Gordon, *Question*, 111–12.
25. PP, 385–89. Bitton, *Cannon*, 192–95.
26. Robert Baskin, *Reminiscences of Early Utah* (Salt Lake City, 1914), 66. Gordon, *Question*, 113–16.
27. *New York Tribune*, July 13, 1859. PP, 373–74.
28. ERSD, August 24, 1870. PP, 380–88.
29. ERSD, November 7, 1870. Edward Bunker, "Autobiography," 18, HL. SoTLDS, 365–72.
30. Nebeker to McKean, April 17, 1874, HL. GQCD, August 26, 1875. Bunker, "Autobiography," 19. Draft of Constitution of Bunkerville, January 1, 1877, Bunker Papers, HL.
31. DN, July 7, 1878. Taysom, *Smith*, 141–43.
32. GQCD, August 29, 1875, April 13, 1877. Bitton, *Cannon*, 346.
33. EBWD, January 7, 1845. WE, May 1, 1879. Madsen, *Wells*, 146–48.
34. Maria Ford, Statement on Her Marriage to William Jarman, April 22, 1884, HL. Maria Ford to George C. Lambert, December 3, 1883, HL. DN, October 10, 1874. Albert Jarman to Maria (Ford) Barnes, before February 19 and

other letters, 1894, HL. See Susan W. Howard, "William Jarman: 'That Anti-Mormon Apostle of the British Isles,'" JMH 43, no. 21 (January 2017): 59–86; S3:40–42.

35. WoC, 106–7. Susa Young Gates to Lucy Bigelow Young, April 18, 1879, in *Woman's Voices: An Untold History of the Latter-day Saints, 1830–1900*, ed. Kenneth Godfrey et al. (Salt Lake City: Deseret Book, 1992), 334. Thomas W. Simpson, *American Universities and the Birth of Modern Mormonism, 1867–1940* (Chapel Hill: University of North Carolina Press, 2016), 18–25.

36. William Hartley, "The Priesthood Reorganization of 1877: Brigham Young's Last Achievement," BYUSQ 20, no. 1: 3–36. WoC, 118–23.

37. WE, April 1, 1881.

38. GCM, January 16, 1848. Gates, quoted in PP, 378. Lisle Brown, "'Temple Pro Tempore': The Salt Lake City Endowment House," JMH 34, no. 24 (Fall 2008): 1–68.

39. GQCD, November 9–10, 1876. Richard E. Bennett, *Temples Rising: A History of Sacrifice* (Salt Lake City: Deseret Book, 2019), 197–98.

40. WWD, January 1, March 21, 1877.

41. WWD, January 15, February 1, 12, 1877. Bennett, *Rising*, 205–17.

42. GQCD, April 10, 1877.

43. Devery Anderson, ed., *The Development of LDS Temple Worship: 1846–2000, A Documentary History* (Salt Lake City: Signature Books, 2011), 36–38, 163–64.

44. GQCD, August 26, 29, 1877. PP, 405–7.

45. EBWD, August 29, 1877. GQCD, August 29, 1877.

46. GQCD, October 6, 9, 1880.

47. GQCD, January 15, 1879. WE, December 1, 1878.

48. *National Citizen and Ballot Box* (Syracuse, NY), May 1879. EBWD, January 13, 17, 21, 1879. GQC to Taylor, January 28, 1879, FPC. SLT, January 8, 1879. Madsen, *Wells*, 183–89.

49. GQCD, March 16, 1878. Gordon, *Question*, 122–30.

50. Gordon, *Question*, 130–45 (quote on 143–44).

51. *A Review of the Decision of the Supreme Court of the United States, in the Case of Geo. Reynolds vs. the United States* (Salt Lake City: Deseret News, 1879), 4. Taylor, *The Supreme Court Decision in the Reynolds Case* (Salt Lake City, 1879), 4. WWD, February 26, 1879. WE, May 15, 1879.

52. GQCD, January 11, 21, May 7, 21, June 18, 28, August 28, 1879. SoTLDS, 397–98. Bitton, *Cannon*, 232–34.

53. Nathan B. Oman, "Natural Law and the Rhetoric of Empire: Reynolds v. United States, Polygamy, and Imperialism," *Washington University Law Review* 88 (2011): 661–706; Tisa Wenger, *Religious Freedom: The Contested History of an American Ideal* (Chapel Hill: University of North Carolina Press, 2017).

54. GQCD, September 29, 1880, December 7, 1881, January 24, 1882. GQC to Eliza Cannon, December 8, 1881, Eliza T. Cannon Correspondence, CHL.

55. GQCD, February 16, 1882. GQC to Eliza Cannon, February 17, 1882, Cannon Correspondence.

56. GQCD, February 3, April 11, 1882.

57. GQCD, February 25, April 19, June 21, 1882.

58. *Atlanta* (GA) *Constitution*, August 26, 1884. Patrick Q. Mason, *The Mormon Menace: Violence and Anti-Mormonism in the Postbellum South* (New York: Oxford University Press, 2011), 35–56.

59. Gary James Bergera, ed., *The Autobiography of B. H. Roberts* (Salt Lake City: Signature Books, 1990), 1, 145. GQC, discourse, August 24, 1884, JD, 25:287–88. GQCD, August 19, 1884. John McAllister to Edward Bunker Jr., October 20, 1884, Bunker Papers, HL. John Sillito, *B. H. Roberts: A Life in the Public Arena* (Salt Lake City: Signature Books, 2021), 95–126.

60. *Pittsburg* (PA) *Leader*, November 12, 1883. GQCD, October 14, 19, 1882; June 27, July 2, 1884. SoTLDS, 393–95.

61. Wilford Woodruff to Emma Woodruff, January 14, 1884. (Emphasis in original.) GQCD, October 24–25, 1884. SoTLDS, 403–4. Gordon, *Question*, 157.

62. GQCD, October 23, 27, November 3–4, 1884. Daynes, *More Wives*, 174.

63. WWD, December 31, 1884. Wilford Woodruff to John Taylor and GQC, January 27, 1885, First Presidency Correspondence, CHL. GQCD, December 23, 27, 29, 1884, January 11, 13, 22, 23, 1885.

64. John Taylor, discourse, February 1, 1885, recorded by Lucy B. Young, 4–5, 7, CHL. GQCD, February 3–4, 1885.

65. John Whitaker, Diary #1, 1, HL.

66. Whittaker, Diary #2, 16, HL. Whitaker, Diary #3, 1–4, HL. "List of those who entertained the Presidents during the Underground years," CHL.

67. GQCD, February 14, 16, March 17, September 15, October 8, 1885. GQC to Cleveland, March 25, June 3, 1885, GQCP. GQC to Daniel Manning, August 7, 1885, GQCP.

68. GQCD, April 6, 11, 21, 29, 1885.

69. Daniel Wells to John Taylor, December 3, 1885, FPC.

70. GQCD, February 27, March 17, 1886. Nebeker to McKean, February 22, 1886, HL.

71. Martha Hughes Cannon to Barbara Replogle, May 1, 1885, Martha Cannon Collection, CHL. John Winder, in GQCD, December 15, 1885. Lewis Allen to Edward Bunker Jr., May 6, 1885, HL. John D. T. McAllister to Ann E. McAllister, October 18, 1888, CHL. C. Layton to John Taylor, May 30, 1885, First Presidency Correspondence, CHL. Bitton, *Cannon*, 282. Gordon, *Question*, 157–61.

72. Sillito, *Roberts*, 133–59.

73. Moroni Brown, diary, August 6, September 25, 1886, CHL. James Mills Paxton, "262 Days in the Penitentiary," December 8, 1889, February 14, 1890, CHL. William Fife to Moroni Brown, March 15, 1886, CHL.

74. WE, May 1, 1886. Madsen, *Wells*, 217–27.

75. Whitaker, Diary #1, 20–23. Whitaker, Diary #3, 17.

76. Whitaker, Diary #3, 7. SLT, September 7, 1886. Kenneth Cannon II, "The Tragic Matter of Louie Wells and John Q. Cannon," JMH 35, no. 22 (2009):126–90; Madsen, *Wells*, 233–58.

77. EBWD, July 16, 1887.
78. ERSCD, September 5, 15, 1884.
79. EBWD, December 7, 1887. WoC, 127–28.
80. GQCD, February 13, July 25, 1887. John W. Young to John Taylor and GQC, February 5, 1887, FPC.
81. GQCD, September 13, 1887. Ronald W. Walker, "Grant's Watershed: Succession in the Presidency, 1887–1889," BYUSQ 43, no. 1 (2004): 195–229.
82. EBWD, June 12, 1888. WoC, 129–34. Madsen, *Wells*, 264–65.
83. Eli Murray to Grover Cleveland, December 1, 1885, GCP. Caleb West to Cleveland, July 21, 1886, GCP. Charles Penrose to John Taylor, February 16, 1887, John Taylor Letter File, UofU.
84. EBWD, January 12, 1887. Gordon, *Question*, 164–81 (quote on 168).
85. Gordon, *Question*, 183–220.
86. Whitaker, Diary #5, 8, HL. GQCD, November 15, 1887. SoTLDS, 416–19.
87. GQCD, October 8, 1887, September 14–17, 1888. EBWD, October 8, 1887. Bitton, *Cannon*, 292–96.
88. GQCD, September 9, 11, 1889. WWD, December 31, 1889.
89. DN, December 21, 1889. *St. Louis* (MO) *Globe-Democrat*, February 9, 1890. (Emphasis in original.) Thomas G. Alexander, *Things in Heaven and Earth: The Life and Times of Wilford Woodruff, a Mormon Prophet* (Salt Lake City: Signature Books, 1991), 266–68. Gordon, *Question*, 211–13. Bennett, *Rising*, 268–78.
90. GQCD, February 17, June 11, July 17, 21, 31, 1890. Bitton, *Cannon*, 307–12.
91. WWD, September 25, 1890. GQCD, September 22–24, 1890.
92. Frank Cannon, *Under the Prophet in Utah: The National Menace of a Political Priestcraft* (Boston: C. M. Clark Publishing, 1911), 102–11. Bitton, *Cannon*, 312–17.
93. EBWD, September 29, 1890. Roberts, diary, 1890–93, 39–40, UofU. S2:602–4.
94. Whitaker, Diary #8, 9–11, HL.
95. Joseph H. Dean, journal, October 6, 1890, CHL. Roberts, diary, 42. Annie Cowley, diary, October 6, 1890, CHL. Zina DH Young, diary, October 6, 1890, RSD:574. B. Carmon Hardy, *Solemn Covenant: The Mormon Polygamous Passage* (Urbana: University of Illinois Press, 1992), 133–35.
96. Hardy, *Solemn*, 206–7.
97. Frank Cannon to Grover Cleveland, May 24, 1888, GCP.

Chapter 5: A Period of Progress, 1890–1920

1. EBWD, April 6, 1900.
2. B. H. Roberts, "Mormonism: A Paper Submitted to the Parliament of Religions at the World's Columbian Exposition," in Roberts, *Defense of the Faith and the Saints*, vol. 1 (Salt Lake City, 1907), 25.
3. Richard Neitzel Holzapfel and Stephen H. Smoot, "Wilford Woodruff's 1897 Testimony," in *Banner of the Gospel: Wilford Woodruff*, ed. Alexander Baugh and Susan Easton Black (Provo, UT: Religious Studies Center, 2010): 327–64.

4. WWD, September 8, 1893. Bennett, *Rising*, 286–98. Reid Neilson, *Exhibiting Mormonism: The Latter-day Saints and the 1893 Chicago World's Fair* (New York: Oxford University Press, 2011). Konden Smith Hansen, *Frontier Religion: Mormons and America, 1857–1907* (Salt Lake City: University of Utah Press, 2019).

5. See Louis Menand, *The Metaphysical Club: A Story of Ideas in America* (New York: Farrar, Straus and Giroux, 2001).

6. DN, October 3, 1893.

7. NYT, February 16, 1893.

8. WWD, December 31, 1893. For overviews of this period, see Thomas G. Alexander, *Mormonism in Transition: A History of the Latter-day Saints, 1890–1930* (Urbana: University of Illinois Press, 1986); Ethan R. Yorgason, *Transformation of the Mormon Culture Region* (Urbana: University of Illinois Press, 2010).

9. Marriner Merrill, diary, September 21, 1890; August 20, 1891, CHL. See Hardy, *Solemn*, 148–50; Alexander, *Transition*, 12.

10. Smith to Mercy Fielding Thompson, November 18, 1890, JFSP. DN, September 28, 1891. Jan Shipps, "The Principle Revoked: A Closer Look at the Demise of Plural Marriage," JMH 11 (1984): 65–77; Hardy, *Solemn*, 141–46.

11. Hardy, *Solemn*, 169–77, 182, 227–32. Alexander, *Woodruff*, 324–28. D. Michael Quinn, "LDS Authority and New Plural Marriages, 1890–1904," *Dialogue* 18, no. 1 (1985): 9–105.

12. SLT, November 3, 1890.

13. See Heather Cox Richardson, *How the South Won the Civil War: Oligarchy, Democracy, and the Continuing Fight for the Soul of America* (New York: Oxford University Press, 2020), 101–3.

14. Abraham H. Cannon, diary, June 10, 1891, in *Candid Insights of a Mormon Apostle: The Diaries of Abraham H. Cannon, 1889–1895*, ed. Edward Leo Lyman (Salt Lake City: Signature Books, 2010), 218–19. Franklin Richards, diary, June 10, 1891, CHL. Gene A. Sessions, ed., *Mormon Democrat: The Religious and Political Memoirs of James Henry Moyle* (Salt Lake City: Signature Books, 1998), 150–51. GCQD, March 23, 1893. See Alexander, *Transition*, 7; Edward Leo Lyman, *Finally Statehood! Utah's Struggles, 1849–1896* (Salt Lake City: Signature Books, 2019), 266–78, 296–99.

15. SLT, June 23, 1891. Joseph F. Smith, *Another Plain Talk: Reasons Why the People of Utah Should Be Republicans* (Salt Lake City: Republican Central Committee, 1892), 15–16. D. Michael Quinn, *The Mormon Hierarchy: Extensions of Power* (Salt Lake City: Signature Books, 1997), 330–31.

16. SLT, July 31, 1891; March 22, 23, 30, 31, April 6, 10, 1893. Lyman, *Statehood*, 290–92, 310–16.

17. Abraham H. Cannon, diary, February 8, July 12, 1892, 301–2, 342–44.

18. DN, January 5, 1893. GQCD, January 5, March 11, 1893. Lyman, *Statehood*, 316–30; Hardy, *Solemn*, 152; Howard R. Lamar, "National Perceptions of Utah's Statehood," JMH 23, no. 1 (1997): 42–65.

19. GQCD, January 4, 1896. John Hartvigsen, "Utah's Mammoth Statehood Flag," *Raven: A Journal of Vexillology* 19 (2012): 27–56.

20. GQCD, October 24, November 7, 19, 1895; January 14, 1896. Lyman, *Statehood*, 343–46; Quinn, *Extensions*, 354.

21. GCQD, April 6, October 5, November 12, 18–20, 1896. Edward Leo Lyman, "The Alienation of an Apostle from His Quorum: The Moses Thatcher Case," *Dialogue* 18, no. 3 (1985): 69–91; Kenneth Godfrey, "Moses Thatcher in the Dock: His Trials, the Aftermath, and His Last Days," JMH 24, no. 1 (1998): 54–88; Quinn, *Extensions*, 350–52; Lyman, *Statehood*, 348–56.

22. Lyman, *Statehood*, 336–37; Jean Bickmore White, "A Woman's Place Is in the Constitution: The Struggle for Equal Rights in Utah," *Utah Historical Quarterly* 42, no. 4 (1974): 344–69.

23. GCQD, August 2, 1897. Martha Hughes, quoted in Jonathan Stapley and Constance Lieber, "Do Some Little Good Work While We Live," in *Women of Faith in the Latter Days*, ed. Richard Turley Jr. and Brittany Chapman, vol. 3 (Salt Lake City, UT: Deseret Book, 2014). Susan Anthony and Ida Husted Harper, eds., *History of Woman Suffrage*, 4 vols. (Indianapolis: Hollenbeck Press, 1902), 4:319.

24. GQCD, December 30, 1899. Hardy, *Solemn*, 247–50. Jana Riess, "Polygamy in the Nation's Capitol: Protestant Women and the 1899 Campaign against B. H. Roberts," in *Mormonism and American Politics*, ed. Randall Balmer and Jana Riess (New York: Columbia University Press, 2016), 32–52.

25. Quinn, *Extensions*, 331–33.

26. GQCD, September 2, 1898.

27. MSS, 33.

28. Dave Hall, *A Faded Legacy: Amy Brown Lyman and Mormon Women's Activism, 1872–1959* (Salt Lake City: University of Utah Press, 2015), 32–34.

29. See Amy Brown Lyman, "Tribute to Karl G. Maeser," Amy Brown Lyman Papers, BYU; Gary Bergera and Ron Priddis, *Brigham Young University: A House of Faith* (Salt Lake City: Signature Books, 1985), 1–13.

30. Hall, *Lyman*, 35–39 (quote on 38). Dunford, quoted in S3, 25.

31. Jane Addams, "Subjective Necessity for Social Settlements," in *Philanthropy and Social Progress. Seven Essays* (1893; Patterson Smith Reprint, 1970), 20. See Rima Lunin Schultz, "Jane Addams, Apotheosis of Social Christianity," *Church History* 84, no. 1 (2015): 207–19; Jennifer Ratner-Rosenhagan, *The Ideas That Made America: A Brief History* (New York: Oxford University Press, 2019), 108–10; Lepore, *These Truths*, 380.

32. Hall, *Lyman*, 40, 45–48.

33. Hall, *Lyman*, 48–50.

34. WoC, 150–51.

35. Alexander, *Transition*, 5–6. WoC, 154–55. MSS, 35.

36. CR, November 1901.

37. Alexander, *Transition*, 5, 95–96, 99–100, 112. SoTLDS, 474–80. See Matthew Bowman, "Eternal Progression: Mormonism and American Progressivism," in Balmer and Riess, *Mormonism and American Politics*, 53–70; William Hartley, "The Priesthood Reform Movement, 1908–1922," BYUSQ 13, no. 1 (1973): 137–56.

38. Richard H. Cracroft, "Nephi, Seer of Modern Times: The Home Literature Novels of Nephi Anderson," BYUSQ 25, no. 2 (1985): 3–15; Ardis Parshall and Michael Austin, eds., *Josephine Spencer: Her Collected Works* (Salt Lake City: By Common Consent Press, 2020); Kylie Nielson Turley, "'Untrumpeted and Unseen': Josephine Spencer, Mormon 'Authoress,'" JMH 27, no. 1 (2001): 127–64. Randy Astle and Gideon Burton, "A History of Mormon Cinema: The Second Wave: Home Cinema (1929–1953)," BYUSQ 46, no. 2 (2007): 45–75.

39. DN, December 19, 1903.

40. Newell, *Sister,* 109–12.

41. Newell, *Sister,* 113–15, 119. Reeve, *Different,* 202. Mueller, *Race,* 201.

42. James, quoted in Henry J. Wolfinger, "A Test of Faith: Jane Elizabeth James and the Origins of the Utah Black Community," in *Social Accommodation in Utah,* ed. Clark S. Knowlton (Salt Lake City: University of Utah, 1975), 148–50. Jane Manning James Autobiography, circa 1902, dictated to Elizabeth Roundy, CHL. See Quincy D. Newell, "The Autobiography and Interview of Jane Elizabeth Manning James," *Journal of Africana Religions* 1, no. 2 (2013): 252–301; Mueller, *Race,* 119–52.

43. W. E. B. Du Bois, *The Souls of Black Folk: Essays and Sketches,* 5th ed. (Chicago: A. C. McClurg & Co., 1904), vii. Du Bois, "To the Nations of the World," in *My Life and Work,* ed. Alexander Walters (New York: Fleming H. Revell Co., 1917), 257.

44. Background and sources for Banks comes from Ardis Parshall, "Elijah A. Banks," CBM. Statistics come from Edwin S. Gaustad and Leigh Schmidt, *The Religious History of America: The Heart of the American Story from Colonial Times to Today,* rev. ed. (San Francisco: HarperOne, 2004), 217–20. See also Nicole Myers Turner, *Soul Liberty: The Evolution of Black Religious Politics in Postemancipation Virginia* (Chapel Hill: University of North Carolina Press, 2020).

45. Church of Jesus Christ of Latter-day Saints, Minneapolis Branch, Sunday School Minutes and Records, February 16, March 9, April 27, 1902, quoted in Parshall, "Elijah A. Banks." Asahel H. Woodruff to P. P. Taylor, February 5, 1904, Northern States Mission, CHL. JI, February 1, 1903.

46. *Liahona: The Elders' Journal* 6, no. 1 (June 20, 1908): 19. See Justin Bray, "John Wesley Harmon," CBM.

47. German E. Ellsworth to Joseph F. Smith, December 24, 1909, Northern States Mission, CHL. Ibram X. Kendi, *Stamped from the Beginning: The Definitive History of Racist Ideas in America* (New York: PublicAffairs, 2016), 290–91.

48. For these inquiries, see Reeve, *Different,* 203–4.

49. Jane Elizabeth James to Joseph F. Smith, August 31, 1903, in Wolfinger, "A Test of Faith," 151. Matthias F. Cowley, quoted in Newell, *Sister,* 131–33.

50. George A. Smith Family Papers, Council Minutes, August 26, 1908, UofU. See Reeve, *Different,* 207–10.

51. George F. Gibbs to Elijah A. and Caroline B. Banks, July 11, 1911, abbreviated typescript in SGKC. First Presidency to Ben E. Rich, May 1, 1912, in *Minutes of the Apostles of the Church of Jesus Christ of Latter-day Saints,* 4 vols. (Salt Lake City: self-pub., 2010), 4:1576.

52. Bray, "John Wesley Harmon, Jr." Parshall, "Elijah A. Banks."

53. See Mohrman, *Queer*, 157–66.

54. GQCD, November 8, 1900. Kathleen Flake, *The Politics of American Religious Identity: The Seating of Senator Reed Smoot, Mormon Apostle* (Chapel Hill: University of North Carolina Press, 2004), 12–13.

55. James H. Howell to Ed Callister, January 18, 1906, SGKC. Alexander, *Transition*, 241; Flake, *Politics*, 5, 33–34, 51–53, 68.

56. *New York World*, March 10, 1904. Flake, *Politics*, 56–57. For Smith's involvement with the trial, see Taysom, *Smith*, 291–92, 307–13.

57. Alexander, *Transition*, 66.

58. Anthon Lund, diary, April 6, 1904, in John P. Hatch, ed., *Danish Apostle: The Diaries of Anthon H. Lund, 1890–1921* (Salt Lake City: Signature Books, 2006), 272. Heber J. Grant to Joseph F. Smith, January 5, 1906, SGKC. Ben E. Rich to Joseph F. Smith, November 15, 1905, SGKC.

59. Reed Smoot to Joseph F. Smith, December 8, 1905, CHL. Smoot to Jesse M. Smith, March 22, 1904, CHL.

60. Flake, *Politics*, 94–102, 144; Hardy, *Solemn*, 264–65.

61. O. N. Malmquist, *First One Hundred Years: A History of the* Salt Lake Tribune, *1871–1971* (Salt Lake City: Utah State Historical Society, 1971), 229. Flake, *Politics*, 145–58; Smith Hansen, *Frontier*, 198–234.

62. Annie Clark Tanner, *A Mormon Mother: An Autobiography*, rev. ed. (Salt Lake City: Tanner Trust Fund, 1973), 223–26. Hardy, *Solemn*, 291, 313–19.

63. Alexander, *Transition*, 67–70.

64. Alexander, *Transition*, 198–203, 261–62.

65. D. Michael Quinn, *Elder Statesman: A Biography of J. Reuben Clark* (Salt Lake City: Signature Books, 2002), 2–4.

66. Frank Fox, *J. Reuben Clark: The Public Years* (Provo, UT: Brigham Young University Press, 1980), 437. Clark's copy of the Smoot proceedings is found in JRCP.

67. Harold B. Lee, "President J. Reuben Clark Jr.: An Appreciation on His Ninetieth Birthday," IE, September 1961, 632. Quinn, *Statesman*, 13–16.

68. J. Reuben Clark, memorandums, quoted in Quinn, *Statesman*, 26.

69. John Augustine Zahm, *Evolution and Dogma* (Chicago: D. H. McBride, 1896). Pope Pius X, *Pascendi Dominici Gregis: Encyclical of Pope Pius X on the Doctrines of the Modernists*, September 8, 1907, Libreria Editrice Vaticana. Andrew Jewett, *Science under Fire: Challenges to Scientific Authority in Modern America* (Cambridge: Harvard University Press, 2020).

70. John A. Widtsoe, *Joseph Smith as Scientist: A Contribution to Mormon Philosophy* (Salt Lake City: General Boards Young Men's Mutual Improvement Association, 1908), 8. See Alexander, *Transition*, 275.

71. JETJ, May 4, 1884. John A. Widtsoe, *Rational Theology as Taught by the Church of Jesus Christ of Latter-day Saints* (Salt Lake City: General Priesthood Committee, 1915), iii. See Simpson, *Universities*, 63, 71–72. Alexander, *Transition*, 140–43, 167; Matthew Bowman, "James Talmage, B. H. Roberts, and Confes-

sional History in a Secular Age," in *Standing Apart: Mormon Historical Consciousness and the Concept of Apostasy*, ed. Miranda Wilcox and John D. Young (New York: Oxford University Press, 2014), 77–92; Miranda Wilcox, "Sacralizing the Secular in Latter-day Saint Salvation Histories (1890–1930)," JMH 46, no. 3 (2020): 23–59.

72. IE 11, no. 7 (May 1908): 523. Simpson, *Universities*, 54–68, 71–72. Alexander, *Transition*, 167.

73. IE, November 1909. Simpson, *Universities*, 72.

74. Horace Hall Cummings to Joseph F. Smith, January 21, 1911, BYU Board of Trustees Minutes, February 20, 1911, in Henry Peterson Papers, USU. See Gary James Bergera, "The 1911 Evolution Controversy at Brigham Young University," in *The Search for Harmony: Essays on Science and Mormonism*, ed. Gene A. Sessions and Crag J. Oberg (Salt Lake City: Signature Books, 1993), 23–41.

75. *Salt Lake City Herald-Republican*, February 23, 1911. SLT, March 16, 1911. Simpson, *Universities*, 78–84. JI, April 1911; IE, April 1911; DN, March 17, 1911.

76. JI, April 1911. IE, July 1911. Henry Peterson, typed autobiographical notes, 112, Henry Peterson Papers, USU.

77. Luciane to JRC, January 6, January 14, and April 9, 1923, in JRCP.

78. JRC to Luciane, July 12, 1923, JRCP. Clark to Cloyd Marvin, December 1, 1956, quoted in Quinn, *Statesman*, 26.

79. Talmage, *The Vitality of Mormonism* (Salt Lake City: Deseret News, 1917), 6.

80. Hall, *Lyman*, 53.

81. MSS, 36.

82. WoC, 174–75. Alexander, *Transition*, 135. Jonathan Stapley and Kristine Wright, "Female Ritual Healing in Mormonism," JMH 37, no. 1 (2011): 40–53.

83. RSM 8 (February 1921): 113.

84. Hall, *Lyman*, 59–62; WoC, 154–55.

85. RSM 1 (January 1914): 1–3. WoC, 187–90 (quote on 189). A bridge periodical, *The Bulletin*, served for one year between the *Exponent* and *Relief Society Magazine*.

86. WoC, 195–96, 215–17, 236–38. Hall, *Lyman*, 5, 84–85. Alexander, *Transition*, 131.

87. CR, October 1914, 7. IE, September 1914, 1074–76. CR, October 1916. CR, April 1917. Richard Bennett, "'And I Saw the Hosts of the Dead, Both Small and Great': Joseph F. Smith, World War I, and His Visions of the Dead," *Religious Educator* 2, no. 1 (2001): 104–25. Alexander, *Transition*, 46–49.

88. IE 22 (December 1918): 148–52. See John M. Barry, *The Great Influenza: The Story of the Deadliest Pandemic in History* (New York: Penguin Books, 2005).

89. Joseph Fielding Smith, *Life of Joseph F. Smith* (Salt Lake City: Deseret News Press, 1938), 476. George Tate, "'The Great World of the Spirits of the Dead': Death, the Great War, and the 1918 Influenza Pandemic as Context for Doctrine and Covenants 138," BYUSQ 46, no. 1 (2007): 10–12.

90. DN, October 31, 1918.

91. IE 22 (November 1918): 80. JETJ, October 31, 1918. DN, November 30, 1918. Smith, *Life*, 466. See Tate, "Great World," 7–9. Taysom, *Smith*, 356–57. A half

century later, the vision was adopted as scripture and added to the Doctrine
and Covenants as section 138.

92. Ronald W. Walker, "Rachel R. Grant: The Continuing Legacy of the Feminine Ideal," in *Supporting Saints: Life Stories of Nineteenth-Century Mormons*,
ed. Donald Cannon and David Whittaker (Provo, UT: BYU Religious Studies Center, 1985): 17–42; Walker, "A Mormon 'Widow' in Colorado: The Exile
of Emily Wells Grant," *Arizona and the West* 25, no. 1 (1983): 5–22.

93. See Ronald W. Walker, *Qualities That Count: Heber J. Grant as Businessman,
Missionary, and Apostle* (Provo, UT: BYU Studies, 2004).

94. Susa Young Gates to the Presidency and Board of the Relief Society, November 4, 1919, in WoC, 216.

95. Madsen, *Wells*, 491–94; WoC, 221–23.

96. EBWD, January 9, 1904.

Chapter 6: The Perils of Reform, 1920–45

1. Sessions, *Mormon Democrat*, 21.

2. Davis Bitton and Maureen Whipple, "Riding Herd: A Conversation with
Juanita Brooks," *Dialogue* 9, no. 1 (1974): 25–27.

3. See Levi Peterson, *Juanita Brooks: Mormon Woman Historian* (Salt Lake City:
University of Utah, 1988).

4. F. Scott Fitzgerald, *This Side of Paradise* (New York: Charles Scribner's Sons,
1920), 282. Walter Lippmann, *A Preface to Morals* (1929; New York: Routledge,
2017), 8. Lippmann, *Drift and Mastery: An Attempt to Diagnose the Current
Unrest* (1914; Madison: University of Wisconsin Press, 2015), 147. See Jennifer
Ratner-Rosenhagen, *The Ideas That Made America: A Brief History* (New York:
Oxford University Press, 2019), 116–17.

5. Juanita Brooks to Dale Morgan, December 28, 1945, SLJB, 72.

6. Harris, quoted in Bergera and Priddis, *University*, 50.

7. Bergera and Priddis, *University*, 1–50 (courses listed on 16, 60). J. Gordon
Daines III, "'By Study and Also by Faith': Balancing the Sacred and the Secular at Brigham Young University in the 1930s and 1940s," BYUSQ 59, no. 1
(2020): 157–82. Simpson, *Universities*, 92–95.

8. Heber J. Grant, BYU Board of Trustees Minutes, April 26, 1921, BYU President's Records, BYU. Charles Penrose to Joseph W. McMurrin, October 31,
1921, First Presidency Letterpress Copybooks, CHL. See Bergera and Priddis, *University*, 50–51; Simpson, *Universities*, 95–97.

9. Casey Paul Griffiths, "Joseph F. Merrill and the Transformation of Church
Education," in *A Firm Foundation: Church Organization and Administration*,
ed. David Whittaker and Arnold Garr (Provo, UT: BYU Religious Studies
Center, 2011), 377–402. Alexander, *Transition*, 168–69.

10. John A. Widtsoe, *In Search of Truth* (SLC: Deseret Book, 1930), 90. Russel
Swensen, "Mormons at the Chicago Divinity School," *Dialogue* 7, no. 2 (1972):
37–39. Simpson, *Universities*, 98–101. Casey Paul Griffiths, "The Chicago

Experiment: Finding the Voice and Charting the Course of Religious Education in the Church," BYUSQ 49, no. 4 (2010): 93–95.

11. Lyon, quoted in Griffiths, "The Chicago Experiment," 101. Swensen, "Mormons at the Chicago Divinity School," 43. T. Edgar Lyon to David Lyon,
August 21, 1931, Lyon Collection, BYU.

12. *Y News* (Provo, UT), February 9, 1927. G. V. Billings to George Brimhall,
March 26, 1926, Brimhall Papers, BYU. Susa Young Gates to Frank Harris,
February 27, 1930; Gates to Harris, March 8, 1930, Harris Papers, BYU. See
Bergera and Priddis, *University*, 56.

13. Richard R. Lyman to Franklin Harris, June 14, 1932, Harris Papers, BYU.
Richard R. Lyman, diary, January 7, 1929, BYU.

14. "Report of the Correlation-Social Advisory Committee to the First Presidency and the Council of Twelve on the Definition and Assignment of Auxiliary Functions and Organizations," April 12, 1921, CHL. See Alexander,
Transition, 153–54.

15. Susa Young Gates, diary, May 1922, CHL. See MSS, 48–49.

16. MSS, 51. Hall, *Lyman*, 81. WoC, 230–31.

17. Amy Brown Lyman, "Achievements of Women, 1926," in Hall, *Lyman*, 30.
RSM 16 (December 1929): 661.

18. Alexander, *Transition*, 264–65, 300–302. Jonathan Stapley, *The Power of Godliness: Mormon Liturgy and Cosmology* (New York: Oxford University Press,
2018), 88–94.

19. Heber J. Grant, diary, February 24, 27, 1928, in Alexander, *Transition*, 135.

20. Hall, *Lyman*, 18, 63–64.

21. May Booth Talmage, "'These Wives,' by May Booth Talmage, Made at Social
Gathering in the Home of Br. & Sister M. J. Ballard, March 28, 1923," Minutes of the Wives of the General Authorities Club, CHL. The poem was one
of several highlighting the ambitious wives of priesthood leaders.

22. See Alison Collis Greene, *No Depression in Heaven: The Great Depression, the
New Deal, and the Transformation of Religion in the Delta* (New York: Oxford
University Press, 2015).

23. RSM 19 (November 1932): 641. RSM 21 (May 1934): 287–89. Garth Mangum
and Bruce Blumell, *The Mormons' War on Poverty: A History of LDS Welfare,
1830–1990* (Salt Lake City: University of Utah Press, 1993), 116–88. See also
RSM 20 (November 1933): 658–59; RSM 21 (November 1934): 685; Hall,
Lyman, 117–22; WoC, 253–54.

24. Susa Young Gates to Franklin S. Harris, September 3, 1930, Harris Papers,
BYU. Sillitoe, *Roberts*. The Roberts collection at the LDS Church History
Library lists 1,385 books that were in his possession.

25. William Riter to James Talmage, August 22, 1921, in B. H. Roberts, *Studies of
the Book of Mormon*, ed. Brigham Madsen, 2nd ed. (Salt Lake City: Signature
Books, 1992), 35–36. B. H. Roberts, *New Witnesses for God*, vol. 2, *The Book of
Mormon* (Salt Lake City: Deseret News, 1909), iii–viii.

26. Roberts to Heber Grant, December 29, 1921, March 15, 1922, and Roberts to
Richard Lyman, October 24, 1927, all in Roberts, *Studies*, 45–47. Wesley P.

Lloyd, journal, August 1933, Lloyd Papers, BYU. JETJ, January 4 and 5, 1922. See Shannon Caldwell Montez, "The Secret Mormon Meetings of 1922" (master's thesis, University of Reno, 2019).

27. Roberts, *Studies*, 143.

28. Givens, *Hand*, 89–116.

29. B. H. Roberts, *The Truth, the Way, the Life: An Elementary Treatise on Theology*, ed. John W. Welch, 2nd ed. (Provo, UT: BYU Studies, 1996), 17, 20, 27, 240, 318. His sources are listed on 743–52. Notably, of all his references to scripture, only 10 percent came from the Book of Mormon, a drastic decrease when compared to his previous volumes. The manuscript still reaffirmed the text's antiquity, but demonstrated a weakened faith in its stability.

30. Joseph Fielding Smith, quoted in James B. Allen, "The Story of *The Truth, The Way, The Life*," in Roberts, *Truth*, 700. The relevant sources for these debates are closed to historians but are summarized and quoted in Allen's article.

31. Committee Report, October 10, 1929, in Allen, "The Story," 700. DN, April 5, 1930. B. H. Roberts to George Albert Smith, April 28, 1930, in Allen, "The Story," 701. On the January meetings, see Allen, "The Story," 705–6.

32. Sterling Talmage to James Talmage, February 9, 1931, Sterling Talmage Papers, UofU.

33. Ronald L. Numbers, *The Creationists: From Scientific Creationism to Intelligent Design*, expanded ed. (Cambridge: Harvard University Press, 2006), 72–101.

34. Matthew Avery Sutton, *American Apocalypse: A History of Modern Evangelicalism* (Cambridge: Harvard University Press, 2014), 149–54. See Michael Lienesch, *In the Beginning: Fundamentalism, the Scopes Trial, and the Making of the Antievolution Movement* (Chapel Hill: University of North Carolina Press, 2007).

35. Alexander, *Transition*, 283–86. "Mormon View of Education," September 1925, in Clark, *Messages of the First Presidency* 5:243–44. IE, October 1925, 1109–31.

36. Smith, quoted in Allen, "The Story," 729.

37. First Presidency Report, April 5, 1931, in Allen, "The Story," 709.

38. See Fox, *Clark*, 447–85.

39. Fox, *Clark*, 446.

40. Quinn, *Statesman*, 42–48.

41. CR, April 1933. Quinn, *Statesman*, 392.

42. Mangum and Blumell, *War on Poverty*, 97, 111–12. Joseph Darowski, "The WPA versus the Utah Church," in *Utah in the Twentieth Century*, ed. Brian Cannon and Jessie L. Embry (Logan: Utah State University Press, 2009), 168–69. See also Charles Peterson and Brian Cannon, *The Awkward State of Utah: Coming of Age in the Nation, 1896–1945* (Salt Lake City: University of Utah Press, 2015), 292–304. MSS, 58.

43. Grant to Clark, October 18, 1940, JRCP. Quinn, *Statesman*, 57–74, 89–91, 94–95.

44. CR, October 1936. SoTLDS, 517–25. LJAD, June 27, 1973, 1:539.

45. Hall, *Lyman*, 145–46. Jill Mulvay Derr, "Changing Relief Society Charity to Make Way for Welfare," in *New Views of Mormon History*, ed. Davis Bitton

and Maureen Ursenbach Beecher (Salt Lake City: University of Utah Press, 1987): 242–72.

46. Luacine Savage Clark to J. Reuben Clark, August 20, 1936, JRCP. NYT, May 25, 1936. Quinn, *Extensions*, 359.

47. SoTLDS, 525. Mangum and Blumell, *War on Poverty*, 112. MSS, 60.

48. See Allison Kelley, "Free Agency, Hard Work, and the Justification of Economic Inequality in the Church of Jesus Christ of Latter-day Saints," MSR 10 (2023): 10–20.

49. Sessions, *Mormon Democrat*, 32, 288.

50. Marianne Watson, "From Nineteenth-Century Mormon Polygamy to Twentieth-Century Mormon Fundamentalism: Three Contemporary Perspectives on John W. and Lorin C. Wooley," in *The Persistence of Polygamy: Fundamentalist Mormon Polygamy from 1890 to the Present*, ed. Newell Bringhurst and Craig Foster (Independence, MO: John Whitmer Books, 2013), 144–80.

51. *Truth* (Salt Lake City), July 1939. Quinn, *Statesman*, 244–52; Hardy, *Solemn*, 342–43. Cristina Rosetti, "'Hysteria Excommunicatus': Loyalty Oaths, Excommunication, and the Forging of a Mormon Identity," JMH 47, no. 3 (2021): 22–43.

52. *Truth*, June 1, 1935. See Cristina Rosetti, *Saint Joseph W. Musser: A Mormon Fundamentalist* (Urbana: University of Illinois Press, forthcoming).

53. Martha Sonntag Bradley, *Kidnapped from That Land: The Government Raids on the Short Creek Polygamists* (Salt Lake City: University of Utah Press, 1993), 18–39.

54. Elisa Eastwood Pulido, "Margarito Bautista, Mexican Politics, and the Third Convention," MSR 8 (2021): 48–56.

55. Margarito Bautista, *The Evolution of Mexico: Its True Progenitors and Its Origin: The Destiny of America and Europe*, trans. Brett Morrison and Fernando Gomez (Provo, UT: Museum of Mormon Mexican History, 2014). "Letter to the First Presidency," in *Informe general de la Tercera Convención* (Mexico, DF: Comité Directive, 1936), 20. Pulido, *The Spiritual Evolution of Margarito Bautista: Mexican Mormon Evangelizer, Polygamist Dissident, and Utopian Founder, 1878–1961* (New York: Oxford University Press, 2020).

56. The Third Convention schism came to a close a decade later, when a majority of the Mexican saints returned to the LDS church. Bautista founded his own polygamous, communitarian community known as Colonia Industrial de la Nueva Jerusalén. See Jason Dormady, *Primitive Revolution: Restorationist Religion and the Idea of the Mexican Revolution, 1940–1968* (Albuquerque: University of New Mexico Press, 2011).

57. DN, August 9, 1938. Scott C. Esplin, "Charting the Course: President Clark's Charge to Religious Educators," *Religious Educator* 7, no. 1 (2006): 103–19.

58. Clark to John Widtsoe, June 29, 1930, JRC. Heber Grant, *Teach What Encourages Faith* (Salt Lake City: Deseret News Press, 1934), 3–4. Quinn, *Statesman*, 236. Bergera and Priddis, *University*, 18.

59. Harold T. Christensen and Kenneth L. Cannon, "The Fundamentalist Emphasis at Brigham Young University: 1935–1973," *Journal for the Scientific Study of Religion* 17, no. 1 (1978): 53–57.

60. Grant to Harris, June 11, 1937, FHP. Heber C. Snell, "Criteria for Interpreting the Old Testament to College Youth," *Through the Years: Occasional Writings of Heber C. Snell* (Logan, UT: Merrill Library, 1969), 95–97. Joseph Fielding Smith to Harris, March 11, 1937, in Richard Sherlock, "Faith and History: The Snell Controversy," *Dialogue* 12, no. 1 (1979): 27. See Griffiths, "Chicago Experiment," 106–7.

61. Clark, "The Charted Course of the Church in Education," in *J. Reuben Clark: Selected Papers* (Provo, UT: Brigham Young University Press, 1984), 251–52. DN, August 9, 1938.

62. Sterling M. McMurrin and L. Jackson Newell, *Matters of Conscience: Conversations with Sterling M. McMurrin on Philosophy, Education, and Religion* (Salt Lake City: Signature Books, 1996), 115. Joseph Fielding Smith to J. Reuben Clark, August 15, 1938, JRCP.

63. Griffiths, "Chicago Experiment," 109–10. Daines, "By Study," 170. Bergera and Priddis, *University*, 60.

64. Daines, "By Study," 170. J. Reuben Clark, *The Mission of Brigham Young University: Inaugural Charge* (Provo, UT: Brigham Young University Press, 1949), 10.

65. Juanita Brooks to Dale Morgan, February 21, 1943, SLJB, 29.

66. Brooks to Morgan, June 4, 1945, in Brooks, *Quicksand and Cactus: A Memoir of the Southern Mormon Frontier* (SLC: Howe Brothers, 1982), xxxiii. Brooks to Morgan, August 27, 1941, April 5, 1942, SLJB, 16, 23.

67. See Terryl L. Givens, *People of Paradox: A History of Mormon Culture* (New York: Oxford University Press, 2007), 287–97; Michael Austin, *Vardis Fisher: A Mormon Novelist* (Urbana: University of Illinois Press, 2021).

68. Quoted in Mary Lythgoe Bradford, foreword to *A Little Lower Than the Angels*, by Virginia Sorensen (1942; Salt Lake City: Signature Books, 1997), x.

69. Quinn, *Statesman*, 204. CN, May 11, 1946. Newell G. Bringhurst, *Fawn McKay Brodie: A Biographer's Life* (Norman: University of Oklahoma Press, 1999), 104–5.

70. Juanita Brooks to Dale Morgan, May 19, 1946, and Brooks to Hugh Nibley, November 7, 1946, SLJB, 75, 84.

71. Thomas O'Dea, *The Mormons* (Chicago: University of Chicago Press, 1957), 222, 224.

72. David Conley Nelson, *Moroni and the Swastika: Mormons in Nazi Germany* (Norman: University of Oklahoma Press, 2015).

73. SoTLDS, 538–41. Quinn, *Statesman*, 283–307.

74. WoC, 298. CR, April 1940. Hall, *Lyman*, 151.

75. WoC, 287–89, 298–99.

76. Richard Lyman to Stephen Richards, April 10, 1956, Michael Quinn Papers, Beinecke Library, Yale. Gary James Bergera, "Transgression in the Latter-

day Saint Community, Part II: Richard R. Lyman," JMH 37, no. 4 (Fall 2011): 179–80.

77. DN, November 13, 1943. Bergera, "Transgression," 183–92.

78. Vera W. Pohlman, Oral History, quoted in Bergera, "Transgression," 193. See Hall, *Lyman*, 161–68.

79. RSM 36 (December 1949): 797–98. Hall, *Lyman*, 152.

Chapter 7: One Family under God, 1945–70

1. David O. McKay, *Treasures of Life* (Salt Lake City: Deseret Book, 1962), 144–45.

2. Ernest L. Wilkinson and W. Cleon Skousen, *Brigham Young University: A School of Destiny* (Provo, UT: Brigham Young University Press, 1976), 746. SoTLDS, 586.

3. Lacee A. Harris, "To Be Native American—and Mormon," *Dialogue* 18, no. 4 (1985): 143–45. For background to the program, which will be discussed later, see Matthew Garrett, *Making Lamanites: Mormons, Native Americans, and the Indian Student Placement Program, 1947–2000* (Salt Lake City: University of Utah Press, 2016).

4. Billy Graham, quoted in Lepore, *These Truths*, 568. CR, October 1947.

5. Harris, "To Be Native American," 147–49.

6. Harris, 151–52.

7. DOMD, January 19, 1953, 50–51. DOMD, November 5, 1952, 43. Quinn, *Extensions*, 360.

8. NYT, December 23, 1952. Lepore, *These Truths*, 545–46. Kevin M. Kruse, *One Nation under God: How Corporate America Invented Christian America* (New York: Basic Books, 2015), 67–68.

9. *Time*, February 2, 1970. Gregory A. Prince and William Robert Wright, *David O. McKay and the Rise of Modern Mormonism* (Salt Lake City: University of Utah Press, 2005), 23. SLT, October 4, 1953. Francis Gibbons, *David O. McKay: Apostle of the World, Prophet of God* (Salt Lake City: Deseret Book, 1986), 263, 347. LJAD, December 13, 1971, 90.

10. Quinn, *Statesman*, 142–60. Prince and Wright, *McKay*, 2.

11. DOMD, December 3, 1956, 157. DOMD, June 3, 1954, 96.

12. IE 48 (November 1945): 711. SoTLDS, 547. Matthew L. Harris, *Watchman on the Tower: Ezra Taft Benson and the Making of the Mormon Right* (Salt Lake City: University of Utah Press, 2020), 14–17. Ernest Wilkinson, diary, May 13, 1963, BYU. Gary James Bergera, "Ezra Taft Benson's 1946 Mission to Europe," JMH 34, no. 2 (Spring 2008): 73–112.

13. CR, October 1944. Kruse, *Under God*, 67–125 (cabinet prayer found on 81–82).

14. Lepore, *These Truths*, 527–28. David M. Kennedy, *Freedom from Fear: The American People in Depression and War, 1929–1945* (New York: Oxford University Press, 1999), 786–87.

15. Prince and Wright, *McKay*, 205–25. SoTLDS, 563–73. Jan Shipps, *Sojourner*

in the Promised Land: Forty Years around the Mormons (Urbana: University of Illinois Press, 2000), 262–63. MIAM, 18–20.

16. Donald Bergsma, "The Lamps of Mormon Architecture," *Dialogue* 3, no. 1 (1968): 19. Givens, *People of Paradox*, 243–46.

17. *Time*, July 21, 1947. SoTLDS, 552.

18. *Time*, August 3, 1953. Bradley, *Kidnapped*, 127–30.

19. *Arizona Daily Star* (Tuscon), July 27, 1953.

20. Bradley, *Kidnapped*, 147–49.

21. Craig L. Foster and Marianne T. Watson, *American Polygamy: A History of Fundamentalist Mormon Faith* (Charleston, SC: The History Press, 2019), 104–10.

22. DOMD, February 3, February 29, 1956, and February 10, 1957, 136–37, 138, 265. Brooks to Ogden Kraut, October 6, 1968, SLJB, 333.

23. DOMD, April 16, 1953, 69. CR, April 1959. Taylor G. Petrey, *Tabernacles of Clay: Sexuality and Gender in Modern Mormonism* (Chapel Hill: University of North Carolina Press, 2020), 59–63. Kristin Kobes Du Mez, *Jesus and John Wayne: How White Evangelicals Corrupted a Faith and Fractured a Nation* (New York: Liveright, 2020), 36.

24. WoC, 304, 308–10, 327–29.

25. RSM 36 (November 1949): 727. RSM 46 (January 1959): 33. WoC, 318–19, 326–27.

26. Betty Friedan, *The Feminine Mystique* (New York: W. W. Norton, 1963). MSS, 66–73.

27. Julie Debra Neuffer, *Helen Andelin and the Fascinating Womanhood Movement* (Salt Lake City: University of Utah Press, 2014), 21–26.

28. Helen Andelin, *Fascinating Womanhood* (1965; New York: Bantam Dell, 2007), 129. Neuffer, *Andelin*, 31, 35–36, 40–47, 68.

29. IE, August 1946, 492. Lowry Nelson to Heber Meeks, June 27, 1947, UofU. First Presidency to Nelson, July 17, 1947, UofU. DOMD, February 25, 1949. Joanna Brooks, *Mormonism and White Supremacy: American Religion and the Problem of Racial Innocence* (New York: Oxford University Press, 2020), 117–33. Quinn, *Statesman*, 342–51.

30. DOMD, January 19, February 25, 1954, 89–90. Prince and Wright, *McKay*, 73–81.

31. Helen Rose John, interview, October 10, 1978, CHL. I appreciate Elise Boxer for sharing her research notes on John's interview.

32. John, interview. See John Birch, "Helen John: The Beginnings of Indian Placement," *Dialogue* 18, no. 4 (1977): 119–29.

33. Margaret D. Jacobs, "Entangled Histories: The Mormon Church and Indigenous Child Removal from 1850 to 2000," JMH 42, no. 2 (April 2016): 28–34.

34. Kimball, quoted in Brandon Morgan, "Educating the Lamanites: A Brief History of the Indian Student Placement Program," JMH 35, no. 4 (2009): 417. CR, October 1960.

35. Elise Boxer, "'The Lamanites Shall Blossom as the Rose': The Indian Student Placement Program, Mormon Whiteness, and Indigenous Identity," JMH 41, no. 4 (2015): 132, 152–57. Garrett, *Making Lamanites*, 59–71. WoC, 319–22.

36. Garrett, *Making Lamanites*, 134. Boxer, "Lamanites Shall Blossom," 163.

Marin D. Topper, "'Mormon Placement': The Effects of Missionary Foster Families on Navajo Adolescents," *Ethos* 7, no. 2 (1979): 147–49, 154.

37. Margaret D. Jacobs, *A Generation Removed: The Fostering and Adoption of Indigenous Children in the Postwar World* (Lincoln: University of Nebraska Press, 2014).

38. Birch, "Helen John." Harris, "To Be Native American," 152.

39. Sterling M. McMurrin, *The Philosophical Foundations of Mormon Theology* (Salt Lake City: University of Utah Press, 1959); McMurrin, *The Theological Foundations of the Mormon Religion* (Salt Lake City: University of Utah Press, 1965).

40. Joseph Fielding Smith, *Man: His Origin and Destiny* (Salt Lake City: Deseret Book, 1954), 9.

41. Thomas A. Blakely, "The Swearing Elders: The First Generation of Modern Mormon Intellectuals," *Sunstone* 10, no. 9 (1985): 12.

42. Blakely, "Swearing Elders," 13. DOMD, August 18, 1954, 104. J. Reuben Clark, *Why the King James Version* (Salt Lake City: Deseret Book, 1956).

43. Brooks to Donald P. Bean, July 11, 1949, SLJB, 114. Juanita Brooks, *Mountain Meadows Massacre* (Palo Alto: Stanford University Press, 1950).

44. Brooks to Charles Kelly, January 5, 1952; Brooks to Dale Morgan, June 10, 1951; Brooks to David S. Grow, December 16, 1974; Brooks to Anthony Bentley, February 2, 1956, SLJB, 143–44, 134, 382, 170. DOMD, November 7, 1951, 15.

45. Leonard J. Arrington, "Historian as Entrepreneur: A Personal Essay," BYUSQ 17, no. 1 (1977): 194. Arrington, *Great Basin Kingdom*. Gregory L. Prince, *Leonard Arrington and the Writing of Mormon History* (Salt Lake City: University of Utah Press, 2016).

46. Armand L. Mauss, *The Angel and the Beehive: The Mormon Struggle with Assimilation* (Urbana: University of Illinois Press, 1994), 84–85.

47. DOMD, June 3, 1966, November 7, 1967, 659, 715. Hugh Nibley, "Prolegomena to Any Study of the Book of Abraham," BYUSQ 8, no. 2 (1968): 171.

48. Hugh Nibley, "Phase One," *Dialogue* 3, no. 2 (1968): 102. Boyd Jay Petersen, *Hugh Nibley: A Consecrated Life* (Salt Lake City: Greg Kofford Books, 2002), 313–24.

49. DOMD, May 24, 1968, 764–65.

50. "An Interview with Sterling McMurrin," *Dialogue* 17, no. 1 (1984): 25. Petersen, *Nibley*, 272–74, 302. Arrington, "The Intellectual Tradition of the Latter-day Saints," *Dialogue* 4, no. 1 (Spring 1969): 24. *Daily Universe* (Provo), May 14, 1963.

51. Tonya S. Reiter, "Frances Leggroan Fleming," CBM. Reiter, "Life on the Hill: The Black Farming Families of Mill Creek," JMH 44, no. 4 (2018): 68–89.

52. Frances Fleming, oral interview by Leslie Kelen, Salt Lake City, Utah, 1983, transcript, in "Interviews with Blacks in Utah, 1982–1988," UofU.

53. Sterling M. McMurrin, speech to NAACP, March 1960, in Russell W. Stevenson, *For the Cause of Righteousness: A Global History of Blacks and Mormonism, 1830–2013* (Salt Lake City: Kofford, 2014), 315–23. DOMD, September 26, 1961, 393.

54. Spencer Kimball to Edward Kimball, June 15, 1963, in Reeve, *Different*, 259. Prince and Wright, *McKay*, 65.

55. IE 49 (August 1946): 492. DOMD, September 26, 1961, 393.

56. John Stewart, *Mormonism and the Negro: An Explanation and Defense* (Salt Lake City: Bookcraft, 1960), 29–30, 44, 50. J. Russell Hawkins, *The Bible Told Them So: How Southern Evangelicals Fought to Preserve White Supremacy* (New York: Oxford University Press, 2021).

57. Adewole Ogunmokun to LaMar Williams, July 29, 1961, CHL. James Allen, "Would-Be Saints: West Africa before the 1978 Priesthood Revelation," JMH 17 (1991): 207–47.

58. DOMD, June 22, 30, July 1, 19, August 16, 1961, January 9, 1962, 371–72, 377, 379–81, 382, 384, 404–9.

59. NYT, June 7, 1963. DOMD, June 5, 7, 1963, 482–83; January 14, 1964, 512–13; November 4, 1965, 618–27. Allen, "Would-Be Saints," 230, 234–35. Attempts to open the Nigerian mission continued, off and on, for several more years, before being officially furloughed in 1967 at the start of the country's civil war.

60. Brooks to Far Decker Dix, March 25, 1964, JBL, 284. CR, October 1963. DOMD, October 4, 1963, 498.

61. D. Dmitri Hurlbut, "Gobert Edet and the Entry of the RLDS Church into Southeastern Nigeria, 1962–1966," JMH 45, no. 24 (2019): 81–104. George N. Walton, "Sect to Denomination: Counting the Progress of the RLDS Reformation," JWHAJ 18 (1998): 39.

62. David Hollinger, *Protestants Abroad: How Missionaries Tried to Change the World but Changed America* (Princeton, NJ: Princeton University Press, 2017).

63. David Gillispie to David O. McKay, June 4, 1967, in Matthew L. Harris and Newell G. Bringhurst, *The Mormon Church and Blacks: A Documentary History* (Urbana: University of Illinois Press, 2015), 86–89.

64. David Lingard to Bishops of Granger, Utah, April 16, 1967, CHL.

65. Shannon Bybee to N. Eldon Tanner, April 25, 1967, CHL.

66. DOMD, April 18, 1967, 690. See Matthew Dallek, *Birchers: How the John Birch Society Radicalized the American Right* (New York: Basic Books, 2023).

67. MIAM, 15, 18, 23–25. SoTLDS, 619. Prince and Wright, *McKay*, 336–37, 354–57. DOMD, November 12, 1957, October 26, 1960, 197, 343–44.

68. *Time*, April 6, 1969. Benjamin Wallace-Wells, "George Romney for President, 1968," *New York Magazine*, May 18, 2012. MIAM, 50.

69. *Nation*, February 3, 1962. *New Republic*, December 3, 1966. MIAM, 2. *LA Times*, November 15, 1966.

70. DOMD, December 15, 1961, January 3, 1962, 401–4. Delbert Stapley to George Romney, January 23, 1964, https://archive.org. MIAM, 40.

71. Ezra Taft Benson, *So Shall Ye Reap: Selected Addresses of Ezra Taft Benson* (Salt Lake City: Deseret Book, 1960), 165. Harris, *Watchman*, 56–60.

72. Joseph Fielding Smith to Alfred A. Hart, March 15, 1954, CHL. Harris, *Watchman*, 45–46.

73. DOMD, July 8, 1958, 225; August 24, November 16, 1961, 387, 399–400; March 5, 1963, 471.

74. DN, January 2, 1963. DOMD, January 23, February 4, 1963, 463, 466; March 5, August 18, 1964, 520–23, 539.

75. DOMD, February 9, 18, 19, March 6, 1966, 642–45. Gregory L. Prince, "The

Red Peril, the Candy Maker, and the Apostle: David O. McKay's Confrontation with Communism," *Dialogue* 37, no. 2 (2004): 37–94.

76. England, "'No Cause, No Cause': An Essay toward Reconciliation," *Sunstone* 125 (January 2002): 33.

77. Interview with Eugene England, 1970, quoted in Terryl L. Givens, *Stretching the Heavens: The Life of Eugene England and the Crisis of Modern Mormonism* (Chapel Hill: University of North Carolina Press, 2021), 64.

78. See Matthew Bowman, "Zion: The Progressive Roots of Mormon Correlation," in *Directions for Mormon Studies in the Twenty-First Century*, ed. Patrick Q. Mason (Salt Lake City: University of Utah Press, 2016): 15–34. Jill Lepore, *If Then: How the Simulmatics Corporation Invented the Future* (New York: Liveright, 2020).

79. Bruce R. McConkie, *Mormon Doctrine* (Salt Lake City: Bookcraft, 1958), 106, 130, 238, 476.

80. Quinn, *Statesman*, 224. DOMD, February 6, March 5, 1959, January 7–8, 1960, 262, 270, 300–304.

81. IE, January 1962, 36. SoTLDS, 596–606, 614–15.

82. WoC, 330–45, 340–46.

83. Esther Peterson, quoted in Maxine Hanks, *Women and Authority: Re-Emerging Mormon Feminism* (Salt Lake City: Signature Books, 1992), 91–92.

84. G. Wesley Johnson, "Editorial Preface," *Dialogue* 1, no. 1 (1966): 6. NYT, December 12, 1965.

85. Kyle Longley, *LBJ's 1968: Power, Politics, and the Presidency in America's Year of Upheaval* (New York: Cambridge University Press, 2018).

86. DOMD, April 16 and October 31, 1966; January 6, March 22, 1967, 651, 670, 680–81, 689.

87. DOMD, November 16, December 2, and December 13, 1966, 672–74.

88. DOMD, February 13, 1968, 737–38.

89. DOMD, February 13, 1968, 739, 741–43.

90. DOMD, November 4, 1965, 622–23; September 1, 1967, 704–6; July 16, 1968, 768–69. MIAM, 47.

91. SLT, June 22, 1968. DOMD, June 26, 1968, 766–67. DN, January 10, 1970. Harris and Bringhurst, *Mormon Church and Blacks*, 79–80.

92. DOMD, October 15, 1962, October 28, 1958, May 12, May 20, 1969, 453–54, 778, 769–98. Harris, *Watchman*, 78–79.

93. Morgan D. King, "The People: A Mormon Student's Reaction to the Radical Movement," *Dialogue* 5, no. 2 (1970): 32–33.

Chapter 8: Fault Lines, 1970–95

1. LJAD, November 11, 1980, 3:127.

2. Laurel Thatcher Ulrich, "The Pink *Dialogue* and Beyond," *Dialogue* 14, no. 4 (1981): 28–39. Claudia L. Bushman, "Women in *Dialogue*: An Introduction," *Dialogue* 6, no. 2 (1971): 5–8.

3. Darius Gray, interview, October 20, 2021, in *Mormon Land*, produced by *Salt Lake Tribune*, podcast. Michael Marquardt notes from interview with Eugene Orr, November 7, 1971, in Harris and Bringhurst, *Mormon Church and Blacks*, 89.

4. Richard A. Viguerie, *The New Right: We're Ready to Lead* (Falls Church, VA: Viguerie, 1981), 55. See Lepore, *These Truths*, 55; Daniel T. Rodgers, *Age of Fracture* (Cambridge: Harvard University Press, 2011).

5. LJAD, November 11, 1980, 3:127.

6. QCP. LJAD, August 28, 1972, 204–7. Gary Topping, *D. Michael Quinn: Mormon Historian* (Salt Lake City: Signature Books, 2022), 33.

7. LJAD, January 26, 1972, 108.

8. LJAD, February 24, August 9, 1972, 1:110, 232–33. Davis Bitton, "Ten Years in Camelot: A Personal Memoir," *Dialogue* 16, no. 3 (1983): 9. See Leonard J. Arrington, *Adventures of a Church Historian* (Urbana: University of Illinois Press, 1998), 74–91; Prince, *Arrington*, 152–91.

9. LJAD, June 16, 1972, 1:167–68. SoTLDS, 603–6.

10. D. Michael Quinn, *The Mormon Hierarchy: Wealth and Corporate Power* (Salt Lake City: Signature Books, 2017), 120–44. See Bethany Moreton, *To Serve God and Wal-Mart: The Making of Christian Free Enterprise* (Cambridge: Harvard University Press, 2009); Darren E. Grem, *The Blessings of Business: How Corporations Shaped Conservative Christianity* (New York: Oxford University Press, 2016).

11. SoTLDS, 651–57.

12. LJAD, December 30–31, 1973, February 25, 1974, 1:634, 38–39, 51. *Time*, January 14, 1974. Edward L. Kimball, *Lengthen Your Stride: The Presidency of Spencer W. Kimball* (Salt Lake City: Deseret Book, 2005), 3–4.

13. SoTLDS, 629–33. Rodney Stark, *The Rise of Mormonism* (New York: Columbia University Press, 2005), 139, 142.

14. LJAD, November 30, December 1, 1972, 1:366–68; April 19, June 11, 1973, 1:480, 526–27. D. Michael Quinn, diary, April 14, 1972, in "On Writing Mormon History, 1972–95: From the Diaries and Memoirs of D. Michael Quinn," in *Writing Mormon History: Historians and Their Books*, ed. Joseph W. Geisner (Salt Lake City: Signature Books, 2020): 238. QCP.

15. LJAD, December 4, 1972, December 7, 1975, 1:370, 2:127. Lester Bush, "Writing 'Mormonism's Negro Doctrine: An Historical Overview' (1973): Context and Reflections, 1998," JMH 25, no. 21 (1999): 256.

16. Bushman, "Women in *Dialogue*," 5–8. Juanita Brooks to Claudia Bushman, December 21, 1971, SLJB, 382. Claudia Bushman, "Mormon Feminism after 1970," in Amy Hoyt and Taylor G. Petrey, *The Routledge Handbook of Mormonism and Gender* (New York: Routledge, 2020), 159.

17. Bushman, "Mormon Feminism after 1970," 159–60. Claudia Bushman, "*Exponent II* Is Born," *Exponent II* 1 (July 1974): 2.

18. MIAM, 75–79.

19. LJAD, November 28, 1978, 2:678–79. MIAM, 81–84.

20. Lepore, *These Truths*, 655–66.

21. MSS, 102–3. Andrew Hartman, *A War for the Soul of America: A History of the Culture Wars* (Chicago: University of Chicago Press, 2015), 87–101.

22. CN, January 11, 1975. Martha Sonntag Bradley, *Pedestals and Podiums: Utah Women, Religious Authority, and Equal Rights* (Salt Lake City: Signature Books, 2005), 51–124. WoC, 367–68. Neil J. Young, "'The ERA Is a Moral Issue': The Mormon Church, LDS Women, and the Defeat of the Equal Rights Amendment," *American Quarterly* 59, no. 3 (2007): 623–44.

23. MSS, 88, 105–7. WoC, 375–77.

24. LJAD, June 27, 1975, 1:871. Givens, *People of Paradox*, 170–71.

25. LJAD, February 15, March 29, 1973, 1:437–38, 471–72.

26. Dixie Snow Huefner, "Church and Politics at the Utah IWY Conference," *Dialogue* 11, no. 1 (1978): 58–76. Ulrich, "Pink *Dialogue* and Beyond," 35.

27. LDSGC, October 1973. Anonymous, "Solus," *Dialogue* 10, no. 2 (1976): 99.

28. "Solus," 96–99.

29. Jerry Falwell, August 13, 1981, University of North Texas Digital Library. Sutton, *American Apocalypse*, 354.

30. Spencer W. Kimball, "Love vs. Lust," January 5, 1965, https://speeches.byu.edu. Kimball, *Miracle of Forgiveness* (Salt Lake City: Bookcraft, 1969), 75–85. LDSGC, October 1977. Boyd K. Packer, *To Young Men Only* (Salt Lake City: Church of Jesus Christ of Latter-day Saints, 1976), 16. Petrey, *Tabernacles*, 65, 69–71, 88.

31. Petrey, *Tabernacles*, 53–92 (quotes on 72–73). Gregory A. Prince, *Gay Rights and the Mormon Church: Intended Actions, Unintended Consequences* (Salt Lake City: University of Utah Press, 2019), 89–92.

32. Ina Mae Murri, "Panel Presentation Sunstone Symposium West," August 30–31, 1987, Ina Mae Murri Papers (1997–2007), UofU. David C., "A Call to Righteousness," *Affinity: Affirmation National Newsletter* (September 1986), UofU. John Donal Gustav-Wrathall, "Mormon LGBTQ Organizing and Organizations," in Hoyt and Petrey, *Routledge Handbook*, 221. I have also drawn from Sara Patterson and Joshua Smith, "'I Know You from Your Inmost Being': Feeling the Spirit in the Lives of LGBTQ+ Mormons," unpublished paper delivered at the 2021 Mormon History Association Conference.

33. Carol Lynn Pearson, *Goodbye, I Love You: The True Story of a Wife, Her Homosexual Husband, and a Love Honored for Time and All Eternity* (New York: Random House, 1986).

34. QCP.

35. Bush, "Writing 'Mormonism's Negro Doctrine,'" 247–48.

36. Stephen Taggart, *Mormonism's Negro Policy: Social and Historical Origins* (Salt Lake City: University of Utah Press, 1970). SLT, May 10, 1970. NYT, June 21, 1970.

37. Bush, "Writing 'Mormonism's Negro Doctrine,'" 237, 240–44, 246. Bush, "A Commentary on Stephen G. Taggart's Mormonism's Negro Policy: Social and Historical Origins," *Dialogue* 4, no. 4 (1969): 86–103.

38. Bush, "Writing 'Mormonism's Negro Doctrine,'" 251, 254–63. LJAD, June 1, 1973, 1:517–18.

39. Lester E. Bush, "Mormonism's Negro Doctrine: An Historical Overview," *Dialogue* 8, no. 2 (1973): 11–68. Bush, "Writing 'Mormonism's Negro Doctrine,'" 265–67.

40. SLT, June 10, 1978. Edward L. Kimball, "Spencer W. Kimball and the Revelation on Priesthood," BYUSQ 47, no. 2 (2008): 35, 40.

41. MIAM, 61–71. Harris and Bringhurst, *Mormon Church and Blacks*, 106–7. *Church Almanac* (Salt Lake City: Deseret News, 1977), 23. LJAD, January 7, 1978, 2:447.

42. Brazil North Mission, 1970, "Lineage Lesson," in Harris and Bringhurst, *Mormon Church and Blacks*, 105.

43. *Ensign*, October 1980. LeGrand Richards, interview, 1978, in Harris and Bringhurst, *Mormon Church and Blacks*, 105. See also LJAD, June 13, 1978, 2:552–53.

44. Kimball, "Revelation on Priesthood," 46–59.

45. Official Declaration #2, https://www.lds.org. SLT, November 20, 1988. MIAM, 71–72.

46. Bruce R. McConkie, "All Are Alike unto God," August 18, 1978, https://speeches.byu.edu.

47. Gray, October 20, 2021, *Mormon Land* podcast. Margaret Blair Young and Darius Aidan Gray, *One More River to Cross* (Salt Lake City: Bookcraft, 2000), xiii. DN, June 10, 1978.

48. LJAD, June 28, 1978, 2:584. SLT, July 23, 1978.

49. AP, July 28, 1978. Christopher Jones, "Repudiating the Pearl of Great Price? More on Reactions to the 1978 Revelation," *Juvenile Instructor*, June 17, 2014. Foster and Watson, *American Polygamy*, 137–48.

50. LJAD, January 30, 1976, October 2, 1979, 2:136–37, 840–41.

51. Quinn, diary, April 14, 1972, 254. Topping, *Quinn*, 108.

52. *Newsweek*, March 4, 1985. Matthew Bowman, "The Evangelical Counterculture Movement and Mormon Conservatism," in *Out of Obscurity: Mormonism since 1945*, ed. Patrick Mason and John Turner (New York: Oxford University Press, 2016), 259–77.

53. MIAM, 101–2, 110–20; Neil J. Young, *We Gather Together: The Religious Right and the Problem of Interfaith Politics* (New York: Oxford University Press, 2015); Daniel Williams, *God's Own Party: The Making of the Christian Right* (New York: Oxford University Press, 2012), 167–78; Du Mez, *Jesus and John Wayne*, 5–11.

54. LJAD, February 8, 1973, 1:430.

55. Sonia Johnson, *From Housewife to Heretic: One Woman's Struggle for Equal Rights and Her Excommunication from the Mormon Church* (1981; New York: Anchor Books, 1983), 94. MSS, 109–18.

56. Sonia Johnson, "The Church Was Once in the Forefront of the Women's Movement," in MF, 70. Johnson, "Patriarchal Panic: Sexual Politics in the Mormon Church," in MF, 73–74. LJAD, October 2, 1979, February 2, 1980, 2:843, 912–13. Bradley, *Pedestals and Podiums*, 342.

57. Robert O. Self, *All in the Family: The Realignment of American Democracy since the 1960s* (New York: Hill and Wang, 2012), 358–60. Neuffer, *Andelin*, 104–8, 118–24.

58. LJAD, December 3, 1979, 2:877–81. SLT, November 27, 1979. Ulrich, "Pink *Dialogue* and Beyond," 37–39. Bradley, *Pedestals and Podiums*, 363–68.

59. LJAD, February 25, March 10, 1908, 2:917–19. MIAM, 92–95.

60. MSS, III. Kimball, *Lengthen Your Stride*, 383–413.

61. Richard E. Turley, *Victims: The LDS Church and the Mark Hofmann Case* (Urbana: University of Illinois Press, 1992).

62. LJAD, August 18, September 5, September 21, September 22, October 22, 1976, 2:222–27, 238–41, 270. Jill Lepore, *The Whites of Their Eyes: The Tea Party's Revolution and the Battle over American History* (Princeton, NJ: Princeton University Press, 2010), 133–35.

63. LJAD, January 1, 1978, June 26, June 30, July 9, December 30, 1980, 2:452, 3:74–75, 97, 139–42.

64. Boyd K. Packer, "The Mantle Is Far, Far Greater Than the Intellect," BYUSQ 21, no. 3 (1981): 259, 261, 263, 267, 269. For the evangelical context, see Randall Stephens and Karl Giberson, *The Anointed: Evangelical Truth in a Secular Age* (Cambridge: Harvard University Press, 2011), 74–83.

65. Quinn, "On Being a Mormon Historian (and Its Aftermath)," in George Smith, ed., *Faithful History* (Salt Lake City: Signature Books, 1992): 77, 82, 87, 89. QCP. *Newsweek*, February 15, 1982.

66. Bruce R. McConkie, "The Seven Deadly Heresies," June 1, 1980, https://speeches.byu.edu. McConkie to England, February 19, 1981, https://www.eugeneengland.org. Givens, *England*, 161–67. LJAD, May 25–26, 1983, 3:301–2.

67. QCP. Topping, *Quinn*, 111–15. The article was also ill-timed as it followed the media coverage of Ron and Dan Lafferty, members of a radical polygamous cult who killed their sister-in-law and her fifteen-month-old daughter. Jon Krakauer, *Under the Banner of Heaven: A Story of Violent Faith* (New York: Doubleday, 2003).

68. SLT, January 3, 1987. LJA to children, September 13, 1986, in LJAD, 3:442.

69. Gaustad and Schmidt, *Religious History of America*, 386–93. Kate Bowler, *The Preacher's Wife: The Precarious Power of Evangelical Women Celebrities* (Princeton, NJ: Princeton University Press, 2020), 38–39.

70. LJAD, August 17, September 18, 1978, January 1, 1979, 2:596, 621, 700–701.

71. Hansen, "Women and Priesthood," *Dialogue* 14, no. 4 (1981): 48–57. Newell, "A Gift Given, a Gift Taken: Washing, Anointing, and Blessing the Sick among Mormon Women," *Sunstone* 29 (1981): 16–25. Margaret M. Toscano, "The Missing Rib: The Forgotten Place of Queens and Priestesses in the Establishment of Zion," *Sunstone* 51 (1985): 16–22.

72. MSS, 118–23.

73. Nancy Ross, David Howlett, and Zoe Kruse, "The Women's Ordination Movement in the Reorganized Church of Jesus Christ of Latter Day Saints: Historical and Sociological Perspectives," MSR 9 (2022): 21–23.

74. Jeff Braithwaite, "The Changing Face of Priesthood in the RLDS Church," JWHAJ 20 (2000): 133–46; William Russell, "Ordaining Women and the Transformation from Sect to Denomination," *Dialogue* 36, no. 3 (Fall 2003): 61–64.

75. Ezra Taft Benson, "To the Mothers in Zion," February 22, 1987, in *Preparing for a Temple Marriage* (Salt Lake City: LDS Church, 2003), https://www.churchofjesuschrist.org. LJAD, June 29, 1995, 3:418. Lavina Fielding Ander-

son, "The LDS Intellectual Community and Church Leadership: A Contemporary Chronology," *Dialogue* 26, no. 1 (1993): 48.

76. Dallin H. Oaks, "Principles to Govern Possible Public Statement on Legislation Affecting Rights of Homosexuals," August 7, 1984, E. Jay Bell Papers, UofU. Prince, *Gay Rights*, 38–43. Petrey, *Tabernacles*, 143–45.

77. *Ensign*, November 1975. LDSGC, October 1975.

78. Armand L. Mauss, *All Abraham's Children: Changing Mormon Conceptions of Race and Lineage* (Urbana: University of Illinois Press, 2003), 81, 89–92.

79. *Daily Herald* (Provo, UT), November 12, 1972. Edward L. Kimball and Andrew E. Kimball, *Spencer W. Kimball* (Salt Lake City: Bookcraft, 1979), 404–5. Edward Blum and Paul Harvey, *The Color of Christ: The Son of God and the Saga of Race in America* (Chapel Hill: University of North Carolina Press, 2012), 247–49.

80. Boyd K. Packer, speech at BYU's Indian Week, 1979, in Mauss, *All Abraham's Children*, 96–97.

81. SoTLDS, 646–50. Jorge Iber, *Hispanics in the Mormon Zion, 1912–1999* (College Station: Texas A&M University Press, 2000), 86, 108. Brittany Romanello, "Multiculturalism as Resistance: Latina Migrants Navigate US Mormon Spaces," *Dialogue* 53, no. 1 (2020): 5–31. Ignacio García, *Chicano while Mormon: Activism, War, and Keeping the Faith* (Madison, NJ: Farleigh Dickinson University Press, 2015). P. Jane Hafen and Brenden W. Rensink, introduction to *Essays on American Indian and Mormon History*, ed. P. Jane Hafen and Brenden W. Rensink, xi–xiii.

82. LDSGC, October 1988. John Turner, *The Mormon Jesus: A Biography* (Cambridge: Harvard University Press, 2016), 44–46. MIAM, 165.

83. "The Lee Letters," *Sunstone* 72 (1989), 50–55. DN, September 10, 1989. SLT, October 12, 1994.

84. P. Jane Hafen, "'Great Spirit Listen': The American Indian in Mormon Music," *Dialogue* 18, no. 4 (1985): 141.

85. LDSGC, April 1989. SLT, August 24, 1992. *Ensign*, November 1991.

86. Anderson, "Chronology," 62.

87. Givens, *England*, 227–29. NYT, August 22, 1992.

88. Maxine Hanks, introduction to *Women and Authority*, xi.

89. Anderson, "Chronology," 61.

90. Claudia L. Bushman, *Contemporary Mormonism: Latter-day Saints in Modern America* (Westport, CT: Praeger, 2006), 160.

91. Avraham Gileadi, a conservative biblical scholar, was the sixth member of the disciplined group, and the oddest fit. He did not identify or associate with the more progressive academics, and was rebaptized within three years. See Sara Patterson, *The September Six and the Struggle for the Soul of Mormonism* (Salt Lake City: Signature Books, 2023).

92. LJAD, September 25, 1993, October 14, 1994, 3:616–17, 631. NYT, September 19, 1993. "Six Intellectuals Disciplined for Apostasy," *Sunstone* 92 (November 1993): 65–79. Bryan Waterman and Brian Kagel, *The Lord's University: Freedom and Authority at BYU* (Salt Lake City: Signature Books, 1998), 258–301. Givens, *England*, 177–80.

93. *Chronicle of Higher Education*, February 24, 1993. LJAD, February 15, September 25, 1993, 3:611, 617. Laurel Thatcher Ulrich, "Border Crossings," *Dialogue* 27, no. 2 (1994): 1–7. MSS, 127–28.

94. "The Family: A Proclamation to the World," September 1995, https://www.churchofjesuschrist.org. Petrey, *Tabernacles*, 139–42.

95. Prince, *Gay Rights*, 48–54.

96. Richard E. Turley, *In the Hands of the Lord: The Life of Dallin H. Oaks* (Salt Lake City: Deseret Book, 2021), 215–16. Gregory A. Prince, "'There Is Always a Struggle': An Interview with Chieko N. Okazaki," *Dialogue* 45, no. 1 (Spring 2012): 136.

97. Petrey, *Tabernacles*, 145–47.

Chapter 9: Showtime, 1995–2012

1. Trey Parker, Robert Lopez, and Matt Stone, "Two by Two," track 2 on *The Book of Mormon: Original Broadway Cast Recording*, Ghostlight Records, 2011.

2. LDSGC, April 1996.

3. "CBS 60 Minutes: Bill Marriot on LDS Temple Garments," *60 Minutes* broadcast from April 7, 1996, YouTube, https://www.youtube.com/watch?v=cCiVHMQmAUw.

4. MSS, 131–32.

5. MIAM, 158–61, 166–68.

6. LDSGC, April 1995. Sara M. Patterson, *Pioneers in the Attic: Place and Memory along the Mormon Trail* (New York: Oxford University Press, 2020), 161–78.

7. DN, February 22, 2002.

8. MIAM, 172–75.

9. *Chicago Tribune*, February 25, 2002. *Ensign*, May 2002. MIAM, 175.

10. LDSGC, October 1997. LDSGC, April 2007.

11. DN, June 21, 2004.

12. David Jackson to Hinckley, October 9, 1995, in Harris and Bringhurst, *Mormon Church and Blacks*, 124–27.

13. Harris and Bringhurst, *Mormon Church and Blacks*, 122–23, 127–29. Armand L. Mauss, *Shifting Borders and a Tattered Passport: Intellectual Journeys of a Mormon Academic* (Salt Lake City: University of Utah Press, 2012), 108–9.

14. LAT, May 18, 1998. SLT, May 19, 1998. LAT, September 12, 1998.

15. *Ensign*, July 1998. MIAM, 175–77.

16. NYT, October 2, 2005. Sujey Vega, "Intersectional *Hermanas*: LDS Latinas Navigate Faith, Leadership, and Sisterhood," *Latino Studies* 17 (2019): 27–47. Aihwa Ong, *Buddha Is Hiding: Refugees, Citizenship, and the New America* (Berkeley: University of California Press, 2003), 200–201.

17. Darron Smith, "The Persistence of Racialized Discourse in Mormonism," *Sunstone* 126 (2003): 31–32. SLT, February 13, 2011. Brittany Romanello, "Not a Country or a Stereotype: Latina LDS Experiences of Ethnic Homogenization and Racial Tokenism in the American West," *Religions* 12 (2021): 1–15.

18. LDSGC, April 2006. SLT, May 21, 2010.

19. "Mormons on the Slopes," *Saturday Night Live*, season 27 (2002), YouTube, https://www.youtube.com/watch?v=db1GgfJYVws.

20. MIAM, 203–4. Krakauer, *Under the Banner of Heaven*. "Church Response to Jon Krakauer's Under the Banner of Heaven," Newsroom, June 27, 2003.

21. Foster and Watson, *American Polygamy*, 168–72. Janet Bennion, *Polygamy in Primetime: Media, Gender, and Politics in Mormon Fundamentalism* (Waltham, MA: Brandeis University Press, 2012), 32.

22. Foster and Watson, *American Polygamy*, 173–78.

23. Bennion, *Polygamy in Primetime*, 2–3.

24. Newsroom, March 6, 2006, September 7, 2007. MIAM, 201–2. DN, March 13, 2003. SLT, March 25, 2003.

25. Bennion, *Polygamy in Primetime*, 182–87. Foster and Watson, *American Polygamy*, 213–14.

26. Foster and Watson, *American Polygamy*, 206. MIAM, 218–20.

27. William Russell, "The Last Smith Presidents and the Transformation of the RLDS Church," JMH 34, no. 23: 46–84. Roger Launius and W. B. Spillman, eds., *Let Contention Cease* (Independence, MO: Graceland, 1991). SLT, December 3, 2004.

28. William Russell, "The Community of Christ and the LDS Church: Closer Friends, Clearer Differences," *Dialogue* 36, no. 24 (Winter 2003): 177–90.

29. SLT, October 3, 2003.

30. WoC, 404–9. MSS, 153–55.

31. LDSGC, April 2004. Caroline Kline, "Saying Goodbye to the Final Say: The Softening and Reimagining of Mormon Male Headship Ideologies," in Mason and Turner, *Out of Obscurity*, 214–33. W. Bradford Wilcox, *Soft Patriarchs, New Men: How Christianity Shapes Fathers and Husbands* (Chicago: University of Chicago Press, 2004).

32. Valerie Hudson Cassler, "Two Trees," MF, 249–52.

33. Kynthia Taylor, "The Trouble with Chicken Patriarchy," MF, 238–39.

34. MSS, 139–41. TNM, 40.

35. Emily Matchar, "Why I Can't Stop Reading Mormon Housewife Blogs," Salon, January 15, 2011. Kristine Haglund, "Blogging the Boundaries: Mormon Mommy Blogs and the Construction of Mormon Identity," in Mason and Turner, *Out of Obscurity*, 234–56.

36. NYT, March 5, 2005. SLT, October 6, 2007. MSS, 175–77.

37. John Welch, ed., *The Worlds of Joseph Smith: A Bicentennial Conference at the Library of Congress* (Provo, UT: Brigham Young University Press, 2006). "Is This an Academic or an Evangelistic Conference?," *By Common Consent* (blog), May 7, 2005.

38. RSR. Richard Bushman, "The Commencement of Mormon Studies," in *New Perspectives in Mormon Studies*, ed. Quincy D. Newell and Eric F. Mason (Norman: University of Oklahoma Press, 2013), 197–213.

39. SLT, September 18, 2010.

40. MIAM, 189–90. Ronald Walker et al., *Massacre at Mountain Meadows*. DN, June 25, 2009.

41. Givens, *England*, 262–66; *Boston Globe*, February 19, 2008.

42. Mauss, *Shifting Borders*, 144–61. Topping, *Quinn*, 120–21. Other endowed professorships have since been created at the University of Utah and the Graduate Theological Union. The University of Wyoming also announced the fundraising for a chair, though without a positive outcome.

43. Jacob Weisberg, "Romney's Religion: A Mormon President? No Way," Slate, December 20, 2006. Andrew Sullivan, "Mormon Sacred Underwear," *Atlantic*, November 24, 2006. MIAM, 212–15.

44. MIAM, 225–26.

45. NYT, December 12, 2007.

46. Mitt Romney, "Faith in America," NPR, December 6, 2007, https://www.npr.org/templates/story/story.php?storyId=16969460.

47. DN, October 10, 2007.

48. NYT, May 22, 1998.

49. David E. Campbell et al., *Seeking the Promised Land: Mormons and American Politics* (Cambridge: Cambridge University Press, 2014), 86. Campbell, Jonathan Green, and Quinn Monson outline how the Mormon political body had become "conservative and cohesive" by this point.

50. *NBC News*, November 6, 2008. LAT, November 7, 2008. "Prop 8 Passes, Triggers Massive Protest against LDS Church," *Sunstone* 151 (2008): 76–79.

51. LDSGC, October 1999. "Proposition 22 Dominates California Wards' Attention, Divides Members," *Sunstone* 122 (2001): 86–92.

52. Newsroom, June 30, 2008. NYT, November 14, 2008. Neil J. Young, "Mormons and Same-Sex Marriage: From ERA to Prop 8," in Mason and Turner, *Out of Obscurity*, 159–61.

53. SLT, November 22, 2008. Prince, *Gay Rights*, 126–74.

54. John Donald Gustav-Wrathall, "Trial of Faith," *Dialogue* 40, no. 2 (2007): 79, 102. See also Fred Matis, Marilyn Matis, and Ty Mansfield, *In Quiet Desperation: Understanding the Challenge of Same-Gender Attraction* (Salt Lake City: Shadow Mountain, 2004). Taylor G. Petrey, "Toward a Post-Heterosexual Mormon Theology," *Dialogue* 44, no. 4 (2011): 106–41.

55. LDSGC, October 1995. SLT, November 10, 2009. Young, "Mormons and Same-Sex Marriage," 154, 166. Petrey, *Tabernacles*, 176.

56. SLT, October 25, 2010.

57. SLT, March 30, April 6, 2012. WP, December 23, 2013. Religion News Service, January 3, 2013. Prince, *Gay Rights*, 206–18.

58. Newsroom, August 4, 2010. LDSGC, October 2013.

59. *Newsweek*, June 5, 2011.

60. Trey Parker, Robert Lopez, and Matt Stone, *The Book of Mormon: Original Broadway Cast Recording*, Ghostlight Records, 2011.

61. Newsroom, October 18, 2011. NPR, March 24, 2011. *Daily Universe*, September 18, 2012.

62. *ABC News*, June 20, 2011. MIAM, 246–47, 270–72.

63. *Colbert Report*, August 10, 2011, https://www.cc.com/shows/the-colbert-report.

64. WP, May 14, 2012. *Bloomberg Business Week*, July 2012. See also *Businessweek*, June 9, 2011; *Harper's*, October 2011; *Economist*, May 5, 2012.

65. WP, February 28, 2012.

66. Newsroom, February 29, 2012. Official Declaration #2, March 1, 2013, https://www.ldschurch.org. "Race and the Priesthood," December 6, 2013, https://www.ldschurch.org.

67. BuzzFeed, August 21, 2012.

68. MIAM, 256.

69. *Boston Globe*, November 14, 2012. AP, November 15, 2012. BuzzFeed, November 14, 2012.

70. LDSGC, October 2005.

Chapter 10: Latter-day Legacies, 2012–Present

1. Carol Lynn Pearson, "Pioneers," MF, 292.

2. DN, December 17, 2010, December 9, 2020.

3. SLT, January 23, 2022. David Archuleta (@DavidArchie), Twitter, June 12, 2021, 3:27 p.m.

4. LDSGC, April 2013. Lepore, *These Truths*, 719–82.

5. TNM, 16–27. SLT, April 22, 2022.

6. AP, August 24, September 28, 2022. TNM, 191–93.

7. LJAD, April 21, 1984, 3:368. LDSGC, October 2008, April 2012.

8. DN, November 28, 2018. CNN, March 24, 2019. Newsroom, December 30, 2020, April 3, 2022. SLT, October 14, 2021.

9. SLT, October 14, 2021.

10. Newsroom, August 16, October 30, 2018. LDSGC, October 2018. SLT, May 1, 2021. Nelson had argued for this change as early as 1990, but received pushback from other leaders, like Hinckley, who remained attached to the name. LDSGC, April 1990, October 1990.

11. For the broader blending of corporate and religious culture, see Kathryn Lofton, *Consuming Religion* (Chicago: University of Chicago Press, 2017), 197–242.

12. *Wall Street Journal*, February 8, 2020. SLT, April 5, 2022. Quinn, *Mormon Hierarchy: Wealth and Corporate Power.*

13. *Wall Street Journal*, February 10, 2023. SLT, February 21, 2023.

14. Newsroom, April 8, 2022.

15. LDSGC, October 2022. SLT, March 22, 2023.

16. WP, January 29, 2012. Reuters, January 31, 2012. NYT, July 20, 2013.

17. Matthew L. Harris and Newell G. Bringhurst, *The LDS Gospel Topics Series: A Scholarly Engagement* (Salt Lake City: Signature Books, 2020), 1–6, 13–15. Religion News Service, October 5, 2016.

18. LDSGC October 2012, March 2013.

19. NYT, November 10, 2014.

20. LDSGC, October 2013. SLT, March 17, 2014.

21. NYT, November 10, 2014. SLT, March 8, June 26, 2015. Harris and Bringhurst, *Series*, 17–22.

22. Frank Newport, "Millennials' Religiosity amidst the Rise of Nones," Gallup, October 29, 2019. Elizabeth Drescher, *Choosing Our Religion: The Spiritual Lives of America's Nones* (New York: Oxford University Press, 2016). Matthew Hedstrom, "Rise of the Nones," in *Faith in the New Millennium: The Future of Religion and American Politics*, ed. Matthew Sutton and Darren Dochuk (New York: Oxford University Press, 2016), 250–68.

23. TNM, 18–24, 53–58, 65, 155–62, 178, 219–28.

24. SLT, September 12, 2013, October 23, 2017.

25. SLT, July 26, 2012, March 12, 2015, September 5, 2019. The following titles were published by Deseret Book: Adam Miller, *Letters to a Young Mormon* (2013); Terryl L. Givens and Fiona Givens, *The Crucible of Doubt: Reflections on the Quest for Faith* (2014); Patrick Q. Mason, *Planted: Belief and Belonging in an Age of Doubt* (2015); Laura Hales, ed., *A Reason for Doubt: Navigating LDS Doctrine and Church History* (2016).

26. SLT, January 17, 2018, August 28, 2022.

27. TNM, 71–79, 107. Glenda Gilmore and Thomas Sugrue, *These United States: A Nation in the Making, 1890 to the Present* (New York: Norton, 2015), 536–38.

28. SLT, December 19, 2012. Kristine Haglund, "Blogging the Boundaries: Mormon Mommy Blogs and the Construction of Identity," in Mason and Turner, *Out of Obscurity*, 248–51. MSS, 184–85.

29. Kelly, "Equality Is Not a Feeling," MF, 266. NYT, June 23, 2014. MSS, 185–86.

30. SLT, October 18, 2013, August 29, 2014. Neylan McBaine, *Women at Church: Magnifying LDS Women's Local Impact* (Salt Lake City: Kofford Books, 2014).

31. "Mormon President Russell M. Nelson's First Press Conference 1/16/2018," 25:20, YouTube, https://www.youtube.com/watch?v=keqbSQtqyOk.

32. Foster and Watson, *American Polygamy*, 206. MIAM, 218–20. Turley, *Oaks*, 242. SLT, February 10, 2018. Carol Lynn Pearson, *The Ghost of Eternal Polygamy: Haunting the Hearts and Heaven of Mormon Women and Men* (Walnut Creek, CA: Pivot Point Books, 2016).

33. Rachel Hunt Steenblik, *Mother's Milk: Poems in Search of Heavenly Mother* (Salt Lake City: BCC Press, 2017); Steenblik, *I Gave Her a Name* (Salt Lake City: BCC Press, 2019). LDSGC, April 2022. SLT, May 21, 2022. Janan Graham-Russell, "On Black Bodies in White Spaces," MF, 267–69. Charlotte Shurtz, "A Queer Heavenly Family: Expanding Godhood beyond a Heterosexual, Cisgender Couple," *Dialogue* 55, no. 1 (2022): 69–98. Fatimah Salleh and Margaret Hemming, *The Book of Mormon for the Least of These*, 2 vols. to date (Salt Lake City: BCC Press, 2020–). See also Tyler Chadwick, Dayna Patterson, and Martin Pulido, *Dove Song: Heavenly Mother in Mormon Poetry* (El Cerrito, CA: Peculiar Pages, 2018); Carol Lynn Pearson, *Finding Mother God: Poems to Heal the World* (Layton, UT: Gibbs Smith, 2010).

34. DN, May 26, 2009. Heidi Hatch (@tvheidihatch), "Julie Beck 15th general Pres. of Relief Society of the Church of LDS church opens Pence rally with

prayer," Twitter, October 26, 2016, 3:50 p.m., https://twitter.com/tvheidihatch/status/791381395436285952?lang=en.

35. Max Mueller, "The New Mormon Mission," Slate, October 8, 2016. DN, October 8, 12, 2016. SLT, October 8, 2016. BuzzFeed, October 9, 2016.

36. Du Mez, *Jesus and John Wayne*, 250–71. John Fea, *Believe Me: The Evangelical Road to Donald Trump* (Grand Rapids, MI: Eerdmans, 2018).

37. SLT, October 27, 2016.

38. "How the Faithful Voted: A Preliminary 2016 Analysis," Pew Research Center, November 9, 2016. SLT, April 1, 2021.

39. Compare Newsroom, September 11, 2008, October 9, 2014, October 5, 2016. NPR, January 2, 2017.

40. NPR, May 21, 2021. "The 'Big Lie,'" Public Religion Research Institute, May 12, 2021. DN, January 13, 2022.

41. Betsy Quammen, *American Zion: Cliven Bundy, God and Public Lands in the West* (Salt Lake City: Torrey House, 2020). Leah Sottile, *When the Moon Turns to Blood: Lori Vallow, Chad Daybell, and a Story of Murder, Wild Faith, and End Times* (New York: Twelve, 2022).

42. Sharlee Glenn, "Women of Faith Speak Up and Speak Out: The Genesis and Philosophical Underpinnings of Mormon Women for Ethical Government," BYUSQ 61, no. 1 (2022): 145–62. LDSGC, April 2021.

43. WP, February 5, 2020, June 21, 2022. DN, October 30, 2020, September 21, 2022.

44. Religion News Service, April 1, 2021. WP, September 27, 2021. TNM, 170–75, 178. For immigration, see Campbell et al., *Seeking*, 122–25. TNM, 170–75.

45. SLT, June 1, 2018. Newsroom, June 1, 2018.

46. RNS, June 6, 2018.

47. SLT, January 30, 2015. Eddie Glaude Jr., *Begin Again: James Baldwin's America and Its Urgent Lessons for Our Own* (New York: Crown, 2020), 6–11. Anthea Butler, *White Evangelical Racism* (Chapel Hill: University of North Carolina Press, 2011). Brooks, *White Supremacy*, 1–13.

48. TNM, 119–21. Janan Graham-Russell, "Choosing to Stay in the Mormon Church despite Its Racist Legacy," *Atlantic*, August 28, 2016.

49. SLT, June 20, 2016, January 21, 2021, June 9, 2022. Caroline Kitchener, "The Women Behind the Alt-Right," *Atlantic*, August 18, 2017. BuzzFeed, March 25, 2017. "Creating More Inclusive Public Spaces," PRRI, September 28, 2022.

50. Newsroom, August 15, 2017. LDSGC, October 2020. SLT, October 9, 2019, October 27, 2020. DN, April 13, 2023.

51. Graham-Russell, "Choosing." SLT, August 9, 2019, May 2, September 24, 2022. Eliza Griswold, "How Black Lives Matter Is Changing the Church," *New Yorker*, August 30, 2020. RNS, May 25, 2021. Craig Steven Wilder, *Ebony and Ivory: Race, Slavery, and the Troubled History of America's Universities* (New York: Bloomsbury, 2013).

52. SLT, January 28, 2021. LDSGC, April 2022.

53. LDSGC, April 2018, October 2019. Newsroom, July 16, 2022.

54. BoM, 29 [1 Nephi 13:12]. King, "The Complications of Columbus and Indig-

nity at BYU," and Draper, "I Am Giving Columbus No More of My Time," both in *Dialogue* 54, no. 2 (2021): 108, 110.

55. Monika Brown Crowfoot, "The Lamanite Dilemma: Mormonism and Indigeneity," *Dialogue* 54, no. 2 (2021): 57, 63. Daniel Glenn Call, "Rubik's Palimpsest: Searching for My Indigeneity," *Dialogue* 54, no. 2 (2021): 79.

56. Chelsea Gibbs, "Seeking Courage, Pride, and Limits," in Kerry Pray and Jenn Smith, *I Spoke to You with Silence: Essays from Queer Mormons of Marginalized Genders* (Salt Lake City: University of Utah Press, 2022), 174. TNM, 145.

57. SLT, November 5, 2015. WP, November 6, 2015.

58. Gibbs, "Seeking," 174–75.

59. NYT, March 12, 2015. Newsroom, November 12, 2021. Marie Griffith, *Moral Combat: How Sex Divided American Christians and Fractured American Politics* (New York: Basic Books, 2017), 273–310.

60. Prince, *Gay Rights*, 257–63.

61. Newsroom, November 6, 2015.

62. DN, November 14, 2015. NYT, November 19, 2015. SLT, February 3, 2016. Prince, *Gay Rights*, 267. TNM, 143–44.

63. SLT, April 4, September 17, 2019.

64. *Daily Universe* (Provo, UT), April 29, 2019. AP, May 6, 2019. DN, January 28, September 8, 2016, August 16, 2017. Benjamin Knoll, "Youth Suicide Rates and Mormon Religious Context: An Additional Empirical Analysis," *Dialogue* 49, no. 2 (2016): 25–43. See also Blaire Ostler, *Queer Mormon Theology: An Introduction* (Salt Lake City: BCC Press, 2021).

65. SLT, Trib Talk with Oaks, January 30, 2015. WP, January 27, 2015. Taylor G. Petrey, "An LDS Leader Signals New Openness on Transgender Issues," Slate, February 13, 2015. Prince, *Gay Rights*, 269–83.

66. SLT, February 5, 2021. Newsroom, October 2, 2019. Petrey, *Tabernacles*, 197–200.

67. SLT, July 30, 2017, October 2, 2019. Naji Haska Runs Through, "Memoir of a Wikita," in Pray and Smith, *Silence*, 23–24.

68. SLT, October 7, 2019. Kris Irvin, untitled poem, submitted to Rachel Hunt Steenblik, April 10, 2021, used with permission.

69. Jeffrey Holland, "The Second Half of the Second Century," Newsroom, August 23, 2021. Holland's "musket fire" rhetoric was borrowed from an address Dallin Oaks had delivered at BYU a few years earlier. *Good Morning America*, November 18, 2022.

70. SLT, March 4, 2021. DN, September 29, 2022.

Epilogue: Longing for Zion

1. Joseph Smith, revision to the Book of Genesis, circa June 1830 [Moses 7:69], JSP.

2. JS, AiH, H1:208.

IMAGE CREDITS

INDEX

Page references in *italics* indicate figures. Page references followed by *n* indicate notes.